CONSTRUCTING RUSSIAN CULTURE IN THE AGE OF REVOLUTION: 1881–1940

Constructing Russian Culture in the Age of Revolution: 1881–1940

Edited by

Catriona Kelly and David Shepherd

OXFORD UNIVERSITY PRESS

This book has been printed digitally and produced in a standard specification
in order to ensure its continuing availability

OXFORD
UNIVERSITY PRESS

Great Clarendon Street, Oxford OX2 6DP

Oxford University Press is a department of the University of Oxford.
It furthers the University's objective of excellence in research, scholarship,
and education by publishing worldwide in

Oxford New York

Auckland   Cape Town Dar es Salaam   Hong Kong   Karachi
Kuala Lumpur Madrid Melbourne Mexico City Nairobi
New Delhi Shanghai Taipei Toronto
With offices in
Argentina Austria Brazil Chile Czech Republic France Greece
Guatemala Hungary Italy Japan South Korea Poland Portugal
Singapore Switzerland Thailand Turkey Ukraine Vietnam

Oxford is a registered trade mark of Oxford University Press
in the UK and in certain other countries

Published in the United States
by Inc., New York

ISBN 0-19-874235-5

Antony Rowe Ltd., Eastbourne

Acknowledgements

The editors wish to record their especial gratitude to Andrew Lockett of OUP for entrusting them with this project, and for his patience during its gestation.

Similarity between the proposal for a book and the end product is often, if not coincidental, at least distant. This is the first of two books arising from a single volume first mooted in 1992. In part this development results from changes in the understanding of Russian culture which have taken place since then, and which we have tried to reflect, and in part from the helpful suggestions of anonymous readers. But it is also in large measure the fruit of a workshop on the theme of 'Russian Cultural Studies' held at the School of Slavonic and East European Studies, University of London, in July 1995, with the generous support of the British Academy and the Leverhulme Trust. Discussions at the workshop opened new avenues and provided fresh impetus; especially important were the frequent contributions made by Robin Aizlewood, Martin Dewhirst, Sheila Fitzpatrick, Maria Gough, Julian Graffy, Barbara Heldt, Geoffrey Hosking, Lindsey Hughes, Robert Service, and Tony Swift. The workshop could not have succeeded in this way without Radojka Miljevic's organizational skills.

The slightly unorthodox genesis of this book has its counterpart in matters of presentation. This is not a traditional volume of essays, each by an individual author. Rather, in the interests of narrative and thematic coherence, material submitted by contributors has in most cases been combined, often with greater than usual editorial intervention, to form lengthy chapters which are credited both to the principal authors and, in some cases, to providers of 'additional material'. The willingness of contributors to accept this unconventional procedure is greatly appreciated.

Thanks are also due to Laurence Waters for his assistance in preparing the illustrations.

Finally, the editors owe heartfelt thanks to Ian Thompson and Jeff Denton for practical and, above all, moral support.

Contents

List of Illustrations

Sources for illustrations

1, 5, 8, 9, 14–19 courtesy the Curators, Taylor Institution, University of Oxford.

2, 4, 6, 10, 11, 12 courtesy Louise McReynolds.

3 courtesy Tret'iakov Gallery, Moscow.

7 courtesy Georgian National Art Gallery, Tbilisi, Georgian Republic.

13 courtesy Catriona Kelly.

20 courtesy Robin Milner-Gulland.

LIST OF CONTRIBUTORS

Lynne Attwood is Lecturer in Russian Studies at the University of Manchester. She is the author of *The New Soviet Man and Woman: Sex-Role Socialisation in the USSR* (1990), and editor of *Red Women on the Silver Screen* (1993). She is currently working on the construction of gender identity in the USSR, focusing on the changing representations of women in the press and in films.

Rosamund Bartlett is the author of *Wagner and Russia* (1995) and co-author, with Anna Benn, of *Literary Russia: A Guide* (1997). The focus of her current research is Russian modernism and the musical structure of Russian prose, and she is editing a collection of articles about Shostakovich.

Neil Cornwell is Professor of Russian and Comparative Literature at the University of Bristol. He is the author of *The Life, Times and Milieu of V. F. Odoyevsky* (1986) and *Vladimir Odoevsky and Romantic Poetics* (1997), and of other Russian and comparative literary studies. He is also the general editor of the *Reference Guide to Russian Literature* (1997), and is currently engaged on projects concerning Henry James and Vladimir Nabokov.

Linda Edmondson is ESRC Research Fellow at the Centre for Russian and East European Studies, University of Birmingham. Her research has focused on issues of gender equality and civil rights in the history of late imperial Russia. She is the author of *Feminism in Russia, 1900–1917* (1984) and editor of *Women and Society in Russia and the Soviet Union* (1992). She is currently completing a monograph entitled *Gender, Citizenship and Authority in Russia, 1860–1920*.

Catriona Kelly is Reader in Russian and Tutorial Fellow at New College, University of Oxford. She is the author of *Petrushka: The Russian Carnival Puppet Theatre* (1990) and *A History of Russian Women's Writing, 1820–1992* (1994), editor of *An Anthology of Russian Women's Writing, 1777–1992* (1994), and co-editor, with David Shepherd, of *Russian Cultural Studies: An Introduction* (also to be published by OUP). She is currently working on a monograph entitled *Refining Russia: Gender, Manners and Morals from Catherine to Yeltsin*.

Louise McReynolds is an Associate Professor of History at the University of Hawaii. The author of *The News under Russia's Old Regime: The Development of a Mass-Circulation Press* (1991), she has also written numerous articles on the press and other aspects of popular culture in late imperial Russia. Most recently she has translated Evdokiia Nagrodskaia's *The Wrath of Dionysus* (1997). She is currently writing a history of Russia's commercial culture at the turn of the twentieth century.

Derek Offord is Professor of Russian at the University of Bristol. His books include *Portraits of Early Russian Liberals* (1985), *The Russian Revolutionary*

Movement in the 1880s (1986), and *Using Russian: A Guide to Contemporary Usage* (1996), and he is co-author, with William Leatherbarrow, of *A Documentary History of Russian Thought: From the Enlightenment to Marxism* (1987). His current research is in the field of eighteenth-century intellectual history.

Maureen Perrie is Reader in Russian History at the Centre for Russian and East European Studies, University of Birmingham. Her most recent book, *Pretenders and Popular Monarchism in Early Modern Russia*, was published by Cambridge University Press in 1995; her other publications have included studies of neo-populism, popular culture, and peasant unrest in pre-Revolutionary Russia. She is currently working on representations of Tsarist Russian history in the Stalin era, with particular reference to the image of Ivan the Terrible.

Cathy Popkin is Professor of Russian at Columbia University. She is the author of *The Pragmatics of Insignificance: Chekhov, Zoshchenko, Gogol* (1993), and is currently completing a book on epistemology and physicality in the works of Anton Chekhov entitled *Bodies of Knowledge: Chekhov's Corpus.*

David Shepherd is Professor of Russian and Director of the Bakhtin Centre at the University of Sheffield. He is the author of *Beyond Metafiction: Self-Consciousness in Soviet Literature* (1992), editor of *Bakhtin, Carnival, and Other Subjects* (1993), and co-editor, with Catriona Kelly, of *Discontinuous Discourses in Modern Russian Literature* (1989). His current research is focused on the intellectual contexts of the Bakhtin Circle.

Steve Smith is Professor of History at the University of Essex. He is the author of *Red Petrograd: Revolution in the Factories, 1917–1918* (1983), and of books and articles on aspects of late imperial Russian social and cultural history. He also works on the social history of China in the republican period and is completing a book of comparative essays on labour in the Russian and Chinese revolutions.

Vadim V. Volkov is Lecturer in and Dean of the Faculty of Political Sciences and Sociology of the European University at St Petersburg. In 1995 he received his Ph.D. from Cambridge University for a thesis entitled 'The Forms of Public Life: The Public Sphere and the Concept of Society in Imperial Russia', and is currently writing a book on this subject. His research interests are in social theory, historical sociology, Russian social history, and issues of civil society.

Faith Wigzell is Reader in Russian at the School of Slavonic and East European Studies, University of London. She is the author (under the name Faith Kitch) of *The Literary Style of Epifanij Premudryj: 'pletenije sloves'* (1976), and editor of *Russian Writers on Russian Writers* (1995). She has recently completed *Reading Russian Fortunes: Print Culture, Gender and Divination in Russia from 1765*, and is currently continuing research on folk belief, Leskov, and popular culture.

Translation and Transliteration

Unless otherwise stated, translations are by the contributors or editors.

With the exception of some commonly occurring names, Russian words are transliterated according to the Library of Congress system (without diacritics).

Introduction:
Literature, History, Culture

Catriona Kelly and David Shepherd

THE idea that Russian literature has traditionally, if not predominantly, been a vehicle for ideology and social criticism has long been familiar in the West, where it has at times been taken to rather bizarre extremes. Thus, the earliest translations of Russian novels were often presented as ethnography rather than fiction, with, for example, an appallingly inaccurate version of Gogol''s *Dead Souls* published at the height of the Crimean War under the title *Home Life in Russia* and contaminated by the translator's own fulminations on the eccentricities of Muscovite barbarians.[1] In more recent times, the quintessential 'Russianness' of writers has frequently been associated, in Britain at least, with a certain artlessness. Tolstoi, a sophisticated writer who was widely read in French and English literature, has tended to be perceived as more 'Russian' than the Slavophile Dostoevskii, one of the few Russian writers almost universally accepted as an international giant, because Tolstoi's language is held to be a transparent veil through which the beating heart of what D. H. Lawrence admiringly called 'life kindled to vividness' may be glimpsed.[2] Such ideas underpin much academic exegesis as well: the yoking of 'literature' and 'society' is a reflex action; it is still possible to come across ruminations, in the manner of William Gehardie, about the success of writers such as Chekhov in capturing, without caging, life in all its fullness; and almost all university courses sooner or later involve an attempt to deal with what has been termed 'the anomaly of Russian literature'.[3]

There can of course be no doubt that Russian literary texts have often been valued above all for their supposed reflection of contemporary reality; indeed, a good many nineteenth-century prose works appear to be little more than lightly fictionalized tracts (with Chernyshevskii's *What is to Be Done?* perhaps the most (in)famous example). The identification between literature and document was enhanced by the fact that social criticism rendered as fiction or literary criticism could more easily pass through the censorship than works of publicistic and journalistic enquiry. So, although due emphasis must be given to texts that have deliberately detached themselves from socially engaged models of art, it would be a patent absurdity for this or any other book to attempt to set out an alternative view by asserting that the Russian literary tradition has in fact been dominated by ideologies of 'art for art's sake'. Nor is there much potential for originality in a further variation on the familiar theme that Russian literature achieved greatness despite, not because of, the 'anomalous' instrumentality that was thrust upon it. The starting point for this project was, rather, dissatisfaction with the somewhat arbitrary and unsophisticated character of the connections between 'literature' and 'society', 'text' and 'context', that have traditionally been drawn. 'Context' has been interpreted as meaning, first and foremost, literary institutions, such as censorship, the decisions of prominent editors, the dicta of literary critics, or Party decrees on the function of literature. These have often been presented as obstacles negotiated by writers more or less successfully according to the degree of their talent. 'Society', on the other hand, includes not only the institutions specific to literature, but other social structures (the class stratification of Russian society), important political and historical events (the Crimean War, the Great Reforms), and the character of the Russian elite (the personal aesthetic tastes of rulers, from Catherine II to Stalin and beyond). The result has been a polarization between, on the one hand, authors and texts, which are held to be unique and in a crucial sense self-determined (where they are of high quality), and, on the other, historical processes, which are interpreted as impersonal and abstract. One well-known historian of Russia, Richard Wortman, has accurately summarized the consequences of this polarization: 'The historian's focus on the collective presumes a preoccupation with change that is alien to the literary scholar . . . Whether the historian looks favorably or critically on the processes of change, the dynamic of history must be a central theme in his discourse'; by contrast: 'The student of literature often shares the antihistorical bias of his subjects who raise existential questions and refuse to find comfort or even understanding in the historical process.'[4]

Moreover, although there is a long and honourable tradition of examining the connections between literature and the history of ideas (as, for example, in Isaiah Berlin's famous essay on *War and Peace*, 'The Hedgehog and the Fox'), there has also been remarkably little study of the relationship between literary texts and other cultural forms. Very little work has been done on, for example, the connections between fiction and journalism, or the links between elite literature and popular culture, exploring how literature assimilated material from popular tradition, or, conversely, how writers attempted to distance themselves from works suitable for 'the people', either by writing hostile commentaries on them, or by pointedly adopting strategies not characteristic of them. Even attempts to synthesize discussion of different 'high-art' forms (painting and literature, literature and dance, music and art) have been rare.

For their part, historians in the Russian field have until recently been wary of the kind of textual scholarship practised by commentators on literature. An unfortunate result has sometimes been the pillaging of material that a textual scholar would recognize as highly conventional (for example, in terms of genre tradition) for factual information: the reading of textual sources as though these were transparent. One instance of this is the use, in an excellent study of Russian child-fostering practices, of Saltykov-Shchedrin's surreally satirical and allegorical novel *The Golovlev Family* (*Gospoda Golovlevy*, 1876) as a source for information about how child-raising was actually carried out in the Russian aristocracy.[5] A further outcome of the literature/history divide has been a reluctance among historians to take into account the linguistic structures of their material—for instance, the precise phrasing of laws, the formulae used in autobiography, the strategies used by informants in court testimony or oral history—as evidence for the history of mentality, rather than as at best irrelevant to, or at worst distracting from, the factual content of the message. As one historian, Mark Steinberg, has argued: 'Over the last couple of decades, a loosely materialist view of human consciousness and behavior has tended to predominate in studies of Russian society. Until recently, most studies explained popular mentalities and behavior, for instance, as logical responses to material conditions and changes (structures of authority in industry or of power in civic life, for example).'[6] The consequence in terms of methodology was that sources (ranging from folklore to autobiography) from which popular mentality was held to be retrievable were glossed as unproblematic responses to, and unmediated reflections of, the material conditions in which they had been composed. And, although the last few years have seen a most productive appropriation by social historians of cultural theory, something of a gulf between 'literary' and 'historical' explications still remains. This is manifested in the continuing preference of historians for material that is, at least at some level, referential (realist prose, popular fiction); conversely, phenomena such as modernist poetry or metafiction have remained the province of 'literary' specialists, who in their turn continue, in many cases, the practice of close reading of texts with little or no reference to the circumstances of their production.[7]

The gap between 'literary' and 'historical' appropriations of texts may be illustrated by the fate of one important early memoir, the life history of Anna Labzina (1758–1828). In Adele Lindenmeyr's recent study of philanthropy in Russia, *Poverty is Not a Vice*, the memoir is interpreted as a source for tracing the patterns of actual eighteenth-century behaviour: 'An unusually detailed account of one mid-eighteenth-century noblewoman's charity by her daughter is especially revealing of the forms personal charity took, the psychological and social conventions connected with it, and the relationship such personal charity was supposed to establish between giver and receiver.' By contrast, in Barbara Heldt's pioneering feminist study, *Terrible Perfection*, Labzina's memoir is read with emphasis on its adumbration of such modern Western values as self-assertion and articulation (albeit indirect) of emotional distress: 'Between the lines of the narrative, we hear outrage, silent protest, the seizing of small opportunities for companionship rather than acceptance of humiliation. There is a sense of her own self-worth that never fails Labzina.'[8] A fuller and more satisfactory reading of the text might mediate between these two approaches, tracing Labzina's rhetorical strategies and capacities for self-expression, as well as her need for self-concealment, to the context in which she wrote the memoir. This was a context determined by, *inter alia*, the Masonic concept of the human life as a struggle for virtue, but in the sense of Protestant self-examination rather than Orthodox *podvig*, and also by Labzina's own peculiar status as a member of the small elite of educated Russian women, part of a female network that also included the poet Elizaveta Kheraskova and the writer Aleksandra Khvostova.

One way of so mediating is to adopt a 'cultural studies' approach. Such a bald statement immediately invites criticism for precisely the shortcomings it is intended to counter: there is no single, direct route through the labyrinth of cultural studies to a space where more sophisticated analysis might take place.[9] The term is used here to denote an approach in which 'culture' has its anthropological sense of the totality of relations obtaining in a given society, and textual expression is understood as part of an intricate network in which symbolism is as important as materialism. Literary texts and other forms of expression—the visual arts, advertising, popular song—are consequently seen as competing but complementary discourses, linked by processes of mutual attraction and repulsion, and connected to the conditions of their production and consumption in ways that are by no means as immediate and amenable to unproblematic recuperation as has traditionally been assumed.

An important aspect of this book's attempt to present a more rounded view of Russian culture has been the attempt to initiate a fuller dialogue between literature and history. Those who have collaborated on the project include social and cultural as well as literary historians, and the issues covered include those more familiar to historians (for example, the rise of a 'civic society' in the late nineteenth century) as well as those more familiar to specialists in literature (for example, 'the crisis of symbolism' in 1910). However, the book is intended neither as a synthesis, nor as an exhaustive cultural history of Russia between 1881 and the early Soviet period, but as an exploration of several key themes: 'commercial culture', or the relationship between culture and the market-place; 'objectivity', or the creation of a new kind of imagined communality in the Russian city, and its relationship to the literary realism of the day; and 'issues of identity', or the perceptions among Russians of national affiliation and selfhood in the late nineteenth and early twentieth centuries. Each of these themes might be defined as 'a field of cultural production', to borrow the category invented by Pierre Bourdieu.[10] The analysis in each case considers various sites of cultural production (the department store, the 'new arts' journal, the learned society, the women's movement, to name only a few instances) and numerous examples of cultural product (fashionable clothes, etiquette books, novels, poems, critical essays, paintings, ballets, and so on), in order to establish links between aspects of Russian society that are not usually considered together. For example, the 'crisis of symbolism' tends to be discussed by literary historians as though it amounted to little more than a dispute between various schools (symbolism, acmeism, and futurism); our discussion is directed towards achieving a broader understanding of the debate about literary language, and to relating this debate to burgeoning anxieties about the commercialization of the city environment in early twentieth-century Russia. Conversely, we hope that the discussion of consumption as a cross-class phenomenon, albeit one in which individual practices were heavily dependent on individual economic resources, offers something of a corrective to traditional historiography of Russia, with its repetitive debates on class conflict, for example the question of whether there in fact was a 'proletariat', or a 'bourgeoisie', in late imperial Russia. The evidence, we believe, suggests overwhelmingly that a 'bourgeois sensibility' was widely present in Russia by the late nineteenth century, whatever the balance of factory-owners and traders in the population. There were striking differences between Russian intellectuals and their counterparts elsewhere in Europe: liberal values played a lesser role in debate; there were extraordinarily high levels of, in Siegbert Prawer's phrase, 'bourgeois self-hatred' among Russian intellectuals; and the Russian intelligentsia's *mission civilisatrice* had a peculiarly agonized character, given both the incompetence of their government, and the extraordinary gap, in terms of education, material well-being, and political power, between intellectuals and the working classes. However, there were also numerous similarities, which are underlined both by the interest that Russian intellectuals took in other countries, from America to Ireland, and by the absorption of key Western texts of an impeccably bourgeois kind, from the novels of Dickens to the self-help books of Samuel Smiles, into Russian tradition, where they had a readership not only among intellectuals but, by the early twentieth century, also among the more privileged workers.

The bulk of discussion in the book concerns the years around the turn of the century, roughly from the assassination of Alexander II in 1881 to the Russian Revolutions of 1917. However, we have also included an epilogue discussing the further history of our themes in the first decades of Soviet rule, and covering such issues as the growth of the Soviet scientific establishment; the evolution of new and different 'programmes of identity' (psychoanalysis, Fordism, biomechanics, 'physical culture', mass song, film, and so on); and the integration of commercial and intellectual values in the new doctrine of *kul'turnost'*, or culturedness. It was not our intention to offer a detailed history of the Russian Revolution and its aftermath: there are many excellent books that already do this.[11] Rather, we set out to offer case-studies that give a more focused sense of change and continuity than the sociological or psychoanalytical abstractions about 'authoritarianism', 'masochism', 'adolescent syndromes', or 'Rustam complexes', that are sometimes advanced as a key to understanding the similarity in difference of Russia before and after the Revolution.[12] A Russian historian, Boris Paramonov, has recently suggested that 'it remains to be seen whether the Soviet regime was a historical aberration or an expression of the country's destiny'.[13] We have preferred an intermediate and, again, mediating view, according to which the ambitions of successive leaders and dominant social groups to alter the nature of Russia and break with the past were themselves altered by practicalities: time and again, it proved a great deal easier to manufacture 'blueprints for identity' than to 'engineer human souls' in the envisaged manner. At the same time, we hope that our focus on the processes of 'everyday life' has helped us escape the Western tendency to represent Russia as extraordinary and different, an exotic land beyond encompassing by the mind. Even in the 1940s, perhaps the least congenial period of recent Russian history, there were many aspects of the country's culture that could have been matched in the West: a worker from Finland or Britain would have felt remarkably at home in the room of a 'cultivated' (*kul'turnyi*) Russian worker, with its improving books, oilcloth tablecloth, doilies, best china, and coloured reproductions of famous national paintings; while the notorious communal flats (*kommunalki*), so often mythologized as a uniquely Russian phenomenon, had their counterparts in Finland, Britain, or Germany until at least the 1960s.

The prologue to the book consists of three short essays on important key words denoting important concepts to which explicit and implicit reference is made in the subsequent chapters. The first two, dealing with *lichnost'* and *narodnost'*, linked by a brief examination of *sobornost'* and *obshchestvennost'*, are surveys of the conceptions of personal and national identity that existed before the era on which we focus, while the third, on *literaturnost'*, is a brief history of the notions of Russian literature that circulated up to the end of the nineteenth century. In a book that in many ways takes issue with the notion of Russia's unique destiny and peculiar identity, it seemed important to begin by exploring historical factors that have made Russia different. These can be briefly summarized as: first, an extremely vexed history of theories of the self, polarized between the individualist ideologies of the Westernizers, and the collectivist ideologies of the Slavophiles; second, a concept of 'the nation' that has been inextricably fused with representations of 'the people'; and third, an insistence on the extraordinary importance of literature in Russia arising at least in part from an uneasy sense that literary culture was 'belated, sudden, foreign, and problematic'.[14] These key-word essays also have the function of providing introductory information about the Russian Empire before 1881, as a background to our discussion of the post-1881 period in the main part of the book.

There might appear to be a suspicious neatness about this choice of a trinity of words, not to mention their blatant morphological kinship. However, the suffix -*ost'* has an interesting history: first entering Slavic languages in the ninth century, it became especially productive in Russian from the end of the eighteenth, as new words were coined to name concepts in the burgeoning fields of science, knowledge, and literature.[15] Furthermore, all the abstract nouns chosen are intimately linked to the debates considered in later sections of the book. Thus, the history of the concept *literaturnost'* is connected with the anxious effort to separate literature from entertainment and commercial activity; the account of *narodnost'* presents a pre-history of concepts of national identity which were to be subjected to a variety of cultural reworkings; and the exploration of *lichnost'* not only outlines the problems that Russian thinkers have had in dealing with Western views of the individual self, but also foregrounds the collectivist principles that have shaped Russian culture, and especially the effects of these on mythologization of the intelligentsia's leading role in cultural change (the *mission civilisatrice*).

We had at first contemplated including a key-word essay on another important concept, *kul'turnost'*; it seemed preferable, in the event, to integrate discussion of that nexus of ideas into analysis of the post-Revolutionary period, when it received its most sustained formulation and was at its most influential. Another possible candidate for a key-word essay, the Russian term for 'vulgarity', 'tastelessness', or 'banality', *poshlost'*, has recently been the subject of an excellent extended discussion by Svetlana Boym.[16] Suffice it to say here that the implications of *poshlost'* are more moralistic than those of 'vulgarity': the word implies poverty of intellect and spiritual qualities, as well as failure of taste. A second important point is that the word *poshlost'*, though often held by Russian commentators to be class-neutral, is in practice used as a synonym of *meshchanstvo*. The latter word is often translated 'philistinism', but is in fact derived from the Russian word for the estate (*soslovie*) of lower-class town-dwellers, 'burghers', a term also pressed into service in the late nineteenth century to calque the French concept of the petite bourgeoisie. It is important to appreciate the connection of 'vulgarity' with the urban lower classes in order to grasp the nature of Russian populism both before the Revolution and after. Other candidates for consideration, such as *gosudarstvo* (state) or *obshchestvo* (society), for all their obvious relevance to developing and contested notions of national identity or civic society, were rejected on the grounds that they might prompt a falling back on the very kind of familiar category whose supposedly self-evident explanatory power we were seeking to call into question.

Finally, a word should perhaps be said about the overall structure of the book, which is not organized as a running narrative in chronological order. As a result, there is some overlap between the material covered in different places. The main discussion of Chekhov's work comes in part II, chapter 1, for example, but Chekhov is also mentioned briefly in later chapters. However, a sense of narrative sequence has, we hope, been preserved: thus, for example, the debates that are analysed in chapter 1 not only go back earlier than those in chapter 3, but also to some extent provoked the latter. While it would have been not only possible, but a great deal easier, to organize the book as a series of short chapters dealing with familiar topics (a section on literature, one on pictorial arts, one on social institutions, and so on), this would have meant reinforcing boundaries, and closing off dialogues, rather than instituting a process that has been collaborative and interdisciplinary, in the full sense dialogic, from beginning to end.

Notes

[1] The text was published in London in 1854: see R. May, *The Translator in the Text: Reading Russian Literature in English* (Evanston, 1995), 15–16.

[2] D. H. Lawrence (Extract from Introduction to *Cavalleria Rusticana*), in H. Gifford (ed.), *Leo Tolstoy* (Harmondsworth, 1971), 197.

[3] See G. S. Morson, 'Introduction: Literary History and the Russian Experience', in Morson (ed.), *Literature and History: Theoretical Problems and Russian Case Studies* (Stanford, 1986), 14–27.

[4] R. Wortman, 'Epilogue: History and Literature', in Morson (ed.), *Literature and History*, 277–8.

[5] See D. Ransel, *Mothers of Misery: Child Abandonment in Russia* (Princeton, 1988), 154.

[6] M. D. Steinberg, 'Stories and Voices: History and Theory', *Russian Review*, 55 (1996), 349.

[7] An important recent contribution to discussion of cultural theory and the historical field, along with exemplary readings, appears under the heading 'Language and Meaning in Russian History', in *Russian Review*, 55 (1996). For an example of historians' preference for referentiality, see even L. Engelstein's otherwise excellent and sophisticated study, *The Keys to Happiness: Sex and the Search for Modernity in Fin de Siècle Russia* (Ithaca, 1992), which analyses Lidiia Zinov′eva-Annibal's simplistic representation of lesbian relations in *Thirty-Three Freaks* (*Tridtsat′ tri uroda*, 1907) rather than the complex and disturbing portrait of 'perverse' adolescent sexuality given by the same writer in *The Tragic Menagerie* (*Tragicheskii zverinets*, 1907). For an example of a reading of metafiction unusually sensitive to conditions of production and reception, see M. Finke, *Metapoesis: The Russian Tradition from Pushkin to Chekhov* (Durham, NC, and London, 1995), esp. the discussion of *What is to Be Done?*, which shows how that 'documentary' novel's self-distantiation from fictional convention in fact serves to highlight its dependence on the complex of discursive formations surrounding the production and reception of fiction (1–5).

[8] A. Lindenmeyr, *Poverty is Not a Vice: Charity, Society, and the State in Imperial Russia* (Princeton, 1996), 21; B. Heldt, *Terrible Perfection: Women and Russian Literature* (Bloomington, 1987), 78; and cf. M. Ledkovsky, C. Rosenthal, and M. Zirin, *Dictionary of Russian Women Writers* (Westport, 1994), 355–6.

[9] On the theoretical and methodological diversity encompassed by the term 'cultural studies', see Catriona Kelly, Hilary Pilkington, David Shepherd, and Vadim Volkov, 'Introduction: Why Cultural Studies?', in Kelly and Shepherd (eds.), *Russian Cultural Studies: An Introduction* (Oxford, forthcoming).

[10] See P. Bourdieu, *The Field of Cultural Production: Essays on Art and Literature*, ed. R. Johnson (Cambridge, 1993), esp. 29–73.

[11] See e.g. S. Fitzpatrick, *The Russian Revolution*, 2nd edn. (Oxford, 1994); E. Acton, *Rethinking the Russian Revolution* (London, 1990); O. Figes, *A People's Tragedy: The Russian Revolution 1891–1924* (London, 1996).

[12] See D. Rancour-Laferrière, *The Slave Soul of Russia: Moral Masochism and the Cult of Suffering* (New York, 1995); I. Kon, 'Moral Culture', and Z. Abdullaeva,

'Popular Culture', in D. N. Shalin (ed.), *Russian Culture at the Crossroads: Paradoxes of Post-Communist Consciousness* (Boulder, 1996), 195, 227.

13 B. M. Paramonov, 'Historical Culture', in Shalin (ed.), *Russian Culture*, 11.

14 Morson, 'Introduction', 23.

15 See N. Shanskii, 'O proiskhozhdenii produktivnosti suffiksa -ost′ v russkom iazyke', *Voprosy istorii russkogo iazyka* (Moscow, 1959), 117–18. We are grateful to Vadim Volkov for this reference.

16 See S. Boym, *Common Places: Mythologies of Everyday Life in Russia* (Cambridge, Mass., 1994).

PART I

Prologue: Key Concepts Before 1881

Lichnost': Notions of Individual Identity

Derek Offord

THE English-speaker has difficulty with the Russian term *lichnost'*, as is so often the case when it is necessary to describe in another language the abstract concepts used by a people to organize its view of the world (*narodnost'*, *pravda*, and *volia* are further examples of terms that perplex the foreign student of Russian thought). The term *lichnost'* is capable of translation in various ways: as 'personality', or 'individual', or even 'selfhood'. These distinctions have come to be reflected to some extent in Russian lexicography. While in Dal''s dictionary the principal definition of the word is merely 'a person, an independent, separate being',[1] authoritative modern dictionaries identify both the sense of 'personality', as a collection of a person's distinctive traits, and the sense of 'individual', conceived in relation to others. Thus, for Ozhegov *lichnost'* is both 'a person as the bearer of certain qualities' and, as a synonym of *litso*, 'a person as a member of society'.[2] Treatment of the concept of *lichnost'* in its first sense of personality entails examination of the debate in Russian thought about the emergence of distinct selves from among the undifferentiated mass, and touches on questions as to the nature and distinctiveness of Russian historical development and the Russian people. Treatment of the concept in its second sense of individual member of society entails consideration of such matters as the relationship between the individual and the collectives in which he or she operates, such as family, commune, Church, or state, the capacity of the individual to affect his or her destiny, and ultimately, therefore, the interplay of freedom and necessity.

Russian versus Western Views of *Lichnost'*

No matter how successfully we manage to translate the term *lichnost'* in any given context, the concept which it denotes has a different place in what Academician Likhachev has recently called the 'conceptosphere'[3] of the Russian from that occupied by such concepts as 'personality' and, in particular, 'individual' in the Westerner's view of the world. The difference is not difficult to account for in broadest outline. Pre-Petrine Russia lacked that sense of worth of the human personality embodied in the concept of *humanitas* inherited by the West from the Roman world, the sense, as it has been described, of the 'dignity of one's own human personality, which is a thing unique and which must be cared for and developed to the full', on the one hand, and a 'recognition of the personalities of others and their right to care for their own personalities', on the other.[4] Rejecting alien influence and shunning cultivation of the intellect, Orthodox Muscovy did not possess a culture of the sort that both reflected and underpinned respect for the human personality in the West; the individual personality, as Marc Raeff has asserted, was not an important element in social and cultural life there.[5] It generated no philosophy that examined the nature of the individual's being, the sources of his knowledge, his ethical nature, or his political status, no imaginative literature that explored his inner world, nor any code of law defining his rights. In the political sphere every subject was at the disposal of the autocrat; the concept of citizenship, a view of the individual as not only bound by obligations but also enjoying rights, could not develop. In the social sphere the serf came to be viewed as a chattel, while the system of *mestnichestvo* (abolished in 1682) defined the position of each noble on the basis of the place of his clan among the aristocracy and the importance of the positions occupied by his ancestors.

It is what Russians know as the 'Petrine reform', the Westernization of Russia in the early eighteenth century by Peter the Great (sole ruler 1696–1725), that opened the way—or at least was felt by Russians themselves to open the way—for the unleashing of personal potentialities and for speculation on the nature and status of the individual human, as on innumerable other questions of ethical, aesthetic, social, and political significance. The Table of Ranks introduced by Peter, it has been claimed, 'provided both the stimulus and the foundation for the development of individualism'.[6] Men of independent cast of mind begin to liberate themselves from the hold of tradition. Thus, Kantemir, perhaps the first writer of a Western sort in Russia, defends in his satires a nobility promoted on the basis of personal worth rather than lineage, and advocates education, conceived in a broad sense, as a means of moulding the virtuous and socially useful individual. Both these concerns—for the creation of a nobility of personal merit and for the spread of education—are central to the thought of Fonvizin, the first distinguished Russian dramatist, who wrote in the age of Catherine (ruled 1762–96). From the late 1770s, in the often powerful poetry of Derzhavin, the subjective ego of the poet, with its joys and anxieties, is for the first time on display. The poet himself assumes importance, becoming a legitimate literary subject in his own right and even a vehicle for the manifestation of God's being. With the advent of sentimentalism in Russia late in the eighteenth century, 'the idea of personal merit', in the words of the Soviet scholar Kochetkova, 'took on a new and different meaning: . . . . man was as great as his power of feeling'.[7] Each individual was now invested with sensibility, and this view of personality extended to the lower orders: 'even peasant women know how to love!', Karamzin infamously assures his readers in 'Poor Liza' ('Bednaia Liza', 1792). In artistic creation, as Karamzin conceives it, the personality and capacity of the author himself to feel were the touchstone of aesthetic success.[8] Finally, the subversive nature of Radishchev's critique of serfdom in his *Journey from St Petersburg to Moscow* (*Puteshestvie iz Peterburga v Moskvu*, 1790) is intensified—in a way difficult for the modern reader to appreciate—by the author's tendency to treat the serfs he portrays as autonomous beings worthy of the attention of the narrator.

It is only in the nineteenth century, however, that the concept of *lichnost'* assumes a position of central importance in Russian thought. From the 1840s the flowering of the personality and its liberation from contingency and oppression of every description—political, social, intellectual—become inextricably associated in the minds of many classical Russian writers and thinkers with their quest to bring civilization to their country. Without a moral personality, as Herzen thought in the 1840s, there could be no movement, stability, or development.[9] The human personality, Pisarev observed a little later, had been a more central preoccupation of Russian literature than had society, for society as such did not yet exist in Russia.[10] Concern to foster the human personality in Russia was all the more marked for the fact that personality was felt, as Belinskii expressed it in 1847, to be 'only just pecking its way out of the shell' there.[11] However, once the concept of *lichnost'* did firmly establish itself in Russia its formulation was inevitably affected by the lateness of its arrival, by the largely unfavourable conditions for the development of the creative personality, and by the intellectual climate that now prevailed. In the first place, various factors— the survival of an autocratic regime and of serfdom, the existence of censorship and the lack of political freedoms, the absence of a developed public opinion, the country's late cultural development—tended to drive thinkers to seek solutions which offered scant protection to the individual or even prohibited individual assertiveness. In the second place, the Western bourgeois order, which extolled individualism, expressed through commercial enterprise, material acquisition, and the ownership of private property, was in the main despised by a nascent intelligentsia which saw itself as an aesthetic and, in particular, a moral elite, and gave precedence to Christian brotherhood or socialist equality. (Herzen's devastating indictment of the mores of the Paris in which he arrived in 1847 eloquently illustrates the point.[12]) In the third place, Russian thinkers of the 1840s had nearly all been deeply influenced by German philosophical doctrines in which the goal of the self had tended to be seen as its self-abnegating communion with some Absolute.

We must, in addition, bear in mind the fact that the proportion of the population on whose lives discussion of the concept can have seemed in mid-nineteenth-century Russia to have an immediate bearing was very small. Westernization in Russia gave rise, as Russian thinkers frequently point out, to a rift between the educated class, particularly that part of it which came to be known as the intelligentsia, and the people, known collectively as the *narod*. Among the subjugated, illiterate mass, governed by the exigencies of serfdom and tradition, concepts of individuality and autonomy cannot have been strong. The view of the peasant as a child, and the peasant's view of the Tsar as a paternal figure, *batiushka*, confirm this sense of a person who has not developed into a responsible adult personality. 'The Russian peasant', wrote Pisarev, 'is perhaps still not able to raise himself to a conception of his own personality, to rise to rational egoism and respect for his own personality.'[13] It has even been suggested that the cowed nature of the pre-Revolutionary peasant who saw no individuality within himself is attested linguistically by the existence, alongside the royal 'we', of a 'peasant "we"', illustrated by one of Tolstoi's depictions of a character from this class who, when asked where he comes from, replies 'We are from the village'.[14]

It is against this complex, distinctive background that an examination of the development of the concept of *lichnost'* during the classical period of Russian culture, which roughly spanned the reigns of Nicholas I (1825–55) and Alexander II (1855–81), must be set. In general, views of *lichnost'* in nineteenth-century Russia follow the same channels down which Russian thought, following its Western models, also flows. That stream of European thought which is associated with the Age of Reason, cherishes enlightenment, adopts a universalistic view of man, and conceives of the possibility of improving social structures and institutions, and which has its most important recent origins in eighteenth-century France, gives rise to a generally positive view of the development of a sense of personality. That counter-current which emphasizes the limitations of reason, seeks transcendent knowledge, stresses ethnic difference and cultural distinctiveness, and exalts an organic type of society, and which emanates from Germany in the late eighteenth and early nineteenth centuries, expresses apprehension about the effect of individualism on community. For the sake of simplicity we shall label these streams 'universalist' and 'particularist' respectively, and will organize our discussion of *lichnost'* in nineteenth-century Russian culture within this broad framework.

'Universalist' Versions of *Lichnost'*

Of particular importance in initiating explicit discussion of the subject of *lichnost'*, as in so many other respects, was the debate of the 1840s and 1850s between the so-called Westernizers and Slavophiles. 'The concept of personality', as Andrzej Walicki has noted, 'was at the roots of all Westernizing thought in the 1840s.'[15] As men who broadly speaking belonged to the universalistic stream of Russian thought identified above, the Westernizers welcomed the emergence of individuality out of the undifferentiated primeval mass, and equated this development with progress and civilization. They believed that the Middle Ages, with their perceived intense Christian spirituality and highly developed code of chivalry, had been a crucial period in the emergence of personality. In Russia, life had been given to the principle of personality by Peter the Great, whom the Westernizers revered. Moreover, the age of romanticism, in which the Westernizers had been formed morally, was conducive to the same development; for romanticism, as Nicholas Riasanovsky has observed, apotheosizes the creative individual, the ego of German idealist philosophy, the thinker or artist of romantic aesthetics, even the individual at odds with his environment.[16] The Westernizers' interest in and viewpoint on the development of personality may be illustrated by reference to four of Westernism's leading representatives in the 1840s and 1850s: Vissarion Belinskii, Aleksandr Herzen, Timofei Granovskii, and Konstantin Kavelin.

Belinskii begins to defend the human personality from late 1840 and through 1841. His defence, which finds its fullest and most famous expression in his copious letters to Botkin, is the more passionate for the fact that it forms part of the self-castigation on which Belinskii embarked as he rejected his own Hegelian phase and his former 'vile yearning to be reconciled with vile reality!'[17] Only the year before, in his notorious review of a book on the Battle of Borodino, Belinskii had set personal interests as nothing by comparison with those of society, the 'highest reality', and warned that individuals who had the temerity to rebel, like Pushkin's Aleko in *The Gypsies* (*Tsygany*), would be crushed beneath the 'leaden weight' of society's 'gigantic palm'.[18] Now, in October 1840, regarding Hegelian philosophy as an oppressive system of thought, and conscious of an analogy with tyrannical political systems such as the autocracy which Hegelianism seemed to legitimate, Belinskii exalted the human personality as the highest value, 'higher than history, higher than society, higher than humanity'. This was the 'idea and the thought of the age'.[19] In December he is upholding the 'idea of liberalism', which he conceives as rational, Christian, and humane, for its aim is to restore the rights of the individual and reinstate human worth; it was for the sake of the individual, after all, that Christ came into this world and suffered on the cross.[20] Again, on 1 March 1841: 'the fate of the subject, the individual, the personality is more important than the fate of the whole world and the well-being of the Chinese emperor [a reference to Hegel's *Allgemeinheit*]'.[21] It is the 'fanatical love of freedom and of the independence of the human personality', he writes in June 1841, that accounts for his obsession with civic virtue, truth, and honour, for without those things the human personality cannot flourish. Indeed, the human personality is a 'point' which he fears will drive him insane.[22] Socialism, which by September 1841 he sees as the 'alpha and omega of faith and knowledge', offers him the promise of an end to the suffering of the personality, the liberation of his brothers in humanity, his neighbours in Christ.[23]

Herzen offers some detailed thoughts on the subject of personality in an unfinished work, 'Some Comments on the Historical Development of Honour', written in 1843 and first published in 1848. Men and women have a need, Herzen contends, to save and respect something of themselves out of the 'whirlwind of contingencies'. At the root of what one reveres is a 'sense of one's own worth and a striving to preserve the moral independence of one's personality'. (It is as one discovers in oneself the measure of one's worth that there develops the concept of honour with which Herzen is chiefly preoccupied in his essay.) Herzen believes that different concepts of human worth, of personality, have characterized the great ages of mankind. In oriental civilization the concept of personality was submerged in the tribe or kingdom. Regarding himself as a slave, the Oriental saw his true personality as residing in something or someone outside himself, of which, or of whom, he was merely a member or an organ. In the Graeco-Roman world, with its highly developed concept of citizenship, the individual was subordinate to the ideal ruling personality of the city or fatherland. Here, cities, such as Athens and Rome, were free, but individuals were not. In the Middle Ages the relationship between personality and the state that had obtained in classical antiquity was inverted: personality came to prevail and *res publica* became immaterial. Out of Teutonic individualism and the Christian insistence on the intrinsic worth of every human, there developed the institution of chivalry. Through the medieval knights-errant, whom collectively Herzen admires as the 'leading phalanx of mankind', with their purity and a strict code of honour which they were prepared to defend with the sword, men learnt to respect the greatness of the human personality. One-sided though the chivalric defence of the individual may have been, the respect for personality which chivalry fostered helped to save Europe during the eventual revolutionary overthrow of feudalism. For revolution, while taking the sanctity of the person as its starting point, inevitably ends up, in Herzen's view, depriving the individual of those rights which had been declared inalienable and measuring a man's worth by the degree to which he is prepared to subordinate his own personality to the interests of the indivisible republic. That is not to say that the medieval view of personality satisfies Herzen any more than the classical view. For while it is true, Herzen believes, that personality is the 'real apex of the historical world', the essence through which everything lives, and that without it the universal is an 'empty abstraction', nevertheless individuals assume full reality only in so far as they operate within society. A true concept of personality, then, cannot be arrived at either when the individual is sacrificed to the state, as in the ancient world, or when the state is sacrificed to the individual, as in the Middle Ages. It will emerge only when the relationship between the individual and the state is formulated in a rational and conscious way.[24]

The more moderate Westernizer Granovskii, who shared Herzen's enthusiasm for the institution of knight-errantry and indeed was himself surrounded by an aura of chivalry, expressed his own respect for the individual, on one level, through resistance to what he saw as the dry, cruel concept of historical necessity, which he believed had superseded the concept of chance in the eyes of modern historians as the chief determinant of historical events.[25] Necessity seemed to Granovskii to treat peoples as means to the fulfilment of some overriding idea and to strip man of dignity by turning him into a 'blind, almost unconscious instrument of fateful predeterminations'.[26] In opposition to the deterministic view of history, Granovskii asserted that the individual was not so much the instrument as an independent 'champion or opponent of a historical law', the 'architect' as well as the 'material' of his history. Thus, the morally enlightened man of learning had a role, in Granovskii's scheme of things. It should be a major purpose for a people to create such individuals and a society which answered to their needs. The enlightened individuals, for their part, would civilize an ever greater proportion of the masses who, left to their own devices, stagnated under the weight of 'historical and natural contingencies'.[27]

Perhaps the most important contribution to the debate on the subject of personality in Russia in the 1840s was made by the young historian and legal scholar Kavelin in his essay 'A Survey of the Juridical Way of Life of Ancient Russia', which was published in 1847 and taken by the Westernizers themselves as a definitive statement of their view of Russian historical development. Searching for the principle which had governed Russian history from its beginnings, according to the chronicles, in the ninth century, Kavelin focused on the infinite, unconditional value with which Christianity endowed the human personality. With the advent of Christianity man was no longer the 'slave of nature and circumstances', but their master; his spiritual energies were released and his moral and individual development became the 'slogans of all modern history'. However, among the Russian tribes the principle of *lichnost'* had not existed in the early stages of their history. Whereas the German tribes, having mingled with the Roman elements in the lands they conquered and having accepted Christianity, founded states of a new type imbued with the 'individual principle', the Russians had adopted at the dawn of their history an exclusively patrimonial form of social organization based on the principle of kinship. They lived originally as one family in settlements under the rule of an elder, recognized no political power or legal authority, devised no laws, set up no administration, and owned no personal property. In time, though, in Russia too the individual began to free himself from the bonds of kinship. Indeed, Russian history could best be periodized in accordance with the stages by which the personal principle advanced at the expense of the patrimonial one. Although the patrimonial principle had begun to decay even in the Kievan and Tatar periods, when already some princes had been prepared to subordinate the interests of the clan to those of the state, it was in the Muscovite period that personality began to operate independently in juridical and civil affairs. Ivan the Terrible in particular hastened this process by establishing a service gentry in place of a hereditary nobility. His work was completed in a more propitious age by Peter the Great, through whom personality renounced 'immediate, natural, exclusively national determinations'; that is to say, in the eighteenth century individuals began to appear with a civic consciousness distinguishable from that of their fellows and not entirely determined by their environment. All Peter's private and public life constituted the 'first phase of the realization of the principle of personality in Russian history'. No less than the other Westernizers, Kavelin welcomed this process, for he believed that the principle of personality was a prerequisite for any spiritual development, and that without it an individual would lack resilience and energy and a people as a whole would play no significant role in the modern world.[28]

We must, however, remind ourselves of the limitations to which these Westernizers' conception of the rights of personality, the entitlements of the individual as against other, was subject. Herzen, after all, revolted by the rampant individualism of the Western bourgeoisie, was shortly to advocate his 'Russian socialism' attuned to the supposedly collectivist instincts of the faceless peasantry. Again, the liberal Westernizers expressed reservations about the emancipation of women, or in practice did not behave as if they fully endorsed it: Granovskii, for example, disapproved of women who aspired to some professional role, while others, such as Botkin, notorious for his sensuality, and Druzhinin, who patronizingly referred to women as *doñas*, tended to view the other sex mainly as a means to male pleasure. Most importantly, they yielded repeatedly to adulation of awesome forces beyond the control of the ordinary mortal, the sort of crushing superhuman political power epitomized by the image of Peter the Great in Pushkin's *Bronze Horseman* (*Mednyi vsadnik*, written in 1833), or the 'heroes' revered by Thomas Carlyle, who so fascinated Botkin in the 1850s. The same Belinskii who demands of Hegel a 'full account of all the victims of circumstance in life and history, all those martyrs to contingency, superstition, the Inquisition, Philip II, etc.' accepts that the kingdom of heaven on earth will not 'come about on its own, in due course, without violent upheavals and bloodshed', and admits that he loves mankind in the same way as Marat: in order to make the smallest part of it happy he would be prepared to destroy the rest of it with fire and sword. Belinskii's heroes in history are now the destroyers of the past, even the terrorists. He considers people so stupid that they must be led forcibly to happiness, deems the blood of a few thousand as of no significance 'when compared to the degradation and suffering of millions', and proclaims, with the Holy Roman Emperor Ferdinand I (1503–64), *fiat justitia—pereat mundus* ('may justice be done, even if the world should perish').[29] Granovskii's formulation of the role of the individual in history is on one level a panegyric to the 'great man', some mighty agent, such as Alexander the Great, Charlemagne, Peter the Great, or even Tamerlane, who is chosen by Providence to fulfil a mysterious purpose at a certain stage in a people's history.[30] This acceptance of a need in Russia for unbridled power enabled Granovskii in 1855 to rue the lack of a contemporary Peter and his 'big stick'.[31] Kavelin too reasoned that the emancipation of personality depended, as Walicki has put it, 'upon the rationalization of social relationships, and the emergence of the centralized state is a necessary stage in this process'.[32] Kavelin depicts Ivan the Terrible (whom Belinskii too had portrayed in startlingly sympathetic terms) as a tragic figure struggling against an environment unready to understand his genius.[33] Thus, while for Western liberals the state would play only a protective role in the promotion of individuality, which they conceived, as John Stuart Mill put it, as 'one of the principal ingredients of human happiness, and quite the chief ingredient of individual and social progress', their Russian counterparts seemed to accept that they still dwelt in an age when, in Mill's words, they had no alternative to 'implicit obedience to an Akbar or a Charlemagne', if they were so fortunate as to find one.[34]

This obeisance to strong state power continued in the period after the Crimean War (1853–6), at the beginning of the reign of Alexander II, when, in freer conditions, the surviving liberal Westernizers had some grounds for their belief that in Russia the best hope for individual liberation lay, paradoxical as it might seem, in the survival of enlightened autocracy. Men such as Kavelin and Annenkov now professed renewed loyalty to and reverence for the ruler who in 1856 had initiated discussion of emancipation, and who in 1861 did abolish serfdom. Similarly, Chicherin, in some respects a successor to the liberal Westernizers of the 1840s, while advocating the establishment of a *Rechtsstaat* in which individual rights would be guaranteed, at the same time sensed danger in proceeding too quickly in Russian conditions and emphasized the continuing need for a strong centralized state. Indeed, it was in the establishment of such a state that the whole sense of Russian history seemed to Chicherin to lie.[35]

Even that most Western of Russian writers, the novelist Turgenev, who in his political sympathies was close to the liberal Westernizers, seems to doubt both the capacity of the individual to achieve personal fulfilment through creative action and even the legitimacy of such selfish striving. In his fiction, as a Hungarian scholar has recently argued, it proves possible to satisfy the impulse to be oneself and at the same time to remain in harmony with nature only by achieving complete self-oblivion through a fusion of love, duty, and sacrifice, or through immersion of selfhood in the elements through art. The search for selfhood entails a sense of guilt and acceptance of punishment: it is as if such characters as

Liza in *A Nest of Gentry* (*Dvorianskoe gnezdo*, 1859) and Elena in *On the Eve* (*Nakanune*, 1860) lived in the world of an Old Testament God who punishes people for their temerity as they stand on the threshold of happiness.[36] Indeed, perhaps we may look on the 'superfluous man', the feckless, egoistic nobleman doomed by excess of reflection to passivity, isolation, and a sense of futility, as a manifestation of the failure of the human personality, in Russian conditions, to liberate itself from the 'immediate, natural, exclusively national determinations' of which Kavelin had spoken.

Chernyshevskii, the leading representative of the radical *raznochintsy* ('estate outsiders', that is, men and women from outside the ranks of the nobility) who were in the ascendancy in the intelligentsia after the Crimean War, makes a no less ambiguous contribution to the cause of the emancipation of the personality and liberation of the individual. Like the older Westernizers, he too, of course, clamoured for the emancipation of the peasantry. He also insisted on treating woman as an autonomous human being, a full equal to man with rights of her own, a rational intellect, and creative potential. This insistence is central to his seminal novel *What is to Be Done?* (*Chto delat'?*, 1863) and is taken up by minor writers influential in their time such as Sleptsov. And yet in other respects Chernyshevskii tended further to enslave rather than to liberate the individual. For the vulgar materialism he espoused, his concern to explain all phenomena, including human morality and behaviour, in the light of supposedly immutable and irresistible laws, made for a rigid determinism which deprived the individual of autonomy. In his essay 'The Anthropological Principle in Philosophy' (1860), in particular, Chernyshevskii belittles the will as a factor in prompting human actions and underlines the role of environment in the moulding of character and the shaping of the individual's destiny.[37] He is, in any case, interested in the material well-being of the collective rather than the abstract, legal, constitutional rights of the individual. The latter are meaningless, he argues elsewhere, without the material means to take advantage of them.[38]

Among the major radical thinkers of the 1860s only Pisarev vigorously asserts the rights of the individual. Russian literature, he argues in an early essay, must be a moral teacher, striving 'with all its might to emancipate the human personality from the various constraints which are imposed on it by the timidity of its own thought, caste prejudices, the authority of tradition, the aspiration to a common ideal, and all the obsolete lumber which prevents a living person from freely breathing and developing in all directions'.[39] And yet Pisarev's nihilism could lead to rejection of claims to individual identity. While Pavel Kirsanov in Turgenev's *Fathers and Children* (*Ottsy i deti*, 1862) holds that 'human personality must be strong as a rock, for everything is built upon it' (chapter 10), his ideological rival Bazarov contends that 'One human specimen is sufficient for one to make judgements about all the others. People are like trees in a forest: no botanist is going to study an individual birch-tree' (chapter 16). At the same time, nihilism, pressed in another direction, endowed the individual with a freedom liable to lead to social disintegration. For in a world in which religious belief was breaking down, the assertive personality, accepting only the empirical evidence of the five senses, ultimately lost belief in anything outside itself, as

Pisarev acknowledged in his essay on Bazarov, and found itself free to choose at random between good and evil.[40] It is a potentiality long feared by the representatives of the particularist stream of Russian thought, to whose countervailing view of *lichnost'* we may now turn.

'Particularist' Views of *Lichnost'*

For thinkers who belonged to the particularist, that is the anti-rationalist, nationalist stream of Russian thought, the ideal development of personality consisted not in the cultivation of individuality but in its voluntary renunciation. Thinkers of this type cherished Russian institutions such as the Orthodox Church, to which the individual seemed to surrender personal identity. Thus, the peasant commune was admired by Konstantin Aksakov, for example, as a 'moral choir' in which the highest aspiration of the individual was to contribute to the general harmony.[41] At the same time they abhorred those features of Western civilization which they considered a threat to Russian institutions. Such features included Roman law, the Catholic Church and the type of learning it was believed to generate, and notions such as honour and chivalry, to which they thought Western assertion of the self had given rise. The view of personality held by such thinkers can be traced, in the classical period of Russian culture, through the various forms in which conservative nationalism manifested itself, from Slavophilism and *pochvennichestvo* (so-called 'native soil conservatism') to pan-Slavism.

Slavophile abhorrence of the condition to which Western absorption with self was supposed to lead perhaps finds its clearest expression in an essay written by Samarin in 1847 in response to Kavelin's 'Survey of the Juridical Way of Life of Ancient Russia', and in Ivan Kireevskii's essay of 1852 'On the Nature of European Culture and its Relation to the Culture of Russia'. Samarin distinguished between two meanings of personality which he felt Kavelin had confused: 'personality in the sense of an exclusive individualism which sets itself up to be the measure of all things', and 'personality as an organ of consciousness' whose role it was to integrate man's divided spiritual forces. Samarin agreed with Kavelin that personality in the first sense had not existed in ancient Russia, but considered that personality in its second sense, as reflected in the spiritual wholeness and strength of ancient Russian monks, princes, and heroes of folk epics, was correspondingly stronger there than in the West. The value of Christianity's contribution to history lay, according to Samarin, in encouragement of a willingness to renounce selfish 'exclusive' individuality and to submit entirely to the community. The concepts 'man' and 'people' were identical. What Samarin shunned was the principle of personality as reflected in Teutonic individuality, which led down a blind alley.[42]

Kireevskii argued in a similar vein that Western civilization, dominated by the legacy of the Roman mentality, was characterized by a dead formalism which distorted natural human relationships. Roman law and poetry, and even the Latin language, all bore this rigidity and artificiality. In these circumstances the only thing governing one's actions was one's 'personal logical conviction', so that each *lichnost'* considered itself not only distinct but also different from other personalities, and could conceive of no relations with them other than relations logically deduced from the external conditions of life. In the medieval world every 'noble personality' strove to become a law unto itself in its relations with others. The knight in his castle was a separate state, oblivious to the interests of his people or the state as a whole and submitting only to laws of honour. There thus developed societies based not on 'public spirit' but on a spirit of 'personal separateness'. In the modern world Westerners lived their lives in a state of personal disintegration, cultivating different selves in conformity with their various personal drives: religious, rational, sensual, ethical, egoistic, aesthetic. Russians, on the other hand, free of individualism and materialism, exhibited a true Christian spirit which led them always to sacrifice themselves for the sake of their family and to strive for 'inner wholeness of being'.[43]

An essentially similar view of the Westerner is taken by the pan-Slavist Danilevskii. In his *magnum opus Russia and the West* (*Rossiia i Zapad*, 1869) Danilevskii argues that it is an excessively developed feeling of personality, of individuality, that leads Westerners to value their own interests so highly, and thus explains the coercive nature of all the peoples of the Romano-Germanic type.[44] However, the most compelling depiction of the sickness thought to afflict the godless Westerner, with his exaggerated view of his individual importance, is provided by Dostoevskii, whose love of paradox fuses easily with the Slavophile inversion of Westernist arguments. The solution to modern problems to which Dostoevskii's writings point is at a polar opposite from the Westernizers' demand for legally guaranteed rights. It is to be found instead in the apparent extinction of self within the Christian fold. This solution, while implicit in Dostoevskii's major novels, is most explicitly advocated in his *Winter Notes on Summer Impressions* (*Zimnie zametki o letnikh vpechatleniiakh*, 1863), his deliberately perverse attempt to define Russian selfhood by contrast with the West, which he had visited for the first time in 1862. The entire West was afflicted, Dostoevskii claimed here, by a struggle to the death between the individualistic principle and the need for people somehow to live together, create a community, and construct a single antheap without devouring each other. While the Westerner talks about brotherhood as the great moving force of mankind, in reality he exhibits the 'principle of the mansion', or place apart (*osobniak*), of 'intensified self-preservation'. He places his ego in opposition to the whole of nature and to all other people like a separate principle of absolutely equal value to everything outside it. Brotherhood could not in fact arise out of such self-exaltation, because real brotherhood comes about not when the self demands equality with other, but when other of its own volition acknowledges the equal value of self. Indeed, the rebellious self should entirely and unconditionally surrender to society. That is not to say that salvation and happiness lay in impersonality (*bezlichnost'*). For to sacrifice oneself completely, unconditionally, consciously, and voluntarily, for the benefit of all, to go to the cross or the stake, is for Dostoevskii the highest development of personality, the highest expression of freedom of will. A strongly developed personality, fully assured of its right to be a personality, has no use other than to give itself up to others so that they too might become happy. This is for Dostoevskii the law of nature towards which the normal human leans. On its basis he constructs his own utopia in answer to that of the French socialists and their Russian followers, who seek to beguile people into surrendering a part of themselves to the community by holding out the prospect of material advantage.[45]

To a degree, the tradition represented by the Slavophiles, by Danilevskii, and by Dostoevskii is continued by the populists. Admittedly, the populists, countering what they saw as Chernyshevskii's 'fatalism', wished to reinstate the autonomy of what Lavrov called the 'critically thinking individual', that is to say the 'repentant nobleman' or the *raznochinets* endowed with free will and fired by a sense of moral duty to enlighten the masses. And yet, at the same time, for the populists, as for the Slavophiles before them, that quality of Russian history which Kavelin had identified as indicative of the absence of the principle of *lichnost'*—a communal, apolitical, unbureaucratic way of life—was a virtue to be cherished and incorporated in a new social order before capitalism and its attendant political forms obliterated the vestiges of it that survived among the peasantry. Moreover, by going to the people and in many cases attempting to assume the identity of peasants, the populists strikingly fulfilled the ambition of so many Russian thinkers to sacrifice their individual personalities to some form of other. The aspiration to merge with the *narod*, which sometimes assumed the quasi-religious character of a spiritual exploit or *podvig*, was emulated by certain revolutionaries who in the 1880s and 1890s conducted propaganda among the urban workers, such as the St Petersburg artisan Tochisskii,[46] and by the Tolstoyans who tried to 'simplify themselves' (*oprostit'sia*).

We might say of thinkers of the particularist stream of thought in general that they are less concerned with finding means of liberating the individual than with defining the collective personality of their people. Under the influence of notions originating in eighteenth-century Germany about national distinctiveness (*Volkstum*), and perhaps also as a consequence of the distance of the educated class from the popular mass, they indulged in large and mainly eulogistic generalizations about the nature of the Russian *narod*. Such speculation merged with the perennial quest to divine the riddle of the national destiny, a riddle symbolized at the end of part I of Gogol''s *Dead Souls* by Chichikov's *troika* flying through the air, inspired by God, like Russia herself, for whom other peoples and states draw aside and make way. And yet the preoccupation with national personality was not confined to thinkers of a nationalist complexion. Thinkers within that apparently universalistic stream, which seemed to share a Western concern for the emergence of the autonomous creative individual, such as Belinskii, Herzen, and Dobroliubov, were also prone to assume that the Russian possessed such qualities as a communal nature, good sense, a clear and practical mind, and sobriety. This widespread preoccupation with national personality is perhaps reflected in the Russian language itself, with its abundance of expressions defining the Russian character. At the same time, the emotive content of such concepts as *otchizna*, *otechestvo*, and *rodina*, denoting entities to which the individual belongs (or, if the Russian does not belong to such an entity, he or she has that nomadic quality detected by Chaadaev among his educated countrymen), test-ifies to a different conception of the relationship of the individual to the world about him from that to which the Englishman is accustomed.

Conclusion

One is therefore tempted finally to suggest that the concept of *lichnost'* should not be equated too closely, when one speaks of the classical age of Russian culture, with the English concepts of 'personality' and the 'individual'. The importance of the Russian concept is relatively slight at all points on the political spectrum. Among the Westernizers of the 1840s, both radical and liberal, it competes with reverence for the great historical individual and yields to an awe of the powerful state which makes for a willingness to overlook curtailment of individual liberty. Among later, more radical Westernizers, 'men of the 1860s' (and from the 1880s among Marxists such as Plekhanov too) the concept is weakened by predilection for supposedly scientific and therefore immutable laws which leave little room for individuals to fashion their own destiny. Among conservative nationalists the concept pales again into insignificance beside the desire for more or less mystical communion with some absolute form of otherness.

Obshchestvennost', Sobornost': Collective Identities

Catriona Kelly and Vadim Volkov

THE distinction between Russian and Western concepts of the individual, as well as the tension between 'universalist' and 'particularist' streams of thought, are underlined by the existence of two concepts that gained currency in Russia during the second half of the nineteenth century—*sobornost'* and *obshchestvennost'*—neither of which is easily translatable into English. The first, evolved by the Slavophile thinker Khomiakov, was derived from the translation, in the Russian Creed, of the word 'Catholic' (as in 'one holy Catholic and Apostolic Church') as *sobornaia* (universal or all-embracing). For all its theological origins, however, *sobornost'* soon came to have resonances that were more social and political than theological:

> As [Khomiakov] used the word, *sobornost'* meant unity in multiplicity, an organic union of believers in love and freedom, and pertained to the church as an idea, not as an institution . . . The peasant commune (*mir*) exemplified *sobornost'*; *sobornost'* was the Russian answer to class conflict, the antipode of the rationalism, legalism, compulsion of the West.[47]

Members of the collectivist community would, by implication, be subjected to the overall governance of a patriarch (if the community followed the pattern of the village *mir*, where a *starosta* or elder directed decision-making). The concept of *sobornost'* did not imply enthusiasm for a society that was 'democratic' in the Western liberal sense, that is to say, a social order characterized by full and equal participation of all citizens, in which decision-makers were subject to control by the ballot-box and by legal checks and governances. It was in any case distinguished by the vague and explicitly religious tone of Khomiakov's thought from the rational concepts of a secular society which appealed to Russians with Westernizing enthusiasms. Later thinkers of a Slavophile cast, such as Dostoevskii and Viacheslav Ivanov, were to re-emphasize these anti-Western aspects of *sobornost'*. In Dostoevskii's *Brothers Karamazov* (*Brat'ia Karamazovy*, 1880), for example, the cohort of small boys gathered by Alesha Karamazov as followers (an instance of Christian values at work in the wider world) represents the antipode of the Western tradition caricatured in the 'Legend of the Grand Inquisitor', in which religion is subordinated to temporal authority and rational philanthropy.

The response of Westernizing commentators was to stress individualism less than a different form of collectivist society, one organized this time round secular and rational values. *Obshchestvennost'* appears to have been coined either by the writer and historian Nikolai Karamzin in his *Letters of a Russian Traveller* (*Pis'ma russkogo puteshestvennika*, 1791–1801) or, according to a different account, by the anti-autocratic thinker and writer Aleksandr Radishchev in 1790.[48] It then disappeared from view for several decades before being revived by radicals of the 1840s and 1850s, such as Belinskii, Herzen, and Ogarev, to mean social solidarity, the specific qualities developed by people living in society. A secondary meaning signified the 'progressive' or rationalist sector of society that was distinguished from the conservative aristocratic elite (*obshchestvo*; the British equivalent is 'high society'). That is, *obshchestvennost'* meant both the qualities of social engagement, and the sector of society most likely to manifest such qualities, the radical intelligentsia. Among Russian liberals, *obshchestvennost'* came to refer to concern with public duties and common deeds (*res publica*, in Russian *delo obshchestvennoe*), and also to 'public opinion' (*obshchestvennoe mnenie*) as expressed in democratic political structures and a free press. Potentially, then, the term supplied a common identity to people of different estates and professions (and varying political views) who committed themselves to social duties. Since *obshchestvennost'* is constituted through concerted action, an individual can be said to be a member of *obshchestvennost'* if and while (and only if and while) he takes part in such action. In other words, the term conceptualized society according to a cross-class, rather than anti-class, ideology, while at the same time constructing a hierarchy according to which those sectors of the population who were engaged in engineering social change (and above all the intelligentsia) were seen as privileged members of the collective. Furthermore, by representing both dirigiste and consensualist views of Russia's ideal political evolution, the concept of *obshchestvennost'* neatly encapsulated the fissuring of public discourse in late nineteenth- and early twentieth-century Russia.

Collectivist rather than individualist, and inscribing (though in very different ways) the notion of an individual's primary loyalty to the larger community, *sobornost'* and *obshchestvennost'* were to prove, for many Russian political thinkers of the late nineteenth and early twentieth centuries, more attractive and productive ideologies than *lichnost'*, or individualism, with its puzzling elusiveness and instability.

Narodnost': Notions of National Identity

Maureen Perrie

Origins

THE term *narodnost'* is one of the most elusive in the Russian language. Its meanings and possible translations range from nationalism, nationality, nationhood, and national identity, through folkways, folksiness, and folklorism, to populism, popularity, accessibility, and comprehensibility. It has been dignified by inclusion in two notorious 'trinities' of Russian cultural history: alongside Orthodoxy and autocracy in the tripartite formula of 'Official Nationality' in the reign of Nicholas I; and, together with ideological correctness (*ideinost'*) and Party-mindedness (*partiinost'*), in the dogma of Soviet socialist realism.

The word *narodnost'* appears to have been first used in 1819 by the poet P. A. Viazemskii in a letter to A. Turgenev. Viazemskii described his poem 'First snow' as having a 'Russian colouring', and he referred to the *narodnost'* of some of its stylistic features. Recognizing that the term was a neologism, Viazemskii added: 'Why not translate *nationalité* as *narodnost'*? After all, the Poles have said *narodowość*!'[49] It is clear from this that Viazemskii intended *narodnost'* to be the Russian equivalent of the French *nationalité* or English 'nationality' (or rather, in the context, 'national character'). But why, in that case, did he feel the need to coin the new term *narodnost'*, when the Russian language already possessed the word *natsional'nost'*? His decision may partly have reflected a distaste for words of foreign origin, typical of some proponents of Russian national consciousness in the late eighteenth and early nineteenth centuries; but it also reflected Viazemskii's awareness that the adjective *narodnyi*, from which the noun *narodnost'* was derived, was the Russian equivalent not only of the French *national* but also of *populaire*: 'we say *narodnye pesni* and *dukh narodnyi* where the French would say *chanson populaire* [popular song] and *esprit national* [national spirit]', he wrote in 1824.[50]

In its turn, the Russian word *narod* can mean both 'nation' and 'people', in the sense of the 'common' or 'simple' people (*prostoi narod*). The term *narodnost'*, when applied to literature, came to refer not only to its 'national character' in the sense of a Russian colouring or setting, but also to elements of folklorism in its style or content. Conversely, folklore and its bearers and transmitters, the *prostoi narod*, came to be seen as the truest exemplars of the Russian national character.

The basis for this identification of the *prostoi narod* as the source of the national character was laid in the late eighteenth century. Russian national consciousness developed among the educated elite of the eighteenth century partly as a form of protest against Western cultural influence. This led to an identification of rural Russia as more truly 'national' than the urban centres, such as St Petersburg and Moscow, where foreign influence was greatest.[51] A number of satires depicted dissolute and Westernized aristocrats, divorced from their native soil, and indulging their taste for foreign luxuries at the expense of their peasants. These parasites were counterposed to true Russian noblemen of the old school, who lived not in the capitals, but on their ancestral estates, where harmonious patriarchal relations supposedly prevailed between lord and peasant. Eighteenth-century writers such as N. I. Novikov and D. I. Fonvizin played an important part in the definition of what came to be regarded as Russian national characteristics. According to Hans Rogger, these were

> values that came to be regarded as national because they were the opposite of the vices which imitation was thought to have produced. They were the simple virtues on which every nation thrown into contact with a more complex civilization tends to pride itself: possession of a generous heart and simple soul . . .; the preservation of a certain roughness of manner . . .; the avoidance of luxury and a proper regard for probity, sincerity, friendship, and honest service.[52]

Once the patriarchal village, where lord and peasant lived together in harmony, had been identified as the true fount of national life and strength, it was only a short step to the depiction of the peasants themselves as embodiments of traditional national virtues. The influence of Rousseau encouraged the notion that rural people lived closer to nature, and hence to God, than did civilized man; the peasants were therefore more truly human, and more profound in their capacity for feeling, than the urbanized and Westernized nobility. And the true expression of national feeling was folklore, the artistic expression of the simple peasantry.

The interest of the educated class in folklore went back to the second half of the eighteenth century; in Russia, as elsewhere in Europe, it was influenced by the growth of nationalism and romanticism. In contrast to the cosmopolitan and universalist neo-classicism of the mid-century, sentimentalism and early romanticism were concerned with indigenous literary and artistic forms. Just as the peasantry came to be seen as the true bearers of the national character, so did their artistic creations appear as the truest expression of the national culture. (Comparative studies have shown that much folklore comprises universal motifs; but this discovery was made later, and did not seriously undermine belief in the national peculiarity of folklore.)

The notion of the peasantry as the authentic embodiment of the nation was not, of course, unique to Russia; like so many other intellectual trends, it was borrowed from the West. But in Russia the reception of this idea was influenced by two specific features. First, Peter the Great's reforms had introduced a greater distinction between the Westernized upper classes, on the one hand, and the 'simple people', on the other, than existed in other European states. And second, the fact that the majority of the *narod* comprised serfs, and that serfdom not only assumed a harsher form, but also lasted longer in Russia than in any other major European country, made the Russian 'peasant question' more acute than it was elsewhere. The idealization of the peasantry by so many nineteenth-century intellectuals may have reflected the guilt of educated nobles whose privileges were derived from serf-ownership.

The concept of *narodnost'* enjoyed a considerable vogue in the 1820s, particularly in discussions of the national character of Russian literature.[53] The incorporation of folk motifs in the poetry of the Romantic era, in Russia as elsewhere, served to give literature a 'national' flavour. But Pushkin, who utilized folk themes in poems such as *Ruslan and Liudmila* (*Ruslan i Liudmila*, 1821), nevertheless insisted that *narodnost'* in literature represented a more profound expression of national character than simply the adoption of local settings and vocabulary.[54] Pushkin's concept of 'true' *narodnost'* was somewhat mystical and elusive; a more superficial variety of *narodnost'*, however, in the guise of folklorism, came to characterize much nineteenth-century literature. Folk art also influenced Russian music: folk melodies and motifs were incorporated into the works of such composers as Glinka, Musorgskii, Borodin, and Rimskii-Korsakov.

But Russian romanticism did not identify *narodnost'* exclusively with the ethnically Russian peasantry. Literary figures close to the Decembrists associated the concept with the peoples of the Empire as a whole. Orest Somov, in his 1823 article 'On Romantic Poetry', insisted that Russian poets should write about the non-Russian nations of the Empire, and utilize the mythology and beliefs of these peoples in their verse. Pushkin, in his Byronic *Captive of the Caucasus* (*Kavkazskii plennik*, 1822), provided an early example of this new imperial literature.[55]

Intellectuals throughout the nineteenth century continued to associate *narodnost'*—as the expression of a truly national and popular form of culture— with the rural peasantry. The growth of towns and cities, with their expanding lower-class populations, was to be accompanied by the development of various forms of urban popular culture: funfairs, circuses, and music-halls, as well as publications addressed to the mass market. Some of this popular literature, such as *lubki* (chapbooks), circulated widely in the countryside as well as the towns. These various manifestations of popular culture, however, were never accepted by educated society as genuine expressions of *narodnost'*: rather, they were seen as reflecting the corrupt, commercialized, and Westernized values of the cities.[56]

The Rise of Official *Narodnost'*

From the early 1830s, the term *narodnost'* was adopted by the government of Nicholas I for its own purposes. In a circular of 2 April 1833 addressed to the officials in charge of the educational districts of the Empire, the newly appointed Minister of Education, S. Uvarov, proclaimed: 'Our common obligation consists in this, that the education of the people be conducted, according to the Supreme intention of our August Monarch, in the joint spirit of Orthodoxy, autocracy and nationality [*narodnost'*].'[57] This three-part formula, subsequently to become known as the ideology of 'Official Nationality', influenced government policy throughout the reign of Nicholas I. Of the three elements, nationality was the least precise and most problematic. Some have claimed that the term was merely a euphemism for serfdom, which it would have been more accurate to list as the third key institution of Nicolaevan Russia. And the historian S. M. Solov'ev noted the irony that the concept of *narodnost'* was advocated as a central educational principle by Uvarov, a man who 'had not read a single Russian book in his life and wrote constantly in French or in German'.[58]

In view of the generally conservative tenor of Nicholas's government, it is tempting to equate Uvarov's *narodnost'* with 'nationalism'.[59] Hans Rogger has identified an early form of official nationalism in the eighteenth century, in the reign of Catherine the Great. This stressed not only the German-born Empress's commitment to Russian principles, in contrast to the allegedly Prussian sympathies of Peter III, the husband she had deposed and murdered, but also her continuation of the achievements of Peter the Great.[60] Military glory and territorial expansion naturally played an important part in this tradition; and in the early nineteenth century Russia's victories in the Napoleonic Wars strengthened national pride. The publication from 1816 of the multi-volume *History of the Russian State* by N. M. Karamzin, the official historiographer, also played its part in strengthening this brand of official nationalism.

Nicholas Riasanovsky has drawn attention to the existence of two distinct concepts of nationality within the government: the 'dynastic' and the 'nationalistic'.[61] The former in effect recognized the reality of the Russian state as a multinational empire, and stressed the importance of the Romanov dynasty as its unifying force. This position was taken to an extreme by Count E. Kankrin, the Minister of Finance, when he said:

> If we consider the matter thoroughly, then, in justice, we must be called not *Russians*, but *Petrovians* . . . Everything: glory, power, prosperity, and enlightenment, we owe to the Romanov family; and, out of gratitude, we should change our general tribal name of *Slavs* to the name of the creator of the empire and of its well-being. Russia should be called *Petrovia*, and we *Petrovians*; or the empire should be named *Romanovia*, and we — *Romanovites*.[62]

The 'nationalistic' view, by contrast, was influenced by romantic concepts of nationalism and national identity, and placed more stress on specific notions of Russia and the Russian people and their historical mission.

This distinction reflects the two different concepts of nationhood that co-existed in nineteenth-century Russia: the 'imperial' concept of the nation as coterminous with the population of the Empire; and the 'ethnic' concept of the Russian people. The adjective *rossiiskii* referred to an inhabitant of the Russian Empire, whereas *russkii* indicated an ethnic Russian. Ethnic 'Russianness' itself was, however, a problematic concept. Official statistics, as late as the 1897 census, used the category 'Russians' (*russkie*) to comprise not only Great Russians (*velikorusskie*), but also Ukrainians (*malorusskie*, literally 'Little Russians') and Belorussians ('White Russians').

Both groups of 'official nationalists' shared a concept of the ordinary Russian people as especially devoted to both autocracy and Orthodoxy, and to that extent it is not coincidental that Uvarov should have chosen to use the word *narodnost'*, rather than *natsional'nost'*, for the third element of his 'trinity'.

Andrzej Walicki has noted that *narodnost'* 'was not only intended to convey a certain nationalistic trend, but also reflected the efforts of the autocratic regime to expand its social base, to rely *directly* on the "people" in the broad sense of the word'; in the aftermath of the Decembrist uprising of 1825, in which scions of the most aristocratic families in the land had attempted to overthrow the autocracy, Nicholas I liked to contrast the loyalty to the throne of the peasantry with the oppositional mood of many of the educated nobility.[63]

This official notion of a union of Tsar and people had its counterpart in peasant concepts of the Tsar as the protector of the ordinary people against exploitation and oppression by bureaucrats and nobles. These 'popular monarchist' ideas found their expression in folklore, especially in positive popular images of rulers such as Ivan the Terrible and Peter the Great, who were notorious for their harsh treatment of the nobility. In the seventeenth and eighteenth centuries, popular rebellions had often centred around pretenders who claimed to be 'true Tsars' leading the peasants against serfdom; in the nineteenth century, peasant 'rebels in the name of the Tsar' claimed to believe that the Tsar had decreed an end to serfdom, but the nobles opposed the implementation of his wishes.

The government itself was not, however, particularly successful in harnessing such sentiments. Occasionally the Tsar tried to take advantage of the symbolism of the myth, as when Nicholas I bowed low to the people of Moscow on a visit to the Kremlin, but in general autocracy as a system was too dependent on the institutions of the nobility and the bureaucracy to risk complementing 'popular monarchism' with its own 'monarchist populism'.[64]

In this notion of the unity of Tsar and people, the 'people' were not necessarily perceived as ethnically Russian. On occasion, the Tsarist government sought to bid for the support of the non-Russian lower classes against the nationalism of the local nobility. The most striking case of this occurred in Russian Poland after the nationalist uprising of 1863. The agrarian reform of 1864 gave the Polish peasants more favourable treatment than their Russian counterparts had received in the Emancipation Act of 1861, as a reward for their loyalty to the throne during the insurgency.

The dynastic and 'nationalist' schools of Official Nationality also differed over their attitudes towards the non-Russian nobility of the Empire. According to the dynastic view, where non-Russian nobles proved themselves to be loyal servants of the state, not only should they not be discriminated against, but they should be allowed special privileges. The most obvious example of this was the case of the Baltic German nobility, whose service was much prized by Nicholas I. The nationalist advocates of Official Nationality, however, were suspicious of the Baltic Germans, and advocated the removal of their privileges and the Russification of the Latvian and Estonian majorities in the Baltic provinces, as a counterweight to the German nobility.[65]

Narodnost' in the Slavophile–Westernizer Debate

Differing concepts of *narodnost'* played their part in the famous controversies between Slavophiles and Westernizers in the 1840s. The ideas that came to be known as Slavophilism were formulated primarily in response to Peter Chaadaev's privately circulated *Philosophical Letters*, which depicted Russia as a backward and benighted country without a history or a national culture. Writers such as Ivan Kireevskii, Aleksei Khomiakov, and Konstantin Aksakov, seeking to defend the Russian national character, found its origins in the traditions and institutions of the common people. For Kireevskii, true Christian principles, as embodied in the Orthodox religion, had survived among the ordinary Russian people, who were unaffected by the Westernizing influences introduced by Peter the Great. Peasant institutions such as the patriarchal family and the commune (*obshchina, mir*) embodied these Christian precepts. (Ironically, the first detailed study of the Russian peasant commune was made in the 1840s by a German scholar, August von Haxthausen.) For Kireevskii, the *narod* embodied the old traditions and the principle of community (*Gemeinschaft*), while educated society (*obshchestvo*) represented modern European civilization, corrupted by rationalism, Roman law, and the principles of private property (*Gesellschaft*). Aksakov was the most fanatical of the Slavophiles in his espousal of the cause of the *narod*: he wore peasant dress and cultivated a beard in order to draw closer to the 'people' who, however, according to Chaadaev, mistook him for a Persian. Aksakov was an uncritical admirer of the peasant commune as an ideal model of *Gemeinschaft*, with its principle of unanimity rather than majority voting. But even for Aksakov, these principles were not peculiarly Russian: they were of universal value, but happened to have been preserved most fully among the peasantry because of accidents of Russia's historical development.

Slavophilism is sometimes characterized as a reactionary form of nationalism that idealized Russian backwardness. But in reality its founders proceeded from a religious standpoint of universalist significance that saw the Russian peasantry as the sole surviving bearers of original Christian principles which would ultimately triumph not only amongst the Russian educated classes, but also in Western Europe. The Slavophiles differed from the proponents of Official Nationality in their rejection of the Petrine state and in their criticism of the Westernized educated society (*obshchestvo*) that had been brought into being by Peter's reforms. Hostility to the autocratic state and to the statist principle (*gosudarstvennost'*) in general was a major part of Slavophile teaching: they set up the *narod* as a counterweight to the state as a focus for national attachment and identity.

A similar distinction to that drawn by the Slavophiles between the *narod* and *obshchestvo* was made by their Westernizer opponents. For the Westernizers, however, *narod* was the inferior category. The literary critic Vissarion Belinskii differentiated between the *narod* and *narodnost'*, on the one hand, and the *natsiia* and *natsional'nost'*, on the other. Pre-Petrine Russia, according to Belinskii, had been a *narod*—a primitive form of society, patriarchal, non-differentiated, and homogeneous. Peter's reforms had begun the process of transforming the *narod* into a *natsiia* by the raising of its consciousness through education. A truly national literature and culture, Belinskii argued, would be characterized not by pseudo-folklorism, but by the development of a more truly national spirit, on the lines of the development of national consciousness in the West.[66]

After the emancipation of the serfs in 1861, the development of the concepts of the 'nation' and the 'people' diverged. The ideas of Official Nationalism evolved in the direction of pan-Slavism. M. P. Pogodin asserted the common heritage of the Slav peoples, both inside and outside the Russian Empire. It was Russia's mission to liberate her Slav brothers currently oppressed within alien empires, and perhaps to bring them together into a single Slav state under the Russian Tsar. But pan-Slavism was full of contradictions. The Russian Empire was not a purely Slav state, and the Tsars denied to both their Slav and non-Slav subjects the rights that the pan-Slavs claimed for the Slav peoples of the Ottoman and Austro-Hungarian Empires. And whereas the Official Nationalist precursors of pan-Slavism had stressed the Orthodox religion, Slavdom was not identical with Orthodoxy: the Poles, the Czechs, and the Croats were predominantly Roman Catholic, while other Slavs were Protestant, and in the Balkans sometimes even Muslim. The Tsars were wary of pan-Slavism when it encouraged or supported Slav nationalist movements abroad, undermining the principles of legitimism on which the domestic stability of the Russian Empire depended. Where it suited Russia's great-power interests, however, the Tsarist government was willing to support Slav nationalisms. This was particularly the case in the Balkans, where Russian expansionism led to war with Turkey in 1877–8; and where Russia's support of Serbia against Austria-Hungary in 1914 led directly to the outbreak of the First World War.

Within the Russian Empire, the rise of non-Russian nationalisms, both Slav and non-Slav, intensified the tendency towards a state policy of Russification that had already been evident in the first half of the nineteenth century. After the Polish rising of 1863, measures to promote Orthodoxy and the use of the Russian language were instituted not only in the Kingdom of Poland but also in the western and south-western provinces of the Empire, where much of the population was Belorussian or Ukrainian. Similar measures were subsequently introduced in the Baltic provinces. Discrimination against the Jews was another element in the Russification policies of Alexander III: quotas for Jewish admissions to secondary and higher education were introduced in 1887; and further restrictions were decreed to Jewish rights of residence, both inside and outside the Pale of settlement. These policies might have been defended as an attempt to create a 'civic nation' of *rossiiane* with a common language and religion that would serve as unifying cultural bonds within the Empire; but the clumsy way in which they were introduced tended to make them counter-productive and to encourage the anti-Russian nationalisms they were intended to forestall. But it must be noted that the Russification policies of the Tsarist government were designed as measures of assimilation and inclusion rather than of racial exclusion: unlike in Nazi Germany, for example, a Russian Jew who converted to Christianity ceased to be regarded as a Jew, and was even accorded special privileges.[67]

If Russian nationalism moved in the directions of pan-Slavism and Russification in the second half of the nineteenth century, conservative thought did retain some elements of Official Nationality right through to the early twentieth century. Some of the right-wing political groupings that formed during the 1905 Revolution, such as the Union of Russian Men and the Union of the Russian

People, embraced neo-Slavophile notions of the union of Tsar and people. They advocated some kind of resurrection of the pre-Petrine Assembly of the Land (*zemskii sobor*) as an alternative to the elected Western-style State Duma. These groups also revived the slogans of Official Nationality: Orthodoxy, autocracy, and *narodnost'*. The Union of the Russian People, in particular, enjoyed some success in recruiting peasant support in 1905–7.[68] If 'popular monarchism' survived into the early twentieth century, so too did 'monarchist populism'. The last, ironic echo of the rulers' belief that they enjoyed the love of the *narod* came with Nicholas II's patronage of Rasputin, an earthy 'man of the people' who symbolized for the Emperor—and even more so for the Empress Alexandra—the closeness of the bond between Tsar and *muzhik* (peasant).

Narodnost' in Revolutionary Thought

In the second half of the nineteenth century *narodnost'* also developed in a very different direction: towards revolutionary populism (*narodnichestvo*). The populists inherited from the Slavophiles a view of the peasant commune as an institution that embodied the principles of social equality and justice; they added the notion that these principles made the commune the embryo of a socialist system (in most of European Russia the commune periodically redistributed the land under its control to its component households on the basis of family size, thereby seemingly implementing the socialist principle of 'to each according to their need'). The populists developed a view of a peculiarly Russian type of socialism that could be created on the basis of existing popular institutions such as the peasant commune and the artisan co-operative workshop (*artel'*). In Western Europe, Marxists envisaged the creation of a socialist society as a result of the development of capitalism, the proletarianization of the small producers, and the revolutionary expropriation of the capitalist class by the proletariat. The Russian populists, by contrast, believed that Russia could achieve socialism without going through the stage of capitalist development. Socialist propaganda among the peasants and artisans would raise them to a level of revolutionary consciousness, and the overthrow of the autocratic state would lead to the creation of a socialist society. The first stage in the revolutionary transformation would be 'black partition': the transfer of all of the land of the large estates into the hands of the peasantry, for them to cultivate on the basis of communal principles.

In Russia, therefore, the social group that the populists identified as the bearers of socialism was not the proletariat but the communal peasantry—the *narod*. Since the recently emancipated peasants were not conscious socialists, however, the question arose of the relationship of the revolutionary socialist intelligentsia to the *narod*. In the early 1870s the 'movement to the people' of several thousand idealistic young people represented an attempt by the revolutionaries to teach the peasants about socialism. Many of the students were to be bitterly disillusioned as a result of their experiences in the villages in the 'mad summer' of 1874. They failed to provoke any kind of popular revolt, and were generally met with incomprehension by the peasants. Hundreds were arrested, some of them denounced to the authorities by the peasants themselves. The failure of the 'movement to the people' led some revolutionaries to develop the idea that, instead of trying to teach the people about socialism, the intelligentsia should serve the interests of the *narod* and subordinate themselves to them. The term *narodnichestvo*, in fact, originally referred to this theory of the hegemony of the masses over the educated elite, which influenced the Land and Liberty (*Zemlia i volia*) organization of 1876–8. When Land and Liberty split in 1879, both its terrorist wing, People's Will (*Narodnaia volia*), and their opponents, Black Partition (*Chernyi peredel*), claimed the term *narodnichestvo* as their own: subsequently, it was to be used by the Russian Marxists as a pejorative label for the older agrarian socialism which had held that Russia could bypass capitalism and proceed directly to socialism through the commune and *artel'*.[69]

Economic developments in the last two decades of the nineteenth century seemed to show that, contrary to populist expectations, capitalism was emerging in Russia in both the industrial and agrarian sectors. Marxist socialist ideas now seemed more attractive and more applicable to Russia than they had two decades earlier. The Russian Marxists identified processes of social differentiation in both town and countryside: the emergence of an urban industrial proletariat, and the separation of the previously homogeneous communal peasantry into a class of petty rural capitalists (*kulakis*), on the one hand, and a rural proletariat or semi-proletariat, on the other. But while the Marxists rejected the very concept of the *narod*, the populists fought a rearguard action. The 'neo-populist' Socialist Revolutionary Party identified a broad revolutionary coalition for socialism that comprised all exploited groups, including not only the industrial proletariat but also the 'toiling peasantry' (*trudovoe krest'ianstvo*) in a single broad working class. This was in essence the *narod* of the earlier populists; and the term *trudovoi narod* (toiling people) often appeared in neo-populist discourse. And indeed, even the Bolsheviks in 1917 implicitly identified the same broad coalition as the mass base of the October Revolution, when Lenin talked of the alliance of the industrial proletariat with the poorest sections of the peasantry: the *nizy*, or lower classes, who opposed the *verkhi*, or upper classes.

Literaturnost': Literature and the Market-place

Neil Cornwell and Faith Wigzell

UNLIKE the other terms considered in these introductory essays, the term *literaturnost'*, literariness, may be translated into Western languages without difficulty. The decision to explain the term here is based less on the intrinsic unfamiliarity of the notions that it conveys to an anglophone audience than on our concern that Western readers should not take it for granted that 'literature' is as well-established a concept in Russian as it is in many Western cultures. One of the most persistent clichés of Western interpretations of Russian culture, at any rate in the twentieth century, has been the idea that Russians accord literature a greater value and reverence than do other Europeans. They are said to read more weighty literature, to know their classical authors better, and to take literature more seriously. The dreadful fates that have befallen many Russian writers, from Pushkin to Mandel'shtam, Pasternak, Akhmatova, and Solzhenitsyn, has been seen as evidence that the Russian and Soviet state, even at its most repressive periods, also understood the importance and value of literature—no democratic culture, it is argued, would think that a poet is worth shooting. All these notions, each of them questionable in itself, have been welded together to underpin one governing idea: that literature is an eternal and unchanging given of Russian culture, and that culture's quintessential expression.

Yet, in fact, the concept of 'literariness' arrived in Russia relatively recently, took some time to become established, and proved as mutable and as contentious as any of the other terms whose genealogy is traced here. For long periods of Russian history, the term *literatura* was not in use at all. Rather than a defence of what is uniquely Russian, then, the debates about literariness can partly be seen as an anxious struggle to domesticate a concept that was unfamiliar and problematic and to make an idea borrowed from other human minds seem (to use the adjective applied to icons) 'not made by human hands', that is, a divinely given form for the expression of national spiritual values (the word was in fact used by Pushkin in his poetic testament of 1836: 'I have raised myself a monument not made by human hands' ('Ia pamiatnik sebe vozdvig nerukotvornyi')). What follows sets out some of the historical processes by which this came about.[70]

'Literature' in pre-Petrine Russia

The term 'literature', when applied to Russian writing before the end of the seventeenth century, presents considerable problems, a fact which has not prevented it being conventionally applied to selected Russian texts: histories of Russian literature begin with texts that accompanied or followed the conversion to Christianity in 988. Those normally included in the category of literature are, unsurprisingly, not legal and other documents, but works that are held to possess clear artistic qualities. Thus, Metropolitan Ilarion's *Sermon on Law and Grace* (*Slovo o zakone i blagodati*), written in the mid-eleventh century, is widely admired for its patriotic tone, its mastery of rhetoric, and the superb logical development of its theme. The late seventeenth-century autobiography of the indomitable leader of the Old Believers Avvakum is distinguished by graphic narrative and vigorous language and portraiture. Yet both were written with a clear functional purpose in mind; the first is a sermon, and the second a combination of polemical religious tract and exemplum, composed in prison to encourage other supporters of the Old Belief to stand firm against the hostility of the official Orthodox Church. In terms of the emphasis on function, there is little to distinguish them from wills, official documents, or polemic tracts.

The conventional division of old Russian texts into literary and non-literary (usually termed in Russian *delovaia literatura*) stems from the application of modern criteria to a different cultural system with its own rules. The absence of a concept of literature, or *belles-lettres*, and hence also of *literaturnost'*, is a consequence of the source and nature of writing in Russia. Kievan Russia acquired writing and written texts in conjunction with the official adoption of Christianity in 988 from Byzantium. Inevitably, the choice of works for translation or copying lay predominantly with monks and other clerics, whose primary aim as cultural intermediaries was the acquisition of devotional materials, though they also copied or translated some secular literature, often of a popular historical character. Overall, the type and range of texts acquired by the East Slavs in the eleventh and twelfth centuries may be compared to the library holdings of a decent provincial monastery in Byzantium. The literature prized by the classically educated Byzantine elite therefore remained largely unknown, as of course did the secular literature of Catholic Europe that developed through the Middle Ages. Writing in Kievan Rus' (from the eleventh to the thirteenth century) was associated primarily with Orthodoxy, and this state of affairs continued into the Muscovite period (fourteenth to seventeenth century). Local *knizhniki* (bookmen), predominantly monks, produced devotional texts based on Byzantine models, while the small corpus of secular or semi-secular texts provided the impetus for local works of a mainly historical or political character (chronicles, treaties, military tales, wills, etc.). This system remained largely intact until the second half of the seventeenth century, although change and evolution occurred within it as a consequence of changing historical and social circumstances and demands.

All written texts performed a specific function which excluded entertainment as a primary aim. Whether ritual, instructional, polemical, or documentary in intention, early Russian writing or *pis'mennost'* saw itself as recording the truth for a specific purpose. Though obviously fanciful or fantastic material often appeared in, say, exaggerated chronicle accounts of battles or popular lives of saints, it was not regarded as anything other than historically accurate. In this system the concept of fiction could not exist, since for it to do so would require an interest in entertainment for its own sake.

The same attitudes led to a disregard of the personal impulse in creativity, and thus to a diminished interest in personal authorship. Many texts are anonymous, since the aim was not to produce an individualized work, but something that could perform its function, and merge without difficulty into the corpus of great works of that genre. It would be wrong to assume that early Russian *pis'mennost'* showed no interest in 'authors', but the differences illustrate the absence of a concept of literature as *belles-lettres*. Although there are instances of an author placing his name to his work, far more important was the tendency for works of a given type 'to agglomerate . . . around authoritative names'.[71] These might be those of the Greek Fathers of the Church, or, with time, known *knizhniki* from an earlier period in Russian history. Attribution of authorship, usually by later copyists, thereby became a way of enhancing the weight and value of a work, and not of designating individuality.

Nineteenth- and twentieth-century scholars have devoted reams of paper to attributing texts to 'real' authors when the work in question appears or clearly is of East Slavonic or Russian origin. Both the obsession with authorship and the preference for native works are largely alien to the literary system of the period. While it would appear that certain works enjoyed considerable popularity as a consequence of relating events that occurred on Russian soil, or describing the lives of local figures, this was not a necessary guarantee of authority. The Russian Church fostered the cult of local saints, but retained the greatest veneration for those worshipped by the whole Christian community. The most popular lives of saints were of general Christian saints like St Nicholas. The distinction between East Slav, or Slav, original works and translated works was hardly relevant, and if anything, the balance of authority lay with translated works.

Attitudes to language and education were also factors militating against the appearance of a concept of literature. The medium of expression for ecclesiastical works of all kinds was Church Slavonic, the South Slav language employed in the ninth century by Cyril and Methodius, the first missionaries to the Slavs, for the translation of devotional texts. In the late tenth century the morphological and phonological differences between it and Old Russian were so slight that comprehension presented no real problem, although the complex Graecized syntax and abstract vocabulary of devotional texts instantly set them apart. A system of linguistic diglossia developed: as Russian evolved, Church Slavonic became increasingly distinct in its archaisms, seen more and more as a sacred language, the only true vehicle for the expression of Christian Truth.[72] When it is also borne in mind that schools did not exist and that literacy was taught (predominantly to clerics) through the memorizing of Holy Writ and other ecclesiastical works written in Church Slavonic, it is easy to see how language and textual content came to be seen as inextricably linked. By the seventeenth century any innovation in Church Slavonic grammar would be deemed the work of the devil, and use of Church Slavonic in inappropriate situations blasphemous. Hence, the attempts by newly arrived Ukrainian scholars, educated in the spirit of the Polish-Ukrainian Baroque, to institute formal study of grammar and so detach medium from message were viewed as the work of the devil.[73] Such rigid views naturally militated against the development of individualized style.

Educational methods as well as attitudes to writing also led to a different concept of style. Since the aim of a *kniẑhnik* was to learn by memorizing and write by imitating, he (and it was always he) generally observed the stylistic and structural norms of texts with the same function. In the case of ecclesiastical works, this led to a concentration on the rhetorical properties of language, ultimately part of a classical heritage in Byzantium but in Russia exclusively connected with religious *pis'mennost'*. No attempt was made to develop the capacity for expression of a notional individual self. Nor could there be any tradition of literary criticism when tradition and the integration of medium and message were dominant. Thus, when in the sixteenth century Prince Kurbskii responded to a lengthy diatribe from Ivan the Terrible by sneering at his convoluted syntax and crude *mélange* of styles, he was criticizing Ivan's shaky grasp of appropriate norms.

The existence of a system of writing that emphasized function and adherence to tradition does not mean that texts necessarily lack artistic qualities. Although ecclesiastical genres such as lives of saints followed structural and stylistic patterns inherited from Byzantium, the author could present episodes with more or less drama or employ a more or less ornate rhetorical style. A writer of a military tale could introduce considerable pathos into his account of a defeat— such as in the *Tale of the Destruction of Riaẑan' by Batu* (*Povest' o raẑorenii Riaẑani Batyem*)—or stick to a bald account of events, preferring factual information to hyperbole. These look like decisions of an artistic nature, but they may owe as much to the type of sources or to the specific audience for whom the work was intended as to individual choice. Nonetheless, it does seem that the popularity of a work, judged by the imperfect criterion of the number of extant manuscripts, may sometimes reflect not only the work's fitness for purpose, but also its appeal to its audience. For example, of the two main works devoted to the martyrdom of Princes Boris and Gleb in 1015, it is the version that corresponds *less* closely to hagiographical tradition, the *Narration* (*Skaẑanie*) rather than Nestor's *Lection* (*Chtenie*), that survives in numerous copies, testifying to its appeal. Emotional appeals, lyrical prayers, and a dramatic tale of death and revenge, as well as a message of support for the ruling clan of princes, struck a chord in Muscovy, emphasizing the need for loyalty to the ruler. When modern literary historians go one step further and declare that the *Narration* is 'better' than the *Lection*, they are deriving their judgements from premises based on modern conceptions of literature and *literaturnost'*, which miss the essential features of the Old Russian system of writing.

It should be possible to integrate some form of judgement about a work's artistic merit into an overall understanding of the system under which it was produced. However, until the late 1950s, no sustained effort had been made to define the system underpinning Old Russian writing. Rejecting the pre-Revolutionary interest in works solely in terms of their value as historical sources and, implicitly, the Marxist obsession with 'progressive' elements (so-called reflections of real life, evidence of class conflict, secularization of literature, etc.), literary historians began to recognize the importance of genre, defining this in the first instance in terms of the pragmatic functions of a text.[74] The Soviet scholar Dmitrii Likhachev took function as one of the markers of genre as a basis upon which to argue that writers followed the stylistic 'literary etiquette' appropriate to that particular genre which had developed on Byzantine models and, in the case of Muscovite works, earlier Russian tradition.[75] The advantage of this theory was that style could now be evaluated in the context of tradition, allowing proper evaluation of the distinctive features of a given work. Nonetheless, the emphasis on style as a determinant of genre reflected a basically belletristic approach, and, as others pointed out, implied that the system of genres was as distinct and well developed as in modern literature. In fact, overlap between genres, anomalies, hybrids, variation within genres, and the use of one text for different functions, all imply a highly flexible, not to say chaotic, system.[76] In recent years, the unsatisfactory nature of all efforts to classify inclusively according to genre has prompted a swing to a socio-cultural approach, developed by a group of German scholars including W.-H. Schmidt, K.-D. Seemann, and A. Ebbinghaus, which suggests that the presentation of the material to a particular community at a particular time rather than structural and stylistic conventions is central to the shaping of a work.[77] Taking the various texts devoted to the cult of the saints Boris and Gleb, Gail Lenhoff has shown that the *Sitz im Leben*—that is, the specific socio-cultural setting of each—interacting with the characteristics and demands of the cult of saints (that is, the need for ritual celebration and record rather than observation of the literary etiquette of a given genre) determined their shape.[78] The advantages of such an approach lie in its emphasis on the community and the literary works produced within that community, although it entirely leaves out questions of artistry or popularity.

The world-view that sustained the Old Russian literary system began to crack in the second half of the seventeenth century. Texts such as the *Tale of Frol Skobeev* (*Istoriia o rossiiskom dvorianine Frole Skobeeve*), a novella about a rogue on the make, were intended solely to entertain, a sure sign of the weakening grip of Church and State on writing. Irreverent parodies like the *Tavern Mass* (*O sluzhbe kabaku*), which travestied the language of the vespers and concluded with a mock saint's life about a drunkard, implied the ability to use linguistic styles to other ends. The position of Church Slavonic as a sacred language indissociable from religious subject-matter was also undermined by scholars educated in the Western tradition of the Polish-Ukrainian Baroque, who believed that both grammar and a system of rhetoric could be taught formally. In this way they were opening the door to the possibility of greater stylistic flexibility and innovation as well as the use of Church Slavonic for non-Orthodox subject-matter.

Nonetheless, seventeenth-century writing still generally lacked the features associated with modern literature. The forcible Westernization of the upper classes by Peter the Great at the beginning of the eighteenth century produced over a number of decades the necessary social conditions for the creation of literature in the modern sense. One of the most significant features of the Westernization of the nobility was the radical changes it produced to the ordering of their leisure hours. The calendar rituals and traditional activities which had for so long regulated leisure hours (separately for men and women, since women were largely segregated in Muscovite times) gave way to genteel activities and pastimes both for men or women on their own and for mixed social occasions. The creation of an elite Westernized group, differentiated from the mass of the population, prompted the appearance of a culture to match, in which books were to play an ever-increasing role.

Westernization meant that the elite classes lost touch with the folk tradition, which dominated the way of life, mind-set, and beliefs of the overwhelming majority of Russians in the pre-Petrine period (indeed, this situation obtained for the peasantry up until the twentieth century). Folklore and *pis'mennost'* had existed as separate systems in the Kievan and Muscovite periods, although folklore, mainly in the form of legends viewed as source material for historical accounts or lives of saints, often appeared in written works. In the reverse direction, the impact was more gradual but equally slight, and came largely with the (often superficial) Christianization of pagan ritual and belief. As folklore ceased to be a vehicle for cultural attitudes, it became a source of artistic material and, suitably sanitized, genteel entertainment. Of course, once this process began, the elite classes brought to bear their own literary attitudes in its appreciation, and, in applying the term 'popular', selected forms that were not necessarily popular in the sense of being known widely among ordinary people. Russian epic songs, the *byliny*, which were admired in the late eighteenth century as colourful expressions of a heroic past and in the nineteenth century as the pinnacle of Russian folk-poetic creativity, were in fact known to only a tiny percentage of Russian peasants living in a few isolated areas, and certainly did not form part of their culture. Even the name *bylina* was invented by folklorists.

The active development and promotion of a Westernized culture naturally lay in the hands of a small number of people, who, working in the 1740s and 1750s within the Academy of Sciences, and subsequently outside as well, sought to establish the basis for a new literary system. In their search for a literary Russian language to replace Church Slavonic, they reflected the new approach to artistic language as a medium with a wide application. The attempts of Trediakovskii, Lomonosov, and Sumarokov to specify appropriate linguistic styles (with a greater or lesser Church Slavonic element) according to subject-matter, and determine the best form of versification for Russian poetry, revealed them as inheritors of a culture that viewed books as instructional as much as subscribers to prevailing Western views of the connection between literature and high moral purpose. Nonetheless, their efforts laid the ground for the establishment of the main Western belletristic genres in Russia (poetry, drama, essays, satire, fiction, etc.).

Establishing a literary language and system of genres proved highly contentious, though the polemic between theorists—writers may be regarded as the first stage in the development of literary criticism. In the absence of any terminology, critical concepts were borrowed from the West through the translation of works such as Boileau's *Art poétique*. However, in the eighteenth century most literary criticism took the guise of vituperative attacks of a highly personal nature. By the end of the century much of what passed for criticism was based on the premiss that the talent of the individual writer, rather than his adherence to set programmes or known groupings, was what mattered.[79]

There could be no book market before Peter, given the absence of necessary factors such as a sizeable educated clientele, an element of consumer choice, adequate book distribution, and reasonable prices. A prerequisite for many of these was printing, which increased book availability and, ultimately, choice. Printing had existed in Muscovy from the mid-sixteenth century (an official typography, the Pechatnyi dvor, under the control of the Tsar and the Metropolitan, was founded in 1563). However, the non-existence of private printing meant that book production prior to the reign of Peter the Great was, first, dominated by the Church (95 per cent of all printed books in the sixteenth and seventeenth centuries were devotional), and, second, still occupied a relatively minor role in the production of *pis'mennost'*.[80] Peter's policies made printing an essential tool of government and modernization,[81] while the founding of the Academy of Sciences in 1725 created a body devoted to the propagation of enlightenment through word and print. Unfortunately, the paucity of qualified Russians meant that three-quarters of Academicians before 1742 were German, who published overwhelmingly in German or Latin, which was not of much positive value to most literate Russians, who formed a small enough group as it was. In any case, most publications were scientific treatises and textbooks of various kinds. Only 15 per cent of all titles published between 1725 and 1755 were *belles-lettres*.[82]

Using printing as an instrument of state control proved so costly that in the 1740s and 1750s economic pressures forced the Academy to try to increase the publication of works in Russian, and even occasionally to try to respond to popular interests. The gradual extension of the right to run printing presses to institutions such as Moscow University and the Cadet Corps in the 1750s and 1760s, and then to individuals in the 1780s and 1790s, slowly resulted in the emergence of a variety of publishers, some of them of merchant origin, interested in producing books for specific tastes and social groups. For example, the entertaining account of the adventures of the famous bandit Van'ka Kain by Matvei Komarov was targeted at the unsophisticated reader, while at the end of the century the spread of literacy from male to female members of the upper classes made the production of reading matter for women feasible.

The eighteenth century was not merely a period of transformation, but one of national literary apprenticeship; by the end of the century many of the cultural processes that had followed Peter's reforms were nearing maturity. With the advent of romanticism, which put the individual in the foreground of literary perception, literary attitudes in Russia in 1800 would engender a fully fledged literature based on more familiar, but still contended, conceptions of *literaturnost'*.

Nineteenth-century Versions of *Literaturnost'*: Functions, Forms, and Factions

The period up to 1800, then, may be considered to have consolidated the movement away from a culture of letters dominated by Church and State towards secularism and progress. This period saw also the development of the Russian literary language, from the three styles of Lomonosov (or *slovesnost'*, *literatura*, and *poeziia*, as Tynianov puts it) to, by the end of the century, the Gallicized salon speech of Karamzin and his followers. The key stage, though, of this linguistic controversy was acted out in the early 1800s between the 'archaists' and 'innovators'—or the followers of Shishkov and Karamzin, respectively. As this confrontation tailed off, with minor victories and notable literary works by both sides, a new synthesis emerged with what is now widely regarded, to some extent simplistically, as the literary language of Pushkin in the role of new and decisive dominant. This is the brand of literary Russian that was to be followed by Lermontov, Turgenev, and their successors.

The same period, and indeed the early nineteenth century, saw an even more fundamental battle between the spoken languages of French and Russian amid the Russian aristocracy, who were now largely, numerically at least, the educated service gentry and who, from the mid-eighteenth century until the rise of the *raznochintsy*, formed the main reading public for the growing Russian culture. Although, from the late eighteenth century, more and more literary writing was being done in Russian, French very largely remained the spoken language of the court and the salons, and the language of private correspondence. It was also the language of literary endeavour for a number of highly educated aristocratic women, from Ekaterina Dashkova, Catherine II's most powerful woman contemporary, through the salon hostess Zinaida Volkonskaia, to Madame de Ségur, née Rostopchina, creator of the famous French children's book *Les Malheurs de Sophie*. The split between 'feminine' Frenchified tradition and 'masculine' language looking back to its Slavonic (or popular) roots was the cause of many anxieties in the 1820s, particularly among male writers espousing a 'Frenchified' literary language. It is evident, for instance, in Pushkin's insistence, expressed in his diaries and letters of the mid-1820s, on the need to create a properly 'virile' style for prose and poetry.

The term *literaturnost'* at this stage in literary history assumes a concern with a number of issues, both stylistic and social. Apart from the literary language and its development—in the sense of the campaign to create a 'national' literature and a style in which to write it—a number of other stylistic questions informed debate on 'literariness' in the early nineteenth century. These included the development of a new, at once flexible and self-conscious, attitude to genre, as the old neoclassical system of odes and elegies broke down in poetry, and prose genres, such as the novel and short story, became increasingly respectable and prominent. With the decay of the old notion that literature should always aspire to elevated subjects and modes of expression came the question of what distinguished 'literature' from other kinds of writing; this was expressed particularly in a concern with the devices and techniques appropriate to *belles-lettres*. There was also a high degree of interest in questions and concepts of authorship, which could be overt or oblique. For instance, the 1820s was a great period for pseudonyms, such as 'Luzhnitskii starets', 'Baron Brambeus', and (though for political as well as literary reasons in this case), 'Marlinskii'. Here, literary-cultural concerns often merged into the social, as 'the author' was seen alternately, or sometimes simultaneously in one text, as the ultimate articulator of romantic individualism, as in Pushkin's

Eugene Onegin (*Evgenii Onegin*, 1823–31), or as the most profound and important expresser of political and social commentary (as in Lermontov's accusation of the Tsarist authorities, 'The Death of a Poet' ('Smert' poeta', 1837)). The often performative role of the author produced as a consequence a particular construction of the reader in the text. Much of the writing of this period verged on the elitist in that it was intended for, or could only be fully appreciated by, an in-group of initiates (it had what has been termed 'circle semantics', *kruzhkovaia semantika*, or, in the more derogatory phrase of F. R. Leavis, was the product of a 'coterie culture'). Address to a privileged in-group was facilitated by the fact that many Russian writers of the day, Pushkin and later Lermontov among them, took a dim view of the intelligence of Russian readers, and in particular of their ability to distinguish fact from fiction, and homily from irony: see, most notably, the preface to Lermontov's *A Hero of Our Time* (*Geroi nashego vremeni*, 1837–40).

Connected with this was the role of the salons and clubs, at which writers read their works to a select audience (including, in the former case, educated women). This facilitated the flourishing of such minor genres as the epigram, the album entry, and the open letter. At the same time, however, the Russian book market was expanding and becoming more professional and commercial. Unlike their later nineteenth-century successors, many early nineteenth-century writers took a very positive view of the new opportunities to earn money (a famous example is Pushkin's 'Conversation between the Bookseller and the Poet' ('Razgovor knigoprodavtsa s poetom', 1824), which ends with the poet jettisoning his high-flown anti-commercial arguments to accept the bookseller's largesse). This was partly because of the nature of the readership at which commercial publishers aimed their materials: literacy levels were so low that the tastes of the lower classes could not impinge much on the book market. Moreover, the possibility of publishing for money seemed to the independent, anti-absolutist, and in some cases even republican-minded young men who were the dominant group in literature after 1820 a preferable alternative to the aristocratic patronage on which their predecessors had often had to rely, since booksellers were less likely to exercise editorial control.[83] This is not to say that all literature produced after 1820 was free of the influence of the court: censorship by the government authorities was often intrusive, especially after the accession of Nicholas I in 1825. The situation was complicated by the collusion of some writers who acted as censors or collaborated with the censorship (Shishkov, Nikitenko, and later Goncharov). It could be a small step from writing literary manifestos or programmatic criticism (activities in which most male writers of the day engaged) to more coercive methods of ensuring political or aesthetic propriety.

Writers and Journals in the Early Nineteenth Century: Two Case-studies

Even the most cursory examination of the case of the towering literary figure of this period, Pushkin, reveals the extensive, not to say exhaustive, range of genres or forms in which he worked, something which is itself emblematic of the dynamically evolving literary period in which he operated. Most famous as a poet, Pushkin of course wrote lyrics, ballads, elegies, and odes, as well as excelling in the epigram, the bawdy, the fairy tale, and the narrative poem, not to mention the novel in verse — this last, arguably, his own generic invention. In the dramatic field he wrote a Shakespearian historical tragedy in blank verse and a complex collection of dramatic miniatures. In the realm of prose fiction he wrote, or attempted, novels, historical novels, short stories, and a cycle of short stories. Most critics would agree that he achieved at least one masterpiece in virtually all the categories mentioned. Apart from prose fiction, he wrote a body of letters (albeit mainly in French), travelogue, history, and critical notes, and was founding editor of one of the century's best-known journals, *Sovremennik* (*The Contemporary*). With very few exceptions — perhaps the serious aesthetic essay, literary translation (though some consider that the 'little tragedy' *A Feast during the Plague* (*Pir vo vremia chumy*, 1830) might come into that last category), and the autobiographical memoir—Pushkin made his mark, to say the least, in just about every literary form of the day in an epoch which boasted manifold literary activity.

Further evidence of the dynamics of the literary process of the early nineteenth century emerges from scrutiny of an influential literary journal: for convenience's sake, we shall take one which (not untypically) ran to only four issues and was then abandoned in the wake of the failed Decembrist uprising. *Mnemozina* (1824–5) was edited by Vladimir Odoevskii and Wilhelm Küchelbecker (the latter was arrested for his active involvement in the Decembrist conspiracy, and was possibly fortunate not to share the desperate fate of Ryleev and others). It was, despite its intellectual success, a financial failure. This publication, subtitled 'a collection of works in verse and prose', was effectively the house journal of the Society of the Lovers of Wisdom (Obshchestvo liubomudrov), and was heavily influenced by German romantic philosophy (particularly that of Schelling and Oken). Nevertheless, its contributors included a wide cross-section of the leading literati of the day, and it stands chronologically at the very centre of the period under discussion, and therefore at a key formative moment in Russian literature: after the Shishkov–Karamzin controversy, but before the hegemony of Pushkin became apparent, and before the establishment of the principal 'thick' journals. Furthermore, it was the most intellectually ambitious journal that Russia had yet seen.

The journal's overall contents are grouped under the following headings: 'Philosophy'; '*Belles-lettres*' (*iziashchnaia proza*), subdivided into 'Apologues', 'Military History', 'Travelogues', 'Tales and extracts from novels' (*Povesti. Otryvki iz romanov*); 'Criticism and Anticriticism'; 'Poetry', subdivided into 'Poetic stories' (*Stikhotvornye rasskazy*), 'Lyrical Verse'; 'Missives'; and 'Miscellaneous'. Also represented are songs in notational form and various illustrations, including cartoons and portraits. In the pages of this extraordinarily diverse publication apologues and philosophy by Odoevskii, campaign notes by Davydov, and travel letters by Küchelbecker (who also contributes an influential essay on Russian lyric poetry) are assembled alongside the more settled genres of the lyric, verse drama, and translation. Griboedov, Polevoi, Pushkin (with the poems 'My demon' ('Moi demon') and 'To the Sea' ('K moriu')), Raich, Shakhovskoi, Viazemskii, and Iazykov all contributed. On a European level, *Mnemozina* promoted German romantic philosophy and paid tribute on the death of Byron. The editors between them contributed well over half the total copy, and were unwise enough to get embroiled in undignified polemics with their vastly more down-market competitors, published by Bulgarin and Grech; when the almanac folded, in 1825, it had a pathetic subscription list numbering just 157.

The Development of *Literaturnost'* in the Later Nineteenth Century: the Rise of 'Mass Literature'

Nicholas I was the last Russian Tsar to take a direct personal interest in the censorship of literary (as opposed to political) works. Alexander II not only permitted a relaxation of the censorship regulations in 1862, but increasingly left to bureaucrats the task of arbitrating what material should be banned and permitted. The last third of the nineteenth century, therefore, was marked by three new developments in Russian literature. The first was a gradual and rather timid increase in the dominance of literary aestheticism, '*l'art pour l'art*', which did not really take hold until the 1890s, but was to make a considerable impact in the twentieth century. The second was that the independence of literary activity from political authority (as distinct from literature's continuing prominence in the 'public sphere') was now taken for granted. In 1847, Belinskii was still needing to emphasize the idea of secular progress: 'Russia needs the success of civilization, enlightenment, humanity; dignity and justice; not mysticism, sermons and serfdom, bribery and corruption.' By the second half of the nineteenth century, even those writers who preferred 'mysticism' to 'enlightenment' saw themselves as independent professionals who had no need for official endorsements of their work, or of ties with the Russian Court.

Finally, and perhaps most importantly, the second half of the nineteenth century saw an immense expansion of the publishing industry generally, and in particular of the production of cheap books aimed at the new readers of the lower classes. Established genres such as *lubochnye knizhki* (pamphlet romances sold by pedlars) were joined by serialized novels in journals and newspapers, detective stories, adventure novels, and romantic fiction (often referred to as 'women's literature', *zhenskaia literatura*).[84] These upstart rivals placed new pressure on the category of *literaturnost'*, which now took on an evaluative coloration, referring not only to particular linguistic strategies, but to their relative aesthetic merits. Like their counterparts in other European countries, Russian writers and critics developed an obsession with distinguishing between 'genuine' literature and 'trash', and considered that the former was distinguished by originality of expression. By the very end of the nineteenth century these concerns were finding expression in theories of literature which emphasized 'form' or manner over 'content' or politico-ideological engagement, both in prescriptions for contemporary practice and in descriptions of what had preceded it.

Russian Theories of Literary Evolution: the Formalist School

Though concern with 'literariness' was, as we have seen, explicit in early nineteenth-century culture, perception of this has, during the last seventy-five years, been inseparable from the literary-historical categories established by the Russian formalists, in particular Iurii Tynianov. According to Tynianov's theories (developed most extensively in his essay collection *Archaists and Innovators*, 1929), genre development takes place by interchange between the 'centre' and the 'periphery'; by a process of 'struggle' and 'replacement' (*bor'ba i smena*); and by a conflict between 'archaism' and 'innovation', involving major figures and their epigones and renewed exploitation of old devices. Old genres may be either enhanced or debased (the neoclassical ode and epic are studied by Tynianov as exemplary instances of these processes). According to Tynianov, there might be periods when all poets wrote 'well', and then the 'bad' poet would write with genius. Nekrasov's verses, criticized originally as 'rotten', were eventually accepted as 'good' because they stifled what had become an automatized verse form and did something new. The combination of these two contentions illustrates the less than fully materialist and relativist attitudes that underlay formalist appreciations: on the one hand literary quality is the result of contingent historical sitting and of reception, but on the other hand those writers such as Nekrasov, who fight against 'automation', are most valued. Similarly evaluative attitudes may be appreciated in Eikhenbaum's distinction between 'literature' and 'sub-literature' or 'para-literature' (*literaturnyi byt*, 'literary life'), following which letters written by Pushkin, say, were able to transform the epistolary genre from 'para-literature' into 'literature', while letters (or indeed poems) written by Pushkin's female contemporaries have attained, in the historiologies of the formalists and their successors, at most the status of 'para-literature' (though this generation included some highly self-conscious women letter-writers, such as the salon hostess Avdot'ia Elagina).

The formalist critics, whether, in the first phase of their activity, when they sought to identify the qualities that distinguished 'poetic' from 'everyday' language, or, later, when they confronted the imperative of taking into account 'extra-literary' history as a factor influencing literary 'evolution', wrote as twentieth-century modernists, for whom *literaturnost'* had taken on a different meaning from that which it held in the early nineteenth century, under the pressure to distinguish book from commodity. But at the same time there was an essential continuity between the enterprise of the formalists and that of their predecessors: *literaturnost'* remained indissociable from a functionality which was now 'laid bare' in literary and critical work alike. The cogency of this position is perhaps masked by the fact that 'literariness' sometimes comes across in their writings as denoting an essence, something that can be identified in ontological rather than functional terms; features which are products, or functions, of a set of relations between the text and its contexts and those of its readers and its critics, are sometimes treated as inherent properties of the literary text, and indeed of 'literature' in general. But in general, the virtue of formalism is that, as Jurij Striedter argues, it 'no more answers the question What is Literature? than it does the question What should literature be?'[85] Rather, it asks: on what basis can we ask these questions? In this sense it is especially valuable for a 'cultural studies' approach, in that it highlights the ways in which, even today, the frequently invoked 'specialness' of Russian literature has tended to depend on a reluctance to analyse the reasons for literature's specificity—a specificity which, as our analysis here has shown, may be traceable both to the recent arrival of 'literature' in the Western sense, and to the accelerated development of a mass readership in the late nineteenth century.

Suggested further reading

Lichnost'

OFFORD, D., *The Russian Revolutionary Movement in the 1880s* (Cambridge, 1986), 141–5.

RAEFF, M., *Origins of the Russian Intelligentsia: The Eighteenth-Century Nobility* (New York, 1966).

WALICKI, A., *The Slavophile Controversy: History of a Conservative Utopia in Nineteenth-Century Russian Thought*, tr. H. Andrews-Rusiecka (Oxford, 1975).

Narodnost'

CHERNIAVSKY, M., *Tsar and People: Studies in Russian Myths* (New Haven, 1961).

MILLER, F. J., *Folklore for Stalin: Russian Folklore and Pseudofolklore of the Stalin Era* (Armonk, 1990).

RIASANOVSKY, N. V., *Nicholas I and Official Nationality in Russia, 1825–1855* (Berkeley, 1959).

ROGGER, H., *National Consciousness in Eighteenth-Century Russia* (Cambridge, 1960).

WALICKI, A., *The Slavophile Controversy: History of a Conservative Utopia in Nineteenth-Century Russian Thought*, tr. H. Andrews-Rusiecka (Oxford, 1975).

Literaturnost'

BROOKS, J., *When Russia Learned to Read: Literacy and Popular Literature, 1861–1917* (Princeton, 1985).

CORNWELL, N., *The Life, Times and Milieu of V. F. Odoyevsky* (London, 1986).

GREENLEAF, M., *Pushkin and Romantic Fashion* (Stanford, 1994).

LIKHACHEV, D. S., *Poetika drevnerusskoi literatury*, 3rd edn. (Moscow, 1979).

MARKER, G., *Publishing, Printing and the Origins of Intellectual Life in Russia, 1700–1800* (Princeton, 1985).

MILLS TODD III, W., *Fiction and Society in the Age of Pushkin: Ideology, Institutions, and Narrative* (Cambridge, Mass., and London, 1986).

MORSON, G. S. (ed.), *Literature and History: Theoretical Problems and Russian Case Studies* (Stanford, 1986).

STRIEDTER, J., *Literary Structure, Evolution, and Value: Russian Formalism and Czech Structuralism Reconsidered* (Cambridge, Mass., and London, 1989).

TYNIANOV, IU. N., *Arkhaisty i novatory* (Leningrad, 1929; repr. Munich, 1967).

Notes

1 V. Dal', *Tolkovyi slovar' russkogo iazyka*, 2nd edn., ii (Moscow, 1881), 259.

2 S. I. Ozhegov, *Slovar' russkogo iazyka*, 20th edn. (Moscow, 1988), headword *lichnost'*. Similarly, the Soviet Academy dictionary gives both 'the personal individual basis in a person' and the 'aggregate of signs and qualities inherent in a person as a social being'.

3 See D. S. Likhachev, 'Kontseptosfera russkogo iazyka', *Izvestiia Akademii nauk. (Seriia literatury i iazyka)*, 52 (1993), 3–9.

4 R. H. Barrow, *The Romans* (Harmondsworth, 1949), 13.

5 M. Raeff, *Origins of the Russian Intelligentsia: The Eighteenth-Century Nobility* (New York, 1966), 146; see also 151.

6 Ibid., 41.

7 N. Kochetkova, *Nikolay Karamzin* (Boston, 1975), 40.

8 See N. M. Karamzin, 'Chto nuzhno avtoru?', in *Izbrannye sochineniia*, ii (Moscow and Leningrad, 1964), 120–2.

9 A. I. Gertsen, 'Neskol'ko zamechanii ob istoricheskom razvitii chesti', in *Sobranie sochinenii* (30 vols.; Moscow, 1954–65), ii, 158.

10 D. I. Pisarev, 'Skholastika XIX veka', in *Sochineniia* (4 vols.; Moscow, 1955), i, 107.

11 V. G. Belinskii, *Polnoe sobranie sochinenii* (13 vols.; Moscow, 1953–9), xii, 433.

12 See Gertsen, 'Pis'ma iz Avenue Marigny', in *Sobranie sochinenii*, v, esp. 15–67.

13 Pisarev, 'Skholastika XIX veka', 101.

14 Quoted in D. E. Rozental', *Prakticheskaia stilistika russkogo iazyka*, 4th edn. (Moscow, 1977), 143.

15 A. Walicki, *The Slavophile Controversy: History of a Conservative Utopia in Nineteenth-Century Russian Thought*, tr. H. Andrews-Rusiecka (Oxford, 1975), 411.

16 N. Riasanovsky, *Collected Writings: 1947–1994* (Los Angeles, 1993), 240–1.

17 Belinskii, *Polnoe sobranie sochinenii*, xi, 556.

18 Ibid., iii, 341.

19 Ibid., xi, 556.

20 Ibid., 577.

21 Ibid., xii, 22.

22 Ibid., 51–2.

23 Ibid., 66, 69.

24 Gertsen, 'Neskol'ko zamechanii', 151–76, esp. 154–5, 157, 159–61, 163, 167–8, 174–5.

25 See A. V. Stankevich, *T. N. Granovskii i ego perepiska*, 2nd edn. (2 vols.; Moscow, 1897), i, 150–1.

26 T. N. Granovskii, 'O sovremennom sostoianii i znachenii vseobshchei istorii', *Sochineniia*, 4th edn. (Moscow, 1900), 25.

27 Granovskii, 'Reforma v Anglii', ibid., 483, and 'Istoricheskaia literatura vo Frantsii i Germanii v 1847 godu', ibid., 439, 445.

[28] K. D. Kavelin, 'Vzgliad na iuridicheskii byt drevnei Rossii', *Sobranie sochinenii* (4 vols.; St Petersburg, 1897–1900), i, 5–66.

[29] Belinskii, *Polnoe sobranie sochinenii*, xii, 23, 52, 72.

[30] See Granovskii, 'Chetyre istoricheskie kharakteristiki: Timur', in *Sochineniia*, 241 ff.

[31] Stankevich, *T. N. Granovskii*, ii, 456.

[32] Walicki, *The Slavophile Controversy*, 406.

[33] Kavelin, 'Vzgliad', 46–53.

[34] J. S. Mill, *On Liberty and Considerations on Representative Government*, ed. R. B. McCallum (Oxford, 1946), 50, 9.

[35] See G. M. Hamburg, *Boris Chicherin and Early Russian Liberalism: 1828–1866* (Stanford, 1992), 85 ff., and my review of this book, *European History Quarterly*, 24 (1994), 309–12.

[36] See I. Nagy, 'Gershenzon chitaet Turgeneva', in Zh. Ziol'dkhein-Deak and A. Khollosh (eds.), *I. S. Turgenev: Zhizn', tvorchestvo, traditsii* (Budapest, 1994), 163–5.

[37] N. G. Chernyshevskii, 'Antropologicheskii printsip v filosofii', in *Polnoe sobranie sochinenii* (16 vols.; Moscow, 1939–53), vii, 222–95, esp. 261 and 264.

[38] Chernyshevskii, 'Bor'ba partii vo Frantsii pri Liudovike XVIII i Karle X', ibid., v, 217–18.

[39] Pisarev, 'Skholastika XIX veka', 103.

[40] Pisarev, 'Bazarov', in *Sochineniia*, ii, 10.

[41] K. S. Aksakov, *Polnoe sobranie sochinenii* (3 vols.; Moscow, 1861–80), i, 291–2.

[42] See Iu. F. Samarin, *Sochineniia* (12 vols.; Moscow, 1877–1911), i, 34–5, 42, 56, 63–4; see also Walicki, *The Slavophile Controversy*, 409.

[43] I. V. Kireevskii, 'O kharaktere prosveshcheniia Evropy i o ego otnoshenii k prosveshcheniiu Rossii', in *Polnoe sobranie sochinenii* (2 vols.; Moscow, 1911), i, 174–222, esp. 186–8, 210, 191–2, 206–7.

[44] See Riasanovsky, *Collected Writings*, 142.

[45] F. M. Dostoevskii, *Zimnie zametki o letnikh vpechatleniiakh*, in *Polnoe sobranie sochinenii* (30 vols.; Leningrad, 1972–90), v, 78–80.

[46] On Tochisskii and his group, see D. Offord, *The Russian Revolutionary Movement in the 1880s* (Cambridge, 1986), 141–5.

[47] N. Riasanovsky, 'Khomyakov and *sobornost'*', in E. J. Simmons (ed.), *Continuity and Change in Russian and Soviet Thought* (Cambridge, Mass., 1955), 183–94 (185). On the later history of *sobornost'*, see B. G. Rosenthal, 'Transcending Politics: Vyacheslav Ivanov's Visions of *sobornost'*', *California Slavic Studies*, 14 (1992), 17–70, and A. I. Mazaev, 'Ot misterii k sobornosti: Viacheslav Ivanov i A. Skriabin o sinteze iskusstv', in *Problema sinteza iskusstv v estetike russkogo simvolizma* (Moscow, 1992), 142–234.

[48] See Ia. Grot, *Filologicheskie razyskaniia* (St Petersburg, 1899), 83–4, and note in *Uchenye zapiski Riazanskogo pedagogicheskogo instituta*, 8 (1949), 147.

[49] Quoted in M. K. Azadovskii, *Istoriia russkoi fol'kloristiki* (Moscow, 1958), 191–2.

[50] Ibid., 192.

[51] See H. Rogger, *National Consciousness in Eighteenth-Century Russia* (Cambridge, 1960), 126.

[52] Ibid., 71.

[53] See L. G. Leighton, '*Narodnost'* as a Concept of Russian Romanticism', in *Russian Romanticism: Two Essays* (The Hague, 1975), 41–107.

[54] See A. S. Pushkin, 'O narodnosti v literature', in *Polnoe sobranie sochinenii*, xi (Moscow, 1949), 40.

[55] See Azadovskii, *Istoriia russkoi fol'kloristiki*, 193–5, and K. Hokanson, 'Literary Imperialism, *Narodnost'* and Pushkin's Invention of the Caucasus', *Russian Review*, 53 (1994), 336–52.

[56] On the 'educated response' to popular commercial literature, see J. Brooks, *When Russia Learned to Read: Literacy and Popular Literature, 1861–1917* (Princeton, 1985), ch. 10.

[57] Quoted in N. V. Riasanovsky, *Nicholas I and Official Nationality in Russia, 1825–1855* (Berkeley, 1959), 73.

[58] Ibid., 70–1.

[59] M. T. Florinsky states that Uvarov's *narodnost'* stood for 'militant nationalism': *Russia: A History and an Interpretation*, ii (New York, 1953), 799.

[60] Rogger, *National Consciousness*, 34.

[61] Riasanovsky, *Nicholas I*, 124.

[62] Ibid., 139.

[63] Walicki, *The Slavophile Controversy*, 46, 420.

[64] See M. Cherniavsky, *Tsar and People: Studies in Russian Myths* (New Haven, 1961), 149, and R. S. Wortman, *Scenarios of Power: Myth and Ceremony in Russian Monarchy*, i. *From Peter the Great to the Death of Nicholas I* (Princeton, 1995), 291–2.

[65] Riasanovsky, *Nicholas I*, 144–6, 232–3.

[66] See Walicki, *The Slavophile Controversy*, 397–421.

[67] See J. D. Klier, 'The Concept of "Jewish Emancipation" in a Russian Context', in O. Crisp and L. Edmondson (eds.), *Civil Rights in Imperial Russia* (Oxford, 1989), 125. L. Kristof has described the policy of nation-building on the basis of religion rather than ethnicity as 'Rossification' (as opposed to 'Russification'): see H. Rogger, *Jewish Policies and Right-Wing Politics in Imperial Russia* (London, 1986), 3–4.

[68] See D. C. Rawson, *Russian Rightists and the Revolution of 1905* (Cambridge, 1995).

[69] See R. Pipes, '*Narodnichestvo*: a Semantic Enquiry', *Slavic Review*, 23 (1964), 441–58.

[70] For a good overview of Russian conceptualizations of literature, see G. S. Morson, 'Introduction: Literary History and the Russian Experience', in Morson (ed.), *Literature and History: Theoretical Problems and Russian Case Studies* (Stanford, 1986), 1–30.

[71] S. Franklin, 'Introduction', in *Sermons and Rhetoric of Kievan Rus*, tr. Franklin (Cambridge, Mass., 1991), pp. lxxii–lxxiv.

[72] The question of the interrelationship between Church Slavonic and Old Russian has been much debated: see B. A. Uspenskii, 'K voprosu o semanticheskikh

vzaimootnosheniiakh sistemno protivopostavlennykh tserkovnoslavianskikh i russkikh form v istorii russkogo iazyka', *Wiener Slavistisches Jahrbuch*, 22 (1976), 992–100, and *Kratkii ocherk istorii russkogo literaturnogo iazyka (XI–XIX vv.)* (Moscow, 1994); G. Hüttl-Volter, 'Diglossiia v Drevnei Rusi', *Wiener Slavistisches Jahrbuch*, 24 (1978), 108–23; D. S. Worth, 'On Diglossia in Medieval Russia', *Die Welt der Slaven*, 23 (1978), 371–93; and A. Issatschenko, *Die Geschichte der russischen Sprache*, i (Heidelberg, 1980), 68 ff.

[73] See B. A. Uspenskii, 'The Language Situation and Linguistic Consciousness in Muscovite Rus′: The Perception of Church Slavic and Russian', in *Medieval Slavic Culture* (California Slavic Studies, 12; Stanford, 1984), 365–86.

[74] R. Jagoditsch argues that medieval Russian writing distinguished work-types rather than art-types: see 'Zum Begriff der "Gattungen" in der altrussischen Literatur', *Wiener Slavistisches Jahrbuch*, 6 (1957–8), 113–37.

[75] The most cogent presentation of his ideas is in D. S. Likhachev, *Poetika drevnerusskoi literatury*, 3rd edn. (Moscow, 1979), 55–79.

[76] See the views of N. Ingham in 'Genre Characteristics of the Kievan Lives of Princes', in P. Debreczeny (ed.), *American Contributions to the Ninth International Congress of Slavists, Kiev, September 7–13 1983*, ii (Columbus, 1983), 223–37, and 'Genre-Theory and Old Russian Literature', *Slavic and East European Journal*, 31 (1987), 234–45.

[77] See W.-H. Schmidt, *Gattungstheoretische Untersuchungen zur altrussischen Kriegserzählung (Zur Soziologie mittelaltlicher Gattungen)* (Berlin–Wiesbaden, 1975); W.-H. Schmidt (ed.), *Gattungsprobleme der älteren slavischen Literaturen (Berminer Fachtagung)* (Berlin–Wiesbaden, 1984); and K.-D. Seeman (ed.), *Gattung und Narration in der älteren slavischen Literaturen* (Berlin–Wiesbaden, 1987).

[78] G. Lenhoff, *The Martyred Princes Boris and Gleb: A Socio-Cultural Study of the Cult and the Texts* (Columbus, 1989).

[79] See W. G. Jones, 'Familiar Solidarity and Squabbling: Russia's Eighteenth-Century Writers', in F. Wigzell (ed.), *Russian Writers on Russian Writers* (Oxford and Providence, 1994), 1–14. The essays by I. Serman and M. Altshuller in C. Moser (ed.), *The Cambridge History of Russian Literature* (Cambridge, 1989), 45–91 and 92–135, offer a good survey of the period 1730–1820.

[80] On printing in seventeenth-century Russia, see S. P. Luppov, *Kniga v Rossii v XVII veke* (Leningrad, 1970).

[81] On printing and publishing in eighteenth-century Russia, see G. Marker, *Publishing, Printing and the Origins of Intellectual Life in Russia, 1700–1800* (Princeton, 1985); and S. P. Luppov, *Kniga v Rossii v pervoi chetverti XVIII veka* (Leningrad, 1973), and *Kniga v Rossii v poslepetrovskoe vremia* (Leningrad, 1976).

[82] Marker, *Publishing, Printing*, 59. Marker assigns odes written to celebrate formal occasions and *belles-lettres* to different categories.

[83] On the development of literary institutions in the first half of the nineteenth century, see W. Mills Todd III, *Fiction and Society in the Age of Pushkin: Ideology, Institutions, and Narrative* (Cambridge, Mass., and London, 1986).

[84] See Brooks, *When Russia Learned to Read*, and C. Kelly, *A History of Russian Women's Writing, 1820–1992* (Oxford, 1994), chs. 1–5.

[85] J. Striedter, *Literary Structure, Evolution, and Value: Russian Formalism and Czech Structuralism Reconsidered* (Cambridge, Mass., and London, 1989), 19.

PART II

Cultural Transformation in Late Imperial Russia

1 The Objective Eye and the Common Good

Louise McReynolds and Cathy Popkin

Additional material by Steve Smith

Introduction

PERHAPS the most significant contribution made to Western historiography by the very various discourses that are collectively labelled 'post-modernist' has been an extensive and wide-ranging debate about the value and significance of the structures, ideologies, and ways of behaviour that European society has inherited from the European Enlightenment. The writings of cultural critics such as Norbert Elias, Jürgen Habermas, Michel de Certeau, and above all Michel Foucault, have stressed the active interventionism that was as central to Enlightenment thinking as was libertarian idealism. They have especially exposed the paradoxical nature of practices which constituted a new view of the sacrosanct nature of privacy, yet also attempted to regulate the individual behaviour of citizens to an unprecedented degree. In this context, historical developments as apparently diverse as the push for universal education, the growth of discourses on hygiene and the care of the body, the emergence of new institutions (laboratories, academies, prisons, and hospitals), and the rise of literary realism, with its emphasis on the capacity of knowledgeable individuals to encapsulate the experience and desires of entire societies, and the possibility of absolute factual knowledge, can be seen as interlinked aspects of a desire to create new collective identities, whose ideal site was the rationally ordered modern city.

Analyses of this kind have a striking relevance to Russian history, given that Catherine II, a model 'enlightened despot', consciously aimed to provide Russia with social institutions and private practices that would, in time, create an ordered and rational society, and pressed the extension of state power over private as well as public life (through measures such as the founding of schools as a replacement for 'erratic' private education, Imperial Foundling Homes centralizing the care of orphans, as well as sponsorship of the translation of behaviour manuals). In the words of a recent historian of philanthropy, 'Catherine did not aim merely to create another bureaucracy, but to stimulate civic involvement by her subjects', a crucial instance being the social welfare boards, cross-class institutions that acted not only as aid institutions, but also as credit banks.[1] From the first, then, 'the growth of a civic society' (that is, the creation of institutions of representative government and associations of social participation), which historians of Russia have long acknowledged as an appropriate subject for their investigations, was established as part of a very wide shift in social consciousness, embracing private as well as public activities and practices.

This shift in social consciousness was characterized by conflict both intellectual and emotional, and cannot be glossed simply as a neutral and consensual move towards 'progress', or a smooth process of 'modernization'. In our emphasis on conflict, we owe much to the insights of Michel Foucault, some of whose work, particularly *Power/Knowledge*, *The Birth of The Clinic*, and *The History of Sexuality*, has also inspired the main areas of investigation explored in this chapter, and our critical examination of late nineteenth- and early twentieth-century discourses on education, science, and the representation of reality. We differ from Foucault, however, in emphasizing the fact that many Russians were themselves aware of the contradictory character of intellectual debate. As Michel de Certeau has argued, rationalism, in both its Enlightenment and its modern manifestations, has necessarily been conditioned by the phenomena that it has attempted to exclude: 'Scientific "reason" is indissolubly wedded to the reality that it meets again as its shadow and its other, at the very moment when it is excluding it.'[2] In order to illustrate this relationship or dialogue, and the anxiety that it has generated in intelligent observers conditioned by scientific reasoning, we finish the chapter with a detailed case-study of one highly self-conscious and sceptical individual with a scientific training: the doctor, improving landlord, writer, amateur photographer, journalist, and would-be ethnographer Anton Chekhov.

The years between 1881 and 1905 were marked by the inherently contradictory policies of political reaction and state-sponsored rapid industrialization. When Alexander III ascended the throne after the assassination of his father, he sought—in consultation with a group of ultraconservative advisers—to reverse what he could of the Great Reforms inaugurated twenty years earlier with the emancipation of the serfs in 1861. Through a series of legislative acts he succeeded in returning an element of gentry control over the peasant commune and shrinking the already unrepresentative pool of electors to city government to favour the wealthiest property owners. The constraints on change were so great that most radical ideas were forced underground, and the floor was held by those many liberals and professionals who believed that substantive change could only come gradually, through the accumulation of piecemeal efforts at reform. Hence, this era is commonly referred to as one of 'small deeds'. Alexander's death in 1894 brought no political relief; his son Nicholas II dashed the 'senseless dreams' of those who petitioned the young Tsar for some form of constitutional guarantees over person and property.

Not all deeds were small, however, as the successive Tsars approved the creation of an anachronism: a modern, industrialized autocracy. The crucial project of the 1890s was the Trans-Siberian Railway, connecting Russia's mineral-rich Asian extremities to its national capital, and sponsored primarily by the politically conservative but economically radical Minister of Finance, and later Prime Minister, S. Iu. Witte, a typical figure of the age. The requirements of retaining great-power status on a continent that was watching the rise of Wilhelm II's Germany necessitated an alliance with France and Britain based on mutual economic and diplomatic interests, and strained Russia's financial capacities to breaking point. Factories expanded, peasants poured into the cities to work in them, professionals received education and training to manage them, and traditional merchants evolved into a proto-bourgeoisie to handle the resultant trade. The Tsars could maintain an aristocratic front around the Winter Palace and in Tsarskoe Selo, the preferred residence of Nicholas II. But the neoclassical façade of power was quickly losing relevance in a society where the circumstances of birth could no longer restrict or advance a person with the same assurance as in the old days. While some Russians became obsessed with inherited status, others fought to remove all remnants of the old caste, or 'estate', system from the legal codes. Projects for new legal codes, institutions of (albeit limited) self-government, increasing numbers of voluntary associations and professional societies, and a mass-circulation press created a public sphere where ideas about citizenship could be aired. Without exaggerating the opportunities for all to enjoy social mobility, it would still be fair to say that many Russians could now try, or even push ajar, doors previously locked in their faces.

The tensions arising from the combination of socio-economic expansion and political contraction found expression in all aspects of the culture, which was itself, as always, contested terrain. The Russian intelligentsia had laid the foundation of what must be considered the dominant culture. From about 1840, poets, novelists, and literary critics had established criteria for evaluating cultural works on the basis of their social utility. The purpose of art was to critique the status quo, which included the obscurantist autocracy, self-interested nobility, and philistine merchantry. Positioning themselves on the moral high ground, the intelligentsia preached a gospel of responsibility for the plight of the peasants and exhorted readers to commit themselves to raising the cultural level on a national/imperial scale. A recurring refrain resounded throughout this debate: Russia's ambiguous relationship to the West. Ashamed at Russian backwardness, many intellectuals insisted upon a nobility of purpose that would mark Russians as ethically superior to their Western counterparts. But what was in part an inferiority complex also generated some of the most salient and powerful features of Russia's national identity.

With industrial strength, however, the foundations of the old national and ethical identity were shaken. A modern, prosperous Russia had no reason to feel second-class, but on the other hand the moral high ground was harder to occupy as well. As industrialization threatened to commercialize culture and to replace the interests of the community with those of the individual, the intelligentsia struggled to defend its leading role; it remained determined to perform a 'civilizing process' that would disseminate intelligentsia ideals to the social strata below without allowing for influence to come from the bottom up. Yet industrialization, by assigning greater economic power both to magnates and to workers, unsettled the 'civilizing process', contesting the autocratic tendencies that the intelligentsia, for all its staunch opposition to autocracy, itself secretly harboured.

The pressure that had been building up, especially since the assassination of Alexander II, finally exploded in 1905. The Revolution of that year is usually explained as an expression of national political protest, its cultural dimension subsumed under that of politics. But it is essential to recall that political protest had developed and found its voice within a public culture that was itself contradictory, having evolved from a multiplicity of paradoxes that made the old ways not only inadequate, but also unacceptable. Increasingly open, cross-class access to cultural resources—education, libraries, political literacy—inevitably resulted in competition among various groups over who had the authority to set the boundaries of acceptability. No single ideology could dominate, and cultural forms were susceptible to the political and economic pressures that they also tried to dominate.

Public Sphere, Public Good

Massive, unmanageable urbanization generated any number of wrenching dislocations. To cite a few statistics: St Petersburg averaged 50,000 new inhabitants annually between 1890 and 1914, becoming a city of approximately two million; Moscow, with a population of one million in 1900, was the world's tenth largest city and also the fastest-growing; in the last half century before the Great War, the population of the port city of Odessa more than quintupled, to over 650,000; that of the ancient capital of Kiev increased tenfold, to more than 600,000.[3] The overwhelming majority of newcomers came from the Russian provinces, sometimes from smaller towns, but much more often from the rural peasantry. Not only did they have to learn to adapt to urban life, but the city folk, too, had to learn to adjust to neighbours with whom they had little in common. Clothing, customs, even language, set up barriers.

Urbanization must be distinguished here from urbanism; the influx of peoples sparked the need for modifications in social behaviour, but the forms that this took were not always similar or predictable. On the one hand, the new influx of population generated anxieties among settled city-dwellers. The Russian press in the late nineteenth century was full of panic about social undesirables: reports of gang rapes, street fighting, drunkenness, and foul language were assimilated into the new concept of 'hooliganism', which suggested that a sinister conspiracy was in play among the lower classes. Russian commentators quickly latched on to theories such as those of Lombroso, according to which crime was a hereditary activity practised by countless generations of lowbrow Cains.[4] Yet, on the other hand, the relentless advance of what everyone saw as 'modernity' worked to smooth down class differences. Changes in time-budgeting affected not only workers but also managers, and eventually even the 'free professions', whose tasks were increasingly institutionalized, and who more and more found themselves required to practise justification by works, rather than by status.

How did the local civic administrations handle increasing demands on resources and help the populace to orient itself? Management of urbanization followed roughly the same divide that marked it in the West, between public, government-run institutions and private charities. Predictably, men dominated in the former and women played a significant role in the latter. Nobles, merchants, and petits bourgeois (*meshchane*) interacted noticeably in the emerging public sphere of urban affairs, their interests overlapping and colliding at critical junctures. A bourgeoisie can be found taking shape here, forming itself around civic values and a vision of how a city might socialize its sundry inhabitants.

The institutionalized origins of both civic government and public charities date back to the enlightened despotism of Catherine the Great. The Tsaritsa's *Charter For Towns* in 1785 implicitly mandated public participation in local politics, though it kept city administrations under the long reach of the state bureaucracy. Catherine also launched a number of philanthropic institutions (notably Foundling Hospitals in St Petersburg and Moscow), of which her daughter-in-law Maria Fedorovna, considered a model of aristocratic benevolence, later took control, ensconcing public charity as an imperial function. Thus, the two different slices of the public sphere found themselves associated, and jointly under central government authority, from the outset. Later, too, it was often impossible to differentiate between public (*obshchestvennye*) and state (*gosudarstvennye*) responsibilities, although the latter exercised final judgement over the former and the state always provided a sizeable percentage of city resources. According to Catherine's charter, the merchant estate, with the assistance of *meshchane* and artisans, administered the urban areas. The central government could not control the actions of the city fathers, who either implemented or blocked the official policies, depending upon how they viewed the best interests of their respective cities.[5] A municipal reform in 1846 brought city-dwelling nobles into government; elections were indirect, based on the curial representation. In the heady atmosphere of the Great Reforms two decades later, the charter seemed to limit more than it empowered local initiative, so the reformers set out to increase self-rule at the municipal level. This call to involve each city's 'best people' had the side-effect of bringing more members of the urbanized nobility into government. Although this increased the number of interest groups competing for authority, it also multiplied the voices expressing opinions about 'public good'. Under these circumstances such figures as liberal historian Boris Chicherin and progressive merchant Nikolai Alekseev could both be elected mayor. Liberals accused merchants of conservatism because the latter tended to favour economic concerns over social welfare, revealing a dispute familiar in all histories of urban growth over whether unimpeded trade should be the locomotive of change.[6] And Alekseev's assassination by a disgruntled city employee in 1893 reflected another, more sombre aspect of modern political attitudes: the accountability of those in public office.

From Catherine's initial charter, studies of Russia's municipal administrations have emphasized the electorate's apathy. Judgements have derived largely from the low level of participation among the eligible electors. However, those who did serve in city governments showed that Russia was not without a dynamic civic consciousness.[7] This was recognized by Alexander III who, fearing the activism of civic administrations, tried to stem what he saw as a liberal tide by increasing property qualifications for the electorate in 1892, hoping to ensure a conservative majority. He mistakenly assumed that the most affluent property-owners would be hostile to the kinds of measure necessary to manage urbanization. But factories could not produce without workers, streaming by the tens of thousands into areas that had no infrastructure to house them. Therefore, industrialists themselves sometimes adopted paternalist measures, offering cheap housing to their workers. Architects also understood the changing demands of housing, and asserted that 'developments in aesthetics do not take second place to the demands of utility. Since the time when man raised the first memorial stones . . . spiritual and moral elements have been an intrinsic part of building.'[8] But functionalism was no less evident, particularly in those accoutrements of the modern city upon which industry depended: electricity, telephones, public transportation, proper sanitation, and the organization of leisure activities. Construction of telephone lines began in 1881, and the demands for instant communications boomed: more than 4,300 telephones were in operation by 1894.[9] In the face of such irresistible pressures, struggles between state and local authorities to control decision-making were a waste of effort; hence, the reactionary statute of 1892 had only limited effects on the history of urban Russia.

Cities were transformed into showcases of the marvels of industry. The two areas most associated with merchants and industry, Moscow and Nizhnii Novgorod—the Volga city which hosted the largest national fair every summer from the early nineteenth century until well after the Revolution—were sites of national exhibitions in 1882 and 1896 respectively. In addition to industry, the cities themselves were on display, symbols of how Russia's towns were metamorphosing into modern metropolises, with paved streets in the centre, public transport, and streetlights. Traditional public spaces had to be rearranged to accommodate new building and crowded streets. Early in the century St Petersburg was still a city of open parks, and the central artery, Nevskii Prospekt, could be closed off for short intervals in the winter for festivals.[10] Various factors, though, began pushing the holiday fairs to the outskirts of the city. Many streets had to remain open to businesses, and the growing number of merrymakers could not be so easily accommodated in a now much larger city. Finally, new standards of public decency meant that traditional street entertainments became increasingly embarrassing. In the 1890s, therefore, the traditional funfairs of central St Petersburg were placed under the jurisdiction of the Directorship of the People's Temperance, and moved to an area at the far end of Nevskii Prospekt from Admiralty Square, before finally closing down before the First World War.[11] In early twentieth-century Moscow, the 'Catkin Week' (that is, Palm Sunday Week) bazaar, selling Easter trinkets for children, was the only regular festivity still held in the centre of the city, on Red Square.

Instead of beer-tents, swings, and roundabouts, city-dwellers began to be offered more sober and decent pursuits. The administration of St Petersburg had long sponsored summer concerts in the imperial parks outside the city, but Moscow's city government presented military-band concerts on Sunday summer evenings on the main boulevard, Tverskaia. By the century's end, these concerts had expanded to include other entertainments, and had moved into the larger park area just beyond the centre, Sokol'niki. The authorities also made attempts to deal with some of the social pressures resulting from urban growth, such as the

Nevskii Prospekt, St Petersburg, c.1908.
Since its construction in the early eighteenth century, this had been the premier shopping street and promenade in the city, analogous to Regent Street in London or the Champs-Elysées in Paris. As the photograph indicates, it was also the centre of modern Russia, with contemporary shop signs, plate-glass windows, and advertising displays, as well as asphalt highways, motor cars, electric trams, and smartly dressed pedestrians. Conditions in most Russian towns were much less redolent of modernity: horse-drawn transport, unpaved roads, wooden houses and sidewalks, and primitive sanitation remained the norm well into the twentieth century (and can still be seen in parts of some sizeable towns to the present day). (Illustration from Harold Williams, *Russia of the Russians*, London, 1914.)

behaviour of rowdies who brought alcohol illegally to the park and harassed young women there.[12] As the centres became increasingly built up, numerous cities tried to save what they could of their open spaces and tree-lined avenues by organizing schoolchildren to plant trees, keeping a symbolic presence of the natural world in the increasingly mechanized city.

Much information about the mundane details of city life can be drawn from the bulletins published regularly by city governments with information about their numerous duties. The number one problem of rapid urbanization, of course, was sanitation. Workers simply flooded in faster than resources for plumbing and clean water could handle them. Traders' wagons created traffic jams in market areas. The sick could not always find beds in already overcrowded hospitals. Rooms opening up for rent had to be investigated to ensure compliance with sanitary regulations. An 1891 inspection of one of the 'fast food' establishments springing up to feed the mobile population painted a repugnant portrait of culinary Moscow:

An inspection on October 4 of the shop selling appetizers owned by the *meshchanin* V. P. Polyshudnikov, Novaia Andronikova, Sergiev Posad, turned up the following: the dishes holding the provisions were dirty, a bottle of vinegar and horseradish was filthy and had flies swimming in it, dirty clothes lay scattered behind the counter, the floor was dirty and the walls and ceiling covered with soot.

Truly, as one peep-show text (*raek*) of the 1880s put it:

Вот вам площадь городская, хорошая такая и убранная к тому же, что ни шаг, то лужи, и украшениам нет счета, где ни взглянь, там болото, а пахнет как будто роза, потому что везде кучи навоза.
    Чисто!

[Here's a town square for ye, fair to see and tidy into the bargain, puddles underfoot, everything real beaut, swamps everywhere you look, and smells like a rose-garden—oh I beg your pardon, that's the manure.
    Clean as a whistle!][13]

Such strains and failures in Russia's urbanization have received great attention, and have been marshalled as evidence of impending revolution.[14] Yet similar strains were felt in Paris, London, and Berlin: no major metropolis, whether in Russia or the West, could cope completely effectively with the health problems posed by inadequate sanitation measures. Descriptions of urban blight have overshadowed the huge symbolic importance of urbanization, the fact that it set so much of the activist civic agenda. Certainly the inability of Russia's city fathers (city mothers were not permitted to stand for election) to meet all of their public duties contributed to unrest, but their successes in meeting some of these should also be recognized if the civic ethic is to be properly understood.

One area of relative success was poor relief, which grew from almost nothing in 1861 to a powerful network in the early 1900s. Before rapid industrialization upended the precarious social balance in Russia's cities, the local administrations paid little attention to the chronically unemployed and culturally disenfranchised element who depended upon the kindness of strangers. The Orthodox Church (through monasteries and convents), the Empress Maria's Foundation, the Ministry of the Interior's Committees on Begging, plus scattered private charities and random alms-giving, gave some aid to the unfortunate, but for the most part the enserfment system was relied upon to keep penury in check. After 1861, the old paternalistic ways came under assault: indigent peasants could no longer be sent back home to their owners. By the 1880s, therefore, the need for better supervision of the burgeoning city population had become clear; more-over, the Tsarist government was now prepared to share with cities the burden of increasing expenditures for poor relief. At this point, too, the science of sociology entered the municipal forum with the argument that society as a whole would benefit from turning the unskilled and unemployed into productive workers.[15] How, though, to single out the deserving from the undeserving poor, and how to turn the latter into productive workers?

Tolstoi's *What, Then, is to Be Done?* (*Tak chto zhe nam delat'?*, 1889) was one famous response to the problem: Russia should return to a pre-industrial society, which Tolstoi ahistorically imagined to consist of self-sufficient male labourers and female child-carers. But such a solution, whatever its considerable appeal to utopian populists, did not attract the practical entrepreneurs who ran city administrations, or pragmatic civil servants. Their response was to set up welfare organizations, such as the Municipal Guardianships for the Poor, founded in 1894. These guardianships, established in all major cities, mirrored the competing interests and financial frustrations of charity as a whole: the government wanted to be able to decide who administered them, but it wanted cities to pay for them, and the cities in turn encouraged whoever they could to volunteer their services and depended in large measure on private donations. The autocracy persisted in its irrational hopes that the wealthy and propertied would take control; in fact, aristocratic and merchant women, and intellectuals (of both sexes) supplied the support personnel. Though many had to be turned away because of insufficient funding, thousands of large families, abandoned wives, and crippled workers received much-needed aid—cash handouts and cheap lodgings were provided, and new employment found.[16] Equally importantly, these guardianships allowed citizens, including women, to learn to define and participate in the commonweal: social welfare was not now seen to trickle down from ever-munificent autocrats to dependent citizens (a metaphor, in fact, frequently used in odes of praise), but as something constructed by citizens themselves, in competition as well as in participation with state institutions.

Charities, both private and state-sponsored, allowed city mothers to play a prominent role in organizing for the public's welfare. The cities' bulletins recorded the extensive activities of charities, including the many and sizeable donations left in women's wills. As in Western cities, charities formed the single significant civic activity that allowed women to participate meaningfully in public life. Thus could the 'feminine' private sphere, recognized as morally superior to the 'dirty' male world of politics since the late eighteenth century, come, paradoxically, to occupy a strategic place in political reform.

The leading female figures in Russia's private charities both came from the *dvorianstvo* (nobility), the class that had benefited most from the reforms to women's education that had been instituted from the 1850s. Countess Sofiia Panina and Anna Filosofova represented two threads of Russia's quasi-feminist movement. Panina, famous for her Ligovskii People's Palace, which offered culture as well as hot food to St Petersburg's needy, personified the Christian moral commitment that eschewed politics in favour of personal devotion. Filosofova, in contrast, involved herself both in charities and in the Higher Courses of Education for Women, because she was first and foremost a social activist and recognized the possibility for charities to function as a way into the public sphere.[17] The 'Charity Lady', a noblewoman expending her largesse on the poor, appeared as a stock figure in late nineteenth-century farces. On one level, this ridiculous character allowed for undeserved derision to be levelled at the sincere efforts of many women activists, but, on another level, her very familiarity indicated the anxieties provoked by the intrusion of private values into public life, and the enhanced possibilities of female power that this offered. Similarly, the great hostility among Russian radicals to philanthropic efforts (reflected also in much Soviet historiography) was largely inspired by the fact that charities and welfare institutions did succeed in siphoning off some of the social discontent which, in the radicals' view, would have been better channelled into revolution. The intersection of political and sexual-political lines of hostility is well reflected in Chekhov's story 'House with a Mezzanine' ('Dom s mezoninom', 1896), in which the artist-narrator's impatience with the charitable efforts of Lida, a reforming landowner, though phrased in the *bien-pensant* clichés of the day, also has strong undertones of a quite irrational sexual aggression inspired by the spectacle of a successful and dominant woman.

The Public Education Movement

Perhaps the central locus of philanthropic efforts, however, was the movement for public education. Successive Tsarist governments, hesitating between the pressure to construct an educated workforce on the one hand, and the fear that education might lead to social unrest on the other, committed themselves only slowly to setting up an adequate network of primary education. In the minds of 'official' Russia, therefore, education was closely linked to concerns about law and order, moral improvement, and social discipline. And the creation of primary schools should be set in the wider context of official attempts to improve the effectiveness of government via such initiatives as the expansion of urban police forces after 1880, the regulation of prostitution, and efforts to improve public health and popular welfare through such initiatives as the institution of factory inspectorates.

But there were also other strands in the official education drive. The first of these was a pragmatic recognition of the need for a properly trained workforce, in order that increasingly complex industrial, and indeed agricultural, processes might be disseminated, and the competitiveness of the Russian economy ensured. The second was admiration for the ideal of 'civilization', towards which Russia should strive if it was to escape cultural, as well as economic, backwardness. This ideal had been particularly assiduously propagandized by the Russian intelligentsia since its formation in the 1840s, but was very widely shared in the Russian elite. Hence, not only the *zemstva* and municipal governments, but 'improving landlords' and even the Orthodox Church, all committed themselves to the mammoth task of expanding popular education.

In the 1860s, a spontaneous movement to expand elementary schools had appeared in provincial towns throughout the country. Even before the Ministry of Enlightenment altered its statute on urban education, municipalities began to fund a large number of new elementary schools. During the 1880s and 1890s, the state made a particular effort to develop the parish schools run by the Orthodox Church.[18] In the countryside, the expansion of schooling largely took the form of converting informal literacy schools into *zemstvo*-supervised and partially subsidized institutions, until 1890, when a programme of new building rapidly got under way. The expansion of schooling in European Russia, measured in enrolments as a percentage of the population, was 1.5 per cent in 1880, 2.9 per cent in 1894, and 4.5 per cent in 1911. Although access to schooling lagged far behind that in Western and Central European countries, the USA, or Japan, it signified a growth of 379 per cent in enrolments in primary education, when the huge increase in rural population at the same period is taken into account. There are statistical difficulties in estimating the actual numbers of children in school, but it appears that more than half of all school-age children were registered on school rolls by 1915 in forty-four of the fifty provinces of European Russia. The proportion of boys was considerably higher than that of girls, but by 1911 the latter represented 32 per cent of school enrolments.[19]

According to the 1897 census, only 29.3 per cent of males and 13.1 per cent of females in European Russia were literate. But this overall rate is somewhat misleading, being explained by the appalling levels of literacy in the countryside —only 17 per cent, as opposed to 45 per cent in the towns. Furthermore, it has been estimated that literacy of the total population increased from 21 per cent in 1897 to 30 per cent in 1913, with the level for the population aged 8 and over reaching 38–9 per cent. By 1920, a third of the population of European Russia was literate, including 42 per cent of men and 25.5 per cent of women; among children between the ages of 12 and 16, 71 per cent of boys and 52 per cent of girls were literate.[20] Despite the low levels of rural literacy, there is evidence that peasants recognized the economic and cultural value of at least limited literacy for themselves and their children. The literate had advantages at many levels of urban employment, and were more likely to migrate than the illiterate, though cities attracted both. Contact with urban life, its shop signs and street names, window displays and price tags, newspapers and kiosks, announcements and bookstalls, also increased the sense that it was necessary to learn to read. Literacy and school attendance among peasants increased, therefore, with their proximity to the city; in cities themselves, male literacy has been estimated at 80 per cent by the 1917 Revolution.[21]

Education was more than a matter of simply raising literacy skills, however. On the eve of the Great Reforms, the renowned surgeon N. I. Pirogov, who had traded a career in medicine for one in education, posed the question that would inform all future debates about pedagogy for the masses: should they receive primarily vocational training, or a broader education in *nauki* (science and humanities)?[22] Pirogov himself favoured the latter, as did most of the self-styled enlightened segment of the population. For example, in a 1911 *zemstvo* survey of rural schoolteachers, nearly 40 per cent of respondents, asked what effect school had on the peasant way of life, replied that it 'raised the cultural level' of students. The most commonly observed changes were alterations in speech patterns, richer vocabulary, heightened curiosity about the outside world, increased respect for science, and an effort to become respectable.[23] 'Raising cultural levels' was also the aim of the many members of the Russian intelligentsia who worked in adult education. The drive for this had begun with the populist 'going to the people' of the 1870s, in which individual activists introduced themselves to lower-class milieux, and attempted, with varying degrees of success, to instruct workmates and neighbours in literacy and elementary radical politics. Later, the adult education campaign became larger-scale, more systematic, and less ideological. By 1895, the Imperial Russian Technical Society had set up thirty-five schools in St Petersburg, attached mainly to large factories. In 1900, there were twenty Sunday and evening schools in the city, not counting element- ary courses put on for workers by other bodies.[24] As a consequence of the 1905 Revolution, the People's Universities were established: these institutions were outside the system of official higher education establishments, but often under municipal control. In 1906 the Society of Civil Engineers founded a People's University in St Petersburg, for which no formal registration was required, just a small entrance fee to lectures. The most famous People's University, though, was the Shaniavskii University in Moscow, which, by the eve of the First World War, had 6,000 mainly part-time students, half of them women. In January 1908, the First All-Russian Congress of Activists of the People's Universities took place, and in 1910 the Society of Popular Universities organized lectures in thirty-six cities, attracting a total of 210,560 students to its sessions.[25] Early twentieth-century guide-books to Moscow and St Petersburg indicate that there were also several museums aimed at working people, intending to instruct them in nature study, history, and so on.

Besides organizing classes, lectures, and displays, the intelligentsia poured its efforts into various methods of distance learning. Political tracts poured from the radical presses operating abroad (in London and Switzerland) or clandestinely in Russia. (The memoirist Ol'ga Sliozberg recalled, in her 1993 memoir *My Path* (*Moi put'*), meeting a woman in prison during the 1930s who had worked for an underground press after the Revolution: one of the press's front operations had been to print the speeches of Nicholas II.) Increasingly, the intelligentsia began to produce didactic fiction, often written in simple language so as to be com- prehensible to inexpert readers. Indeed, the line between tracts and didactic fiction was often so fine as to be nearly invisible, as in Aleksandra Kollontai's *Worker-Mother* (*Rabotnitsa-mat'*, 1914), which juxtaposes the easy child-bearing experiences of the bourgeoisie with the horrendous ordeals of the poor, or Gor'kii's *The Mother* (*Mat'*, 1906), the famous mythologization of a working-class woman's progress to enlightenment. Auto-didactic peasants also became famil- iar figures in texts not aimed so obviously at working people as these: Chekhov's remarkable late story 'The Student' ('Student', 1894) depicts the divided feelings of a youth returning to his native village for a vacation from study in the city, while Ol'ga Shapir's 'The Settlement' ('V slobodke', 1893) portrays the struggles of a working-class boy from a desperately poor township to cope with the demands of education at a *gimnaziia* (classical high school). Among 1890s and 1900s members of the Wanderers (*Peredvizhniki*) group of realist painters, literacy classes became something of a cliché: Nikolai Bogdanov-Bel'skii, himself from a poor peasant background, specialized in such pictures, knocking off in suc- cession *At the School Door*, *Counting Out Loud*, *The Voice Test*, *The Composition*, and, most famously, *Sunday Reading in a Rural School*. Bogdanov-Bel'skii's paintings were immensely well-regarded, several being acquired by the Russian Museum in St Petersburg when it was set up in the late 1890s; they brought con- siderable wealth to the artist, as well as regard, a fact that attracted acid comment from some of his acquaintances.[26]

The drive to bring education to peasants and workers was vitally important to the intelligentsia's self-image, both before the Revolution and after: the
reformed Ministry of Enlightenment, now the Commissariat of Enlightenment,
was to amalgamate the 'official' and 'unofficial' literacy drives, presiding over
rabfaki ('worker faculties') and reading rooms in city and countryside, as well
as over primary, secondary, and tertiary education. After the Revolution, too,
peasants and workers acquiring literacy skills and culture were to be ubiquitous in fiction and painting, as well as in tracts, posters, and other kinds of political propaganda. How much did the education drive contribute, though, to the
involvement of workers and peasants in the commonweal, to the identification
of these politically almost powerless groups with the cultural agenda that was
proposed for them by the elite?

There is no simple answer to this question. As will be explained in our later discussion of commercial culture, the intelligentsia's commitment to raising cultural
levels was powerless to prevent many workers from continuing to enjoy gambling, reading penny dreadfuls, watching film melodramas, buying new clothes,
indulging in other attractions of the modern city, or indeed in such time-honoured
pursuits as fighting, drinking, energetic sex, and cruelty to animals. However, a
small but strategic group of workers did warm to the promise of educational
and moral advancement offered by the intelligentsia. These self-styled 'conscious' workers, sometimes known as the 'worker-intelligentsia', sought to raise
their cultural level and to internalize a new set of values, based on individuality
(*lichnost´*) and respectability. By definition, they were untypical of the mass of
workers, whom they criticized fiercely for the squalor and ignorance in which
they were, apparently, content to live. Boris Ivanov, a young teenage baker,
wrote: 'Drunkenness, card games, prostitutes, the bondage of the job, sottish
and filthy company—otherwise nothing. Did it have to be like that?'[27] Such
animosity was reciprocated by the less 'conscious' workers, in whose eyes the
worker-intelligentsia, as one young samovar-maker recalled, were less frank
and sincere than their fellow workers, as well as less rowdy, sang with sensitivity
rather than gusto, did not fight over girls or get drunk 'from sorrow', and were
consequently dubbed 'students of the cold life'.[28]

Conscious workers looked to the intelligentsia to provide them with a means
of escape from a life of degradation and exploitation. 'What we wanted to hear
from outsiders, from students, was something out of the ordinary, something novel,
something that would open new horizons to us.'[29] One paramount aspiration of
the conscious worker was familiarity with the literary canon: 'The biggest part
of the money in the *kassy* [workers' defence funds] went on buying literature
(mainly legally published literature).'[30] But workers did not necessarily appreciate all classic authors in the same way. Turgenev, Pushkin, and Chekhov left
many lukewarm; as is perhaps scarcely surprising, the problems of the well-off
'superfluous man' seemed the reverse of interesting. Kanatchikov quotes workmates who thought that 'your Onegin and your Lensky . . . should have been sent
to a factory to fit cylinders to a vice'.[31] A skilled turner interviewed by Kabo
liked *Crime and Punishment* better than *War and Peace*: 'I didn't understand a
lot of it, for example that stuff about Freemasons, and I didn't like the heroes

because I couldn't understand their experience.' Much more popular was the political poetry of Nekrasov: 'How well that man could write about the poor, and how he hated the rich', wrote Kanatchikov. The melodramatic stories of Leonid Andreev were also among the favourite reading of lower-class literates. But most popular of all, perhaps, was Maksim Gor'kii, whose working-class image was so strong that A. Frolov was rather shocked to discover that he looked like an *intelligent* rather than the shoemaker of his portraits (though he was also flattered that 'the great Russian writer of the people even shook my callused hand'). As one skilled turner said, 'when you read *The Mother*, it's as though it was written about you'.[32]

Workers themselves began to write in the period after 1905. Some writers' groups began to publish handwritten journals, such as that produced by a group of workers in the Nevskii district of the capital with the title *Gusli-mysli* (*Thoughts of a Psaltery*—that is, a Russian folk instrument rather like a zither). 'Perhaps at first the sounds of our psalteries will seem discordant, our thoughts unclear. But, striving to study, we will help one another. Let our journal be an instrument of self-help, a centre around which our circle spreads out.' Kleinbort, who studied these journals, called them a 'howl of the spirit' on the part of the educated worker. He judged much of the writing derivative; again, it was Nekrasov and Gor'kii, rather than Pushkin, Lermontov, or Saltykov-Shchedrin who were the models, to Kleinbort's evident annoyance.[33] Like women writers, workers were pressed for time, and so found poetry a suitable vehicle. Like women writers, too, workers were gripped by a sense of the precariousness of existence, and by a longing for escape—images of life in prison sit alongside representations of factory experience. Typical is a poem by E. Terent'ev, 'The Weavers' ('Tkachi'), which appeared in the journal of the textile workers' union in 1917. The first verse ran:

> Огромные трубы поднялись, как лес,
> Над ними из черного дыма навес.
> Пропитана копотью черной земля.
> А где-то есть счастье, луга и поля.
> Вон звездочка в небе далеком зажглась
> Но даже и звезды горят не для нас.

> [Giant chimneys rose up like a forest
> A curtain of black smoke hung over them,
> The earth was soaked in black soot.
> Somewhere are happiness, meadows, fields.
> There a small star caught fire in the distant sky.
> But even the stars do not burn for us.][34]

The fact that such work dwelt on suffering meant that it was not truly 'proletarian' in Bolshevik terms, or in the eyes of Soviet critics. Here, as in commentators' evident embarrassment with workers' failure to enjoy Turgenev, Saltykov-Shchedrin, or other writers admired by intellectual radicals, a tension emerges. Intellectuals both attempted to provide workers and peasants with the means of thinking independently, and resented it when they did. Yet this was nonsensical: as a contributor to the newspaper *Nadezhda* (*Hope*) put it in 1908, 'the need for education . . . can be fully satisfied only when the workers themselves take matters into their own hands and create their own workers' enlightenment institutions, which can provide them with unfalsified spiritual nourishment.'[35] Such assertions of proletarian independence reflected not only a new confidence, born of the success of the workers' movement in 1905, when strikes had forced the Tsarist regime to major democratic concessions, but increasing disillusionment with the intelligentsia, many of whom lost their enthusiasm for revolutionary politics after 1905, preferring instead to work through the new constitutional and legal channels—to which workers and peasants had very limited access—for social and political change. When the Bolshevik regime took over the intelligentsia's mission to civilize Russia, it also took over these tensions, which were expressed in the often acrimonious disputes between grassroots cultural organizations, such as Proletkul′t, and intelligentsia *Kulturträger*, who were determined to propagandize the nineteenth-century classics, and/or twentieth-century modernism, among workers and peasants.

'Distance Learning': the Birth of the Russian Mass Newspaper

In the late nineteenth century, the dominance of printed books and 'thick journals' (heavyweight monthly magazines) in shaping public opinion was increasingly challenged by a new source of information, the newspaper. In the first six decades of the nineteenth century, the Tsarist regime's imposition of preliminary censorship on Russian newspapers had hindered the development of political journalism. However, from 1865 the requirement for vetting of newspapers before publication was dispensed with, allowing them to develop along the lines of their European counterparts for the first time. Although Alexander III, in the first wave of counter-reforms following on his accession, returned more power to censors by allowing them to keep specified topics out of newspapers, hence restricting public debate, the demand for information far outstripped the Tsar's ability to control the public agenda. Despite harsher censorship, the number of newspapers in Russia rose between 1883 and 1913 from 80 to 1,158.[36]

Two of Russia's most influential mass-circulation dailies began to make their mark early in the 1880s: N. I. Pastukhov's *Moskovskii listok* (*The Moscow Sheet*) and S. M. Propper's *Birzhevye vedomosti* (*The Stock Market Gazette*), a general newspaper on the pattern of today's *Wall Street Journal* or *Financial Times*. These two papers entered the circulation wars with several other dailies that had appeared since 1865. However, as the most influential of them, the liberal, nationally circulated *Golos* (*The Voice*), died a slow death at the censor's hands just as *Birzhevye vedomosti* was establishing itself, Propper's prime competitor was A. S. Suvorin, whose relatively conservative *Novoe vremia* (*New Times*) also published out of St Petersburg and reached a national audience. Both publishers supported modernization, but Propper believed in a faster programme than did Suvorin, and enjoyed a mutually beneficial relationship with the architect of rapid industrialization, Witte. Through the rival editorial points of view, readers learned much about different aspects of the changes they saw going on around them. The newspapers provided them both with opinions, and with crucial background information.[37]

Birzhevye vedomosti and *Novoe vremia* circulated among the better-educated and more moneyed sectors of society. Readers with less reason for interest in national political questions were less likely to spend hard-earned money on such discussions. As a paper catering to those outside the elite, Pastukhov's *Moskovskii listok*, founded in 1881, was the first of its kind in Moscow. St Petersburg already had two less expensive papers designed for the middle-class urban reader, and in Moscow Pastukhov went even further in making gossip, especially about local merchants, a staple of news items. 'Human interest' stories, close to the material circulating in oral tradition, made the papers more accessible for those who were not practised readers, and hence a more integral part of urban life. For all their sensational tone, too, the street sheets had an explicitly didactic function: they raked the muck of corruption, keeping readers informed about the problems of city life and about measures being taken to resolve them, thus bringing those who were not eligible for city office into the process of municipal administration.

The newspapers focused on the basic issues that had to be addressed if cities were going to be able to enter the twentieth century with a pluralism of publics able to negotiate with each other, as well as adjust to change. For all their variety in editorial opinion and presentation, the papers all operated according to nineteenth-century principles of objective reporting. Relying on descriptions rather than interpretations, the press encouraged readers to develop skills of rational analysis, of thinking the issues through for themselves, of basing conclusions on reasoned assessment of the facts. If the papers failed to create the perfectly logical reader (probably a mythic beast in any case), they nonetheless offered concepts of how an urban community was supposed to function, and suggested to them the benefits of successful modernization. The press worked as an active agent of change, teaching readers the difference between *obshchestvennye* and *gosudarstvennye* institutions, and encouraging identification with the former.

Social Identity and the New Urban Culture: from Social Estate to Social Class

Industrialization shook the foundation of a social system still officially described in the rigid terms of hereditary estates (*sosloviia*): the *dvorianstvo* (nobility/gentry), *meshchanstvo* (burghers, petits bourgeois), *krest'ianstvo* (peasantry), and *dukhovenstvo* (clergy). The system of estates had been formalized by Catherine II so as to avoid intermingling between the different social orders, though in fact social mobility was never impossible. High-ranking civil servants whose origins lay outside the gentry classes were promoted to life or hereditary nobility depending on the class of their employment; the system also recognized unclassifiable 'estate outsiders' (*raznochintsy*, originally army officers who had been granted permission to buy land), and also *sostoianiia*, categories based on occupation, such as 'tradesman'. Perhaps the most important instrument of social mobility, though, was the fact that merchants (*kuptsy*) could come from any estate, since the *kupechestvo* was a system of taxation allowing trading privileges, and levying duties, according to the sum of an entrepreneur's capital. Though few merchants were *déclassé* nobles, many, especially in the lower guilds (that is, tax brackets), were peasants or petits bourgeois who had made their fortunes as market-traders or the owners of workshops. As richer merchants married into the nobility, or made their way into it through city office, and richer peasants rose into the *kupechestvo*, the merchant category had the potential to be a clearing bank of social change.

In the late nineteenth century, the potential of capital to act as a social leveller was further enhanced by the Tsarist authorities' decision to streamline the merchant guilds, and to introduce trading certificates (*promyshlennye spravki*), a simplified form of registering traders which brought many small entrepreneurs who might previously have operated illegally into the official net. Not long afterwards, there was a decision to boost the commercial schools—primary and secondary institutions offering a vocational education based on such commercial skills as bookkeeping. The number of such schools jumped from 12 to 191 between 1896 and 1905. As a result, tens of thousands of less privileged Russians (including many Jews) were able to acquire commercial skills and enter the business world.[38]

But in a society that remained both traditional and hierarchical, many obstacles to social mobility remained. The better-off merchants, such as the Mamontovs and Morozovs of Moscow, tended either to intermarry for dynastic reasons, or to marry out of the merchant estate altogether. They often wanted their children, especially their daughters, to have a 'European' education, rather than one that prepared them for a life in business. Moreover, a significant number of merchants belonged to the Old Believer sect, a conservative and traditional Orthodox group that aimed to keep alive ecclesiastical tradition as it had been prior to church reforms in the mid-seventeenth century. Though the Old Believers valued education—including education for women—hard work, and commercial success more highly than many Orthodox, they were also notoriously wary of outsiders and of change. Unlike Western societies, too, Russia had no history of a craft guild system that would have brought merchants prestige, and furthered the development of particular trades and industries. Finally, many nobles were also hostile to the social change that seemed likely to erode their own prestige. If some Russians anticipated the end of the estate system with glee, others took refuge in a snobbish (and often anti-Semitic) attachment to the aristocratic ideal, which is evident in some turn-of-the-century memoirs (such as those of Aleksandra Sokolova), as well as in the predilection of serious historical journals (*Russkii arkhiv, Russkaia starina, Stolitsa i usad'ba*) for genealogy, family history, and indeed supercilious aristocratic memoirs. Yet if industrialization was to succeed, the system of social estates had to be transformed into one based on social class. To paraphrase Marx, people had to draw the basis for their social identity from their position in the material economy rather than from their lineage. The Tsarist government, with its incongruous desire to rely on a nobility that had much to lose in the projected modern environment, hindered rather than helped. It pitted merchants against bureaucrats, though formulating economic policies that required co-operation to work at all. By the 1890s, however, a number of factors converged to give the proto-bourgeoisie a fixed sense of itself and its direction. Increasing numbers of the highest government servants, members of the State Council who directly advised the Tsar, now came from outside traditional aristocratic circles themselves.[39] Furthermore, even aristocratic landowners did not necessarily despise commerce, now that land-ownership was no longer a guarantee of wealth, and now that there was growing convergence between the lifestyles of at least the wealthiest industrialists and those of the aristocracy. Finally, there was a growing number of cultural institutions that furthered the self-confidence of the proto-bourgeoisie itself, places where it could promote the notion of industrialization as progressive or, like the charity ladies, contribute to easing its strains.

The original sites where identities could be established were the private clubs and societies that had been a part of the cultural landscape from the era of Anglomania at the end of the eighteenth century. The clubs were largely estate-based: the nobles had theirs, the merchants theirs, and, as the intelligentsia perceived itself as a unique *soslovie*, they, too, had their private circles meeting on regular days in the week. Foreign communities also had their own clubs, which opened membership to Russian friends. Interdictions against political discussion could hardly be enforced; indeed, the character of Zaretskii, a bibulous tattler from the 'English Club', the grandest Moscow institution, in Griboedov's 1824 play *Wit's End* (*Gore ot uma*) illustrates that social change was the subject of chat even in the first quarter of the nineteenth century. Later, the split between Slavophiles and Westernizers in the 1840s that epitomized Russian politics for decades was institutionalized in the formation of warring intelligentsia circles (Avdot'ia Elagina's salon on the one hand, Avdot'ia Panaeva's on the other).

Clubs served a dual political/cultural function. Primarily, they offered men a place to share drinks and information with others of their background. Wives and children were not, however, completely excluded. Some clubs, for example, formed theatre groups and staged amateur productions. Others instituted reading groups. At social events too, such as balls, the two sexes mingled. But the political function of clubs was emphatically masculine, and here clubs and societies offered sites for gradual politicization in that they helped members to develop a taste for public activity. As the century progressed, they also became less segregated according to estate.

Alongside the tradition of private social clubs, Russians began, from the era of the Great Reforms, to form voluntary associations that had more specifically political objectives. By the turn of the century few special-interest groups did not enjoy some form of organized status. In fact, a Moscow city directory in 1912 listed more than 600 voluntary associations. These ranged across the broad spectrum of professional groups, charities, and learned societies. They evolved in a natural response to the 'increasing division of labor of the urban economy'.[40] Pitted against a state that kept them disenfranchized from making public policy, voluntary associations took it upon themselves to carve out a sphere in which their actions affected the commonweal.

Although these societies did not have uniform goals, to the extent that a common denominator could be identified it would be in the area of public welfare. Apart from societies promoting education and popularizing science and the humanities (discussed elsewhere in this chapter), public health and hygiene were the two most important areas of activity here. The most abhorrent facets of urbanization inspired some of the most activist associations, for example the ubiquitous temperance societies and the Commission for Diffusion of Knowledge about Hygiene. The devastating famine of 1891 galvanized popular participation in the relief effort on an unprecedented national scale: intellectuals and writers, such as Tolstoi, not only helped in the organization of food kitchens, but also donated royalties from publications to famine relief. The late nineteenth century also saw the foundation of numerous benevolent organizations offering relief to impoverished professionals, such as the Literary Fund, which gave out grants to struggling writers.

Social engineering was by no means the only purpose of the societies, however. People began to develop hobbies, a sign both of increasing time for leisure and of active involvement in concerns beyond the necessary business and domestic chores. Specialized publications connected these societies across the empire. For example, the Society of Lovers of Aquariums and Houseplants began publishing its own journal in 1893, a sure indication of the aesthetic response to living amidst urban blight. Tourism had become increasingly affordable, and not only to the aristocrats and merchants who had been able to afford it earlier. V. V. Bitner, famous for his role in self-education, published paperback tour guides for walking expeditions, for example. Emphasis on health and hygiene brought tourist-patients to the resorts in the Caucasus, which had expanded greatly to include many more than wealthy nobles. The Black Sea coast earned the designation of the 'Russian Riviera'. Cruise ships stratified customers according to ticket prices, but still offered a substantively enlarged acquaintance with the Empire. When Alexander III died unexpectedly in Yalta in 1894, he was, like many of his compatriots, relaxing away from urban life. Athletic clubs offered yet another place in which new social identities could be forged. Originally, organized sports were play for noblemen: horse-racing, for example, or hunting, or yachting. Tolstoi offers an accurate representation of a 'gentlemen's steeplechase' (*dzhentel'menskie skachki*) in *Anna Karenina*, while the Imperial Yacht Club in St Petersburg remained so grand up to the Revolution that Dominic Lieven, historian of the Russian elite, has quite seriously proposed membership of it as a dividing line between true aristocrats and parvenus. But by the 1880s horse-racing at least brought the mass of humanity to the tote to parlay pay cheques into easy winnings (or losses). The new popularity of the sport meant that a jockey club had to be organized on the same principles as in England, to distance the wealthy from the riff-raff at the tracks.

Social exclusivity in the face of the penetration of new social groups into redefined public spaces, however, offered only one reason to found an athletic

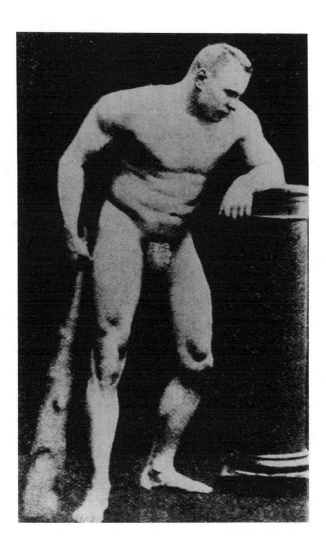

Publicity photograph of the Estonian wrestler Sergei Lurikh as Hercules, complete with pilaster, club, and figleaf.

Such neoclassical references, like the association of sport with 'healthy' and 'clean-minded' impulses, rendered respectable imagery whose overt sensuality might otherwise have pushed it close to pornography. Lurikh, the son of a Revel merchant who was educated at a *real'naia gimnaziia*, was one of the most successful and prominent sportsmen of his generation, and had the reputation of being sharp-witted and a ladies' man.

club. These were also places where men could develop the competitive instincts necessary to compete in the capitalist world. Moreover, the nightclubs, operettas, and flourishing consumer culture threatened to undermine masculine strength: athletics, on the other hand, got men out of the crowded city and into the fresh air, an increasing obsession as the cultural elite took up sedentary pursuits and lived in housing without direct access to space for walking. Apart from workers and peasants, who got a great deal more physical exercise than they wanted or needed, most members of Russian society shared the obsession with fresh air and exercise. Tsar Nicholas II, with his daily constitutionals, and his preference for suburban Tsarskoe Selo over the Winter Palace, typified the age. Building up physical strength metaphorized the parallel struggle to build up the economy. French visionary Pierre de Coubertin organized the first modern Olympics, held in Athens in 1896, according to the ideal that 'neither birth nor fortune gave any man advantage'.[41]

Sandow the Magnificent embodied the virility of the British Empire, and body-building raged from the West to Russia. The first significant body-building club in Russia was organized in 1885 by V. F. Kraevskii, a St Petersburg doctor who turned his office into a weight room and allowed in men from all social estates. Exercise built character and lent brawn to the brain. As one Kiev-based journal editorialized:

> We want you to understand that *Sport* is not some naïve magazine for children, unsuitable for grown-ups. On the contrary, we want to persuade everyone that *Sport* is rational entertainment, spiritual food of the highest quality that nourishes and develops the body, mind, and soul, and that the only mature adult is one who participates in sports and thus amuses himself sensibly. We will give you examples from the West, from Europe and America, where no one could say that people do not know how to live, how to make use of their free time. Sport engulfs all levels of society there like a gigantic wave.[42]

Body-building was closely associated with wrestling, a wildly popular sport at the turn of the century. Its admirers included the poet Aleksandr Blok, who wrote of 'French wrestling' at the Ciniselli Circus in St Petersburg: 'There were real artists among the wrestlers. I shall never forget the fight between a hideously lumpish Russian heavyweight and a Dutchman whose outstandingly beautiful muscular system had the perfection of a musical instrument.'[43]

As Blok's rather supercilious remarks indicate, wrestling opened opportunities not only for outstandingly beautiful Dutchmen, but also for Russian peasant boys. Some of these, such as Ivan Poddubnyi and Ivan Zaikin, achieved international fame, allowing them to move into dramatically different social circles. In medieval Russia, and indeed up to the early twentieth century, an indigenous pastime called *kulachnye boi* (fist battles) had pitted whole villages against each other in mass tugs of war, boxing, and wrestling matches, a recreation that carried over into city culture, as factory vied with factory on Sundays and holidays. But the participants in such matches were unpaid, and their competence varied widely. Professional wrestling required skill and grace as well as muscle, and carried with it fame because wrestlers fought in organized competitions before a paying audience.

Like body-building, wrestling could be a source of national pride: wrestlers carried their national banners with them when they competed abroad. It could also symbolically overturn class barriers: noted wrestlers would be invited to work out at Kraevskii's with wealthy men such as the playboy sportsman Count Ribopierre. The impresario Tumpakov staged renowned matches at his Farce Theatre on Nevskii Prospekt, while Russia's most popular impresario, manager, and announcer, Ivan Lebedev ('Uncle Vania'), used his university credentials to bill himself as a 'doctor of physical culture' and impart respectability to what was essentially a circus act.[44]

In terms of popular participation, the bicycling craze involved the greatest number of active participants. Cycling combined all the necessary attributes of healthy athletics: it could be done singly or in groups, competitively or non-competitively; it was an out-of-doors activity; and it was financially feasible for the thousands who were cut off by insufficient means from equestrianism. It also made possible inexpensive outings, increasing the desire for tourism. It did not require great wealth to take a train out of the city at the weekend, and rent a bicycle with friends in some suburban resort or village. Hundreds of bicycle clubs appeared all over the empire; journals catered to the new craze. Cycling's accessibility to women was also important. It 'sharpened the woman question' because it allowed women to enjoy unprecedented degrees of independence, even conditioning them for the competitive business world.[45] As women cycled and toured, they claimed part of the public space as their own; the simplified clothes required for cycling and other active sports also had their effects on what was considered appropriate public costume.

Organized sports followed rational business principles. The clubs arranged competitions to develop manly athletic skills, and to prepare men to assume leadership roles in the future. Despite the institutional prejudice of athletic clubs in favour of the noble and the wealthy, the objectives they advanced were hardly those of conservative retrenchment. Like the scouting movement, which also spread to Russia from the West in the early years of the twentieth century, physical culture sought to transform the personalities of those who followed it, to create a new kind of person, 'a man with backbone', prepared to master the modern industrial city and to command in the new world. The sporting craze also brought commercial spin-offs in terms of equipment manufacture and especially sports journalism, as specialist publications mushroomed to cover new interests, contributing in their own right to economic growth. The involvement of the trading classes in such ventures indicated a new pride and assertiveness.

As merchants' significance to the national economy increased, so too did their pride and self-awareness. Pavel Riabushinskii, a Moscow banker and manufacturer and a leader of the new merchantry, gave a Russian spin to the French notion of *noblesse oblige* with his *bogatstvo obiazyvaet*, or *richesse oblige* (wealth brings obligations).[46] The number of industrialists who agreed with Riabushinskii was not enormous, but they included a number of important figures in the two capitals, among whom there was a time-honoured merchant tradition of donating to charitable causes at least the tenth part of their incomes required by biblical stipulation. Where earlier generations of merchants had funded churches and monasteries, their successors, who have been aptly described by one recent commentator, Mark Steinberg, as 'an entrepreneurial intelligentsia', preferred to give their money to secular causes—hospitals, soup kitchens, and night-shelter hostels. Two women from the wealthy Abrikosov and Prokhorov families, A. A. Abrikosova and E. I. Beklemisheva, were involved in such activities: the former founded a lying-in hospital on Miusskaia Square, Moscow, at a cost of 100,000 roubles, while the latter set up a soup kitchen and typhus hospital in the Chernigov Region during the Great Famine of 1891–2.[47]

For other merchants, charitable efforts began closer to home. Conditions in the average Russian factory, most particularly in the provinces and in smaller metropolitan enterprises, remained horrendous. Industrial accidents and occupational diseases were rife, working hours were long, employees were often forced to sleep where they worked, and induced, by manipulative credit systems, to buy substandard goods in factory-run shops (sometimes even the products of their own labour). The factory inspectorate, consisting of high-minded (in the best sense) Russian intellectuals, campaigned to publicize abuses and to bring offenders to book. But in a society where regulation of health and safety, conditions of employment, and fair pay was wholly inadequate, there was a good deal of leeway for exploitative employers who wished to turn a profit at all costs.[48] For all that, some industrialists, such as the printer Suvorin, were influenced by current notions of 'progress' and 'civilization' into ameliorating work conditions for their employees—purchasing the latest machinery, commissioning architect-designed factories, constructing basic hostel-type housing, and laying on cheap canteens and factory schools as well as 'rational leisure'—that is, programmes of entertainment that would distract the workforce from drinking, the main spare-time activity of manual labourers in Russian cities (see below).[49]

The temperance movement, like the philanthropy campaigns with which it was closely allied, was another instance of how *obshchestvennye* and *gosudarstvennye* interests could, on occasion, work together in order to assure ends that were universally recognized as being in the common good. Legislation and government programmes were widely welcomed by the educated Russian public, who in turn contributed their own efforts to the furtherance of sobriety. The tide of anti-drunkenness feeling, which had risen since Emancipation, turned once and for all during the 1890s, when, in 1895, the Tsarist regime introduced a state monopoly on alcohol, taking control of wholesale and retail trade in vodka, and becoming sole purchaser of the products of the distilleries. However, though private outlets for spirits were officially suppressed, illegal bootlegging and drinking dens continued to survive, and consumption of vodka appears actually to have increased (from 0.58 *vedro*, or approximately 21 pints, in 1909 to 0.63 *vedro* in 1913). During the First World War, the government took the remarkable step of introducing complete prohibition on alcohol (in December 1914), which at first reduced the level of public drunkenness and alcoholism, but led in due course to a rise in the sale of alcohol substitutes, such as methylated spirits.[50]

The experience of prohibition underlined a truth that had in fact been evident to the Ministry of Finance from the beginning: that restrictions on alcohol sales would have limited effects unless accompanied by positive measures to encourage sobriety. During the 1890s, therefore, it set up 'temperance guardianships' (*kazennye popechitel'stva o narodnoi trezvosti*, literally 'guardianships of popular sobriety'), which were intended to offer cultured alternatives to the tavern—tea-rooms selling *kvas* (a low-alcohol small beer) as well as hot drinks. Such efforts were supported by the organization of popular readings: the Society for the Dissemination of Useful Books and the Society to Encourage Industriousness organized 'spiritual-moral public readings and magic-lantern shows' at the Belov cafeteria. The traditional *narodnye gulian'ia*, seasonal funfairs held in St Petersburg, were given into the hands of the guardianships in the late 1890s, a move that irrevocably changed their previously rather drunken and frivolous character. Most important of all, the guardianships founded a number of 'people's palaces', *narodnye doma*, the most important of which was set up in Ligovka District, St Petersburg, in 1900, under the direction of Countess Sof'ia Panina. With a 1,500-seat theatre and adjoining amusement park containing two outdoor stages, this People's Palace attracted some twenty million visitors during its first ten years of operation.[51] The government's campaigns were matched by the efforts of non-government groups. During the 1890s, *zemstva*, rural co-operatives, schools, and private philanthropists all worked alongside temperance guardianships in the countryside, setting up village and *volost'* (district) libraries, popular readings, and magic-lantern shows. The Orthodox Church also began sponsoring thousands of temperance societies in town and countryside. In 1912, Father V. A. Akimov reported on the activities of the temperance society of the Pokrovsko-Kolomenskoe Parish in St Petersburg. Its 2,000-plus members were almost all men, 34 per cent of whom worked in the construction trade, mostly as seasonal migrants. Members were required to take a solemn pledge before an icon of the Virgin to stay sober for a few months. Those who took the pledge received a certificate, which had economic value, since it assured employers that temporary workers would remain sober.[52] As this piece of information suggests, industrialists had a particular interest in ensuring the sobriety of their employees. By 1900, many of the larger factories in St Petersburg had their own theatres, in the attempt to encourage workers to drink less freely and work more productively. The 'Bavaria' beer factory on Krestovskii Island in St Petersburg, for example, had its own pleasure garden offering a variety theatre and entertainments at low prices to local workers. Further theatres on Vasil'evskii Island, one of the main industrial districts of the city, offered mixed programmes of comedies, vaudevilles, and adaptations of the classics on Sundays and holidays, particularly during the summer. Prices were deliberately kept to a minimum, in order to undercut the cost of even a moderate evening's drinking, and attract the largest possible number of attenders.

Associated with the temperance movement on the one hand, the 'people's theatres' drive was linked, on the other, to the campaigns for popular education. The *narodnye doma* and factory theatres alike offered material that conformed to the programme for public readings outlined by the St Petersburg police prefect, General A. A. Trepov, in 1872: to promote 'the struggle against drunkenness, the elimination of coarse manners, and the improvement of the moral and intellectual level of the people'. Similarly, A. R. Lednitskii opined that 'it is not enough to give the stomach food or the hands work: one must give spiritual food, establish mental hygiene, freshen the sensations of man's soul with noble amusements and moral books'.[53] Encouragement of the popular theatre was inseparable from efforts to regulate it: in 1888 a special censorship was set up for works performed on the popular stage, and in the 1900s, a commission of inquiry urged the administrators of state-run defence factories to expand theatre facilities for their workers, but also to take care what material was offered:

> The repertoire should consist of plays which will appeal to the working public, without indulging bad taste. Plays with too crude or vivid a tendency should be excluded. Everyday plays of a realistic genre, unfortunately, are not very accessible to the mass of workers because of their low artistic development. There remain plays of a historical content, which foster love of the motherland, and melodramas, whose shortcomings can be overlooked in view of the 'good feelings' which they stir up in the audience.[54]

It was indeed such historical, naturalistic, and moralistic works that tended to be offered on the stages of both *narodnye doma* and factory theatres.

Divisions within the Intelligentsia: Science, Knowledge, and Scepticism

What has been said so far in this chapter has emphasized co-operation between various sections of the cultural elite—industrialists, government officials, members of the intelligentsia—in the struggle to build a 'modern', civic society in late imperial Russia. We have shown how the struggles between 'reaction' and 'revolution' that have often been emphasized in chronicles of the era did not disrupt the formation of a consensus based on common notions of the value and meaning of progress and modernization. Yet the Russian intelligentsia's participation in the late nineteenth- and early twentieth-century civic ethos left it at once energized and frustrated. The creation of new, social rather than governmental institutions offered ways of working towards the public good which, though legal, were not within the final control of the autocracy. But these institutions also gave room to the opinions of those who did not necessarily share the intelligentsia's confidence in its own leading role. And practical philanthropy, too, with its many difficulties and disappointments, made it clear that the *mission civilisatrice* would not be as effortless in the concrete as it seemed in the abstract. Even the most treasured project, the propagandization of education, sometimes seemed to be in doubt. One report from the countryside declared that 'in terms of moral fibre our literate peasants are not much better than the illiterate'. In the aftermath of the 1905 Revolution, especially, it was feared that a wave of rural crime and disorder was sapping the nation's strength and threatening the state's ability to uphold the law.[55] At the same time as dealing with these external struggles, the intelligentsia was having to deal with a struggle of its own, one that sometimes threatened to force it apart. The nature of this crisis was epistemological; it reflected the pressures of knowledge, of expertise, and of the professionalism that began to consolidate around them.

The chief manifestation of this potent shift in sensibilities is the rise and rapid development of science in its many forms, with its documentary discourses and practices which advanced a unique claim to objective truth and promised a special contribution to the realization of the utilitarian ideal, 'the greatest good of the greatest number'.

The state itself had helped set the stage for the development of the scientific paradigm in Russia in the second half of the nineteenth century, as it mobilized, in the wake of the Crimean War, to rectify the nation's technological disadvantages. Conflating a deficit of knowledge with a lack of power, in 1855 the Minister of Education identified science as 'our first need. If our enemies are superior to us, it is only because of the power of their knowledge.'[56] The injunction against instruction in chemistry, biology, physiology, and geology in the secondary schools was lifted, and the classical curriculum that had dominated the *gimnazii* (high schools modelled on the Prussian Gymnasium) was supplemented with a new set of courses in science. These more technical fields were now open to middle-class and female pupils as well. The gymnasium statute of 1864 divided secondary education into two tiers with divergent curricula—the classical gymnasium, which was attended by the wealthier students as a college preparatory course, maintained its primary commitment to Greek and Latin in spite of the inroads made by science instruction; the 'real gymnasium', where the middle class was more of a presence, emphasized the natural sciences above all. At the same time, new secondary schools were opened for girls.[57] From their inception, women's *gimnazii* taught scientific subjects such as physics, mathematics, and natural history, which proved popular for a generation of young people whose main enthusiasm was radical socialism of a new, materialist and practical, rather than utopian and idealistic, orientation. Had Bazarov, the hero of Turgenev's famous novel *Fathers and Children* (*Ottsy i deti*, 1862), had a sister, she would have been as likely to have felt the attractions of 'rational' scientific enquiry. One real-life example of a 'Bazarova' (though from a far more privileged family background) was Sofiia Kovalevskaia, who achieved international renown as a mathematician despite being forced to study in Germany because tertiary education in Russia was denied to her. Many less famous contemporaries followed Kovalevskaia into the sciences and into study abroad, Zurich being a particularly popular destination for the pedagogical refugees.

More dramatically still, the university system underwent an unprecedented expansion of facilities, personnel, and, most importantly, academic freedom. New disciplines were introduced into the course of study, a post-graduate system was initiated in 1863, laboratories were founded, research institutes flourished, and tremendous advances were made in the biological sciences, especially physiology (both plant and animal); in mathematics (non-Euclidean geometry in particular); in chemistry (newly appropriated from its traditionally German practitioners); and in the earth sciences like geology, which had long been an almost exclusively Western European affair, but which now spawned the native Russian speciality of soil science. In this climate of discovery and possibility, science was not the only source of enlightenment, but it was regarded as the highest form of intellectual accomplishment, as Russia celebrated what it needed and was beginning to know.

The intellectual explosion of the 1860s, as scholars have noted, can be understood as an integral component of the social and political emancipation that was partly achieved by official reforms in the 1860s, and for whose further expansion the radicals pressed. The commitment to progress, the emphasis on experimentation of all kinds, and the individual freedom to interpret experimental data announce this as an age of epistemological emancipation in which truth is discoverable rather than received as dogma. The intelligentsia championed *obrazovanie* (intellectual stimulation and edification) over the moral indoctrination, *vospitanie*, that had been stressed in the reigns of Catherine, Paul, Alexander I, and Nicholas I; the state lifted its monopoly on the publication of textbooks, and enquiry as such became the primary intellectual goal in all disciplines. Furthermore, social and cultural aspirations were inseparable: scientific materialism, with its emphasis on utility, appealed to non-aristocrats alienated by the former concentration, in both public and private schools, on education as accomplishment; the opening up of the curriculum in universities was, not at all coincidentally, contemporaneous with a drive to have women admitted to Russian universities. Though this possibility was frustrated, the founding of the university-level 'Higher Courses of Education for Women' in the early 1870s brought high-level training in scientific subjects as well as the humanities within the grasp of many women. In 1872, the first medical school for women was opened, putting Russia well ahead of many more 'advanced' countries in so far as such opportunities in this field went. By the 1880s, *zemstvo* 'lady doctors' were familiar in many Russian villages; by the early twentieth century, some Russian women, such as Vera Gedroits (who later developed a second career as a writer under the pseudonym Sergei Gedroits), had even begun practising as surgeons. The Soviet measures outlawing discrimination against women at work, therefore, reflected not only the aspirations but also the practical achievements of some three generations of Russian women.

The freeing of the serfs in 1861 coincided not only with a boom in science generally, but also with the arrival of Darwinism in Russia. *The Origin of Species*, first published in 1859, was translated into Russian in 1865, and Darwin became an honorary member of the St Petersburg Academy of Sciences in 1867. The revolutionary theory of evolution held particular appeal for the 'men of the sixties' who began to translate its insights into the sphere of social change. The 1860s also heralded the ascension of sociology as a discipline in Russia. However, the association of science with radicalism also hastened the wholesale withdrawal of government support for such 'free thinking' as evolutionary science, held to undermine Church dogma and agitate for social change. Knowledge could obviously be turned squarely against the (autocratic) power that sponsored it. In 1871, therefore, the Minister for Education Count D. A. Tolstoi, an anti-scientific reactionary with a strong personal enthusiasm for the classics, stopped the process of educational reform. Both Greek and Latin were now requirements for university entrance (a measure that, like so many other reforms in Russian history, immediately stumbled on an unenvisaged practicality—in this case, the lack of competent classical Greek teachers—but which nevertheless remained in force until 1902). Science was declared by Tolstoi to foster 'materialism, nihilism, and the most pernicious self-importance' in the young.[58] Accordingly, the *real'nye gimnazii* were downgraded to *real'nye uchilishcha*, becoming feeder institutions for technical colleges rather than for universities. Science subjects could still be studied at universities, but suffered, like other areas of academic investigation, from measures to root out dissent (that is, freedom of enquiry) instituted in the 1870s and especially the 1880s, after the assassination of Alexander II.

But, while the legislative spirit of renewal waned as political reaction took hold, the intellectual upsurge ushered in by the age of reform had its own, unstoppable, momentum. Despite the severe new limitations imposed on academic freedom in the university community, public interest in scientific thought was never greater than in the last quarter of the nineteenth century. Leading scientists (such as the plant physiologist K. A. Timiriazev) and social thinkers alike popularized Darwin's ideas in widely accessible publications that made the theory of evolution a matter of public debate. Learned societies were founded not only as professional organizations but also explicitly to make scientific knowledge available to those who were unable to pursue an advanced education themselves, as well as to those who had completed their training but wanted to keep up with subsequent developments. Scholars gave papers, which were published and widely circulated. Greater exposure still was facilitated by the extensive public exhibitions organized by various societies to disseminate the findings of naturalists, geologists, anthropologists, ethnographers, and zoologists, and in both the major cities and the provinces people flocked to these installations, which became important cultural events. Medical societies played a similar role in the proliferation of modern knowledge. The emergence of *zemstvo* medicine produced a physician committed not only to curing village patients, but also to educating them, and, in the process, to collecting and reporting statistical data that would increase the fund of medical knowledge. By comparison, popular audiences for the officially sponsored secondary-school subjects of Greek and Latin were minute: the Society of Classical Philology and Pedagogy, familiarly known as the 'Classical Society', had groups in only two cities, St Petersburg and Kiev, and a report of 1908 stated that meetings had been attended by 'no fewer than ten' members, suggesting a total membership of perhaps 100. Worn out with conjugating verbs and declining nouns (tuition was heavily grammar-based and involved little reading or even translation), most *gimnaziia* pupils wanted nothing to do with the classics ever again.[59]

In contrast, the Russian scientific societies had large and vigorous audiences. The Geographical Society, with more than 900 members, perhaps best exemplified, and most successfully realized, the activist spirit of outreach that inspired all academics of the day. Its guiding light was the explorer N. M. Przheval'skii, whose readable accounts of his exploits made fantasies of exploration into a national pastime. Geographer-explorers, such as Przheval'skii and Petr Semenov, given the sobriquet 'Tian-Shanskii' because of his 'discovery' in 1855 of the remote Tian Shan mountain range, Kashgaria, traversed Central Asia and penetrated into

Chinese and Mongolian territories, especially the recently annexed Ussuriisk area, amassing vast quantities of data of everything from orthography to ethnography. Their reports, crafted with some flair, combined a scientist's encyclopaedic urge to categorize and classify with an adventurer's impulse for lively narrative. Przheval'skii referred to his own work as 'scientific reconnaissance'. The extent of the raw material that he and others accumulated can be appreciated by visiting the public displays and especially reserve collections of the Ethnographical Museums in St Petersburg and Moscow (founded in 1889 and 1867 respectively as the Imperial Academy of Sciences Ethnographical Museum and the Dashkov Ethnographical Museum). The Geographical Society's well-publicized expeditions to unknown lands, and especially the exhibitions it organized to share its new-found intelligence, testified to the general expansive optimism about making the unknown known. With branches in Tiflis, Kiev, Irkutsk, Vladivostok, Khabarovsk, and Omsk, the Geographical Society spanned the provinces, reaching more people than any other scientific institution. The widely disseminated work of physical and human geography offered compelling scientific explanations for the workings of the universe and the nature of earth and its human inhabitants. And while the society's mission became increasingly theoretical and focused on methodological advances, the thinking it disseminated and made so popular was essentially democratic, 'originating not in the revelations of unchallengeable sacred authorities but in man's secular and challengeable search for objective wisdom'.[60] Besides the Classical and Geographical Societies, many other such popularizing learned societies flourished in the last two decades of the century: technical, medical, surgical, archaeological, juridical, even those devoted to such specific subjects as cereals. Among the most famous were the Moscow Society of Naturalists and the Moscow Society of Admirers of Natural Science, Anthropology, and Ethnology. The St Petersburg Society of Naturalists was the leader in popularizing the biological sciences. Its proceedings, which published many of the important papers of mineralogist V. I. Vernadskii, crystallographer E. S. Fedorov, physiologists I. M. Sechenov and I. P. Pavlov, botanist I. P. Borodin, and microbiologist D. I. Ivanovskii, were sent without charge to schools, museums, and libraries. The society also organized natural history expeditions led by experts and open to ordinary citizens. Similar, if less publicly oriented, organizations existed for specialized, advanced scientists in fields such as mathematics and physics. The learned discourses of the era are saturated with faith in the human ability not only to amass knowledge but to process it intelligently and apply it for the common good. This rhetoric of critical examination, thorough investigation, authoritative classification, and especially responsible dissemination of information, is evident, for instance, in the public medical discourse of late nineteenth-century Russia, which, as Laura Engelstein has shown, substituted 'pathological' explications for 'moralistic' ones, tending, for example, to attribute the spread of diseases like syphilis in Russian villages to the peasantry's ignorance rather than to 'immoral' practices: infection was traced to social customs such as the use of communal eating vessels, rather than to sexual promiscuity. The sense of social responsibility also manifested itself, as Nancy Mandelker Frieden's study of Russian medics

The famous chemist Dmitrii Mendeleev (1834–1907), creator of the Periodic Table of the Elements, wearing the robes of the honorary doctorate awarded him by the University of Oxford after he had been refused full membership of the Russian Academy of Sciences in 1884 (watercolour by Il'ia Repin, 1885).
Mendeleev (father-in-law of the poet Aleksandr Blok) was a man whose liberal views (he was a prominent campaigner for intellectual freedom in the universities) and staggeringly polymathic interests were typical of the late imperial Russian intelligentsia. His works included not only the scientific publications that made him famous, but also treatises on sociology (a fact suggested by Repin's decision to show him at his books, not at the laboratory bench). He and his second wife, Anna Popova, a former art student, hosted a salon in St Petersburg that was visited by many prominent intellectuals and artists of the time. Repin skilfully suggests the exceptional character of his subject: quizzical, crusty, and eccentric.

has demonstrated, in the social-demographic orientation of Russian *zemstvo* medical personnel, who, unlike some of their Western counterparts, had implicit faith that knowledge (rather than government policy) would improve peasant welfare.[61] Late nineteenth-century liberalism, just as much as radicalism, reflects this faith in science and education's capacity to elevate the standard of living of the Russian nation, particularly of its masses, urban and rural, and to move the country towards modernity, towards a rule of law over autocracy. Though the most radical judicial reforms had come in 1864, with the introduction of jury trials and the right to defence representation, the 1880s and 1890s were devoted to a revision of the civil and criminal codes in order to bring actual practice in line with legal theory, and especially to bring the law to bear on such pressing social problems as prostitution. Highly trained legal 'experts' were convened, learned commentaries drafted by the dozens, and law, during this time, became an important arena for the constitution of a body of knowledge. Law joined medicine as a major force for regulating social behaviour.

To be sure, neither field could exercise the authority that it did in Western Europe, given the relative underdevelopment of professional traditions and associations (even the 'craft guilds' system was alien to Russia), as well as the stringent government control. Still, doctors in particular had a discursive and practical advantage because of their demonstrable—and desirable—expertise.

As Nancy Mandelker Frieden has shown, two institutions helped effect the real professionalization of physicians: one publication, *Vrach* (*The Physician*, 1880–1901), and one professional organization (The Society of Russian Physicians in Memory of N. I. Pirogov, 1883–1917). *Vrach* became the principal organ for circulating data on *zemstvo* medicine, and the Pirogov society significantly advanced the practice of community medicine in its research agenda. What emerged from these institutions was an idealized image of the altruistic, self-sacrificing doctor devoted to the 'common good'. Doctors were no longer seen as the beleaguered and embittered individuals they had represented in the 1860s, or as the vulgar quacks that they had appeared to be (some foreign-trained specialists apart) in the first half of the nineteenth century. The active engagement of local *zemstvo* physicians in the efforts to alleviate the suffering during the famine of 1891–2 and the cholera epidemic of 1892 fostered this faith in the medical profession all the more strongly, especially as their power to help was viewed as distinct from the centralized power of the state.[62] Russia had indeed changed a great deal since the 1830s, when (according to the German traveller Kohl) a doctor was attacked in St Petersburg by a raging mob, who blamed him for the cholera epidemic that afflicted the city.

The state, for its part, feared not science *per se*, but its intellectual basis —its questioning and, above all, its foundation in experimentation; ministers of education, from D. A. Tolstoi in the 1860s and 1870s to post-Revolutionary commissars, made efforts to emasculate that epistemological trajectory (chiefly in terms of funding). Nevertheless, by the end of the century, the university had become a centre for Russian science, and the hub of this activity was the laboratory. After all, concrete advances in medicine and the like may have been facilitated by professional organizations, but they were made possible by the modernization of facilities and methodology for collecting and interpreting empirical data, particularly in the biological sciences. Physiologists such as Pavlov set the tone in designing experiments and discerning patterns in the data. All of Pavlov's theorizing derived concretely from evidence he himself had gathered.[63] Truth, it would seem, could be derived from data, and good, objective documentation could harness the truth. Soil science, physical anthropology, physics, microbiology, chemistry, and geology all thrived in this climate.

'Science, along with *belles-lettres*', remarked Timiriazev, had 'attained more maturity and creative power in Russia than any other form of intellectual expression.'[64] In short, as Vucinich comments, science was not only an element of late nineteenth-century civilization (that is, a source of material data); it had become a key force in late nineteenth-century Russian culture, a source of values and modes of thought. Empiricism, positivism, diagnosis, categorization, the collection and dissemination of material, the generation of knowledgeable discourses —these impulses are visible in all arenas: in the flowering of experimental science; in ethnography with its vast data banks and increasing interest in classification by ethnic type;[65] in geography with its expeditions and exhibitions; in the journals and proceedings and congresses generated by the ever more active learned societies. Technological advances only increased the general faith in the human ability to document, influencing artistic and journalistic as well as scientific enterprises. The documentary practice of photography, for example, which emerged in the second third of the nineteenth century, was well ensconced and flourishing in Russia by the 1860s; it seemed to testify to the inherent observability, recordability, and knowability of the world with the objective eye (whose observations were rendered more permanent and more distributable by the camera, and more acute and accurate by the microscope; the invention, in the late nineteenth century, of microscopic photography felicitously combined the two possibilities, offering experts and lay people alike a view of worlds formerly unrecordable, if not invisible).

A veritable cult of objectivity developed. In publicistic, ethnographic, sociological, and even literary discourse, objectivity meant sincerity, and only empiricism could vouchsafe the truth. Representations of the peasantry are a good example; the image of the *seryi* (uneducated, uncultured) *muzhik*, ostensibly unadorned and unromanticized, implied that this was the real thing, eminently capturable in learned—that is, objective—discourse. The literary sketches of G. I. Uspenskii and N. N. Zlatovratskii are a case in point, registering beliefs and anxieties about the *ozverenie naroda* (bestialization of the people) that now seem melodramatic, but which were also reflected in the non-fiction of the time, as Russian commentators registered the social upheavals afflicting the Russian village in the wake of Emancipation.[66]

At the same time, though, it would be wrong to say that objectivity 'reigned', or at any rate that its reign was uncontested. The more that information about the material world became available, for instance, the more vociferous grew the debate over the value and reliability of such data. Was this the 'real', the 'whole', the 'final' truth? The nihilist fervour for empirical methods was countered not only by the more reactionary ministers of education in the 1870s and 1880s, but by metaphysical and religious thinkers such as Vladimir Solov'ev, and later Sergii Bulgakov and Nikolai Berdiaev, heirs to the Slavophile and anti-rationalist traditions, who upheld the primacy of spirit and cited the divine as the source of true knowledge. The scientific ethos thus faced a determined challenge from an epistemological idealism that located 'absolute knowledge' not in matter but in the idea or the spirit. By the 1890s a new and vigorous philosophy of science was born to question the epistemological foundations of empirical research and to speculate on the nature of the knowable: knowledge itself had become an object of knowledge in Russia.

Neo-Kantian philosophers of science, such as Aleksandr Vvedenskii, maintained that the 'thing itself' was inaccessible to science, that so called 'positivism' in fact involves judgement, intuition, and, hence, subjectivity.[67] Their epistemological scepticism had been anticipated (from a quite different perspective) by the two greatest Russian realists of the mid-nineteenth century, Tolstoi and Dostoevskii. Dostoevskii, who took a close interest in contemporary medical studies of his own pathological condition—epilepsy—and whose Petersburg novels accept the capacities of 'sickness', both intrinsic (as illness) and exogenic (as environment), to influence human behaviour and destroy organic wholeness, was also a notorious anti-materialist, in whose novels the analyses of doctors, while not so openly ironized as those of political theorists, are only so many different voices whose clamour rises in the disorganized cacophony of the narrative. Tolstoi, some of whose earlier work had employed the techniques of the 'physiological sketch' (a term borrowed from early French realism) and espoused its claims to naturalism (as in his detailed account of gentry life, 'Morning of a Landowner' ('Utro pomeshchika', 1856)), turned similar insights into a full-scale critique of the so-called scientific method in his Confession (Ispoved', 1879). Empirical observation, he held, does not give us the world directly; rather, 'reality' is mediated through consciousness—our mental representation of our sense experience. What we 'know' this way is thus twice removed from matter and illusory at best. There is no prospect for discerning ultimate truth through the 'materialist' and 'determinist' reasoning of science.[68]

Such assertions were unsurprising in a writer whose view of medical practice had ranged from the alienated (in the Sebastopol Sketches (Sevastopol'skie rasskazy, 1855–6)) to the sardonic (in Anna Karenina, where a doctor's gaze, in curious anticipation of Foucault, is seen as necessarily lascivious as well as intrusive). Tolstoi's assault, in the name of common sense, on academic historians in War and Peace was also a preparation for his late anti-rationalism.

More surprisingly, however, some scientists were prepared to question the idea of objectivity too. Vernadskii, the mineralogist, embraced the subjective aspect of scientific reasoning and acknowledged the relativistic value of scientific knowledge; he emphasized the compatibility of science, philosophy, and religion in the human quest to understand the world. For Pavlov, the physiologist, on the other hand, science not only could be, but was an objective method of human thought and practical work that provided genuine and systematized knowledge of the external world. Anything that did not measure up to those objective standards was to be excluded. Famous for his experiments in behaviourism, for instance, Pavlov disavowed psychology altogether as a discipline because it was too introspective and subjective.[69] Hard physiological evidence was admirable; speculations about 'mind' were not. 'To escape subjectivity [Pavlov] went to the lab, not to correlate mind and body, but to eliminate mind.'[70]

Yet Pavlov was himself a religious believer and a churchgoer, who therefore presumably accepted the existence of the soul, if not of the mind. And in fact the mind/body problem became the key locus of the era's epistemological debates, not only in Cartesian terms, as a persistence of the classic question 'can the mind know the body?', but in the light of the ongoing interest in such conditions as hysteria, where the emotional 'materializes' as the corporeal, confirming the connection between mind and body and raising the possibility that the body knows the mind, even if the reverse does not apply. Indeed, the burgeoning discipline of psychiatry became a fertile field for the development of complementary modes of diagnostic discourse and the working-out of questions of objectivity and observation. In France, Jean-Martin Charcot, the pioneer in studies of hysterical illnesses, for instance, saw himself as profoundly objective. His famous 'clinico-anatomic method', developed and practised at the renowned Salpêtrière school in the mid-1880s, is pure nosology. With perfect faith in the visibility of truth, Charcot conducted what he called objective demonstrations of hysteria, exhibiting his patients, describing the clinical phenomena in exhaustive detail, and classifying the observable symptoms into clearly delineated archetypes: 'something about them makes them all the same'.[71] As such, the disease is thoroughly knowable and treatable. Though conceding the emotional origins of hysteria, Charcot took no interest in what his patients had to say, relying solely on the visible stigmata of hysteria. His patients were as devoid of subjectivity as his own procedure, based on a notion of empiricism that separates physician and patient into omniscient observer and passive, eminently available object. Having studied psychiatry with Charcot, V. M. Bekhterev, Pavlov's principal rival in psychoneurology, logically (and polemically) called his own school 'objective psychology', thus establishing a healthy conceptual divide on the nature of psychiatry in Russia.

Could—and should—studies of psychopathology lay claim to the objectivity so valued in the scientific world? Charcot insisted yes, invoking the consummate metaphor of the objective eye, the camera: 'But in fact all I am is a photographer. I describe what I see.'[72] Indeed, Charcot's fascination with visual records of all kinds, photography most of all, was unparalleled. A pioneer in the use of projection aids in teaching, he commissioned detailed drawings of his patients by Paul Richer and established the first section of medical photography in his Salpêtrière clinic, the legacy of which is the famous *Iconographie photographique de la Salpêtrière*. These icons of pathology were Charcot's tribute to the visuality, accessibility, generalizability, recordability, and comprehensibility of physical disturbance with psychic origins. The panoptical mastery that Foucault identifies as informing nineteenth-century criminology and the disciplines of the human sciences is definitely the dominant paradigm here.

At stake is not only the eye as the primary organ of observation, but also the visual nature of the document. The late nineteenth century saw illustrated magazines develop from quaint collections of prints whose decorative purpose was often clear (sheets from publications such as Timm's *Russkii khudozhestvennyi listok* (*Russian Art Sheet*) might be detached, hand-coloured, and used for mounting on walls) to faithful and self-consciously unimaginative realizations of news stories and topical features such as appeared in the popular 'thin journal' *Niva* (*The Cornfield*, founded in 1869). Yet the emphasis on a moment's dramatism could mean that composition and execution pulled different ways; so, too, in documentary easel-painting, such as the work of Vasilii Vereshchagin, whose canvases—immensely popular in Britain as well as in Russia—were in their day as topical as the illustrations in *Niva*. Their stark, almost photorealistic, lighting and colouring can seem facile, but are strikingly effective in Vereshchagin's best-known image, *The Apotheosis of War* (1870–1), the epilogue to a series painted during the Russian invasion of Turkestan. A pyramid of skulls, attended by birds of prey, commemorates the fallen, the conscious, Baroque artifice of construction forming a disturbing contrast to the 'photographic' clarity of line and monotony of shading. Though dedicated by the artist to the 'great conquerors' of history, the painting seems more an evocation of martial horrors than an 'apotheosis' of glory, most particularly since it was meant as the culmination of a series concentrating on Russian defeats at the hands of 'tribal warriors'. It is scarcely surprising that the key motif of the composition could be borrowed by a recent painter, Petr Belov, in his painting *Hourglass* (1987), which symbolizes the oppressions of the more recent past: here, Stalin smugly contemplates an hourglass in which skulls replace sand, trickling into the lower globe to form a pyramid. The reception of Vereshchagin's image has been as ironic as the circumstances of the original image's production, though in neither case was the irony necessarily a matter of conscious intention.

It was not only in painting that such tensions between different modes were observable. In psychiatry too the development of the genre of the case history can be seen as a concerted effort to integrate two modes of discourse: first, the 'pictoral', based on a set of visible, clinical signs that make knowledge about the patient a matter of seeing and reconstituting a clinical picture (concretized in Charcot's photographs), and second, the 'narratological', enquiry based on eliciting in words what has befallen the patient and the reconstitution of a clinical story. The latter method, which privileged plot over image cluster, viewed the patient as a *bona fide* subjectivity with a story to tell and demanded knowledge of that individual, not just a classificatory grid. It was Freud who fully succeeded in reconciling the two modes in his early studies of hysteria, treating hysterical symptoms as the visible manifestations of the part of the story the patient resisted telling (repressed). The body remembers (and makes visible) what the mind forgets (and silences). The connection between event (origin) and symptom, plot and picture, is then forged in the interpretive gesture of the case history. The patient's dissociation is ended and the 'objectively' visible symptom is replaced by the reappropriation by the self of the explanation. However, since Freud's theories were not popularized in Russia until the 1920s, the tension between 'pictoral' and 'narratological' lines was to remain, for the present, incipient and unresolved in Russian psychiatry.

The Development of Photography

Visuality, then, was not uncontested. Even the image of photography as the pinnacle of objective perception was flawed. S. M. Prokudin-Gorskii, commissioned in 1909 by the Tsar to produce a collection of photographs from all over the Russian Empire, was a chemist by training, a member of the Imperial Russian Photographic Society, the editor of *Fotograf-liubitel'* (*Amateur Photographer*, which began publishing in 1890), and the author of popular technical books on photography. He was passionately convinced of photography's educative potential, and an ambitious pioneer of 'scientific' colour-processing. But in his construction of a collection that 'would show students in every school the grandeur of Holy Mother Russia' his role as chronicler of fact clashed with a (perhaps unconscious) process of aesthetic editing. In scenes akin to those presented in landscape and genre paintings of the period, peasants in Sunday best are posed to perform agricultural chores, or a splendid tomato-and-white stuccoed church on a rise stands outlined against silvery clouds. Attractive personal histories are sought out everywhere: one image displays an 84-year-old lockkeeper, Pinkhus Karlinskii, who had been in service for sixty-six years when the photograph was taken, and who stands proudly by his lock in his uniform coat. For all his specialist, scientific interest in the genre, Prokudin-Gorskii sensed the ritual, as well as documentary, impulses in photography as surely as did his subjects, or the many other working-class and peasant Russians who had their photographs taken by less illustrious local photographers, stiff in seldom-worn finery before painted fantasy backgrounds.[73]

Such contradictions were rooted in the theoretical and practical history of photography as 'scientific art' or 'artistic science', which Florentii Pavlenkov, a publisher, had termed 'a perfect violin, brought into being by an organic process involving chemistry and the heart, optics and emotion, apparatus and thought'. If the 'Cartesian perspectivalism' current in the visual arts since the high Renaissance emphasized the observer as privileged organizer of inert material, the pressure to catalogue phenomena in the external world could at the same time displace the centre of observation, as a canvas (or more generally, image) was filled with more and more material unrelated to any textual function.[74] The panorama, where a longitudinal prospect is organized around one fixed viewpoint, remained popular among working-class audiences right up to the Revolution, but in Russia, as in other European countries, was replaced as a form of 'scientific' image, in the second half of the nineteenth century, by representations that were either more concentrated or more saturated, from close-ups of individual, but typical phenomena, to long shots of the teeming and undifferentiated masses. If the customary early nineteenth-century image of the city had been a high-quality print in which human subjects appeared as accoutrements of colonnades and street vistas, the preferred view at the turn of the century emphasized the city's populousness, the ubiquitous overcrowding that made architecture seem at best a bulwark against formlessness. Yet at the same time the traditional panoramic image persisted, not only in fairground panoramas, but also in the new genre of the picture postcard, which rose to prominence in the early years of the twentieth century.[75]

Photography had then been known in Russia for over sixty years, the Academy of Sciences having been informed of the invention in 1839 by a corresponding member. In the early 1840s, Sergei Levitskii, the 'grand old man' of Russian photography, embarked on a career that was to last several decades; by the 1860s, the work of Russian photographers was being honoured at exhibitions abroad. In 1882, the 'Pan-Russian Exhibition' held at Moscow became the first Russian show at which photography was allotted a special place; the first dedicated exhibition was held in St Petersburg during 1888. At both these exhibitions, the links between photography and technology were stressed: in 1882, the specified range of exhibits included everything 'concern[ing] the dissemination of education and knowledge: the printing industry, musical instruments . . . educational books . . . lithography, chromolithography, typography, and finally photography, which represent a direct connection with printing'.[76] In 1888, photography was explicitly compared with two other inventions that had contributed to scientific progress in the nineteenth century: steam and electricity. The scientific links of photography were also evident in the fact that the first photographic association in Russia was the Fifth Section of the Imperial Russian Technical Society, which was founded soon after the society's inception in 1866. Yet the artistic aspirations of photography were quickly recognized too: in 1889, debate on the requisite criteria for photographic awards drew attention not only to technical merit, but also to artistic excellence, held to be inseparable from 'thought' (that is, intellectual process). In 1896, the laws of artistic copyright were extended to photography, whose close links with the arts can also be adduced from the fact that writers were to be the subjects of many of the most memorable photographic portraits of the late nineteenth and early twentieth centuries. From the tensely angular studies of Dostoevskii in his fifties to the ethereal visions of Blok or Anna Akhmatova, photography played a vital role in the creation of writerly personae and their reception by the public, and also contributed to the popularity of vaudeville and cinema stars, whose portraits, alongside topographical shots, challenged the place of the traditional *lubok* (engravings and etchings) and of the lithograph as a means of decorating walls, trunk-lids, and other areas of personal space.[77]

Objectivity in Realist Fiction

If, as is so often said, nineteenth-century Russian realism and the exact sciences developed 'side by side' (to which the postscript is usually added that these were the two greatest accomplishments of nineteenth-century Russia), one might expect that it would be possible to trace a relationship between the two traditions, especially since the aftermath of the 1860s had made the late nineteenth-century Russian intelligentsia more aware of scientific practices than its counterparts in the West. The many writers and cultural activists who had been exposed to specialized scientific training included the realist authors P. D. Boborykin (physics and mathematics), V. G. Korolenko (forestry), N. K. Lebedev (natural sciences), Valentina Dmitrieva (medicine), and Chekhov (medicine), the writer and theorist Aleksandr Bogdanov (physics), and the editor and critic Angel Bogdanovich (medicine). It is scarcely surprising that characters with a scientific training, particularly doctors, are prominent in the realist fiction of the 1890s and 1900s, or that the 'science fiction' that developed in Russia after 1910, and exemplified by works such as Bogdanov's *Red Star* (*Krasnaia zvezda*, 1907) and *Engineer Manny* (*Inzhener Menni*, 1913), should have been a utopian, rather than escapist, tradition that emphasized the importance of science in creating rational and egalitarian societies. Programmatic statements of the day, too, often stress parallels between the procedures of realist fiction and those of science, particularly the 'diagnostic' techniques of medicine, parallels which were also evident in the practices of the Znanie publishing house, founded by K. Piatnitskii in 1898 as an outlet for popular science and educational material, which was to become the most prestigious outlet for realist fiction in the early twentieth century.

But if realist fiction aspired to the 'objectivity' of science, it also inherited the fierce debates around the very notions of objectivity that had characterized scientific discourse in the late nineteenth century. The work of Gork'ii, Andreev, or Kuprin, to name only three of the most prominent realists of the early twentieth century, can in no way be described as 'objective' in the sense that it detachedly observes and records phenomena; it is, rather, invariably didactic and tendentious in its ambitions, concerned not merely to 'diagnose' problems, but to press for their solution. Furthermore, late nineteenth-century realist writing was heir not only to the pro-scientific discourses of the 1860s, but also to the traditions of anti-scientific argument that had been volubly expressed in the works of Dostoevskii, and particularly Tolstoi, who on many occasions expressed his sarcastic contempt for doctors (intrusive busybodies who, if they do not murder their patients, at the very least subject them to psychologically devastating humiliation and power-hungry manipulation). Perhaps as a result, Russian naturalism, though often the creation of trained scientists, and often taking for granted certain scientific orthodoxies of the day (as in, say, its stereotyping of social deviance), was in fact more reticent about its scientific ambitions than Western naturalism. No Russian writer followed Zola in purporting to write 'a social and natural history' of his or her time, and there was a small step between the sceptical anti-scientism of Dostoevskii or Tolstoi and the ambitions of Belyi (the son of an artistic mother and mathematician father) or Solov'ev (an 1860s radical who had rebelled against rational atheism) to synthesize mysticism, religion, art, and science. It has been rightly stated that 'the idealism and mysticism of Russian modernists rested on a solid positivistic substratum':[78] so much was evident not only in Russian modernists' fascination with pseudo-sciences such as anthroposophy and theosophy, but also in Belyi's regretful admission that the philosophical and scientific underpinnings of Otto Weininger's writings on gender difference were shaky. Even the most extreme anti-materialists among the Russian symbolists did not deny the existence of the material world, although they could and did argue that it was inferior to, shaped by, and secondary to the spiritual world that they preferred to investigate or to invoke.

They shared the eschatological preoccupations of Orthodox Christianity, but also its ambitions to regulate and denominate the opposed and contrary sphere of scatology.

In the last two decades of the nineteenth century, however, the epistemological dilemmas of materialism/idealism, body/soul, pictures/words, objectivity/subjectivity, general/particular, are perhaps best crystallized in the work of Anton Chekhov. As a man of several disciplines himself, Chekhov was keenly aware of the multiplicity of ways of knowing the world and its inhabitants, and he sensed both the possibilities and the pitfalls of those various attempts to posit knowledge. Trained in medicine and science, he maintained a positivist's faith in the evidence of the physical world, yet he harboured certain apprehensions about the expertise such special knowledge bestowed. As an artist he shunned certainty—in a famous letter to Suvorin of 30 May 1888, he stressed that the artist's task was to pose questions rather than to answer them, referring to Voltaire and to Socrates, whose greatest wisdom consisted in knowing what they did not and could not know:

> An artist must not be the judge of his characters and the subjects they choose to talk about, but only an impartial observer. I have heard a chaotic conversation between two Russians about pessimism which resolves nothing whatsoever, and I must communicate that conversation exactly as I have heard it; it is the jury, i.e. the readers, who have the task of passing judgement . . . It is time for writers, and especially authors, to admit that you can't understand anything in this world, as Socrates once admitted, and Voltaire too.

Chekhov's own work reveals an abiding concern with the element of power inherent in presuming to know and the potential violence associated with making people—even patients—into objects of knowledge. Some of the most eloquent of his characters are those, such as the artist-narrator of 'The House with a Mezzanine', who express hostility to those philanthropic efforts at social improvement to which Chekhov himself, as an 'improving landlord', was wholly committed in life. Yet unlike Tolstoi (with whose ideas some of Chekhov's most important stories, such as 'Ward no. 6' ('Palata no. 6', 1892) and 'My Life' ('Moia zhizn'', 1896), are directly engaged), Chekhov did not regard texts which placed themselves beyond or above reason—the sermons of the priest or sage—as a more positive model for literature. He held that writers should be as objective as chemists, yet the scientific report—the doctor's case-notes—is not necessarily a document of unassailable authority either. Indeed, the story actually entitled 'A Doctor's Case-Notes' ('Sluchai iz praktiki', 1898) involves an impeccably Charcotian diagnosis of the causes behind the central woman character's symptoms of depression and apathy: 'it's high time she was married'. But it attributes the diagnosis to a doctor whose highly subjective—fluid, self-interested, emotional—impressions of the woman's milieu are the main focus of the story. A doctor's human, snobbish, perhaps also erotic, response to a woman patient cannot be separated from his professional knowledge of her condition.

Yet Chekhov throughout his later life maintained a commitment to specialist knowledge in both his roles, as writer and as doctor. Careful to keep up with the literary works of his contemporaries (his meticulous orders to his bookseller survive in his papers), he also subscribed to medical journals such as *Vrach*, and kept abreast of the proceedings of the growing number of medical congresses. He also industriously submitted statistics from his own practice to the research association that collected them, speculating that, as a field, statistics might well provide the link between the biological and social sciences.[79] In short, it appears that Chekhov embraced a kind of inter-disciplinary perspective, maintaining his professional and intellectual commitment to science even as his literary activity came to the fore, and emphasizing the complementarity of different disciplines in his own writings—a commitment recognized by his nomination to the Society of Admirers of Natural Science in 1890.

A most striking instance of Chekhov's dual role as scientist and *littérateur* was his dazzling 'scientific reconnaissance' mission to Sakhalin Island, at the eastern extreme of the Russian Empire, and, as a 'prison island', at its cultural as well as geographical margins. No doubt inspired by Przheval'skii and others like him, Chekhov embarked in 1890 on this study in a confident spirit of scientific optimism and empirical rigour. He planned not only to examine the hygienic conditions, a task self-evidently proper to his position as *zemstvo* physician, but also to act as ethnographer, geographer, and meteorologist, fusing the expertise and data collection aptitude of the social scientist, the natural scientist, and the explorer. But the enterprise ultimately collapsed under the sheer weight of the unknowable. Chekhov's documentary account of his trip, *Sakhalin Island: Travel Notes* (*Ostrov Sakhalin: Putevye zametki*, 1893–5), not only records the complete failure of the human and natural sciences, everything from geography to criminology having collapsed in the extraordinary environment of Sakhalin Island; his own account falters, too, as his confidence in his own ability to acquire the projected expertise is hopelessly undermined.

Chekhov personally confronted the limitations of the statistical data with which both Russian officialdom and the scientific establishment of the day were obsessed. Given their subordinate and rightless condition, the convicts on the face of it seemed the perfect 'laboratory' material, available for every conceivable form of scientific scrutiny—medical, statistical, sociological, ethnographic, criminological, demographic—and Chekhov expected to return from his voyage with a veritable treasure trove of data, which he would then 'write up' and publish. In accordance with the proper ambitions of objectivity, he had hired the photographer I. I. Pavlovsk to photograph a specific list of corroborating scenes. (There were also personal reasons for the decision, given that Chekhov himself was something of a photography enthusiast, whose own private archive of photographs—some of which had been taken by him—was extensive.) Chekhov took his exercise in empiricism, his magisterial attempt to gather, dissect, document, and disseminate data, extremely seriously. He studied for months before his departure, transcribing and recording materials; he had in fact drafted the first two chapters of his study before reaching Sakhalin. But once he was there his control evaporated and planning proved futile.

What Chekhov experienced was the undoing of his carefully drawn distinctions, a dissolution that led to a full-blown epistemological crisis, and ultimately to the collapse of his project. His goals—drawing distinctions and amassing data—are announced in the finished text with clarity and confidence. But in the course of Chekhov's discussion, virtually all his easy oppositions, his neat categories, are undercut, and the projection of expertise falters, producing an impression, finally, of radical disorientation instead of the anticipated mastery. As it turned out, none of his pre-assigned categories applied to empirical material; his 10,000 pre-printed cards were useless. In the total absence of competent authorities on the island, and of authoritativeness in Chekhov himself, panoptical mastery proved impossible. *Sakhalin Island*, the bizarre document that belatedly resulted, was a negation of the principles of late nineteenth-century Russian criminology, where a Lombrosian emphasis on deviance that might be systematically categorized was balanced (or off-balanced) by a contradictory emphasis on equally classifiable social forces (poverty, deprivation). Where professional criminologists appended representative, carefully chosen case-studies to lucid overviews of method, Chekhov reveals a positive mania for information of all kinds, often bafflingly trivial and relevant to no obvious arguments. The swollen footnotes exacerbate the confusions of the main text. The carefully commissioned photographs were abandoned, since the principle of illustration as subordination had fallen away, now that there were no key points to focus on.

When confronted with a reality in which nothing was clear or distinct, Chekhov seemed to be plunged into epistemological distress of the sort Descartes could only dream of with horror. And since both disciplinary and authorial authority depend on appropriate knowledge, both Sakhalin Island (the place) and *Sakhalin Island* (the book) fail in their attempts to capture, contain, and control their subjects—whether inmates or insights, convicts or convictions. Yet the 'crisis' Chekhov experienced on Sakhalin was less an apocalyptic loss of formerly secure epistemological bearings than a powerful renewal of his enduring anxieties about intellectual presumption. The perfect vision/perfect knowledge projected by Bentham and described by Foucault represents an extreme epistemological hubris, and the fantasy yet failure of this panoptical mastery on Sakhalin closely reproduces the distance between Chekhov's own scholarly aspirations and his long-standing reservations about expertise, between his unshakeable faith in empirical science and his equally strong sense of its limits. The ambitious positivism of Chekhov's information-gathering project reflects the optimism associated at this time with the rise of the social sciences; Chekhov was clearly taken with such documentary discourses as ethnography and documentary/artistic practices like photography. His own documentary discourse falters in the face of the disarray of Sakhalin, but it does at least document 'objectively' his subjective epistemological distress.

Even before the Sakhalin débâcle, Chekhov's fiction evinced acute anxiety about such epistemological issues. 'An Attack of Nerves' ('Pripadok', 1889), written a year before his research trip, is in form and content a veritable case-study of the possibilities of study, of learned discourses, of gathering material (particularly about the social underclasses usually targeted by criminologists), of the status of objectivity (the objective eye and the common good), and the physiological basis (physicality) of knowledge, together with speculation on the genre of the case-study itself.

So far from manifesting 'objectivity' as serene detachment, then, Chekhov's writings indicate the beleaguered status of the concept even before the arrival in Russia of modernist ideas in the early twentieth century. And the dual perception of science and knowledge, *nauka*, was to have far-reaching effects after the Revolution also, as the Soviet authorities poured funding into selected areas of scientific enquiry, and invoked science in metaphor as a touchstone of accuracy and dependability ('scientific communism'), yet displayed a still greater suspicion of independent scientific and scholarly enquiry than their Tsarist predecessors had, subjecting specialists from engineers, doctors, and physicists to medieval historians, lawyers, philosophers, and linguists to harassment, exile, imprisonment, and execution.

Suggested further reading

Urbanization and Local Government

BRADLEY, J., *Muzhik and Muscovite: Urbanization in Late Imperial Russia* (Berkeley, 1985).

BROWER, D. R., *The Russian City between Tradition and Modernity, 1850–1900* (Berkeley, 1990).

CLOWES, E. W., KASSOW, S. D., and WEST, J. L. (eds.), *Between Tsar and People: Educated Society and the Quest for Public Identity in Late Imperial Russia* (Princeton, 1991).

HAMM, M. (ed.), *The City in Late Imperial Russia* (Bloomington, 1986).

OWEN, T., *Capitalism and Politics in Russia: A Social History of the Moscow Merchants, 1855–1905* (New York, 1981).

THURSTON, R. W., *Liberal City, Conservative State: Moscow and Russia's Urban Crisis, 1906–1914* (Oxford, 1987).

ZASOSOV, D. A., and PYZIN, V. I., *Iz zhizni Peterburga 1890–1910-kh godov* (Leningrad, 1991).

Education, Print Culture, the 'People's Theatre'

BROOKS, J., *When Russia Learned to Read: Literacy and Popular Literature, 1861–1917* (Princeton, 1985).

EKLOF, B., *Russian Peasant Schools: Officialdom, Village Culture, and Popular Pedagogy, 1861–1914* (Berkeley, 1986).

McREYNOLDS, L., *The News Under Russia's Old Regime: The Development of a Mass-Circulation Press* (Princeton, 1991).

SWIFT, E. A., 'Fighting the Germs of Disorder: The Censorship of Russian Popular Theatre, 1888–1917', *Russian History*, 18 (1991), 1–49.

THURSTON, G., 'The Impact of Russian Popular Theatre, 1886–1915', *Journal of Modern History*, 55 (1983), 244–8.

Philanthropy and Social Welfare; the Temperance Movement

CHRISTIAN, D., *Living Water: Vodka and Russian Society on the Eve of Emancipation* (Oxford, 1990).

HERLIHY, P. 'Joy of the Rus': Rites and Rituals of Russian Drinking', *Russian Review*, 50 (1991), 131–47.

LINDENMEYR, A., 'A Russian Experiment in Voluntarism: The Municipal Guardianships of the Poor, 1894–1914', *Jahrbücher für Geschichte Osteuropas*, 30 (1982), 429–51.

—— 'Public Life, Private Virtues: Women in Russian Charity, 1762–1914', *Signs: Journal of Women in Culture and Society*, 18 (1993), 562–91.

RIEBER, A. J., *Merchants and Entrepreneurs in Imperial Russia* (Chapel Hill, 1982).

RUCKMAN, J.-A., *The Moscow Business Elite: A Social and Cultural Portrait of Two Generations, 1840–1905* (De Kalb, 1984).

STEINBERG, M. D., *Moral Communities: The Culture of Class Relations in the Russian Printing Industry, 1867–1907* (Berkeley, 1992).

The Worker Intelligentsia

BONNELL, V. E., *Roots of Rebellion: Workers' Politics and Organizations in St Petersburg and Moscow, 1900–1914* (Berkeley, 1983).

KOENKER, D., *Moscow Workers and the 1917 Revolution* (Princeton, 1981).

SMITH, S. A., *Red Petrograd: Revolution in the Factories 1917–1918* (Cambridge, 1983).

ZELNIK, R. E. (tr. and ed.), *A Radical Worker in Tsarist Russia: The Autobiography of Semën Ivanovich Kanatchikov* (Stanford, 1986).

Science, Knowledge, Intellectual History

ENGELSTEIN, L., *The Keys to Happiness: Sex and the Search for Modernity in Fin de Siècle Russia* (Ithaca, 1992).

FRIEDEN, N. M., *Russian Physicians in an Era of Reform and Revolution, 1856–1905* (Princeton, 1981).

FRIERSON, C. A., *Peasant Icons: Representations of Rural People in Late Nineteenth-Century Russia* (Oxford, 1993).

GUSTAFSON, R. F., *Leo Tolstoy, Resident and Stranger* (Princeton, 1986).

JORAVSKY, D., *Russian Psychology: A Critical History* (Oxford, 1989).

MACLEAN, H., 'Realism', in V. Terras (ed.), *Handbook of Russian Literature* (New Haven, 1984), 363–7.

PAPERNO, I., and GROSSMAN, J. D. (eds.), *Creating Life: The Aesthetic Utopia of Russian Modernism* (Stanford, 1994).

POPKIN, C., 'Chekhov as Ethnographer: Epistemological Crisis on Sakhalin Island', *Slavic Review*, 51 (1992), 36–51.

VUCINICH, A., *Science in Russian Culture 1861–1917* (Stanford, 1970).

—— *Social Thought in Tsarist Russia: The Quest for a General Science of Society, 1861–1917* (Chicago, 1976).

Notes

1 Adele Lindenmeyr, *Poverty is Not a Vice: Charity, Society and the State in Imperial Russia* (Princeton, 1996), 34.

2 M. de Certeau, *The Writing of History*, tr. T. Conley (New York, 1988), 40.

3 M. Hamm (ed.), *The City in Late Imperial Russia* (Bloomington, 1986), 13, 51, 212.

4 See e.g. D. Zhbankov, 'Polovaia prestupnost'', *Sovremennyi mir*, 7 (1909), 54–91. An excellent general survey of anxieties about crime is J. Neuberger, *Hooliganism: Crime, Culture and Power in St Petersburg, 1900–1914* (Berkeley, 1993). An example of Lombrosian work on criminology is P. Tarnovskaia, 'Zhenskaia prestupnost'', *Severnyi vestnik*, 5 (1887), sect. 1, 132–49.

5 B. Mironov, 'Bureaucratic or Self-Government: The Early Nineteenth-Century Russian City', *Slavic Review*, 52 (1993), 233–55.

6 D. R. Brower, *The Russian City between Tradition and Modernity, 1850–1900* (Berkeley, 1990), 118.

7 Mironov, 'Bureaucratic or Self-Government', *passim*, and Brower, *The Russian City*, esp. ch. 3.

8 'Zadachi arkhitektury XIX veka', *Artist*, 46 (1895), 56.

9 'Telefony v Rossii', *Elektronicheskii vestnik*, 13–15 (1895), 58–9.

10 'In recent years city officials have been closing Nevskii [on New Year's Eve] for revellers' ('Staryi Peterburg', *Stolitsa i usad'ba*, 43 (1915), 1).

11 See A. Benois's introduction to A. Leifert, *Balagany* (Petrograd, 1922).

12 On the planning of entertainments, see the Moscow City Archive, *fond* 179, *op*. 51.

13 *Izvestiia Moskovskoi gorodskoi upravy*, 12, sect. 1 (1891), 24; the *raek* text is quoted in A. M. Konechnyi, 'Raek v sisteme Peterburgskoi gorodskoi kul'tury', *Russkii fol'klor*, 25 (1989), 135.

14 See Brower, *The Russian City*, esp. ch. 5. All the contributors to Hamm (ed.), *The City in Late Imperial Russia* point to the relationship between uncontrolled urbanization and revolution; see also Neuberger, *Hooliganism*. Clearly, rapid urbanization and revolution did interdepend to some extent, but failure in the former by no means results inevitably in the latter, as such modern cases as Cairo, Bangkok, or Calcutta make clear.

15 On the development of sociology, see A. Vucinich's survey, *Social Thought in Tsarist Russia: The Quest for a General Science of Society, 1861–1917* (Chicago, 1976).

16 A. Lindenmeyr, 'A Russian Experiment in Voluntarism: The Municipal Guardianships of the Poor, 1894–1914', *Jahrbücher für Geschichte Osteuropas*, 30 (1982), 429–51.

17 A. Lindenmeyr, 'Public Life, Private Virtues: Women in Russian Charity, 1762–1914', *Signs: Journal of Women in Culture and Society*, 18 (1993), 562–91.

18 Brower, *The Russian City*, 155.

19 B. Eklof, *Russian Peasant Schools: Officialdom, Village Culture, and Popular Pedagogy, 1861–1914* (Berkeley, 1986), 289–94, and O. Crisp, 'Labour and

Industrialization in Russia', in P. Mathias and M. M. Postan (eds.), *Cambridge Economic History of Europe*, vii, pt. 2 (Cambridge, 1978), 131.

[20] A. G. Rashin, 'Gramotnost′ i narodnoe obrazovanie v Rossii v XIX v. i v nachale XX v.', *Istoricheskie zapiski*, 37 (1951), 37; *Naselenie Rossii za 100 let (1811–1913 gg.)* (Moscow, 1956), 311; and *Formirovanie rabochego klassa Rossii* (Moscow, 1958), 580–1.

[21] B. A. Anderson, *Internal Migration during Modernization in Late Nineteenth-Century Russia* (Princeton, 1980), 109; J. Brooks, *When Russia Learned to Read: Literacy and Popular Literature, 1861–1917* (Princeton, 1985), 12; and G. Guroff and S. F. Starr, 'A Note on Literacy in Russia, 1890–1914', *Jahrbücher für Geschichte Osteuropas*, 19 (1971), 525.

[22] On Pirogov, see Eklof, *Russian Peasant Schools*, 51.

[23] Ibid., 432.

[24] *Istoriia rabochikh Leningrada, 1703–fevral′ 1917*, i (Leningrad, 1972), 146–7, and Ia. V. Abramov, *Nashi voskresnye shkoly: ikh proshloe i nastoiashchee* (St Petersburg, 1900), 318.

[25] R. W. Thurston, *Liberal City, Conservative State: Moscow and Russia's Urban Crisis, 1906–1914* (Oxford, 1987), 164–5, and V. Leikina-Svirskaia, *Russkaia intelligentsiia v 1900–1917 godakh* (Moscow, 1981), 76–7.

[26] For reproductions of works by Bogdanov-Bel′skii, see E. Kridl Valkenier (ed.), *The Wanderers: Masters of 19th-Century Russian Painting. An Exhibition from the Soviet Union* (Dallas, 1990), plates 5–6; on his career, see E. Kridl Valkenier, *Russian Realist Art* (New York, 1989), 163.

[27] B. Ivanov, *Po stupeniam bor′by: Zapiski starogo bol′shevika* (Moscow, 1934), 49.

[28] A. Frolov, *Probuzhdenie* (Kiev, 1923), 531.

[29] R. E. Zelnik (tr. and ed.), *A Radical Worker in Tsarist Russia: The Autobiography of Semën Ivanovich Kanatchikov* (Stanford, 1986), 93. Cf. J. Rancière's remarks about similar workers in France in *La Nuit des prolétaires* (Paris, 1981), 32.

[30] K. M. Takhtarev, *Ocherk peterburgskogo rabochego dvizheniia 90-kh godov* (Petrograd, 1921), 10; S. Kanatchikov remembered being 'irresistibly drawn' to 'books in beautiful, dark bindings' (165).

[31] Zelnik (tr. and ed.), *A Radical Worker*, 106.

[32] On Nekrasov, see Zelnik (tr. and ed.), *A Radical Worker*, 75–6. On Tolstoi, Dostoevskii, and Gor′kii, see E. R. Kabo, *Ocherki rabochego byta* (Moscow, 1928), 67, and cf. A. I. Shapovalov, *Po doroge k marksizmu: Vospominaniia rabochego-revoliutsionera* (Moscow, 1924), 44. On Gor′kii, see also Frolov, *Probuzhdenie*, 167–8. On Andreev, see M. Gor′kii, 'O pisateliakh-samouchkakh', *Sovremennyi mir*, 2 (1911), 178–209.

[33] L. M. Kleinbort, 'Rukopisnye zhurnaly rabochei Rossii', *Vestnik Evropy*, 7–8 (1917), 278, 282.

[34] *Tkach*, 1 (1917), 17.

[35] Quoted in V. E. Bonnell, *Roots of Rebellion: Workers' Politics and Organizations in St Petersburg and Moscow, 1900–1914* (Berkeley, 1983), 333.

[36] P. Kenez, *The Birth of the Propaganda State* (Cambridge, 1985), 21, and Leikina-Svirskaia, *Russkaia intelligentsiia*, 123. See also the appendix to L. McReynolds,

The News Under Russia's Old Regime: The Development of a Mass-Circulation Press (Princeton, 1991).

37 See McReynolds, *The News*, ch. 6.

38 See T. Owen, *Capitalism and Politics in Russia: A Social History of the Moscow Merchants, 1855–1905* (New York, 1981), and A. Rieber, *Merchants and Entrepreneurs in Imperial Russia* (Chapel Hill, 1982).

39 Of the State Council in 1894–1914, 30.7 per cent are classified as 'bourgeois' in D. Lieven, *Russia's Rulers under the Old Regime* (New Haven, 1989), 63; this did not, however, lead to more effective co-operation between the Tsarist regime and the new elites, mainly because of the 'disorganization in institutions caused, above all, by remaining elements of monarchical absolutism' (289).

40 J. Bradley, 'Voluntary Associations, Civic Culture, and *Obshchestvennost'* in Moscow', in E. W. Clowes, S. D. Kassow, and J. L. West (eds.), *Between Tsar and People: Educated Society and the Quest for Public Identity in Late Imperial Russia* (Princeton, 1991), 136–7.

41 J. MacAloon, *This Great Symbol: Pierre de Coubertin and the Origins of the Modern Olympic Games* (Chicago, 1981), 141. Unlike its Soviet successor, the Russian government considered the Olympics a waste of money and offered no support to Russian athletes, few of whom could afford to compete.

42 *Sport*, 1 (1897), 1.

43 A. Blok, 'Predislovie k *Vozmezdiiu*', in *Stikhotvoreniia* (Leningrad, 1955), 524.

44 V. Merkuriev, *Ivan Poddubnyi* (Krasnodar, 1976). Information on sports also comes from Lebedev's journal, *Hercules*, and from dozens of other contemporary sports journals. For a general introduction to the period, see also J. Riordan, *Sport and Soviet Society: Development of Sport and Physical Education in Russia and the USSR* (Cambridge, 1977), ch. 1.

45 So argued a contributor to *Sport*, 6 (1897), 80.

46 See J.-A. Ruckman, *The Moscow Business Elite: A Social and Cultural Portrait of Two Generations, 1840–1905* (De Kalb, 1984).

47 See M. D. Steinberg, *Moral Communities: The Culture of Class Relations in the Russian Printing Industry, 1867–1907* (Berkeley, 1992); Buryshkin, *Moskva kupecheskaia* (New York, 1954; repr. Moscow, 1991) also contains much information on merchant philanthropy.

48 The poor work and living conditions among the Russian working classes are very widely documented: see e.g. S. A. Smith, *Red Petrograd: Revolution in the Factories 1917–1918* (Cambridge, 1983), and D. Koenker, *Moscow Workers and the 1917 Revolution* (Princeton, 1981).

49 Steinberg, *Moral Communities*, esp. 60–8.

50 D. Christian, *Living Water: Vodka and Russian Society on the Eve of Emancipation* (Oxford, 1990), 380, and V. I. Binshtok and L. S. Kaminskii, *Narodnoe pitan'e i narodnoe zdorov'e* (Moscow, 1929), 45–6.

51 See Brower, *The Russian City*, and E. A. Swift, 'Fighting the Germs of Disorder: The Censorship of Russian Popular Theatre, 1888–1917', *Russian History*, 18 (1991), 1–49.

52 S. Frank, 'Confronting the Domestic Other', in Frank and M. D. Steinberg, *Cultures in Flux: Lower-Class Values, Practices and Resistance in Late Imperial*

Russia (Princeton, 1994), 96, and P. Herlihy, 'Joy of the Rus': Rites and Rituals of Russian Drinking', *Russian Review*, 50 (1991), 143.

[53] Brower, *The Russian City*, 182, and J. Bradley, *Muzhik and Muscovite: Urbanization in Late Imperial Russia* (Berkeley, 1985), 353.

[54] N. M. Lisovskii, *Rabochie v voennom vedomstve* (St Petersburg, 1906), 203.

[55] Eklof, *Russian Peasant Schools*, 423, and Frank, 'Confronting', 90–1.

[56] The minister in question was Avraam Norov: see K. A. Timiriazev, 'Probuzhdenie estestvoznaniia v tret'ei chetverti veka', *Granat-Ist*, vii (n.d.), 2, cited in A. Vucinich, *Science in Russian Culture: A History to 1860* (Stanford, 1963), 380–1.

[57] A. Vucinich, *Science in Russian Culture 1861–1917* (Stanford, 1970), 40–2. We are indebted to this volume of Vucinich's study for the discussion here and below of educational reform and scientific institutions in nineteenth-century Russia; the drift of the discussion also owes much to the feminist approaches of, for example, the contributors to L. Alcoff and E. Potter (eds.), *Feminist Epistemologies* (New York, 1993).

[58] S. V. Rozhdestvenskii, *Istoricheskii obzor deiatel'nosti Ministerstva Narodnogo Prosveshcheniia (1802–1902)* (St Petersburg, 1902), 520.

[59] F. A. Vinogradov, 'Obshchestvo klassicheskoi filologii i pedagogiki v 1908 godu', *Zhurnal Ministerstva Narodnogo Prosveshcheniia*, 9 (1909), sect. 4, 9–16.

[60] Vucinich, *Science in Russian Culture 1861–1917*, 227.

[61] L. Engelstein, *The Keys to Happiness: Sex and the Search for Modernity in Fin de Siècle Russia* (Ithaca, 1992), ch. 5, and N. M. Frieden, *Russian Physicians in an Era of Reform and Revolution, 1856–1905* (Princeton, 1981).

[62] Frieden, *Russian Physicians*, 105–12, 116, 118, 122, 127, 135, 145.

[63] Vucinich, *Science in Russian Culture 1861–1917*, 200–3, 298–301.

[64] K. A. Timiriazev, *Nasushchnye zadachi sovremennogo estestvoznaniia*, 3rd edn. (Moscow, 1908), 6, cited in Vucinich, *Science in Russian Culture 1861–1917*, 201.

[65] The inventor of the familiar racial categories such as 'Caucasian' and 'Negroid', Joseph Deniker, was a French citizen, but was married to a Russian and educated in Russia, where his theories were well known, *Les Races et les peuples de la terre* appearing in Russian in 1902, only two years after the French edition.

[66] C. Frierson, *Peasant Icons: Representations of Rural People in Late Nineteenth-Century Russia* (Oxford, 1993), 27–8, 117–18.

[67] Vucinich, *Science in Russian Culture 1861–1917*, 249.

[68] R. F. Gustafson, *Leo Tolstoy, Resident and Stranger: A Study in Fiction and Theology* (Princeton, 1986), 221–2.

[69] Vucinich, *Science in Russian Culture 1861–1917*, 411, 247, 307–8.

[70] D. Joravsky, *Russian Psychology: A Critical History* (Oxford, 1989), 148.

[71] J.-M. Charcot, *Charcot, the Clinician: The Tuesday Lessons*, tr. C. G. Goetz (New York, 1987), 104. One Russian memoirist, Elizaveta D'iakonova, has left an account of being treated by a follower of Charcot: see her *Dnevnik russkoi zhenshchiny* (Paris, 1900–2; repr. St Petersburg, 1905).

[72] Charcot, *Charcot, the Clinician*, 107.

73 R. H. Allshouse, 'Introduction', in Allshouse (ed.), *Photographs for the Tsar: The Pioneering Color Photography of Sergei Mikhailovich Prokudin-Gorskii, Commissioned by Tsar Nicholas II* (London, 1980), pp. ix–xxiii.

74 Quotation from Y. V. Barchatova, *Introduction to A Portrait of Tsarist Russia: Unknown Photographs from the Soviet Archives*, tr. M. Robinson (New York, 1989), 7. The drift of argument here draws on M. Jay, 'Scopic Regimes', in H. Foster (ed.), *Vision and Visuality* (Seattle, 1988), 9.

75 On the growth of the picture postcard, see particularly N. S. Tagrin, *Mir v otkrytke* (Moscow, 1978).

76 Barchatova, *Introduction to A Portrait of Tsarist Russia*, 16.

77 Ibid., 7–27.

78 I. Paperno, 'Introduction', in Paperno and J. D. Grossman (eds.), *Creating Life: The Aesthetic Utopia of Russian Modernism* (Stanford, 1994), 4.

79 See J. Tulloch, *Chekhov: A Structuralist Study* (New York, 1980), 86.

2 Commercial Culture and Consumerism

Steve Smith and Catriona Kelly

Additional material by Louise McReynolds

Introduction

To think about the history of consumption in late imperial Russia is to confront yet again Russia's backwardness. In this case, it is not only the lateness of Russia's development of a consumer society that is at issue, but the lateness of historians in recognizing that an embryonic consumer society was emerging in the period after the emancipation of the serfs. Historians of Britain and North America, and lately of Western Europe, have devoted considerable attention to the growth of the market, the dissemination of commodities (durable household goods, new groceries, luxury articles, etc.), and the chronology and geography of changing consumer patterns. The publication of McKendrick, Brewer, and Plumb's *The Birth of the Consumer Society* in 1982 was a milestone in this regard. Since then, scholarly endeavour has gone beyond exploring the involvement of populations in the purchase of commodities, in order to engage with the symbolic meanings that attached to commodities, exploring such issues as the cultural representation of goods, and their link with the emergence of new social identities. Simon Schama's *The Embarrassment of Riches*, for example, explored the tensions between Dutch commercial prosperity and the Calvinist animus against extravagance and avarice. And feminist historians have examined families as units of consumption, and the interaction of discourses of separate spheres with women's domesticity and consumption patterns.[1]

By contrast, historians of late imperial and Soviet Russia have hardly anything to say on issues relating to consumption. Some would argue that the reason for this is simple: historians have shown no interest in these matters because Russia was never a consumer society. They could point to the fact that in 1913 agriculture still contributed over half of Russia's national income and provided three-quarters of all employment. They might insist—quite rightly —that the majority of Russian peasants were extremely poor, and lacked the resources to become consumers in the ordinary sense. Yet agricultural production had undergone rapid commercialization since the emancipation of the peasantry, and the peasant economy was significantly involved in the market. It is estimated that in 1913, 22–5 per cent of gross agricultural production was marketed outside rural areas, and that over 40 per cent of grain production net of seed was marketed (a figure that does not include the substantial amount of grain conveyed to market by cart).[2] Sale of agricultural produce, earnings from handi-craft production, and, above all, money wages earned outside the village meant that peasant incomes were very probably rising in the last decades of the *ancien régime*, despite persisting concentrations of chronic poverty. The peasantry was consuming more cotton, sugar, and kerosene, and was beginning to purchase new consumer durables. Moreover, historians of consumption in other countries have shown that straitened material circumstances were no bar to the increas-ing desire for consumer goods.[3] At the same time, we should not exaggerate the extent to which Russian peasants were enmeshed in the market economy. A large part of peasant production of food, and to some extent of handicrafts, was consumed by the families producing these, and the ability of the peasantry to withdraw from the market was amply illustrated during the years 1914–21, when food shortages in the city were chronic.

Nevertheless, all this cannot explain why economic historians, for example, have shown little interest in analysing the social depth of the market, per capita consumption of individual commodities, changing patterns of spending, the reorganization of retailing, or the links between consumption and increasing social mobility and differentiation; or why social historians have ignored the social functions and symbolic meanings of consumer goods, or the links between consumption and changing social identities. The fundamental reason for these omissions surely lies in the fact that the Soviet order firmly subordinated con-sumption to production, and invested great energy into sustaining the belief that citizens should constitute their collective energies around their place in the social division of labour. Taking their cue from Soviet ideology, Western his-torians have tended to write the history of late imperial Russia and the Soviet Union from within the same problematic, fixing upon industrialization and the social relations of production, and disregarding the changes in consumer taste and preference that were their necessary counterpart.

The Beginnings of a Consumer Society

It was in Russian cities that the development of a consumer society was most advanced. The urban population of Russia rose from 5.2 million in 1856 to 12.2 million in 1897. From 1897 to 1914, the proportion of the urban population increased from 12.4 to 14.6 per cent (from 15 to 17.5 per cent if one uses the definition of 'urban' in the 1926 census). Russia's historic capitals, together with Warsaw, were among the ten largest cities in Europe.[4] Urban growth came about largely as a result of peasant migration. In 1900 in Moscow, the typical immigrant was a male aged 21–2, married, slightly more literate than his more sedentary fel-low villagers, and slightly less literate than his Moscow-born peers. Immigrants were drawn to the city in search of work, by a desire to escape village burdens and routines, and by the presence of kin and fellow villagers. Peasant males found employment not only as industrial workers, but as day labourers, ser-vants, shop assistants, and odd-jobbers. In 1897, more Russians were employed in trade, private service, restaurants, and as day labourers than in industry. Far more men migrated than women, but the number of female migrants gradually increased. In 1897, for every 1,000 men in the overall population of St Petersburg and Moscow, there were, respectively, 826 and 755 women.[5]

Most women who left their villages were single or widowed, or from impoverished households. Unskilled, usually illiterate, most of them found jobs as servants, cooks, and nursemaids, or in the textile industry, where they earned about half of what men did. Barbara Engel, author of a recent study of migrant women, emphasizes their vulnerability in the urban environment, reflected in the high rates of illegitimate births (in 1897 these represented 26.4 and 22.2 per cent, respectively, of all births for the cities of Moscow and St Petersburg). Yet migration provided some with the opportunity to be their own mistresses, raised their standard of living and level of literacy, reduced their fertility, and altered consumption patterns, bringing them into line with the settled city population.[6]

It was the growth of commerce rather than of large-scale industry that was the most significant force behind the huge expansion of Russia's towns and cities. In Moscow in 1902, 21 per cent of the population was engaged in commerce, a larger proportion than in St Petersburg or Odessa, and one exceeded only by Paris among the major cities of Europe. Wholesale and retail trade constituted the largest subdivision of commerce, with more than 92,000 people working in over 7,500 shops and stores (or more than 19,000 if all the self-employed shopkeepers and vendors are included).[7]

The structure of retailing was still very traditional: the vast majority of urban consumers bought their goods in open markets and fairs, directly from artisan producers, or from hawkers, chapmen, and pedlars. In the heart of Moscow, for example, were many open-air markets, such as the stalls ringing Red Square, and the bazaar-like Trading Rows. Even when Walter Benjamin visited Moscow in 1926, he recalled that street-markets still flourished, and that 'you seldom see signs giving the names of a particular firm in a way that is legible from a distance; mostly there is just the name of the kind of goods sold, or sometimes the signs have clocks, suitcases, boots, furs, etc. painted on them'. James Bater writes of the capital city that 'specialised shops, centrally located or otherwise, took a supporting role when it came to the vast volume of transactions done in scruffy cellars, within evil-smelling sheds along side streets, or over the trays by pestilential peasant tradesmen'. Salesmen of berries, ice cream, balloons, milk, *kvas*, toys, and even water, still roamed the streets of all big cities crying their wares, and shopkeepers' manners were still those of the Eastern bazaar, with haggling the norm in many places.[8]

Yet it was the emergence of the store, especially the department store, that captured the contemporary imagination. And it is the distinction between the shop (*lavka*) and the store (*magazin*) that illustrates the transformation in retailing that was under way. According to one contemporary, the new stores beckoned customers with bright signs and advertisements, a luxurious interior, fancy display windows, and a variety of merchandise. In St Petersburg such stores included the Singer Building (later to become the House of Books), the Eliseevskii delicatessen (later to be Gastronome no. 1, and which retains its extraordinary *art nouveau* appointments), and the four-storeyed Nevskii Passazh

The front of Miur i Meriliz (Muir and Merrilies).
Russia's most famous department store (foreign-owned like many late imperial enter-prises, in this case by Scots), a model of commercial *style moderne* with its stone-faced walls, plate-glass windows separated by fine steel uprights, and discreet panels of dec-orative enamel with delicate trefoil patterns. Workers window-shop, while behatted bourgeois stroll past or gossip nonchalantly, underlining the role of the department store as a space for fantasy as well as a site for acquiring goods.

arcade, housing sixty retail outlets for high-quality clothing, jewellery, and lux-ury items. In Moscow they included the Upper Trading Rows (later GUM), and Muir and Merrilies, opened in 1907 on the Petrovka. Such speciality and luxury stores impressed foreign visitors; even Walter Benjamin, who generally found Moscow a provincial place, thought the Eliseevskii grocery in Moscow amaz-ingly luxurious, while Theodore Child, who visited Russia in the 1880s, recalled that 'here shop windows are full of the inventions of Western civilisation: easy chairs, jardinieres, statuettes, china, cravats, silk stockings, parasols, photo-graphs of French actresses and ballet girls, yellow-covered French novels and the last number of *Vie Parisienne* and *Journal Amusant*'.[9] The department store thus emerged as a pivotal site of identity formation for the growing urban population. Displaying commodities as spectacle, using goods and promotional images to con-struct fantasies, it powerfully moulded the modern, urban consumer, educating her (women were specifically targeted as customers) in fashion and good taste. It was, of course, principally a place where the urban bourgeoisie constructed its class and gender identities, learning how to dress, furnish its homes, spend its leisure time. But at the same time these stores were agencies of diffusion, school-rooms where members of the lower orders, particularly women, could learn the

A street vendor in St Petersburg, c.1910.
The many traders of this kind at market stalls or temporary pitches in Russian cities sold goods ranging from seasonal foodstuffs to items manufactured in Russia's cottage industries—here, feather dusters, bast storage boxes, wooden spoons, and a variety of toys, from wheeled horses to fashion dolls. The badge worn by the toy-seller is a permit indicating that he is trading legally. (From W. Barnes Steveni, *Things Seen in Russia*, London, 1913.)

fashions of the day, criteria of taste, standards of 'respectability' and 'comfort', if only through working in the shops themselves. Muir and Merrilies, which had a mail-order service covering every part of the Russian Empire, could stimulate and realize the fantasies of those too far away, or too shy, to enter its august portals themselves.[10]

Clothes were among the most significant items purchased in the new shops. Many of the grandest clothing shops were owned by foreigners, and the adoption of 'German [that is, foreign] dress' was routine among migrants to cities. Costume served as a communicative device through which social identity could be worked out and transformed. In the Russian village, clothing was a marker of social standing, linked to age, marital status, and the like (married women were expected to cover their heads, and to dress more soberly than young ones, for example).[11] Even before the surge in migration to the cities, ready-made cotton goods were the most widely disseminated mass-produced consumer items. 'Peasant girls hardly ever wear homespun cotton, they mostly wear cotton prints . . . If they do wear some homespun cotton, it is usually half-and-half with machine fabric', wrote one observer.[12] But it was the impact of the town that liberated clothing from the hold of tradition and local custom, and subjected it to the forces of the market. And clothing, *par excellence*, is a measure of the growth of fashion, of the triumph of style over utility. Mikhail Isakovskii, whose sister migrated to Moscow from Smolensk to work in a textile mill, remembers that her dream was to buy the fashionable *sak*, a loose-fitting coat draping from the shoulders. 'Women saved because you could not live without a *sak*, women workers had endless conversations about buying a *sak*. And if they bought one, they wrote to the village at once, to tell everyone that the long-desired *sak* had been purchased.'[13] Working women's taste was thus influenced by the clothing displayed in the department stores and in the pages of women's magazines. In 1908, an elegant, rose-coloured cashmere dress, trimmed with white, machine-made lace and rose-coloured satin ribbons cost the 18-year-old weaver P. T. Galkina three roubles. She paid a seamstress to copy it from a magazine. Single women workers spent more money on clothing in absolute terms than single men, and clothing represented a far higher proportion of their budget—about 20 per cent.[14]

This does not mean that male workers were indifferent to looking good; on the contrary, it was crucial to look smart when one went out, despite the extremely limited purchasing power of the average worker. As a young apprentice at a samovar factory in Tula, A. Frolov refused to dress in the 'uniform' of a worker —that is, 'simple boots, a smock, wide trousers, a jacket and a peaked cap'. Instead, he wore a hat and a European suit, ignoring gibes from his workmates.[15] The young Semen Kanatchikov bought himself a holiday outfit, a watch, and, for the summer, a wide belt, grey trousers, a straw hat, and some fancy shoes: 'In a word, I dressed in the manner of those young urban metal-workers who earned an independent living and didn't ruin themselves with vodka.'[16] Dressing well in public was an assertion of self-respect, and designed to command the respect of one's peers and superiors. As some young workers said in 1926: 'To go into town you have to dress as well as everyone else . . . They don't actually ask if you're a worker, but they can tell from the way you look. Why should you go out just to get laughed at?'[17] Through clothes, young workers—men as well as women —shaped their appearance, visually asserted themselves, and sought to improve their social status. Clothing also helped, of course, in attracting a sexual partner, another important route to status in working-class or peasant society.

By taking home their tastes in fashion, home decorating, and diet, as well as consumer durables, peasant migrants acted as cultural brokers, diffusing new patterns of consumption among the rural masses. In wealthier regions, particularly those from which there was extensive out-migration, contemporaries observed a high degree of modernization and urbanization of taste. When building new cottages, peasants now preferred 'white' ones, that is, ones with proper chimneys, in which people lived in smoke-free comfort but at greater expense (chimneys waste fuel); they aspired to furnish them with manufactured furniture rather than with rough-hewn, fixed wooden benches and shelves.[18] Above all, contemporaries noted the presence of samovars, wines, tobacco, German-cut dresses and jackets, umbrellas, mirrors, table lamps, pen and ink, watch-chains, rings, and accordions.[19] We know very little about the combinations of utilitarian, ornamental, and status meanings that attached to such goods, or how these meanings connected to changing notions of social identity and ideology. But it does appear that consumer goods were crucial to the assertion of individuality by the younger generation, who jibbed at the conservatism and conformism of village society. There were regular complaints of *dendizm* (dandyism), and the tastes of some certainly bordered on the eccentric. A correspondent for a clerical journal in 1904 reported the return of a peasant 'wearing a short coat, a fantastic shirt, dashing cocked hat and boots with rubber bottoms—all that could separate him from the crowds of simple, "grey" villagers. They look on him as a marvel. The village beauties make up to him. The schoolboys run after him as after a miracle.'[20] And there is other evidence that individualism was stirring in the village by the end of the century. The *zemstvo* survey of Iaroslavl' *guberniia* (district) in 1896, for example, remarked that 'liberation from serf dependence and the long-standing association of the more active section of the rural population with town life, have long since roused the desire in the Iaroslavl' peasant to uphold his "ego", to get away from the state of poverty and dependency . . . to a state of sufficiency, independence and respect'.[21]

The meanings of new commodities were, in part, constituted by wider discourses which sought to regulate consumer behaviour through concepts of luxury, self-sufficiency, prudence, restraint, hospitality, novelty, gentility, refinement, respectability, cleanliness, and so forth. In Russia, such discourses generally came from within mass culture itself: behaviour manuals, newspaper articles, magazine illustrations, advertising, the representations in popular novels, plays, and films, all played their part in shaping tastes and triggering desires. The intelligentsia was too devoted to things of the mind, too distrustful of base materialism, to view consumption indulgently. Purchases of samovars, lamps, and other items for the home, increasingly central to peasants' own notions of respectability, clashed with the intelligentsia's stereotype of the peasantry as having simple needs and unsophisticated tastes: 'Striving to be like the petty bourgeoisie (*meshchanstvo*)

. . . they allow themselves all sorts of extravagances with which true peasants do not even bother.'[22] In particular, 'tasteless and useless dandyism' was condemned. One observer remarked: 'In many areas the normal peasant dress is being replaced by urban styles, which cut deep into the peasant's slender budget, hindering major improvements to other, far more important sides of peasant life.'[23] But it was another symbolic expression of modernization, mass entertainments, which was to cause most anguish among intellectual observers.

'Boulevardization': the Evolution of Mass Culture

To Russian intellectuals, the emergence of cultural forms created to make a profit was seen not only to undermine the higher aesthetic and moral purposes of elite culture, but also to threaten pristine, authentic *narodnost'*, folk culture. Commentators sadly noted the preference of peasant communities for 'corrupt' genres of song, such as the 'cruel romance', and the *chastushka* over the *bylina* (folk epic) and the *istoricheskaia pesnia* (traditional ballad), and the ousting of round dances by new urban dances. They proposed using peasant choirs to revive folk-songs 'that are now nearly forgotten', and called for Rural Unions of Enlightenment to preserve traditional entertainments. The commercial arts were, for Russian ethnographers and supporters of popular education generally, the antithesis of the *kul'tura* that they were concerned to promote. A self-explanatory (and international) game called 'climbing the greasy pole for prizes' was thought to epitomize the venal and degrading nature of the spectacles on offer.[24]

Such anxieties were partly brought about by a misunderstanding of the history of urban entertainments, which had begun to be commercialized and Westernized by, at the latest, the end of the seventeenth century. The central site for popular entertainments in cities during the eighteenth and nineteenth centuries was the *narodnye gulian'ia*, literally 'mass promenades', but best translated as 'funfairs', the most important of which were held at Shrovetide and Easter. The entertainers at these expected to be paid (if only with a handful of copecks), and the material that they performed included imported genres (the glove-puppet show, the peep show, the pantomime, the harlequinade) as well as Russian choruses and clown shows. However, the nineteenth century had seen a considerable increase in the number of permanent, non-seasonal entertainments on offer to those who could not afford the imperial or private theatres. In 1800 there were perhaps a dozen theatres in the Russian Empire (excluding private theatres); by 1899 there were 2,134 entertainment establishments in the Empire, including 216 theatres (186 in European Russia), 32 concert halls, 42 circuses, 768 clubs, 248 dramatic, literary, musical, singing, and other societies, 266 military and 4 naval clubs, and 192 outdoor stages (*estrady*) in pleasure gardens. Popular musical theatres included the Bouffe and Berg Theatres in St Petersburg, the Solodovnikovskii Passazh in Moscow, as well as dozens of smaller theatres in the Sokol'niki and Petrovskii Park districts of Moscow, and the Krestovskii Island area of St Petersburg. The mass-market book industry had expanded hugely, offering a vastly greater number

Fanny Tarnovskaia, 'Russian Song and Dance Operetta Artiste'.
Publicity photograph from the professional magazine *Artist i stsena*, the 1910s. The
advertisement refers to Tarnovskaia's 'chic and luxurious costumes' (*shikarnye kostiumy*),
obligatory for women music-hall stars; it also states that she has been 'the toast of Tomsk'.
Though Tarnovskaia was evidently not among the first rank of stars, this commendation
is less of a put-down than it might seem, given that the vast mineral wealth of Siberia
had drawn large numbers of entrepreneurs, both Russian and foreign, to the area, and
brought about a boom in the towns there.

and variety of titles to its readers. And in 1896, the Lumière brothers brought to Russia their new invention, the movie camera; as everywhere else in Europe, the cinema rapidly became a craze, and hundreds of theatres, from the vast and palatial down to fly-blown cinema-miniatures, showing film shorts alongside variety programmes, sprang up in every town of any size. At first, films were mostly foreign-made, but during the First World War, when imports became difficult, a Russian industry was established, and the products of directors such as Evgenii Bauer and Iakov Protazanov soon became as popular with audiences as their foreign competitors.[25]

Not only the size of the entertainments industry, but its character, too, had altered considerably. In the past, only the grandest pleasure gardens, such as the 'Artificial Mineral Water Gardens' (later Demidov Gardens) founded in St Petersburg in 1834, and the two or three biggest *balagany* (fairground theatres) had offered their audiences luxurious entertainments, with expensive costumes and scenery. Now, though some old-style street entertainments survived (people sang, did acrobatics or conjuring tricks, or gave puppet shows, in city courtyards right up until the cultural revolution of the late 1920s), a forest of mid-priced and middlebrow entertainments had also grown up. This was particularly evident in the case of the *estrada* theatre, a generic term approximating to the English music-hall, and covering everything from louche *cafés chantants* to pleasure gardens and even zoos (which often had an *estrada*, outside stage, alongside the cages of animals), where operettas, variety shows, dance programmes, *feerii*, fantasy spectaculars, and firework shows were all offered.

In 1856, Alexander II, the 'Tsar Liberator', in an uncharacteristic fit of illiberalism, extended the Imperial Theatres' monopoly, which gave the theatres the right to regulate dramatic performances in the two capitals. The opening of new private dramatic theatres was now banned; six years later, in 1862, a still more draconian order provided that existing ones be closed. The musical theatre, not subject to the same constraints, began to flourish, and from this point on, dozens more opened, giving golden opportunites to entrepreneurs capable of ensuring a plentiful supply of frothy, refreshing fare. Often the names of the theatres were plagiarized from French originals—a guidebook to St Petersburg published in the 1860s lists the Monplaisir, Chateau des Fleurs, Folies Bergères, Alcazar, Hermitage—but many of the impresarios were Russian. The most successful included K. N. Nezlobin, S. A. Pal'm, Mikhail Lentovskii, Vera Nemetti, and the 'Russian Barnum', P. A. Tumpakov; and they promoted Russian artists whenever possible. For decades Offenbach and Franz Lehár in translation had dominated the Russian operetta. But Lentovskii and Tumpakov introduced V. P. Valentinov, whose operettas *Secrets of the Harem* (*Tainy garema*) and *The Queen of Diamonds* (*Koroleva brilliantov*) delighted audiences at the Hermitage and the Bouffe.

So far as variety shows were concerned, the Russian music-halls, cabarets, and pleasure gardens offered mixed-genre spectacles very like those to be found in any capital city (dance numbers alternating with stand-up comedy alternating with soppy songs). But local tastes were assiduously cultivated too. There was less in the way of conjuring tricks or displays of little-known but interesting facts than in the British music-hall; songs, on the other hand, were even more popular than in the West. In the 1860s, Grendor (*Grain d'or*) and 'the queen of the Paris operetta', Anna Zhiudik, attracted crowds with their suggestive ditties. Apart from *double-entendre*-filled *chansonnettes*, the genre that dominated was the gypsy romance, melodramatic, passionate, sublimely suitable for sentimental wallowing. Among the earliest stars of the Russian *estrada* were Vera Zorina and A. V. Davydov, both specializing in gypsy songs. Later, two superstars of the 1900s, Anastasiia Vial'tseva and Vera Panina, moved from gypsy chorus to gypsy soloists (the latter was a rare instance of a soloist who was actually an ethnic gypsy).

The variety theatres catered for a public whose levels of prosperity differed quite widely. Some theatres were grander than others, and within the same theatre or pleasure garden, tickets at different prices were available, as one member of the Bouffe theatre recalled:

> At 6 p.m. the garden opened to the public. The entrance fee was 40 copecks; seats in the theatre were expensive. First would come the less well-off spectators who wanted to listen to the brass bands and, more important, grab a spot at the fence at the back of the stalls so they could see the operetta for their 40 copecks (even if they had to stand while doing it). Most of these operetta fans were students, artisans, and petty bureaucrats, and they were also quite poorly dressed . . . This group did not eat in the restaurant, where the prices were extremely high. For example, a beer that normally cost 9–11 copecks would sell for 40 in the Bouffe. Likewise a bottle of champagne would sell for 12 roubles instead of the usual 2–4 roubles for that quality. At 8 p.m., at the start of the operetta, there would be heavy traffic in carriages: women in huge hats with ostrich feathers and great capes, men in bowler hats with expensive walking sticks, dazzlingly handsome officers, their spurs jangling.

The popularity of the variety theatres, and such cunning pricing strategies, made them massively profitable: the same observer comments: 'The operettas were staged handsomely and luxuriously; Tumpakov did not stint on the expenses, knowing they would come back to him with interest.'[26] Such unashamed, brash commercialism was also reflected in much of the material on show. The shows staged, and songs sung, in cabarets, pleasure gardens, fairgrounds, and city streets represented characters who were the antipodes of the earnestly self-educating peasants and workers represented in realist fiction and painting. The main aim of these individuals was to make money, and, having made it, to spend it on all the luxuries that the city could offer: smart clothes, jewels, cigarette-cases, fancy hairstyles, and city pleasures. A music-hall song called 'The Iaroslavl' Muzhik', for example, is narrated by a peasant boy who has come to town and turned himself into a dandy:

> Кончен, кончен прежний путь,
> Скучный и постылый —
> Сладко будет отдохнуть
> Мне с подружкой милой!
>
> Лишь вошеі — от всех поклон,
> Ласки и приятство!

Вот что значит миллион,
Что значит богатство!

Закормлю всех на убой,
И друзья к нам кучей!
Заведусь теперь женой
Я на всякий случай.

Что я был? Мужик простой,
Бедный ярославец!
А теперь, гляди, какой
С Невского красавец!

Стянут там как раз бока,
Фраком плечи сузят,
А за деньги русака
Немцы офранцузят!

Нет волос — дадут парик,
Брейся как татарин:
С головой а ля мужик,
С рыла а ля барин!

[I have left my former path,
My path so long and weary,
How good's the thought that I can rest
In comfort with my dearie.

As soon as I come in the room,
People rush to greet me:
Because I am a millionaire
They're careful how they treat me.

I order food for everyone,
My friends rush round to eat some.
I think I'll get myself a wife,
Who knows when I might need one?

Who was I? A Iaroslavl′ muzhik,
Plain man, not worth a penny,
But just you look where I've fetched up,
A dandy on the Nevskii!

They know just how to cut a suit,
And pad you out, those Prussians,
And if you've got the ready cash,
They'll Frenchify the Russians!

If you've no hair, then buy a wig,
Shave like an Oriental man,
Your head may be à la muzhik,
Your mug is à la gentleman!][27]

Alterations to bodies, and indeed bodies themselves, can be purchased as easily as new sets of clothes: there could hardly be a text that better exemplifed the values of popular city life once commercial culture had taken hold. But the song is typical also in the self-ironizing flavour that was so often missed by Russian commentators at the time, and also in the touching modesty of the ambitions that it reflects: a smart new outfit, female company, plenty of food, popularity, and the opportunity to treat one's friends.

'The Muzhik from Iaroslavl'' manifests one of commercialization's best-known side-effects: the fact that women start to be seen as commodities, available to any men who can purchase them. However, sexual go-getting was not limited to men in the turn-of-the-century popular theatre. The *shanson'etki* sung by the women stars of the musical stage were equally explicit in the expression of their desires to make money and enjoy themselves: in one typical example, a singer spins an elaborate tale about opening a boutique as a way of stating that she is in control of what she sells:

> Торговля эта ясно
> Приносит мне барыш,
> Но все-ж она опасна:
> Вдруг да погоришь.
> И вот, поддавшись ражу,
> Решила я всему
> Назначить распродажу
> Товару моему!
> > Но цены без запроса,
> > В кредит не продаю,
> > Не суй без денег носа;
> > Без денег не даю!

> [And I can tell you frankly
> There's money in my trade,
> But it's a risky business:
> You go bust if you're not paid.
> So, bearing that in mind, then,
> Not wanting trade to fail,
> I've bitten on the bullet,
> And I'm going to have a sale!
> > But I don't like to haggle,
> > And credit's not my way:
> > No goods without the money,
> > Pay cash, or go away!][28]

Though cabaret theatres were largely attended by men (women who visited had, or risked, a dubious reputation), the songs of the Russian music-hall made their way, through song-books and gramophone recordings, to parlours and street-corners everywhere. The sorrowing, deceived males and raunchy females that they portrayed became some of the key images of the age. The 'new woman', a heroine liberated from conventional constraints on behaviour, could also be found in popular fiction, most notoriously in Anastasiia Verbitskaia's best-selling, and twice filmed, blockbuster novel *The Keys to Happiness* (*Kliuchi schast'ia*, 1908–13), whose heroine Mania, a beautiful dancer, was shown attaining love, sexual fulfilment, fame, and world travel.

It was perhaps the cinema, though, where the most innovative portrayals of the 'new woman' were to be found, particularly in films made by Evgenii Bauer, known to his contemporaries as 'the woman's director'. In his 1915 feature *A Child of the Big City* (*Ditia bol'shogo goroda*), we observe the rake's progress of Masha, who, when we first see her, is a young seamstress in a sweatshop making blouses. When out in the street staring wistfully through the windows of grand shops at clothes she cannot afford, she is picked up by two wealthy young men, and goes with them to the private room of a restaurant, where she suffers the expected 'fate worse than death'. Her fall is not, however, the prelude to disgrace and disaster, nor even to torments of guilt. Instead, Masha exploits the wealth of one of her admirers to lead a life of perfect hedonism; then, when even his considerable financial resources begin to run dry, she deserts him for the next rich man, while he retires to live in a miserable garret. The final scenes show him visiting the luxurious apartment block where Masha is now ensconced, and then collapsing and dying outside on the street when a servant descends, at Masha's direction, to repulse him with an insulting donation of alms. The film ends as Masha leaves the flat and, with an expression of irritation and disgust rather than any other emotion, steps over his prone corpse on her way to yet another evening of sybaritism at Maxim's Restaurant.

Whether Masha was perceived by her original audiences as heroine, as villainess, or as the woman they loved to hate (one suspects that, like Alexis in the 1980s American soap opera *Dynasty*, she probably came into this last category), she was certainly a remarkable creation. Her use of sexual attraction in order to better herself makes her the female counterpart of the male adventurers, such as Frol Skobeev, cross-dressing social climber and rapist, who had peopled Russian popular fiction during the seventeenth, eighteenth, and nineteenth centuries.

Glamorous, self-serving, and powerful, Masha was an innovative character in terms of Russian popular culture, which had tended, in the past, to represent women only as victims of male authority, or at the very least accoutrements of it. As women from Russian villages began to follow their brothers and male neighbours to the city, and became part of the audience for popular entertainments, so entertainments altered to suit their tastes.

That said, the effects of 'boulevardization' were not uniform. If the 'adventuress' role was a striking novelty, there were still abundant instances of more conventional types: virtuous, victimized wives, *ingénues* led astray by handsome, but perfidious, male seducers, and men and women whose non-conformity was forced upon them by the exigencies of fate, or the evil actions of others, rather than desired. Nor did the prominence of predatory sexuality necessarily mean that women invariably did well out of commercial culture. The emphasis on luxury that went with high budgets brought with it considerable financial duress upon performers, most particularly women performers, who were expected to dress as glamorously as entrepreneurs, producers, and their public demanded. Music-hall singers might boast on stage about their dominance over men, singing 'He's the puppet and I pull the strings', but after the show the roles were often reversed as, to supplement their meagre salaries, they turned to prostitution or posed for cheesecake photographs (in the first volume of his memoirs, the writer Il'ia Erenburg recalled purchasing, as a schoolboy, photographs of music-hall stars 'preferably with no clothes on' at stationers in Moscow during the early 1900s).[29]

Gender-bending was, in any case, only one strategy according to which bou-levard entertainments achieved their fundamental aim: to provide their public with violent sensations, shocking and thrilling them at the same time. The titles of the material on offer effectively advertised its aims: L. Kleinbort noted in 1915 that lower-class readers were devouring penny dreadfuls under banner titles such as *Satan's Crag* (*Utes Satana*), *Evil Charms* (*Zlye chary*), or *The Fateful Button* (*Rokovaia pugovitsa*).[30] Often, the shock-horror effects of the material were increased by the insistence that these were real-life, true stories. Where traditional popular entertainments, such as the puppet show Petrushka, had represented violent, but archetypal events, such as the murder of petty tyrants (policemen, recruiting sergeants, German doctors), not necessarily impossible in the present, but not immediately connected with it, audiences were now drawn by the sense that something not only could happen, but had happened. Popular newspapers, in their features and *feuilletons*, narrated success and hard-luck stories whose characters often made their way directly into popular fiction and later into film. An indicative member of the new tribe was Vasilii Churkin, a rogue peasant who appeared in news stories, serial literature, and cheap book-lets. As one anonymous author introduced the ruffian:

Not so far away from Moscow, in Bogorodskii county, in the village of Barskii, an honest father and mother gave birth to a son. This baby was Vasilii Churkin, who sub-sequently became a bandit and murderer, wreaking fear and terror with his crimes in all the villages of Bogorodskii county, and then in other areas. From earliest child-hood Churkin exhibited his stubborn and evil character, so much so that his father truly did not know what measures to take to discipline his son. The future bandit did not fear the birchrod, the leather strap, or the lash; he was afraid of nothing. Sometimes his father would grab the delinquent by the hair and begin lashing him with a strap for some brash shenanigan; he would beat and beat until he was exhausted, but Vas'ka would sit there like a corpse, not uttering a sound, as if he had not been flogged.

'Damned kid!' his angry father would cry, striking out at his son. But Vas'ka would sit in the shop, scratching his back, taunting, 'Da, Da, buy me some gingerbread; I behaved badly, but you beat me goodly.'[31]

The Churkin craze was probably the most infamous enthusiasm in popular fiction—so infamous, in fact, that the Tsarist government intervened and forced the newspaper serial version of the fictional bandit to be killed off. The phe-nomenon of transferring protagonists/antagonists from real life to literature, however, continued. Not all the wicked adventurers were men: they included 'Lightfingered Son'ka', the nickname of pickpocket and suspected murderess Sofiia Bliuvshtein, who ultimately became the lead character in Russia's first silent movie serial. In newspapers, fiction, street ballads, and movies, 'true crimes' were the staple: another example of the tendency was *Merchant Bashkirov's Daughter* (*Doch' kuptsa Bashkirova*), a film melodrama directed by Nikolai Larin and released in 1913, which shows a flirtation ending in tragedy as the mer-chant's daughter of the title hides her gentleman friend under layers of feather beds to escape detection, only to find that he has suffocated there when she attempts to get him out. Here, an apparently low-key subject was embroidered with much high-pitched gesture, and representation in copious detail of how the unfortunate boyfriend's corpse was disposed of.

Self-censorship and the Market-place: Didacticism in Popular Culture

The products of the boulevard enraged the intelligentsia with their garishness and their vulgarity (the Russian term for which, *poshlost'*, suggests banality, triviality, and sexual filth all in one). It was hard for the traditional Russian intellectual, shaped by his or her ascetic commitment to public service, to accept that tastes in pleasure varied according to changing norms for personal fulfilment. Women who bought booklets on how to style their hair, like men who purchased joke books to help them out in social situations, were making perfectly appropriate uses of their literacy skills, if not ones that had been anticipated by their teachers. Moreover, as in these two cases, what seemed purposeless trash to outsiders was often valued by its consumers partly, or indeed precisely, in terms of its function, a consideration that applied just as much to literature as to how-to manuals of fortune-telling or house management, or to the church calendars that were ubiquitous in peasant households right up to the Revolution. Russian commentators were inclined to confuse what was commercial in the sense of selling well, with what was commercial in the sense of advocating commercial values. Though the two things overlapped significantly, they were not identical by any means.

It is remarkable, for instance, that one of Russia's most passionate voices against the intrusion of commercial values into Russia, Lev Tolstoi, sold well in the late nineteenth and early twentieth century. What is more, there was a strongly ironic or satiric vein in many popular entertainments, often directed at the very sectors of society that were most likely to be watching. Aleksandr Ostrovskii, the most famous initiator of assaults on what the influential 1860s radical critic Nikolai Dobroliubov termed 'the kingdom of darkness', had his plays premièred in the merchant city of Moscow, where they played at the Malyi Theatre before audiences packed with members of the very groups he satirized. Possibly this was because the aspirant merchants who attended the Malyi saw Ostrovskii's plays as attacks on benighted members of their class, but it is equally possible that the spectators were happy to laugh at themselves, and flattered with the chance it gave them to display a new self-confidence and worldly wisdom.

In this sense Ostrovskii can be seen as a transitional figure, standing between the late eighteenth- and early nineteenth-century writers, such as Mikhail Chulkov, Mariia Zhukova, Pushkin, Gogol', and Lermontov, whose representations of lower-class individuals were most certainly not designed for the consumption of the lower classes, and later writers, such as Petr Boborykin (1836–1921), Nikolai Leikin (1841–1906), and I. I. Miasnitskii (1854–1911), all of whom produced explicitly middlebrow fare, serialized in newspapers and in the massively popular illustrated journal *Niva* (*The Cornfield*, founded in 1869), as well as in book form.

Of the three, Boborykin, rather misleadingly dubbed 'the Russian Zola', had the greatest intellectual pretensions. Whereas Leikin came from one of St Petersburg's oldest merchant families, and started by selling gossip to local newspapers, and Miasnitskii was the adoptive (and probably illegitimate) son of the publisher K. T. Soldatenkov, Boborykin came from a landowning family, had a degree in physics and mathematics, and published in such weighty journals as *Russkii vestnik* (*The Russian Herald*), *Vsemirnyi trud* (*Universal Labour*), and *Russkaia mysl'* (*Russian Thought*). However, his works were popular enough to be issued in cheap editions, he enjoyed his entrée to merchant social circles, and wrote with sympathy of their role in Moscow life in some of his many works of popular history. In his most renowned novel, *Kitai-gorod* (1882), named after the area of central Moscow which contained the main covered markets, he chronicled the effects on prominent families of the new wealth and prestige that had come to them with industrialization. Although not whitewashing the weaknesses of individuals, *Kitai-gorod* offered rare positive images both of the industry likely to carry Russia into the future, and of the individuals that would see it through. Interestingly, the characters included a determined woman entrepreneur, loosely based on Boborykin's friend Varvara Morozova, member of the Morozov textile dynasty, industrialist, and sponsor of the arts, whose presence constitutes a rare recognition by a Russian writer that merchant women were not always the cowed wives of tyrannical, chauvinist husbands.

Flouting his connections to important merchant families, Leikin, who published in cheaper organs than Boborykin, such as the mass-market *Peterburgskii listok* (*Petersburg Sheet*), offered instead portraits of smaller fry, the shopkeepers of Gostinyi Dvor, Petersburg's central covered market. Some of these middle-ranking traders (Gostinyi Dvor was by far the grandest market in St Petersburg, abutting as it did on the prestige shopping districts of Nevskii Prospekt and Sadovaia ulitsa) were quite possibly among the readers of Leikin's stories, no doubt recognizing themselves, or more likely their acquaintances, in light-hearted characters such as two merchants taking the obligatory tour of Europe required of the *nouveaux riches* depicted in *Where the Oranges Ripen* (*Gde apel'siny zreiut*, 1892):

'But do oranges really grow in Italy?' asked Ivan Kondrat'evich, sipping from his wine glass and breathing heavily.

'What?' laughed Nikolai Ivanovich. 'You're a fruitseller yourself, you run a fresh and dried fruit stall in Petersburg, and you don't know where oranges grow? What a hick!'

'Yeah, well how am I supposed to know? We buy oranges for the stall in crates from that German, Karl Bogdanych. I thought oranges came from Orangia.'

'I think there's a place called that in Italy—maybe a province or a district maybe,' said Nikolai Ivanovich.

'Stop being so silly!' cried Glafira Semenovna. 'There's no such place as Orange Province, or Orange District for that matter. Oranges only grow in Italy.'

'So how come we sell Jerusalem oranges?' objected Ivan Kondrat'evich.

'They're some sort of Jewboy oranges, grown by the Jerusalem nobility.'

'On the contrary, they're the best ones.'

'I don't know anything about that. The main thing is that oranges grow in Italy, and so Italy's called the land of oranges.'[32]

Such texts taught readers and spectators what they ought to know, what constituted the proper knowledge of a refined person. In the same way, the audiences of popular films could watch the life and behaviour of moneyed individuals, laughing at its absurdity, but also absorbing half-admiringly the rules of behaviour for entry to a new class.

Miasnitskii, whose copious output probably outstripped even Boborykin's, penned everything from vaudevilles to the serious novel *The Merchants of Gostinyi Dvor* (*Kuptsy Gostinogo Dvora*, 1889), which, like *Kitai-gorod*, brought to life the social changes in merchant circles. He also sketched hundreds of vignettes, largely for the popular press, giving glimpses behind the façade of business, as in this conversation set in a popular Moscow nightclub, 'Hermitage':

In one of the side booths . . . two men in late middle age sat gossiping over a bottle of Château-Lafite.

'Oh, how she loved me, God help us!' confessed one to the other, stopping every now and then for a drink of wine. 'Not a day went by that she wouldn't send me a little note. "My wicked little fatty," she'd write, "I get so bored without you, without your health to worry about"—and so on, and so on like that. Oh, I'd bring her a bracelet, earrings, and she'd say, "Do you think that's what I'm in this for?" and burst out crying. . . . And boy did I invest a lot of money—spend, spend, spend. . . . The wife would get one dress, Anfiska'd get two. The wife'd get stuff all, but Anfiska'd get a whole surprise package . . . "If you ever stopped loving me, I'd infect myself with smallpox and die, or maybe I'll drink a whole bottle of acid or take to the bottle! I'm Traviata, you're Alfred . . ." '

'So did she die?' asked his companion.

'Don't I wish! I ran into her not long ago—face so fat you think it'd burst!'

'Some Traviata, eh!'

'A real Bitchiata she turned out to be, not a Traviata! There I was, dying for love, when suddenly I got an anonymous letter telling me my Traviata was being visited by some guitar-playing troubadour from the telegraph office! So she swaps Alfred for a guitar—fine kind of instrument! . . . Couldn't she even have found herself a drummer? At least that would have had more style.'[33]

In the early nineteenth century, the market for this kind of light reading had usually been served by foreign writers in translation, such as the Gothic novelist Ann Radcliffe. Although translated fiction still enjoyed high esteem, sustenance could now be drawn from native products as well. Other writers of the late nineteenth century who produced similar light reading for a middle-class or lower-class readership included the woman writers Kapitolina Nazar'eva ('E. Nikulina'), Ol'ga Bebutova, Aleksandra Sokolova, Natal'ia Lukhmanova, and the massively popular children's writer, Lidiia Charskaia.

The stress fracture between intelligentsia and popular, between didactic and commercial, can also be seen particularly clearly in the Russian theatre. As the most obviously commercial of traditional art forms (without spectators it is doomed to extinction), yet one which has been seen as particularly suited to the exposition of aesthetic and moral values for a mass audience, theatre confronted the Russian intelligentsia with nearly insuperable dilemmas. In the late nineteenth century, the rise of private theatres to challenge those run by the government illustrates how moral concerns (the refusal to be bound by censorship, the determination to confront social inequality, the use of the theatre as a weapon of education) were intertwined with, and to some extent undermined by, efforts to attract an audience in order to make private theatres financially viable, and able to communicate their didactic ideas to a representative part of the population.

Until 1882, when the monopoly of the imperial theatres was finally suspended, the development of a diverse and energetic dramatic tradition in the capitals was severely hindered. The imperial playhouses displayed extreme artistic as well as political conservatism. Hesitating to innovate, they offered the classics, primarily Shakespeare, Molière, Schiller, and the Russian comedies of Fonvizin and Gogol'. Once Ostrovskii became critically established, his works became the mainstay of the Malyi. For their part, the music and ballet theatres staged classic Italian and French operas (Wagner did not appear on their stages until 1890), though the ballet companies were a little more innovative, performing new works by their own *baletmeistery*, such as Marius Petipa.

The Russian intelligentsia, headed by important writers such as Ostrovskii, had long chafed against the monopoly. But when Alexander III rescinded it, he was responding less to anti-censorship pressures than to the demands of private enterprise. A determined young actress from the Malyi company, Anna Brenko, had challenged the monopoly by organizing 'Actors' Voluntary Performances', and the growing number of private clubs and voluntary associations also sponsored amateur productions. Invited guest stars received money under the table, which clearly defied the spirit of the ban. Brenko, however, could not make a financial go of her venture. The first entrepreneur to take immediate advantage of the opportunity also proved to be the most successful, F. A. Korsh, a lawyer who preferred the stage to the courtroom and had likewise produced various 'literary musical evenings' before 1882. His theatre opened in August 1882 with Gogol''s *The Government Inspector*. Within three years he moved into a larger building, turning the old one over to another revolutionary in theatre circles, the young merchant Konstantin Alekseev, who had just changed his name to Stanislavskii. The latter's Moscow Arts Theatre would exercise greater influence on universal theatrical concepts, but Korsh's enterprise better represented the idea of popular theatre as a site of cultural variety and conflict. For example, although playwright Anton Chekhov's name is linked inextricably with Stanislavskii's, it was Korsh who first produced Chekhov's works as part of a larger endeavour to introduce new talent to the Russian public.

No single theatrical genre characterized the Korsh Theatre. Korsh depended on profits to an extent that the state theatres, which could write off losses to the Treasury, did not. His repertoire often paralleled that of the cross-class Malyi Theatre, although Korsh proved far more ready to take theatrical chances. He almost lost his theatre in its second season following the failure of his lavish production of the medieval melodrama *The Death of Vasilii Shuiskii* (*Smert' Vasiliia*

Shuiskogo, 1883), whose author, curator of the Kremlin armoury, insisted on authenticity of costumes and sets. This expensive lesson forced Korsh to reorganize on principles learned in his first, legal, career. He strove relentlessly to balance artistic and commercial approval. The list of plays premièred in Russia by him includes, besides Chekhov's *Ivanov* and *The Bear*, Tolstoi's *The Power of Darkness*, Edmond Rostand's *Cyrano de Bergerac*, and Henrik Ibsen's *A Doll's House* and *An Enemy of the People*. He offered inexpensive matinées for students almost weekly, and devoted many Friday nights to showcasing new writers. Clearly, he felt a strong commitment to the intelligentsia's social utilitarian principles of art.[34]

Yet Korsh also depended upon comedies and farces, especially those translated from French, to subsidize his elitist fare. Throughout the 1880s and 1890s, Miasnitskii's burlesques underwrote the serious dramas. The prolific V. A. Krylov, famous for his Russianized versions of popular French comedies, also had many of his own plays produced here. Korsh staged his most financially successful production in 1895, his own translation of Victorien Sardou and Émile Moreau's farce *Madame Sans-Gêne* (*Madame Cheeky*, 1893), starring the popular beauty Lidiia Iavorskaia. The advance publicity highlighted Iavorskaia's trip to Paris to view the original production and select the loveliest French gowns. This was theatre become spectacle, fashion show rather than a social commentary.

Did Korsh himself see his theatre primarily as a place for entertainment, or as one for enlightenment? It is impossible to say. The celebration for the thirtieth anniversary of his theatre brought testimonials from all political and theatrical factions. He had successfully negotiated the delicate pluralism characteristic of modern societies. Korsh exemplified a new breed, made both possible and necessary by cultural transformation: a commercially successful *intelligent*. His critical and commercial successes pressured the imperial theatres to readjust to the theatre-going public's opinion.

Not only the legitimate stage, but also less 'respectable' forms of entertainment reflected such contradictions. Late nineteenth-century Russian zoos, in which displays of animals communicated the thrill of exoticism as much as broadening knowledge of the natural world, and where concerts of light music and fairground entertainments were set alongside the menageries, exemplified the contradictions of city pleasures. Cabaret and fairground theatres performed patriotic pageants (*The Fall of Sinope*) or evocations of global travel alongside harlequinades and circus acts. All these factors were overlooked by commentators who saw only the mindless side of popular entertainments. When a liberal reviewer dismissed Verbitskaia's immensely popular *Keys to Happiness* as a 'real department store', where the reader found bargain-basement versions of the 'social question, the theory of heredity, Darwin, Nietzsche, Oscar Wilde and the history of art',[35] he ignored both the issue of where else the common reader was supposed to find information about Darwin and Nietzsche, and also the fact that the popular novel, like the department store, could be an arena of fantasy, an education in desire, which represented opportunity rather than travesty, the best he or she could afford.

Irrational Recreations: Popular Leisure after 1881

For all their worthy goals, none of the branches of Russia's educational system could control how people used skills once gained. Literacy as practice was no more homogeneous than literature itself was as an art. But nowhere was the failure of the *mission civilisatrice* more publicly visible than in the area of popular leisure, where, as one commentator complained, '[t]he lower classes, lacking a permanent place of residence', were drawn to 'countless numbers of taverns, restaurants, beer halls and bars'.[36]

Drinking was indeed a main activity of the lower classes in Russian cities and villages at the turn of the century, and there does in fact seem to be some evidence for an increase in public drunkenness. In his authoritative recent study of Russian alcohol consumption, David Christian has attempted to explain this as a transition from what he calls 'traditional' to 'modern' drinking cultures. Traditional culture was rural, collective, associated with festive occasions, while modern drinking culture was more urban, individualistic, recreational, associated with a cash economy. In both cultures drinking was heavy and concentrated, and getting drunk was the aim, but in traditional culture it was periodic (confined to holidays and quiet times of the agricultural year), and controlled by the social group. Christian sees the tavern as pivotal to the transition between 'traditional' and 'modern' drinking patterns: once a tavern was established, it was difficult to resist the temptation to drink on days that were not traditional holidays, particularly once cash images were on the increase.[37] Patricia Herlihy, in another recent study, concurs that 'traditional' drinking was largely confined to holidays, important family events, hospitality, and business transactions, but suggests that social differentiation in rural society, the growing demand for wage labour, and the introduction of compulsory military service in 1874 were other factors eroding the controls that limited drinking to ritual occasions.[38]

In the towns, per capita consumption was almost certainly higher than in the countryside. One factor was the diffusion of stronger, purer, more potable drink. Another was the multiplication of taverns. As early as 1865, St Petersburg had 1,840 taverns or public houses (*kabaki*), 562 inns, 399 alcoholic beverage stores, 229 wine cellars, and miscellaneous other places where vodka was sold.[39] As important in explaining the breakdown of traditional controls on the use of vodka, though, was the growing association of vodka with urban rituals of leisure and work. A newly hired or promoted worker was expected to treat his fellow workers to drink. This was known as a *magarych* (originally a drink sunk to seal a bargain at market), or a *prival'noe* (originally the word for a fee paid to dock a boat at a pier, and later for the vodka or tea given to barge-haulers for bringing a boat safely to port).[40] Vodka celebrated entry into the workplace, it was a reward for a job well done, and it marked holidays. Although unskilled labourers were most heavily represented among those treated for alcoholism, skilled workers, such as printers and tailors, were also notorious drunkards.[41] The importance of the tavern for the nascent proletariat is emphasized in F. M. Reshetnikov's novel *Where is it Better? (Gde zh luchshe?*, 1868). The particular tavern frequented by joiner Petrov and his comrades has about 150 steady customers from five local factories. The heavy drinking takes place on Saturday nights (Saturday being the usual pay-day), after the workers have visited the bathhouse for their weekly bath. Drinking begins at a slow pace and then builds up rapidly, noisy carousing ending in squabbles and brawls.

Drinking rather poignantly illustrates the gendered division of leisure. In the villages, it had been customary on festive occasions for women to drink with men, but in the cities women apparently rarely visited the *kabak* or *traktir*. In 1908, St Petersburg textile workers spent 16.8 roubles (2.9 per cent of annual income) on vodka. However, a single male was likely to spend 11.2 per cent of income on drink and a married man with a family in the village 11 per cent; but a married man residing with his family spent only 3 per cent, and female textile workers spent next to nothing. Married women suffered at the hands of drunken husbands, not only through domestic violence, but also because drinking strained the family budget; hence, stories of wives standing outside factory gates on pay-day, beseeching their feckless husbands to hand over their wage packets, were legion. Temperance initiatives were not organized only by upper-class philanthropists: during the 1905 Revolution, women textile workers launched the Popular Campaign Against Drunkenness in Nevskii district, which provoked the derision of male workers, but gave a lead to the nascent strike committees and trade unions in combating this social evil.[42]

Card-playing and gambling were also widespread among men and boys. Buzinov writes:

> The passion for cards was almost universal, and seized even the greenest of youths. Usually the players would gather on a Saturday in someone's apartment, which those who were 'cleaned out' would leave soon, but others would leave only on the Monday when summoned by the factory whistle. They played exclusively 'Twenty One', and they played avidly, breaking off now and again to down a tot of vodka or a glass of beer. Then back to the cards. Forty sleepless hours a session turned the players into red-eyed roaches, and you could always spot them on the street.[43]

The scene is oddly reminiscent of the opening passage of Pushkin's famous story 'The Queen of Spades', but gambling attracted much greater concern when its practitioners were not aristocrats. During 1917, factory committees and trade unions took strict measures to try to curb the gambling craze. Apart from punting on cards, workers would sometimes stake a few copecks on a kind of roulette in which they bet that a top would land on certain squares marked on a board, or tried to put their fingers into a ring that was moved about rapidly, or guessed which of three cards was a face card.[44]

A survey of the time budget of seventy-six working-class families, carried out in Petrograd, Moscow, and Ivanovo-Voznesensk in 1922, reveals some interesting differences in leisure patterns according to gender, which are undoubtedly relevant for the late nineteenth and early twentieth centuries as well. Male wage-earners spent 2.1 hours a month in taverns or teahouses, 2.4 hours playing football, skittles, or skating, 0.5 hours hunting, and 1.5 hours on chess or draughts. Female wage-earners spent 4 hours a month dancing, compared to only 1 hour spent by male wage-earners (though housewives spent only 0.6 hours); 5.3 hours in singing and music, compared with 0.8 hours among men (though housewives spent nothing); and 15.8 hours visiting and receiving friends (housewives spent 7.7 hours), compared with 9.8 hours among men. Moreover, female wage-earners spent 3.7 hours at church (housewives 3.1), whereas male wage-earners spent only 1.5 hours. The only activities that were approximately equally liked were visits to the cinema or theatre (4.5 hours for men, 2.6 for women, 2.3 hours for housewives) and card games (females spent 1.1 hours versus 1.9 hours for men). However, in the last case, 'card games' probably meant different things for each gender: gambling for men, and fortune-telling for women.[45]

Though leisure was definitely gendered, and workers (and indeed peasants) tended to spend most time in the company of their own sex, there were occasional mixed-gender occasions—name-day parties, holiday celebrations, and so on. All the evidence seems to suggest that the most popular forms of recreation for mixed-gender groups, whether in the city or in the village, were dancing or singing to the tune of an accordion, guitar, or mouth-organ. In the last quarter of the nineteenth century, the *chastushka*, a short, usually four-lined, rhymed ditty, was the genre most often performed on these occasions. The *chastushka* is generally agreed to be a relatively late form of folklore, which gained astonishing popularity in the last quarter of the nineteenth century, and was most widely popular at points of contact between village and city, 'the small *guberniia* and *uezd* capitals, the outskirts of large cities, the bustling villages on major roads, and the areas of railroad construction'.[46] Migrant labourers and itinerant craftsmen, returning soldiers and villagers travelling to other villages, all spread the genre round the country. The *chastushka* varied in character; some were quite close to the traditional *liricheskaia pesnia*, expressions of love or lament for lost lovers; young men might be metaphorized as *sokoly* (falcons), and items from traditional village culture, such as sarafans or shirts, might figure. More commonly, though, the *chastushka* was used as an impromptu epigram, a witty comment on some topical phenomenon, or a satirical and frequently also ribald reaction to the behaviour of an acquaintance. The first substantial collection of *chastushki*, made by the woman ethnographer E. Eleonskaia in 1914, has a strong bias towards rural and 'poetic' material, but it includes some of the topical variety too:

> Мил часы на грудь повесил,
> Думал, буду уважать:
> Мне часы, как в поле ветер,
> Не пойду я провожать.

> [My beloved hung a watch
> On his shirt to make me love him;
> I couldn't give a fig for that,
> I won't go to the station with him.][47]

In another *chastushka* collected by Eleonskaia, a woman boasts of her beloved's three shirts—woollen, raspberry-coloured, and, best of all, pink with braid round the outside; in a third, the female speaker vaunts her affair with an accordion-player (nos. 1266, 1327). Such urban influences were clear, too, in the prevalence of terms for newly fashionable items of clothing—jackets, *kaloshi* (galoshes), *plat'ia* (dresses). City culture also leaked into the *chastushka* through song-books, whose texts could become standards of the oral repertoire only slightly varied in transmission, and through the homogenizing influence of the accordion, which César Cui, the composer, termed 'a barbarous instrument that reduces any song to two chords'.[48]

On the other hand, contemporary commentators were inclined to exaggerate the repetitive character of the *chastushka*. As with any genre of folklore, there were more- or less-talented performers, who owed more or less to personal inspiration. The best of them used standard tunes and metres as a launching point for original flights of fantasy, as recalled by Eduard Dune, who had encountered one such when working in Moscow as a loader during 1915 at the Provodnik rubber works:

> I remember with warmth our masters of improvisation who never once, not even in one *chastushka*, repeated themselves. The *chastushka* would be about something topical—a foreman or a gang-leader, a woman or a young girl, a priest or deacon. Each leader had his own speciality. I recall a fat heavy-faced youth who was completely illiterate, and who on pay-day would drink away his wages, but who was a master of the sharp-witted *chastushka*—admittedly of rather an obscene variety. For every passer-by he would invent some clever and totally unexpected jingle. He would break into an improvisation as the figure drew near, and then subside as they drew away. The appearance of the next person—whether young or old, handsome or ugly, fat or thin—would spark some new association, which would spontaneously form itself into words and rhyme.[49]

With two or more such masters at work, the performance of *chastushki* could turn into a real insult contest, and one to which women, as well as men, could contribute.

Less subject to improvisation was the genre of 'cruel romance', or street ballad, which was dominated by songs sung in the music-halls and circulated on gramophone records or in cheap song-books, or picked up by street-singers and performed to the barrel-organ before being passed on. But even here there were sometimes innovators: as late as the 1920s, the Soviet folklorist I. Sokolov found a street-singer performing an account of a hair-raising murder, in which a husband 'skewered his wife and child' because he was in love with his sister-in-law, and then bribed the building's janitor to help 'clear up the mess'.[50]

Though they depended on commercially available goods in one form or another—new possessions, factory-made instruments, song-book texts—none of these forms of 'irrational leisure' was commercialized in quite the same way as the shows at pleasure gardens, circuses, or theatres. The sums of money involved were relatively insignificant, and the relationship between performers and audience close even in those activities where the division between 'performers' and 'audience' had a significance. Additionally, many workers spent their time in activities that were not commercialized at all. A standard form of recreation among men was, as it had been since medieval times, street-brawling.

This sometimes involved organized battles, the *kulachnye boi*, with hundreds of young men taking part; the two sides, each representing a different street or factory, would form 'walls', struggling for control of a disputed no man's land. Enthusiastic onlookers gathered and placed bets on the outcome. There were rules—no hitting in the eyes or injuring someone who had fallen, no use of weapons—but injuries were frequent. There were also more spontaneous bouts of fighting, as two rival groups of young men competing for girls ran into each other on the street and let fly with their fists. Other young men would hunt birds (in Tula, gangs known as *liutye*, the fierce ones, would spend Sundays catching goldfinches or doves).[51] The urban environment also provided its own, free entertainments. Kanatchikov recalls that around the turn of the century, 'we never missed a fire, and no matter how tired, we would run at breakneck speed to see these free spectacles'.[52]

However, the difficult question of how far peasants and workers actually were affected, or infected, by commercialism was one to which many Russian intellectuals had the answer: far too much. Fears of the corrupting influences of commercial culture were expressed in depictions of commercial entertainments. In stories such as Iuliia Bezrodnaia's 'Tales From the Street' ('S ulitsy: rasskazy'), S. Elpat'evskii's 'Pictures from a Fairground' ('Iarmarochnye kartiny'), or V. Garshin's 'The Bears' ('Medvedi'), fairground and street entertainments are seen as degrading to their observers and, especially, their participants, whether human or, as in the last case, animal. Scruples of this kind were shared by the worker intelligentsia too, who saw popular music (polkas, waltzes, marches) as lacking ideological content. They also disapproved of the Petrushka puppet show, and of circuses as 'pandering to crude instincts'. Cheap literature was also heavily criticized: a carriage-cleaner who worked at the northwest railway depot in St Petersburg asked: 'Dear comrades, why do you think you have a head on your shoulders? To put a hat on it? Why won't you think, use your brain?' *Gazeta-kopeika* (*Copeck Paper*) was said to 'poison the soul of the proletariat'.[53] Prejudices against entertainments and against their producers and consumers reinforced each other; those who enjoyed or propagated such material were seen as vulgar, and their products, accordingly, as the tools of engineering false-consciousness in the human brain. All this had its effects not only on how entertainments were represented, but on the way that the modern city was perceived in literature and in painting, which we will examine in detail in the remaining sections of this chapter.

Commercialism and Language

Though it is customary, in cultural histories, to see realism and the 'new arts' movements (symbolism and post-symbolist schools such as acmeism, cubo-futurism, etc.) as polar opposites, the idea that commercialism was a source of irritation rather than inspiration was shared to a greater or lesser extent by all Russian writers and artists. Part of the reason behind this was the growth of a specific business lexicon in late nineteenth-century Russia, in which words barbarous to the Russian ear were well represented, and which overturned ideas of *kul'turnost'* that were widely held in the Russian intelligentsia.

One manifestation of the changes was a shift in the etiquette of the business letter. Flowery formulae of epistolary deference, the props of a politeness culture that dated back to the early days of Westernization in the reign of Peter the Great, were replaced by new and specific locutions; the business letter now articulated its aims far more directly. The change becomes almost comically evident if one juxtaposes the following two letters. The first comes from a general letter-writing manual published in 1791, whilst the second is taken from a guide to Russian commercial correspondence published in 1916. For the sake of maximally effective comparison, letters touching on similar subjects have been chosen. The first is a response to a request from a business associate for the extension of a loan, the second a demand that the sum covered by a bouncing cheque should be remitted to a creditor forthwith:

1. Reply of another lender to a letter like no. 25.
You are ruined, and now your desire is to ruin others. Was that what I expected when I made you loans of money and goods, and over a period of several years at that? Is this the gratitude you offer me for my pains? What consolation is it to me that it was your elevated ambitions that brought you down? I have long been aware that all that aims high must soon be destined to plummet; but you were able to soothe me by flattery, assuring me that you had reliable support for your efforts, and so on. —Do not expect that I shall in any way consent to your suggestion; but either return to each what he is due in full, or prepare to give account of all your actions at a court of law. I have also applied to Mr B... for his reactions on this matter; he is of course certain to share my opinions; if by some chance he should happen not to share them, then let each follow his own inclinations; for my part I shall never be persuaded to accept the great loss to which you refer in your letter.
I remain, Sir,
Your most undissembling servant,

2. Confidential. Registered Post
                 23 December, 1915
To Mr Fedor Rudnev, Vologda.
To our astonishment, we have today received from the Vologda Branch of the Moscow Merchants' Bank the bill of hand in the sum of 2,345 Roubles (silver) which you issued to us, with a notice that the bill has been protested for non-payment.
   We have the honour to inform you that if a sum to cover the amount of the bill, together with the protest expenses of 23.50 Roubles, is not received by us within ten days, we shall be placed under the necessity of handing the same over for the recovery of the amount and the protest expenses by taking legal proceedings.
   We, however, remain in hope that you will relieve us of this unpleasant necessity, and remain,
Yours very truly,
A. Shatrov and P. Zubov.

The letters are similar not only as to subject-matter, but also in brandishing a threat to take 'legal proceedings', a threat which, however, carries greater weight in the case of the 1915 letter, since Messrs Shatrov and Zubov's business language is akin to contemporary legal language in its exact use of terminology, and also in its impersonality. The anonymous writer of the model 1791 letter, on the other hand, displays an interesting division of identity: he appeals not only to the authority of the law, but also, and more particularly, to the codes of honour that should regulate contact between gentlemen. A high-pathetic emphasis on betrayal of trust is evident in the letter-writer's description of himself as 'your most undissembling servant' (which, unlike 'yours very truly', is not a standard concluding formula), and in the series of reproaches and rhetorical questions of which the first part of the letter is composed.

The emphasis on personal honour as the fundament of business relations that was evident in the commercial-letter formulae set out by Bogdanovich was to continue its existence for a very considerable time in Russian culture. A letter-writing manual produced nearly a century later, in 1882, includes a request for the return of a loan that is far closer, in its phrasing and intonation, to the traditions of 1791 than to those of 1916. The writer, an intermediary rather than the lender himself, respectfully requests a defaulting debtor to return a loan, taking a great deal of time to come to the point, and referring only delicately, and in passing, to the possibility of legal redress. The persistence of the ethics of politeness for the best part of a century is the more remarkable given that the subtitle of the 1882 manual, *samouchitel'* ('teach yourself'), indicates that this book was aimed at merchants, workers, and peasants attempting to do without the services of a scribe, rather than at the members of the aristocracy to whom Bogdanovich had addressed himself in 1791.[54]

In a period of just over thirty years, between 1882 and 1916, business correspondence had changed so much as to be scarcely recognizable. No doubt this was largely the result of contact with the business practices of Western firms; letter-writing formulae were assimilated from Western equivalents, as business lexicon in a more general sense had been: new borrowings such as *akkreditirovat'*, *annulirovat'*, *konosament* (bill of lading), *ambalazh* (*emballage*, that is, packing), *domitsilirovat'*, and even *aktseptirovat'*, joined earlier business terms such as *veksel'*, *aktsiia*, and *arendator*.[55] Exceptionable only in its baldness, the new Russian business lexicon did not offer nearly such obvious material for parody as earlier manifestations of *kantseliarshchina* (officialese), such as the language of legal petitions and civil service memos, had done. However, the peremptory intonations of business correspondence do seem to have sent shock waves across Russian culture, as is suggested by stirrings in two quite different areas: advice on etiquette and debate upon the specifics of the literary language.

Etiquette and Private Life

The first side-effect of business language's new harshness seems to have been an increasing complication and formality in some aspects of private behaviour. Forms of address were now becoming less elaborate in some respects. Forward-thinking aristocrats, such as Lev Tolstoi, preferred to be addressed by name and patronymic, rather than as 'count' or 'your highness'; the deferential particle -*s*—a contraction of *sudar'*, *sudarynia* (sir or madam)—was no longer in use among social equals. Other elements in social intercourse, however, had become more complicated. The late nineteenth and early twentieth century saw the publication of books on etiquette and behaviour manuals in much larger numbers than had formerly been the case in Russia, and these manuals also manifest a change in orientation. Whilst the advice on courtesy in the abstract, and its moral underpinnings, could be taken straight from the translations of French and German behaviour books published in the 1780s and 1790s, there is now a new stress on the material culture that is essential to the communication of refinement. Alongside counsel on deportment at table, one now finds advice on place-settings and the appropriate contents of every well-conducted person's sideboard (silver, or at the very least white metal knives and forks, porcelain plates, and one salt-cellar for every two place-settings). Yet the interior of the house is to be decorated in a discreetly opulent manner, which only whispers of the very considerable sums that have been expended:

> The boudoir should contain a writing-desk, a work-table for needlework and embroidery, and relaxing low divans and armchairs, as well as those countless small objects that, depending on the taste and requirements of the lady of the house, contribute so much to comfort and which it would take too long to enumerate here . . .
>
> Plants and flowers are one of the most attractive decorations for a room. A single big plant whose beauty has not been impaired by the restricted circulation of air, a screen covered in plush, or a flower-vase always create a pleasant impression . . .
>
> Upon the writing-desk should be placed small, but tastefully selected, knick-knacks of metal, porcelain, or bronze, and of elegant manufacture.
>
> This is also the proper place for a carefully chosen small library of ladies' books.[56]

As the decor of early twentieth-century films, and the collection of turn-of-the-century objects in the Museum of the History of St Petersburg, indicate, such directives on the *bon ton* of interiors were taken very seriously. The elaborate Victorian and Edwardian fashions of plush portières and screens, the lace curtains and the antimacassars, the lumpish fireplaces and elephantine sideboards, all made their appearance in Russia as well, suiting the English suburban-style dachas and *kottedzhi* in which they were located, though the English emphasis on comfort was less frequently exported. Harry Smith, scion of a British expatriate family, recalled the house of the plutocratic Morozov family as dauntingly museum-like: 'there were so many costly ornaments that it was impossible to walk about freely'. Naturally, the food that was served on the heavy dining-tables also veered away from simplicity: for their part, cookbooks of the day updated established classics, such as beef à la Stroganov, incorporating a wider range of ingredients and more elaborate methods of preparation.[57]

Decoration of the self was a matter requiring just as much thought; here, too, great effort had to be expended on dodging the Scylla of ostentation, whilst also managing to slip past the Charybdis of insufficiency. Besides advice on entering rooms and making conversation, hints on how to dress were now given by behaviour manuals. Suitably for an age which saw the publication of the first Russian fashion glossy, *Damskii mir* (*Ladies' World*), there was a proliferation of garments and accessories. Each part of the day required a different attire, and a lady, the manuals pointed out, should have gloves and shoes to match each different ensemble, at breakfast, lunch, tea, and dinner. For all the considerable financial outlay required by this, however, there was a taboo on obviously expensive items, such as jewellery (to be kept for balls and banquets), and gentlemen were to confine themselves to watches, pearl studs, and discreet tie-pins.

One function of etiquette guides, as has often been pointed out in the case of their Western counterparts, was the education of Russian 'new money' into the ways of Russian 'old money' (and also, no less importantly, to educate Russian 'new money' on how to adapt itself to Western tastes in clothes and furnishings). But the emphasis on elaborate rituals and behavioural practices, on the need to construct an edifice of gentility, can also be seen as a way of emphasizing the division between office and drawing-room, work and home. As business rituals became balder, so domestic rituals expanded and proliferated; as business ethics increasingly forbade time-wasting, so the proper wasting of time at home became more and more important. Behaviour manuals also reflected, and helped to construct, a world in which homogenization of taste was increasingly evident. As members of the Russian royal family had their rooms decorated in the peacock-feather style of the bourgeois-Bohemian department store Liberty of London, and built houses that resembled vast versions of the villas of Ascot or Dahlem, so lower-class Russians, bettering themselves, invested in lace curtains, pot plants, and sometimes even household pets, and insisted that they were addressed by the polite, plural form of the verb.[58]

Discussions of the Literary Language

Given that the Russian intelligentsia had since the 1840s, and more particularly the 1860s, championed ascetic self-sacrifice in the service of social and political renewal, another effect of the elaboration of manners was to strengthen the association, in the minds of intellectual Russians, between the simple life and political or aesthetic probity. As an ethic of bourgeois genteelism increasingly made itself felt amongst the Russian rich, whether aristocrats or financial magnates, and amongst those of the Russian poor who had the resources and the opportunity, so Russian writers and other artists imagined utopias distinguished by rational simplicity and plainness of behaviour.[59] Conversely, as business language inclined more and more to terseness, indeed harshness, discussions of literature, most particularly poetry, underlined the right of artistic language not to say what it meant concisely and directly. In his essay of 1909, 'On Contemporary Lyricism', the poet and critic Innokentii Annenskii articulated this point obliquely:

> Every branch of knowledge seems to want to free itself from the shackles of metaphor, the mythological nets of speech—not in the cause of stylistic elegance, of course, but in order to escape into terminology, soundlessness, letter-writing, Morse code. What could it do—just tell me—with poetry, that singing genius of the world, which assures it of Proteus's eternal existence and of the immortality of legend, forever created anew?

And who would have any use for unsystematic philosophy, or all the more for poetry that refuses to be personal, irrational, divinely unpredictable?[60]

Annenskii, a schoolmaster and the author of academic articles, is concerned in the first place with a contrast between scholarly or scientific discourse ('branches of knowledge') and poetry. But his opposition of 'the shackles of metaphor, the mythological nets of speech' (themselves, of course, mythical figures of speech, with their suggestions of Prometheus in the first instance, and Venus and Mars trapped by Vulcan's net in the second), and 'Morse code' has (perhaps unconscious) relevance to the new prominence of business language too. '*Kratkost', iasnost' i prostota*' (brevity, clarity, and simplicity) was the triad of virtues preached by manuals of business correspondence, and, as one such manual sternly warned, 'The man of commerce must on no account attempt to shine, in his letters, with *recherché* phrases; they are quite superfluous and offend against the simplicity requisite in correspondence.'[61]

Annenskii's insistence in 'On Contemporary Lyricism' on the need for a poetic language that was 'mythic' not in terms of its references to esoteric legends taken from Greek and Latin culture, but because it was at once personal and universal, and so quite obviously opposed to the impersonal and specific languages of scholarship and commerce, is an early example of the growing sensitivity, in Russian poetry and poetics around 1910, not only to the importance of formal considerations within literature, but also to the literary language's place within the stratification of language in Russian society as a whole. The first phenomenon, the revival of a concern with form, can be seen as a return to the preoccupations expressed by the Russian romantics, and a rebellion against the content-led views more or less uniformly expressed by Russian critics between 1840 and 1900, as a result of the radical movement's almost total domination of critical discourse. But the second phenomenon, discussion of literary language's relations with other types of language, its need to differentiate itself from them, acquired a new urgency and a new complexity in the early twentieth century. Rather than relating the language of poetry to 'society conversation', as the followers of Karamzin did, or to 'the language of the Russian people', as the associates of Admiral Shishkov—the so-called 'archaists'—had, the early twentieth-century theorists of poetry insisted on literature's autonomous status, its separateness from every other type of linguistic activity, an exclusivity which was, paradoxically, held to make it more 'universal' than any other type of language. In a key manifesto for the times, Mikhail Kuzmin called for the 'clarity' also demanded in commercial communications; but by qualifying it with the word 'sublime', he prefigured that the 'everyday' referentiality of post-symbolism would apply itself to the world of parks, cathedrals, and flowerbeds, rather than to that of banks, factories, and false cuffs.[62]

Here it is important to state the limitations of the argument expressed so far. It would of course be absurd to suggest that the axis around which Russian culture revolved between 1881 and 1921 was a distaste for the language used in business letters. But, as we shall see, the symbolic aspects of commercial culture did in fact play at least as large a role in Russian interpretations of contemporaneity as any direct engagement with the implications of commercialization in a strictly economic sense. Russian writers and thinkers at the turn of the century had, in any case, every incentive to think of commercial language and commercial culture as degraded, given that they were products of a school system which had, between 1860 and 1900, favoured education in the humanities over vocational training. The prestigious *gimnazii*, high schools whose curriculum was based around the teaching of the classics, acted as feeder institutions for the universities and the professions; the same role was adopted by a number of equally well-regarded private institutions (for example, the Tenishev and Gurevich schools in St Petersburg). A much lower social place was occupied by another form of high school, the *real'naia gimnaziia* (or *real'naia shkola*), whose curriculum had a bias towards maths and sciences; a third type of institution, the *kommercheskoe uchilishche* (commercial school), which acted as elementary and secondary school combined, had a catchment of children from the merchant and lower classes, whose caste association with trade it had originally been designed to further. However, the early years of the twentieth century witnessed a volte-face in official educational policy, which now began taking vocational education far more seriously. By 1912, there were 465 institutions in the Russian Empire (excluding Finland) offering commercial studies, with a total of 96,838 pupils (including 18,818 women), as against only 10 commercial institutions in 1894. As the effortless superiority, both numerical and cultural, of *gimnaziia* and university graduates came under threat, it was small wonder that sensitivity towards the prominence of 'half-educated' businesspeople should become increasingly evident.[63]

Representations of the Commercial City

If discussions of poetic language can be hypothesized as, in part, an unconscious response to the new dominance of commercial language (which was a great deal more of a novelty in Russian culture than academic discourse, this latter having begun to emerge in the early years of the nineteenth century), there were many intellectual responses to the commercialization of Russia (as it was seen) that were both conscious and overt. The first and most typical reaction was a condemnation of capitalist activity as 'non-Russian'.[64] Hostility to capitalism was most particularly evident in discussions of the effects of industrialization on Russian villages, the standard line being that migrancy had at one and the same time sapped the human resources of the peasantry, and led to a corruption of traditional values by infecting village culture with the rapacious cynicism of town-dwellers. Such views were propounded by large numbers of essays and pieces of realist fiction published in the last two decades of the nineteenth century, and the first two decades of the twentieth. In Tolstoi's late story *Master and Man* (*Khoziain i rabotnik*, 1896), a substantial episode only tangentially related to the main plot shows the two central characters, the merchant Brekhunov and his worker Nikita, visiting the household of an extended family. The self-sufficient peasant community which Tolstoi had celebrated nearly twenty years earlier in

Anna Karenina is on the point of decay. Several sons are now working in Moscow: one who remains at home has absorbed city tastes in terms of his pastimes (he has an untutored interest in books which Tolstoi represents sardonically); the women are at loggerheads and pushing for the break-up of the household; no one any longer heeds the head of the formerly patriarchal household. A similar interpretation of the decline of peasant well-being, this time in actuality rather than in prospect, is given in the populist woman writer Valentina Dmitrieva's 1896 memoir 'Round the Villages' ('Po derevniam'), a study of the appalling poverty and degradation evident in some southern Russian villages in the years after the famine of 1891–2, and also in Aleksandr Engelgardt's *Letters from the Country*, a memoir originally published in the journal *Russkii vestnik* between 1872 and 1887.[65] Perhaps the most striking representation of the corruption of the 'Russian people' by capitalist culture, though, comes from the pen of the supposedly non-committal Chekhov, whose story 'In the Ravine' ('V ovrage', 1900) represents an entrepreneurial peasant household in a rural industrial settlement as a nightmarish haunt of avarice, sexual misdemeanour, and eventually murder.

This is not to suggest that there was no plausibility in populist representations of Russian peasants as victims of the greed of the merchant middle-men (or women) who purchased their goods and crops, and of factory-owners' exploitative work practices. The ethnographical articles and stories of the late nineteenth and early twentieth centuries published in Russian journals reflected more than their authors' prejudices about change in the countryside; the problems of drunkenness, wife-beating, and malnutrition that they depict are attested in oral history sources too, and representations in fiction were frequently based on the personal experiences of authors who had worked in the countryside on philanthropic missions aimed at alleviating the suffering that they described. The ideological charge of populist representations is evident less at the level of the phenomena described (though selection processes had of course gone on here), than at the level of their interpretation. For example, many Russian radicals who commented on village culture attribute the collapse of patriarchal family structures to pressure from women in the household (a plausible enough observation). But they see the women as the instruments of urbanized social decadence and avarice, rather than associating the atomization with the exploitation of younger women in extended families whose horrendous realities they themselves, ironically, so frequently recorded. As Engelgardt put it in the seventh of his *Letters from the Country*:

> But suddenly the old man dies. . . . The babas begin to eat away at their husbands. 'It's slavery to work for someone else's children.' 'Look, Senka left the land, hired himself out to the lord as a herdsman, he receives seventy-five roubles with meals and he sets his wife up in a little house. She doesn't reap, she doesn't plough, she sits like a lady and does spinning just for herself,' and so on and so forth. The force which united the family and held it together in one household has cracked.

The conclusion is that the subordination of women is necessary if the collective (whose status as an efficient economic entity is never questioned) is not to disintegrate: 'I have decidedly observed that those villages where babas rule, where babas have mastered the men, live more poorly, work worse, do not farm as well as those where men are the masters.'[66]

Even in the relatively 'pure' domain of the Russian village, commercialism was accounted a force with almost occult powers of corruption (and as with witchcraft, women were assumed to be the first objects of Satanic seduction). In depictions of the city, which the neoclassical pastoral tradition eagerly borrowed by Russians since the late eighteenth century had in any case conventionally portrayed as a sink of vice, the wickedness of commercial culture was naturally still more frequently referred to, though there was often an odd vagueness in depictions (perhaps because the case was so generally accepted that its rightness seemed self-evident). Anti-pastoral could be as distant from reality as pastoral: early twentieth-century Russian representations of the city were often as little concerned with actual work practices and living conditions as the idyllic rural visions of the eighteenth century had been. Sober depictions of the actualities of poverty as evident in slum tenements, unsafe and unsanitary work conditions, alcoholism, child prostitution, infanticide, and the desertion of small children were set down in the essays of philanthropists, but the authors of literature often preferred to give their critiques from the mouth of Hell rather than elaborating the horrors of the inferno itself. The ambitions of industrialists, managers, shop assistants, and hairdressers to acquire a veneer of culture were the subject of many derisive portrayals in literature, and the ragged, emaciated figures of factory workers might be sketched, but the intricacies of machine operation, industrial relations, and wage-bargaining, the stuff of industrial life itself, went largely unobserved. In Chekhov's 'A Doctor's Case-Notes' ('Sluchai iz praktiki', 1898), for example, the physician-protagonist records the external appearance of a factory, plus the vulgar interior of the owners' house; these two halves, placed together, acquire the sense of an adequate representation of the whole of industrial culture. For his part, Aleksandr Blok, in the early poem 'The Factory' ('Fabrika'), again represents the industrialization of the city through the metonym of the factory's outside walls. And his famous short poem 'Night. Street. Streetlight. Pharmacy' ('Noch'. Ulitsa. Fonar'. Apteka', 1912) moves, in a series of equally carefully selected metonyms, from eternal verities through the historically dignified realities of cities to the ugly innovations of the modern commercialized street (electric light and 'pharmacy' less as haven for the sick than as a place where relief for the exhausted half-men of the modern city may be purchased).

A comparable use of a rather different metonym is to be found in Kuprin's novel *The Pit* (*Iama*, 1908), the tale of a provincial bordello full of pimps and prostitutes as given to 'philosophizing' as the characters in a Chekhov play, and where the selling of human bodies seems at most marginal to the organization of wearisomely discursive symposia upon morality. The 'pit' of the title rapidly emerges as a metaphor for Russian society (and intellectual society at that) in its imbrication with commercialized sexuality, rather than as the setting for a dissection of prostitution *per se*. In Tolstoi's short story *The Kreutzer Sonata* (*Kreitserova sonata*), written two decades earlier in 1889, society had been described by the crazy *raisonneur* narrator, Pozdnyshev, as a *maison de tolérance*; in *The Pit* a *maison de tolérance* figures as society. Neither approach allows for any dissection of the commodification of sexuality as such; Tolstoi's short story is, as well as far more narratorially sophisticated, a much more profound and wide-ranging attack upon sexual *idées reçues* than Kuprin's lumpy bestseller (the question of whether Pozdnyshev is *raisonneur* or dangerous crank remains open), but *The Kreutzer Sonata*'s wrath is for all that directed against the celebration of sexual pleasure in all non-Christian and secular societies, rather than against the commercialization of pleasure in *fin de siècle* Russia as such.

Literary Culture and 'Boulevardization'

The conversion of motifs from commercial and industrial culture into literary tropes allowed Russian writers to express their (perfectly genuine) concern about social and economic transformation, whilst keeping personal anxieties at bay, and enforcing their own authority, by failing to question the extent of literary culture's own involvement with the commercial culture that it critiqued. Another aspect of this defensiveness could be seen in the fact that the economic props of literary culture were seldom, if ever, mentioned. Though some turn-of-the-century writers (notably Chekhov) made a great deal of money out of their publications, the profitability of writing as a profession was a taboo issue; though several 'new arts' journals were funded by money that had been made in industry, the issue of sponsorship was seldom raised. Another important phenomenon passed over in silence was that of literary image. When Sergei Makovskii, the editor of *Apollon*, accepted work by the exotic Hispano-French countess 'Cherubina de Gabriak' (in fact written by a home-grown poet, Elizaveta Vasil'eva, whom Makovskii had rejected under her own name), this was the subject of much irony. But the equally powerful part played by image in reception of the work of more famous poets—such as Aleksandr Blok or Anna Akhmatova—went unanalysed (indeed, this feature of 'Silver Age' literary life still awaits detailed commentary). Untainted (in its own account) by commercialism, the literary establishment was, also in its own perception, utterly distinct from the 'trivial' products of commercial publishers ('*lubok* fiction', as it was contemptuously described), and also from such popular entertainments as music-halls, funfairs, circuses, and other forms of paid performance, which were seen by commentators as scarcely less significant evidence of the evils of commercialism than factories or brothels.

Unlike their colleagues in the 'illegitimate' theatre or the editorial offices of cheap newspapers, members of the Russian literary establishment were disinclined, then, to celebrate making money in its own right. Attitudes to commercialism did, at one level, create a division between popular and elite culture. However, there were also deep-lying forces that undermined the division. The activists of elite culture themselves, whether they recognized it or not, belonged to a world that was becoming more and more commercialized in the first decades of the twentieth century. Up to the turn of the century, the standard method of publication for most Russian literature, at any rate for fiction, was serialization in the so-called 'thick journals', literary and political monthlies such as *Vestnik Evropy* (*European Herald*), *Russkaia mysl'* (*Russian Thought*), and *Russkoe bogatstvo* (*Riches of Russia*). After 1900, however, as the publication industry expanded, separate editions of novels and other fiction proliferated. Verbitskaia's *The Keys to Happiness*, Aleksandr Artsybashev's scandalous tale of a Russian provincial disciple of Nietzsche, *Sanin* (1907), Mikhail Kuzmin's account of Platonic homosexual love in *Wings* (*Kryl'ia*, 1907), and Lidiia Zinov'eva-Annibal's short story about two lesbian lovers, *Thirty-Three Freaks* (*Tridtsat' tri uroda*, 1907) were only the most notorious examples of fictional works that bypassed publication in the thick journals altogether, though all were by authors who could have (and in some cases who previously had) published in 'respectable' literary journals. For the first time since the early nineteenth century, Russian authors again had a choice between prestigious, but not necessarily remunerative publication in a literary journal, or remunerative, but not necessarily prestigious publication in a separate edition whose print run was likely to ensure them financial, if not literary, success.

The natural result was a significant thematic congruence between at least some of the fictions produced by avant-garde writers, and those that circulated for a wider and more impecunious public in cheap books and cinema melodramas. In what has been termed 'boulevard culture'—the urbanized literature and cinema of the early twentieth century—themes of sexual deviance and gender fluidity were ubiquitous. Adultery, sado-masochism, incest, and homosexuality were only the most obvious of such themes. The 'new woman', a heroine liberated from conventional constraints on behaviour, appeared in every level of fictional creation, from those early poems by Anna Akhmatova which show an unchaperoned woman dining in a restaurant with a male admirer, and the lyric plays of Aleksandr Blok, or the memoirs of the painter Mariia Bashkirtseva, to the novels of Verbitskaia and her colleague Evdokiia Nagrodskaia, or cinema melodramas such as Evgenii Bauer's *A Life for a Life* (*Zhizn' za zhizn'*, 1916), in which the two daughters of a woman factory-owner both fall in love with the same man, a silver-tongued, self-serving prince.

There was also a growing assimilation between technical and artistic standards across the 'high' and 'low' arts. The sheer amount of money available to impresarios meant, for example, that many popular theatrical shows of the 1910s displayed a much greater sophistication than their predecessors, making full use of better lighting and new mechanical procedures; the production values of some music-halls were undoubtedly higher than those of the more amateurish avant-garde cabarets. Bronislava Nijinska, whose father was a notable *maître de ballet*, recalled in her memoirs that he was earning more on tour in provincial fairgrounds and pleasure gardens than he would have done as an employee of the imperial theatres.[67] Once the Russian cinema got going, it, too, made use of expensive and sophisticated sets, glamorous costumes, and complex techniques. Evgenii Bauer, who was criticized by Eisenstein for making static, 'theatrical' films, certainly broke no conventions of linear narrative (indeed, how could he, as he needed to create them for the Russian cinema?). However, he was an exceptionally talented director, whose scenes are rich in visual interest, using slow approach shots to heighten the effect of carefully posed figure groups, and to tantalize the viewer's desire with visions of remote luxury. Iakov Protazanov was another pre-Revolutionary director making films of considerable cinematic quality as well as popularity. It is true, of course, that other pre-Revolutionary films, especially comedies, could be fairly feeble efforts, indifferently scripted, poorly shot and acted; they represent, one suspects, in flickering black and white the average efforts of a fairground booth or small music-hall. Similarly, whilst there is little to choose, in terms of literary merit, between Kuzmin's *Wings*, a turgid, improbable, and sentimental book by a generally well-regarded writer, and Verbitskaia's *The Keys of Happiness*, a turgid, improbable, and sentimental book by a writer who was widely vilified in her own time and has continued to be so since (and who wrote many much better books), there is a vast gulf in complexity of versification and in choice of lexis between the poetry of Kuzmin and the average music-hall song (though the gulf between the poetry of Kuzmin and the poetry of many of the writers whose work was published by the poetically insensitive editors of many 'thick journals' was equally wide). And if there is evidence that working-class readers enjoyed some modernist writers, such as Leonid Andreev, Aleksandr Blok, Igor' Severianin, or Anna Akhmatova, it is also clear that there were many modernist writers who were not, and never have been, popular outside a narrow circle of highly educated readers (for example, Belyi or Mandel'shtam). For all that, though, the turn of the century did see a growing congruence between intellectual and working-class tastes; this was one reason behind the emergence, in the late nineteenth century, of larger numbers of talented writers from working-class backgrounds than had been seen in Russian literature at any time since the eighteenth century. Fedor Sologub, Maksim Gor'kii, Sergei Esenin, and Nikolai Kliuev are only the better-known examples of an era whose less illustrious alumni included Ivan Pridvorov, pseudonymously 'Dem'ian Bednyi', who was later to become the poet laureate of the early Soviet period.[68]

Populism and the Avant-garde

The reasons for the increasing pluralism in literature lay not only in the effects of 'boulevardization' as an unconscious force in early twentieth-century culture, but also in the conscious and explicit cultivation of 'vulgar' material by the avant-garde writers of the time. Commercialization as a phenomenon in itself, the idea of 'art for sale' in the abstract, might be frowned on, but the products of commercial culture—from gleaming steel machines, aeroplanes, and motorcars to shop signs and high-rise buildings—could be perceived as exciting examples of a new and challenging aesthetic. Admittedly, the Russian avant-garde did not absorb technology quite as readily as its Western counterparts. Use of industrial motifs by writers and painters who wished to celebrate 'modernity' was as selective as the employment of such motifs had been in critiques by realist writers. The cubo-futurist manifestos of 1912–14, with their famous references to 'throwing Pushkin overboard from the ship of modernity', or the paintings of Larionov and Goncharova, in which factory chimneys or looms were used for decorative purposes, were typical of early avant-garde work. The practice of poets and painters, in the meantime, payed only lip-service to the 'machine-age' aesthetic that was evoked by the programmatic documents. Until the founding of the constructivist movement in 1921, eulogies of individual machines were far more common than commitment to a true functionalist aesthetic.[69] Unlike the vorticists, whose paintings were modelled directly on the hard edges, smooth surfaces, and relentless momentum of machines, Russian futurist works usually had the homeliness of cottage gardens: the intersecting planes suggested sprouting vegetation rather than the relentless grinding of cogwheels or the inexorable pulsing of conveyor belts. In Goncharova's painting *The Woman Weaver* (*Tkachikha*, c.1913), for example, the great drum of the loom resembles a tree-trunk, its sprockets and stretchers aspidistra leaves, and even the light fitting looks more like a child's sketch of the sun peeping out from clouds than the latest technological gadget. Though the figure of the weaver herself is totally absorbed into the delineation of the machine, the painting suggests restful harmony; this is symbiosis rather than reification.

Domestication of the urban by means of animal imagery (buses as elephants, cranes as swans) is also found in what are perhaps the most original literary evocations of the city before 1921, the stories of Evgenii Zamiatin, whose visit to England in 1916–17 had provided him with suggestive material for fantasizing the city of the future, from underground railways to Zeppelins. Otherwise, myths of the city essentially remained those of French symbolism (looming buildings, 'the scent of lilacs and petrol', absinthe addicts in cafes) or of Russian romanticism (yellow fog and yellow buildings, public monuments as the symbols and fetishes of political authority). Representations of the machine as such rarely rose much above the level of jejune whimsy. In 1914, for example, the poet Vasilii Kamenskii produced the following celebration of his experience as a pioneer of aviation, the latest craze in the Russian capital; as the poet rises on his propellered Pegasus through the clouds, he defies a death visualized in the hackneyed terms of the *poètes maudits*:

КАКофоНию ДУШи
МоТОрОВ <u>симфонию</u>
----- ф р р р р р р р р р
это Я это Я
футур=Ст-ПЕСНЕБОЕ́Ц и
ПИЛОТ-АВИАТОр*)
ВАСИЛИЙКАМЕНСКИЙ
       эЛаАсТичНыМ пРопеЛерОм
ВВИНТИЛ ОБлАкА
киНув ТАМ
       за визит
ДряБлой смерти КОКЕТКЕ
       из ЖалоСти сшитое
ТАнгОВое МаНтО и
       ЧУЛКИ с
       ПАНТАЛОНАМИ

*) диплом ИМПЕРАТОРСКОГО всероссийского Аэроклуба № 67 выдан 9 ноября 1911 г.

[CACOPHOny of the SOUl
symphony of the MoTOrS
-----f r r r r r r r r r r
It's ME iT's ME
futur=ST-SONGWARRIOR and
PILOT-AVIATOr*)
VASILII-KAMENSKII
    with my eLaAsTiC pRopeLleR
WINDING UP the CLoUdS
flInGinG DOWN
    as payment
to death that FroWsY TART
    a TAngO MaNTeaU
made of PitY
    anD STOCKINGS anD
    PANTALOONS
*) Diploma of the IMPERIAL Russian Aeroclub no. 67 issued 9 November 1911.][70]

Much the same selectivity was evident in Russian writers' and painters' orientation to the 'commercialized' popular arts of Russian cities. Because commercial art was so widely lambasted as 'vulgar', it had considerable appeal to the avant-garde's emphasis on art as *épatage*. Sharing the perceptions of their conservative colleagues, but standing traditional aesthetic values on their heads, avant-garde artists valued the commercial arts precisely for their crudity and harshness, and also for their associations with the coarse and 'primitive' life of the Russian streets. As Eisenstein and his fellow 'eccentrics' wrote in 1922: 'A Pinkerton [cheap detective story] cover is worth more than the whole of Picasso.' About fifteen years earlier than this, the texts of fairground theatre, of street ballads, and cheap cabaret acts, the motifs of shop signs, painted wooden carts, and popular prints, had become a central reference point for many Russian modernist writers and painters, inspiring such famous texts as Aleksandr Blok's playlet *The Puppet Booth* (*Balaganchik*, 1906), Stravinskii and Benois's ballet *Petrouchka* (*Petrushka*, 1911), Larionov's ballet *The Fool* (*Shut*, 1921), and paintings and graphic works by Dobuzhinski, Sudeikin, Goncharova, Larionov, Lebedev, Grigor'ev, and Benois.

Inspiring as such modernists found the commercial culture of the streets, however, their enthusiastic imitations were in some ways as distant from their material as the negative appraisals set out in the commentaries of radicals hostile to the supposedly corrupting influence of commercialized material. The Russian peasants and workers who were the main consumers of cheap popular entertainments were naturally not inclined to see these as 'barbarian', 'vulgar', 'shocking', or even 'exotic': they were simply an accessible way of passing the time. Further, Russian writers and artists became interested in the specificity of urban popular culture at precisely the moment when that specificity began to come under threat. As Russian workers exchanged traditional peasant wear (red shirts and baggy trousers, sarafans and blouses) for mass-produced, Western-style suits, hats, and dresses, so artists and writers adopted 'Russian shirts', wide trousers, and billowing peasant skirts as 'rational' workwear. The hiatus between the actual culture of the streets and its literary or artistic reflections was also evident in the fact that artists and writers tended to prefer mass-cultural forms that they saw as 'traditional', rather than those that were actually popular amongst the working class in their own time. So Benois, in designing the sets for *Petrouchka*, turned to 1830s and 1840s engravings of the St Petersburg fairground, rather than studying the street Petrushka players of his own day. And such genuinely popular, but artistically unappealing, phenomena as the cheap newspapers of the 'yellow press' (for example, the *Gazeta-kopeika*, with its true crime stories and sexual scandals), or the penny-dreadful novels of the cities, found no imitators. The popular literature of the late seventeenth and early eighteenth century appealed to some (such as Mikhail Kuzmin and Fedor Sologub, who used popular motifs in some of their dramas); the popular literature of the early twentieth century interested no one.

Distinctions between Verbal and Visual Arts

Fastidious attitudes to street culture were particularly evident in the verbal arts, as opposed to the visual arts; turn-of-the-century writers continued the tradition first developed by Russian radicals in the 1860s, according to which the commercial entertainments of cities were held to exemplify the degradation of national-popular culture. Of all popular art forms, only the cinema escaped this general disapproval. With historical hindsight, this exception seems paradoxical, given that cinema was the first properly industrialized and effectively commercialized art form; but it is important to realize that it was not so perceived in turn-of-the-century Russia. Although the owners of 'electric theatres', and later the owners of Russian studios, film-makers, and silent-film stars enjoyed considerable financial success, the cinema's primary importance for commentators was that this art form, whose admirers ran the whole gamut of Russian society, from the Tsar down to street urchins, promised at last to realize the social consensus through art for which socialists and mystics had alike been longing. In his essay 'The Cinematograph', Andrei Belyi articulated this idea with particular insistence. He opposed the early cinema, with its truly democratic character, both to the mystical symbolist notion of spiritual renewal through a revival of classical tragedy (as advocated by Viacheslav Ivanov), and to the tainted collectivism of the popular theatre, either in its original form, or as adapted by symbolist poets, such as Blok in his *Fairground Booth*:

> [The cinematograph] is the place where those disillusioned in the possibility of unification through love or literature may enjoy unification. . . . The cinematograph is the democratic theatre of the future, a *balagan* [fairground theatre] in the noblest and most elevated sense of the word. Anything you like but a *Balagan-'chik'*[playing on the title of Blok's play]. . . . I discovered the cinema by chance, after leaving a dinner in Paris organized by French writers who had all been blabbering the most vulgar nonsense imaginable. I wanted to wash the gluey residue from my brain, so I went to a café-concert. True, it was a considerable improvement on literary chat,

but all that hysterical emotion . . . who needs it? So off I went wandering down the brightly-lit boulevards. I arrived at the cinematograph by accident, but I left it as though it had been a church, with a prayer in my heart: they were showing a religious procession, and from a dark corner a pale French lady with a wonderful dramatic soprano voice was fervently singing the Ave Maria.[71]

Not all Russian observers were as unintentionally comical in their enthusiasm as Belyi, but almost all of them, from the writer Leonid Andreev to Lenin, did believe that the cinema had the potential to be a truly and newly democratic art form. Celebration of it was ubiquitous, even in poetry, the most exclusive of the arts. Blok, Mandel′shtam, and Ada Chumachenko were only three of many poets whose works used the flickering melodramas of the early 'electric theatres' as metaphors for the inconstant, seductive pleasures of city life in general.[72]

Otherwise, however, arts and entertainments perceived as 'commercial' were rarely cited directly, unless for the purpose of parody. Typical was 'Pchelkin the Artist' ('Zhivopisets Pchelkin', 1908) by V. I. Gorianskii (1888–1944), a satirical poet working for the intellectual journal *Satirikon* (Satyricon), which published many comic ventriloquizations of lower-class voices ('The Song of the Lovesick Hairdresser', and so on). Typically, Gorianskii's piece is presented through the admiring eyes of a half-educated philistine, whose artistic experience so far extends to the works of Repin, a famous realist painter hostile to the avant-garde whose paintings were widely displayed in museums of national art, such as the Alexander III Museum (founded in 1898), and the Tret′iakov Gallery (founded in 1875). The whole joke lies in the fact that the speaker not only knows what he likes, but likes anything he sees:

> У кого к чему способности есть,
> Кому шофером быть, кому стричь бороду.
> А у Пчелкина вывески — глаз не отвесть,
> Ходи да рассматривай по городу.
>
> . . .
>
> Табачная лавка — тропический сюжет:
> Арап на столе ли, на верблюде ли,
> Там гирлянды висят монополь-манжет,
> Там скорняк — и на вывеске скачут пудели.
> Куда тебе Репин? Хорош, да не то!
>
> [Every person has something he can do,
> Like shaving beards, or driving cars around,
> And you should see them signs that Pchelkin paints too,
> Just go and look: they're all over the town.
>
> . . .
>
> Something nice and tropical for the tobacco shop,
> A Moor sitting on a table, or on a camel's back;
> Or a lovely white garland all made of false cuffs,
> Or poodles for a furriers, curly all over and black.
> Eat your heart out, Repin! You can't do half as well.][73]

Even parodistic citations of this kind were relatively rare. Commoner was the evocation of popular-cultural material for decorative purposes (as in Briusov's poem 'The Fairground Booths' ('Balagany', 1915), which celebrates the bizarre freak-shows of the Russian fairground), or as 'degraded' background for a lyric or dramatic protagonist's visionary experiences of an elevated 'other world' (as in Blok's poem 'The Strange Woman' ('Neznakomka', 1906)). The most famous street-culture-based verbal text, Blok's *The Fairground Booth*, still further extends the tradition of employing street culture as mere background by confecting a high-symbolist fiction of a marginalized alter ego as languishing, moon-faced Pierrot, in conflict with an assertive Harlequin for the heart of a perfidious Columbine. The wordless marionette drama of the fairground becomes a vehicle for a poetic *crise de foi*, and the optimistic transformation pantomime transmutes into an exceedingly pessimistic representation of the self as inadequate and unimpressive, but still intellectualized, mask. Russian writers of later generations, most particularly such members of the OBERIU (the absurdist Association for Real Art) as Kharms or Vvedenskii, were to exploit the language of the streets in order to craft texts that genuinely were shocking in their dead-pan allusions to unmentionable violence, but Alfred Jarry's *Ubu* plays did not inspire equivalents, at least amongst the published works of his Russian contemporaries.[74]

The exuberant fusions of high and low culture, the exotic and the banal, supported by a zestful use of pretentious neologisms, made Igor' Severianin perhaps the most popular early twentieth-century Russian poet. Poems such as 'Lilac Flavoured Ice Cream' ('Morozhenoe iz sireni', 1913) or 'Pineapples in Champagne' ('Ananasy v shampanskom', 1915) drew cleverly on the urban lust for novel forms of gratification; that Severianin touched a nerve can be seen in the fact that his work inspired cabaret songs and even films. But his celebration had inverse results so far as his literary colleagues were concerned. After 1914, in particular, his success was seen as an indication of imminent catastrophe for high art. For Gumilev, writing in the post-symbolist arts magazine *Apollon*, Severianin was the herald of a 'barbarian invasion', speaking in 'newspaper Volapük' to those who 'talk of love to their hairdresser and brilliantine to their mistress', and accessible to this broad public as Goethe and Pushkin (and by implication Gumilev himself) were not. Though conceded to be 'broadening the boundaries of art', Severianin is at the same time a poet whose writings conveniently emphasize, for Gumilev, the necessary existence of those boundaries, standing as they do 'outside art altogether with their cheap theatricalism'. A rather similar instance was another popular writer, the short-story and sketch author Nadezhda Teffi, whose fame even led to her having a brand of chocolates named after her. Teffi's excursions into poetry were slammed (Briusov branded her collection *Seven Jewels* (*Sem' ognei*) as 'paste every one'), and the literary sophistication of Teffi's stories, universally described as 'entertaining', was seldom recorded, though their supposed appeal to shop assistants frequently was.[75]

Only amongst émigré writers after the Revolution, once they had become part of an elegiacally evoked lost world, did popular arts regularly begin to figure as the objects of art, and also as artistic objects. This was above all the case in émigré memoirs of childhood (such as Nabokov's *Speak, Memory*, or the autobiographies of the painters Benois and Dobuzhinskii), in which nostalgia for lost Russia was reinforced by the established Russian tradition of representing the gentry childhood as idyll.[76]

Matters in the visual arts were rather different, since here a receptivity towards popular material was evident from a far earlier stage. True, hostility towards such material was sometimes articulated. The poet and painter Maksimilian Voloshin was exceedingly scathing about the technical crudity and artistic ineptitude of the primitivist 'Donkey's Tail' group.[77] But painters were, as a group, far closer to the spirit of 'cheap theatricalism' than their literary counterparts. In Dobuzhinskii's decorations for Petr Potemkin's adaptation of the Petrushka puppet show, staged at the Strand cabaret in 1906, a view of a St Petersburg street, used as backdrop to the booth in which the human puppets performed, not only cites shop decorations (a massive painting of a top-boot, an oversized gilded pretzel, a glazed-looking hairdresser's dummy), but also itself imitates the distortions of linear and aerial perspective characteristic of the shop sign. Still closer to street signs were the early still lifes of Goncharova and Larionov, which imitated the signs hung outside vegetable shops in terms of composition —fruit, vegetables, and objects are scattered arbitrarily in blank space—and in the manner of applying paint—pigment has been dabbed on with a stiff brush, creating blocks of unshaded flat tones. Besides shop signs, avant-garde painters such as Goncharova, Dobuzhinskii, Sudeikin, and Kustodiev were inspired by the *lubok*, Russian popular print, with its crude hand-colouring, strong outlining, and use of semantic perspective (the representation of figures in terms of their narrative importance, rather than according to the principles of perceptual geometry), whose rhyming captions, on the other hand, were imitated by poets only in highly specific cultural contexts (such as the construction of pro-war propaganda in 1914–17, and of pro-revolutionary propaganda thereafter).[78]

The performance arts were just as receptive as the visual arts to citations from 'commercial' pieces (indeed, as the Dobuzhinskii design mentioned above indicates, some of the most innovative appropriations of popular arts were to be seen in work for the theatre). If the verbal effects of the popular theatre had left writers cold, its visual effects were enthusiastically imitated by producers and designers. In Meyerhold's famous staging of Blok's *The Fairground Booth*, indeed, the avant-garde production values were notably at variance with the conventional symbolist aesthetic of the play.

There is abundant evidence, then, that Russian visual artists and theatre directors were far less timid in evoking the commercial world of the Russian streets than their writer colleagues were. The evidence explaining this situation is more elusive. However, one may hypothesize various causes. One may be that Russian secular culture, no doubt as a result of its need to break away from religious culture's emphasis on the sacral nature of the icon, has traditionally valued verbal representation more highly than visual representation. This was reflected in the dominance, in nineteenth- and twentieth-century art, of narrative- and *realia*-based traditions of painting, such as those adhered to by the *Peredvizhniki* (Wanderers), the nationalist and socially conscious group that had dominated Russian painting between 1863 and 1900, and whose most famous representatives

Shop sign for 'cold beer' (properly *kholodnoe pivo*) painted for a Tiflis beer bar by the famous self-taught Georgian sign-painter Niko Pirosmani (1862– 1918).

Pirosmani's work was much admired, and imitated, by the Russian neo-primitivists, such as Mikhail Larionov, who organized the hanging of pictures by Pirosmani and other sign-painters at the Target exhibition in Moscow, 1913. Work by Pirosmani was also displayed at the 'Art of the Peoples of the USSR' exhibitions held in Moscow in 1927 and in 1937 for the tenth and twentieth anniversaries of the Bolshevik Revolution.

were Repin, Surikov, and Kramskoi. It also influenced the symbolism used by the worker movement in Russia: whereas trade unions in the West used visual symbolism on their banners, Russian unions and workers' groups gave prominence to written slogans.[79] In popular entertainments, too, the word appears to have been more highly valued than the image. The peep-show (perspective box) of Western Europe was treasured by its lower-class public because it communicated visual images, but Russian audiences and showmen were far more concerned with the novelty of the comic verbal explication that accompanied the demonstration of the images. Panoramas seem to have been relatively little valued for their own sakes; it was the *son* rather than the *lumière* to which Russians gravitated.

Another, and perhaps more significant, factor, though, was that visual artists (and theatre directors) were themselves involved in the commercial world to a far greater extent than their literary colleagues, since they depended upon individual patrons (or upon theatre audiences) for their survival. Russian writers certainly also felt a need to sell their work, in the sense of publishing it; but the writers and poets who placed their work in avant-garde journals, even if sponsored by *nouveaux riches* looking for respectability, could feel buffered from the vulgar world of money-making by the fact that they invariably had contact with an editor as intermediary. Poets who placed work with *Vesy* (*The Balance*) knew they had to cater to the taste of Briusov, its editor, not to that of Sergei Poliakov, whose inherited industrial wealth allowed the magazine to run. By contrast, painters who sold their work direct to factory-owner collectors were confronted with plutocratic reality through the nature of the transaction itself. Still more was this the case when artists sold their work for overtly commercial purposes, taking advantage of the opportunities available in the huge new advertising industry that sprang up in Russia at the turn of the century. Even the staid 'thick journals' now carried small advertisements not only for books and magazines, but for nostrums purporting to cure pimples, syphilis, impotence, and fatigue; Russian beers, perfumes, cosmetics, ready-to-wear clothing, or cabarets had their contesting merits trumpeted in posters every bit as colourful as those in France, Britain, or America. Well might a guide for British businessmen published in 1917 advise its readers that 'a well-composed advertisement brings good results, even in Russia'.[80] Russian consumers had already grown used to advertising of quality. From the Art and Craft movement artists, such as Bilibin, who produced illuminated *style russe* menus for city dinners, or the architects who designed stations and villas, Russian artists from 1900 were increasingly aware of commercial opportunities, and showed themselves able to exploit them.[81] And, if some literary magazines, such as *Vesy* and *Apollon*, with their vignettes and black-and-white plates, were opulent by the standards of the 'thick journals', or of today's 'little magazines' of poetry, they were humble by comparison with the luxurious standards of the art journals proper, such as *Mir iskusstva* (*World of Art*) and *Zolotoe runo* (*The Golden Fleece*), which regularly carried superb full-page colour reproductions complete with protective veils of tissue, as well as sumptuous black-and-white illustrations and decorations to such literary texts as could be squeezed in between the artworks.

A montage of small ads from the popular illustrated weekly *Niva*, 1899, for branded goods (Einem's cocoa, Ceylon tea, *Armin* beard and moustache lotion, and Leongardi's inks, the last company warning against 'inferior imitations' of its goods), and also Esperanto and handwriting manuals, premium bonds, and a historical novel by Count Salias, *In Old Moscow*.

Typical in the range of goods they promote, the advertisements also illustrate the variety of styles employed, from plain boxes to well-designed and imaginative displays. The first Russian advertising agency, Mettsel's, was set up in 1878, and by the early twentieth century advertising was ubiquitous, though still practically unregulated. According to the Brockhaus–Efron *Encylopaedia*'s 1899 article on advertising (*Reklama*, vol. 52, pp. 527–8), one company advertised its perfume as made from a monastery spring that had rendered incorruptible the bodies of monks buried there. The only dubious claim here, that Ceylon tea is 'very good for the health', pales by comparison.

Generally, too, artists seem to have felt less rancour about their dependence on sponsors' taste than Russian writers have traditionally felt about their
dependence on the whims of readers. In around 1906, for example, Natal′ia
Goncharova paid a visit to Southern Russia in order to design a poster for an agricultural exhibition. She had her own ideas about the composition, but these were
overruled by the sponsor. Rather than dispute the point, Goncharova calmly
altered her original plan:

> She went to Tiraspol′, to an agricultural exhibition for which she'd been commissioned
> to paint posters . . . 'They wanted pedigree cows on them. The client didn't think mine
> suited the landscape. But the main problem was, they didn't suit him because they weren't
> pedigree enough. I wanted skinny-looking, expressive cows, the client insisted on great
> fat ones. So I painted the capitals of columns instead.' (Ionic, off the pillars in the hall.)[82]

Later in her career, too, during the 1930s and 1940s, Goncharova was to recognize commercial pressures, turning increasingly to theatre design and to the
production of flower-paintings, since these genres were then the most market-
able. A similar transition, though in the other direction, was earlier visible in the
work of Serov, who moved from *pleinairisme* in his early easel paintings to the
hauntingly decadent manner most familiar in his famous nude of the dancer Ida
Rubenstein.

That the symbiosis between art and commerce was more tranquil than the
coexistence of literature and commerce was evident, too, in the well-known
fact that the vast majority of important Russian purchasers of adventurous
contemporary art were industrialists or successful merchants. Two of the best-
known of them, Savva Morozov and Ivan Shchukin, directed their tastes (until
the First World War stopped communications) largely towards the purchase
of French art, accumulating important holdings of Gauguin, Cézanne, Picasso,
and Matisse; but other collectors, such as Ivan Morozov and Ivan Riabushinskii,
made important purchases of Russian art, and also furnished Russian architects
with prestigious private commissions. If the artists benefited financially, the purchasers themselves did hardly less well from their transactions: the vigorous,
energetic paintings of the avant-garde, with their strong ties to popular art, far
better represented the vigour and confidence of early twentieth-century Russian
commerce and industry than pallid conventional art would have done. In mid-
nineteenth-century Russia, the conservative tastes of Russian merchants had
been expressed in their preference for figurative art, and most particularly for
family portraits; in the twentieth, the purchase by Riabushinskii and Poliakov
of impressive oils by Larionov was a most impressive statement of the emancipation of merchant taste, and of its new social and cultural dominance. The
owners of factories might select sentimental images of the Russian countryside
in order to sell their goods to the public—images of brawny, bearded ploughmen
appeared as brand symbols on everything from sewing machines to soapflakes
—but their preferred images of their own taste reflected a much more vigorous
and innovative attitude to Russian folk tradition. True as it may be that 'capitalism survives by forcing the majority, whom it exploits, to define their own interests as narrowly as possible', the converse is that the elite can afford, in all senses,

to indulge its interests with magpie-like eclecticism.[83] The jewelled, chased-silver *kovshi* (scoops) made by Russian craftsmen between 1890 and 1917, the perfectly beautiful, perfectly functionless imitations of the humble wooden vessels used by generations of Russian peasants in order to portion out food and grain, are effective symbols of Russian capitalist taste in one of its manifestations, but Goncharova's vintage panels represent another and quite different direction of taste. The white-and-gold, eighteenth-century-revival rooms of Shchukin's Moscow mansion, hung with paintings by Matisse, Gauguin, and Picasso which had been bought from the artists' studios, and in some cases specially commissioned, show that early twentieth-century taste could be schizophrenic in the proper sense of the word: not a division along binary lines, but a shattering into dozens of unreconciled pieces. Shchukin, who made enormous efforts to educate himself in contemporary art (though almost defeated by Picasso's *Les Demoiselles d'Avignon*), and who left his collection in Russia when he emigrated, so that it could be enjoyed by the Russian public, was also an illustration that commercial acumen was not always separable from aesthetic and moral sensibilities that would have done credit to any member of the intelligentsia.[84]

Conclusion: on 'High', 'Low', and the Market

Cultural practices and processes in late imperial Russia cannot be understood outside the context of class and state power. We have seen that the onset of industrialization, urbanization, and money economy caused the authorities, and also a wider swathe of the educated public, to feel that the culture of the urban—and later rural—populace was degenerating. This led, on the one hand, to efforts to 'raise the cultural level of the people' and, on the other, to a drive to eliminate customs deemed to be at odds with modernity and social order. This was a systematic effort to acculturate the popular classes into the national, 'high' culture, and to extirpate backwardness, ignorance, and dissoluteness. The effort seems to have failed as often as it succeeded: the urban and rural masses resisted attempts to change their ways, to dispossess them of what they did not themselves see as backwardness, but as their own traditions. The failure of the temperance movement is the most persuasive example of such staunch, if unheroic, resistance.

Continuing this interpretation, we can see the post-Revolutionary period as one in which the classes pressing for change finally acquired the political and social authority to achieve the transformation of 'low' culture that they desired. There was certainly a sense in which the Bolsheviks typified radical intelligentsia attitudes towards backwardness. In *Literature and Revolution* (1923), Trotskii wrote: "'Give us,' they say, "something pock-marked but our own." This is false and untrue. A pock-marked art is no art and is therefore not necessary to the working masses.' Lunacharskii, whose attitude towards popular culture was relatively liberal, wrote of 'purifying' and 'adapting' popular art forms, such as the circus, popular novels, the *chastushka*, and the 'cruel romance', so as to make them acceptable in a new society. The assault on commercial arts began immediately after the Revolution, when non-Party advertising was banned in a decree of 1917, and publishing nationalized in 1918. The non-Party intelligentsia might worry about the closing of the oppositional press, but they were much less concerned about assaults on commercial art. With the onset of the cultural revolution in 1928, the commercial arts were caught in a pincer movement between economic and cultural centralization, doomed because of their association with capitalist economics on the one side, and backwardness on the other. (On the cultural revolution, see the Epilogue.)

From this perspective, cultural power seems to be operating analogously to political and economic power—from the top down—and seems to induce a similar kind of resistance from below to that which is traced in studies of social and political conflict. Yet a note of caution should be sounded. One of the most suggestive models for grasping the changing contours of class relations in late imperial Russian society has been that of 'dual polarization', developed by Leopold Haimson.[85] Haimson's model proposes that especially after the 1905 Revolution, *obshchestvo* (civil society) was increasingly at odds with the state, whilst the growing working class was at odds with both the state and the *obshchestvo*. So far as changing cultural patterns are concerned, however, one is struck by the extent to which state and *obshchestvo* were bound together by cultural habits and aspirations. The intelligentsia may still have perceived itself to be at odds with official Russia, yet its *Kulturträger* initiatives had more in common with those of government and ecclesiastical officials than it was prepared to concede. As Richard Stites puts it, 'intellectuals, censors, priests, physicians and revolutionaries—however sharply they differed among themselves—were often united in their animosity to the new culture which they linked directly to vice'.[86] Similarly, it is difficult to see a working-class culture that is clearly distinguishable from that of the urban lower orders in general. A working-class culture did exist, centred on the workplace, but its boundaries were porous, and it flowed into a broader, 'mass' or 'lower-class' culture, in which workers, servants, traders, and shopkeepers participated.

Shifting patterns of culture, then, did not neatly match the changing contours of class relations. Indeed they are rather a poor guide to these. A society of *sosloviia* was mutating into a society of classes, and cultural consumption and appropriation were central to this mutation. But rather than being reflective of coagulating class identities, cultural patterns were more expressive of individual aspirations, of aspirations to social mobility rather than expressive of structural fixity. It was through culture that ordinary people came to terms with social change and sought to impose meaning and aspiration on it. Perhaps the closest links that could be made between new cultural practices and class formation would be in relation to the emergent bourgeoisie, where the links between urban patterns of consumption and bourgeois class-consciousness were sketched in. Yet the fate of that class was soon cut short, and it has not been the object of systematic treatment.[87]

In general, however, our study of how commercialization and consumption of culture was related to social change has indicated that use of cultural forms was related less to class formation than to the emergence of modern individuality, 'modern' gender identities (especially for women), and—one might add, though this has not been a theme of this chapter—of new renditions of national identity. Of course, this may be partly an optical illusion brought about by our particular vantage point: if we examined culture in relation to work and pro-duction, for example, instances of class-based cultural practices would almost certainly become more apparent.

Whatever the contests between different sectors of the elite, the fact remains that the gap between 'high' and 'low' was perhaps greater in Russia than in any other European country of the late nineteenth century (at any rate, any country that had experienced industrialization). Possession of education and 'culture' was at least as important as the possession of wealth in determining social status, and marked out the narrow band of its possessors from the 'dark' masses. Nowhere was the attitude of the educated to the non-educated more condescending. And yet nowhere, perhaps, were the interactions between 'high' and popular culture so intense and creative: if only because they disliked it so much, Russian intellectuals often had a uniquely close relation with the 'other' of popular culture.

Moreover, fifty years of 'culturalism' on the part of the intelligentsia had not been without effect on popular culture. If the latter often rejected the highmindedness of 'high' culture, insisting on the pleasure principle, it in fact absorbed certain elements of that moralism which was intrinsic not only to the intelligentsia tradition, but to the deeply religious character of popular life as well. Not for nothing were popular theatres often given titles such as *Razvlechenie i pol'za* (Entertainment and Usefulness). Therefore, post-1928 Soviet culture, with its cult of 'Mother Russia' and various sainted heroes, its ubiquitous expressions of love, patriotism, self-sacrifice, and friendship, and proliferation of candyfloss variety shows and musical comedies, was in some senses a logical and adequate continuation, not just of efforts to repress commercial culture, but of that culture itself in unrepressed form.

Relations between 'high' and 'popular' were more interactive, therefore, than the standard model allows. Further, popular culture proved remarkably adapt-ive to negotiating social change, as is illustrated by the growth of new genres, for example the *chastushka*, the 'cruel romance', and the *chansonnette*. The charac-teristics of popular culture were less ones of 'conservatism', 'traditionalism', or 'decline' than of adaptation, appropriation, recycling, and hybridization. Such characteristics marked even the most commercial forms of mass culture, such as the amusement park and the *estrada*. We are, therefore, far from a situation in which the popular classes were simply rendered passive—subject to 'social control', to the forcible imposition of an alien culture by those with wealth and polit-ical power, or by an impersonal market. It was possible for those who did not respond positively to the massive 'top-down' effort to reform popular manners to appropriate these to their own ends. There were, for instance, cases where peasants turned tearooms or libraries into gambling or drinking clubs, and cases where didactic dramas were watched for their sensationalist potential (such as an adaptation of *Anna Karenina* for the popular theatre, which attracted crowds drawn by the chance of seeing the heroine jump under the train at the end).[88] There is equally striking evidence of popular agency where commercial mass culture is concerned. In an atmosphere of increasing social conflict, commercialized forms of culture could even, in extreme cases, be made to legitimize revolution. Thus a classic piece of schlock, such as Pastukhov's tale of the bandit Churkin, which ran in *Moskovskii listok* as a *feuilleton* from 1882 to 1885, could fire up textile workers in Orekhovo-Zuevo to demand that they 'plunder' the factory-owners for having 'plundered' them.[89] And, of course, for a relatively broad swathe of the urban and rural populace, literacy—even when it extended only to reading *lubochnaia literatura* (penny dreadfuls)—proved crucial to the development of new political affiliations and social movements. This is most strikingly evident in relation to the worker-intelligentsia, who rejected mass culture, but whose appropriations of the 'national' canon served to promote class identity, thus disproving the long-held intelligentsia assumption that the dissemination of culture would bring social unity. But for wider layers too, culture in all its forms was an arena of popular agency, notwithstanding the constraints on the lives of the popular classes set in place by state oppression, class exploitation, and poverty. In the context of the turbulent political developments which characterized late imperial Russia, the development of urban and commercial forms of culture served not merely to advance forms of individuality, but in certain circumstances to shape and even inspire resistance to the social and political order.

Suggested further reading

Industrialization, Development of the Commercial City

BATER, J. H., *St. Petersburg: Industrialization and Change* (Montreal, 1976).

BRADLEY, J., *Muzhik and Muscovite: Urbanization in Late Imperial Russia* (Berkeley, 1985).

BROWER, D. R., *The Russian City between Tradition and Modernity, 1850–1900* (Berkeley, 1990).

DAVIDOVICH, M., *Peterburgskii tekstil'nyi rabochii v ego biudzhetakh* (St Petersburg, 1912).

DUNE, E., *Notes of a Red Guard*, tr. and ed. D. P. Koenker and S. A. Smith (Urbana, 1993).

JOHNSON, R. E., *Peasant and Proletarian: The Working Class of Moscow in the Late Nineteenth Century* (Leicester, 1979).

RUANE, C., 'Clothes Shopping in Imperial Russia: The Development of a Consumer Culture', *Journal of Social History*, 28 (1995), 765–82.

SMITH, S. A., *Red Petrograd: Revolution in the Factories 1917–1918* (Cambridge, 1983).

VON GELDERN, J., 'Life in Between: Migration and Popular Culture in Late Imperial Russia', *Russian Review*, 55 (1996), 365–83.

ZELNIK, R. E. (tr. and ed.), *A Radical Worker in Tsarist Russia: The Autobiography of Semën Ivanovich Kanatchikov* (Stanford, 1986).

Consumer Culture in the Countryside

ENGEL, B., *Between the Fields and the City* (Cambridge, 1994).

FRANK, S. P., 'Confronting the Domestic Other: Rural Popular Culture and its Enemies in Fin-De-Siècle Russia', in Frank and M. D. Steinberg (eds.), *Cultures in Flux: Lower-Class Values, Practices and Resistance in Late Imperial Russia* (Princeton, 1994), 74–107.

FRIERSON, C. A. (tr. and ed.), *Aleksandr Nikolaevich Engelgardt's Letters from the Country, 1872–1887* (New York, 1993).

Entertainments, 'Boulevardization'

BROOKS, J., *When Russia Learned to Read: Literacy and Popular Literature, 1861–1917* (Princeton, 1985).

CHRISTIAN, D., *Living Water: Vodka and Russian Society on the Eve of Emancipation* (Oxford, 1990).

ENGELSTEIN, L., *The Keys to Happiness: Sex and the Search for Modernity in Fin de Siècle Russia* (Ithaca, 1992).

HERLIHY, P., 'Joy of the Rus': Rites and Rituals of Russian Drinking', *Russian Review*, 50 (1991), 131–47.

KELLY, C., *Petrushka: The Russian Carnival Puppet Theatre* (Cambridge, 1990).

—— 'Better Halves? Representations of Women in Russian Urban Popular Entertainments, 1870–1910', in L. Edmondson (ed.), *Women and Society in Russia and the Soviet Union* (Cambridge, 1992), 5–31.

KONECHNYI, A., 'Shows for the People: Public Amusement Parks in Nineteenth-Century St Petersburg', in S. Frank and M. D. Steinberg (eds.), *Cultures in Flux: Lower-Class Values, Practices and Resistance in Late Imperial Russia* (Princeton, 1994), 121–30.

—— 'Peterburgskie narodnye gulian'ia na maslenoi i paskhal'noi nedeliakh', in N. V. Iukhneva (ed.), *Peterburg i guberniia: Istoriko-etnograficheskie issledovaniia* (Leningrad, 1989), 21–52.

—— 'Raek v sisteme peterburgskoi narodnoi kul'tury', *Russkii fol'klor*, 25 (1989), 123–38.

KUZNETSOV, E., *Iz proshlogo russkoi estrady: Istoricheskie ocherki* (Moscow, 1958).

NEKRYLOVA, A. F., *Russkie narodnye gorodskie prazdniki, uveseleniia, i zrelishcha: Konets XVIII–nachalo XX veka* (Leningrad, 1988).

SCHULER, C., *Women in Russian Theatre: The Actress in the Silver Age* (London, 1996).

Silent Witnesses (10 videocassettes of early Russian films, British Film Institute) (London, 1992).

STITES, R., *Russian Popular Culture: Entertainment and Society since 1900* (Cambridge, 1992).

TAYLOR, R., and CHRISTIE, I. (eds.), *The Film Factory: Russian and Soviet Cinema in Documents, 1896–1939* (London, 1988).

TSIV'IAN, IU., *Early Cinema in Russia and its Cultural Reception*, tr. A. Bodger (London and New York, 1994).

ZASOSOV, D. A., and PYZIN, V. I., *Iz zhizni Peterburga 1890–1910-kh godov* (Leningrad, 1991).

ZORKAIA, N. M., *Na rubezhe stoletii* (Moscow, 1976).

Modernism in Literature and the Theatre

BARRATT, A., and RUSSELL, R. (eds.), *The Russian Theatre in the Age of Modernism* (London, 1990).

CLAYTON, J. D., *Pierrot in Petrograd: The Commedia dell'arte/Balagan in Twentieth-Century Russian Theatre and Drama* (Montreal, 1994).

MARKOV, V., *Russian Futurism* (Berkeley, 1968).

—— (ed.), *Manifesty i programmy russkikh futuristov* (Munich, 1967).

PYMAN, A., *A History of Russian Symbolism* (Cambridge, 1994).

RUDNITSKY, K., *Russian and Soviet Theatre* (London, 1988).

Visual Arts, the Art Market

BOWLT, J., *The Silver Age: Russian Art of the Early Twentieth Century and the World of Art Group* (Newtonville, 1979; repr. 1982).

—— *Russian Stage Design: Scenic Innovation 1900–1930: From the Collection of Mr and Mrs Nikita D. Lobanov-Rostovsky* (Jackson, 1982).

—— 'The Moscow Art Market', in E. Clowes, S. D. Kassow, and J. L. West (eds.), *Between Tsar and People: Educated Society and the Quest for Public Identity in Late Imperial Russia* (Princeton, 1991), 101–30.

BURRUS, C., *Art Collectors of Russia: The Private Treasures* (New York, 1994).

DUDAKOV, V. A., *Il Simbolismo russo: Sergej Djagilev e l'Età d'argento nell'arte* (Milan, 1992).

ELLIOTT, D., and DUDAKOV, V., *100 Years of Russian Art: From Private Collections in the USSR* (London, 1989).

The Great Utopia: The Russian and Soviet Avant-Garde, 1915–1932 (Guggenheim Museum, New York, 1992).

KEAN, B. W., *All the Empty Palaces: The Merchant Patrons of Modern Art in Pre-Revolutionary Russia* (London, 1983; repr. 1995).

MILNER, J. (ed.), *A Dictionary of Russian and Soviet Artists, 1420–1970* (Woolbridge, 1993).

Notes

1 N. McKendrick, J. Brewer, and J. H. Plumb, *The Birth of the Consumer Society: The Commercialization of Eighteenth-Century England* (London, 1982); S. Schama, *The Embarrassment of Riches: An Interpretation of Dutch Culture in the Golden Age* (London, 1987); and L. Davidoff and C. Hall, *Family Fortunes: Men and Women of the British Middle Class* (London, 1987).

2 R. W. Davies, 'Introduction: from Tsarism to NEP', in Davies (ed.), *From Tsarism to the New Economic Policy* (London, 1990), 12.

3 L. Tiersten, 'Redefining Consumer Culture: Recent Literature on Consumption and the Bourgeoisie in Western Europe', *Radical History Review*, 57 (1993), 116–49.

4 S. G. Wheatcroft and R. W. Davies, 'Population', in Davies, M. Harrison, and S. G. Wheatcroft (eds.), *The Economic Transformation of the Soviet Union, 1913–1945* (Cambridge, 1994), 59, and A. G. Rashin, *Naselenie Rossii za 100 let (1811–1913 gg.)* (Moscow, 1956), 99.

5 Rashin, *Naselenie*, 323, and J. Bradley, *Muzhik and Muscovite: Urbanization in Late Imperial Russia* (Berkeley, 1985), 34.

6 B. Engel, *Between the Fields and the City* (Cambridge, 1994), *passim*, and A. J. Coale, B. A. Anderson, and E. Harm, *Human Fertility in Russia since the Nineteenth Century* (Princeton, 1979), 252–3.

7 See Bradley, *Muzhik*, 79, and D. R. Brower, 'Urban Revolution in the Late Russian Empire', in M. Hamm (ed.), *The City in Late Imperial Russia* (Bloomington, 1986), 324.

8 W. Benjamin, *Moskauer Tagebuch* (Frankfurt am Main, 1980), 53. For general information on the growth of retail culture, see J. H. Bater, *St. Petersburg: Industrialization and Change* (Montreal, 1976), 268; Bradley, *Muzhik*, 64; *Istoriia Moskvy*, iv (Moscow, 1954), 164; and W. Barnes Steveni, *Petrograd* (London, 1915).

9 T. Child, *The Tsar and His People* (New York, 1891), quoted in Bradley, *Muzhik*, 62, and Benjamin, *Moskauer Tagebuch*, 53. See also H. Pitcher, *Muir and Mirrilies: The Scottish Partnership that Became a Household Name in Russia* (Cromer, 1994), *passim*; Bradley, *Muzhik*, 83; Bater, *St. Petersburg*, 264; and *Istoriia Moskvy*, v (Moscow, 1955), 51. The analysis of consumption patterns here and below owes much to G. McCracken, *Culture and Consumption: New Approaches to the Symbolic Character of Consumer Goods and Activities* (Bloomington, 1988), and to P. Glennie, 'Consumption within Historical Studies', in D. Miller (ed.), *Acknowledging Consumption* (London, 1995), 164–203.

10 Pitcher, *Muir and Mirrilies*, 147, 169. The profit of the company (store and mail order combined) was 6 million roubles p.a. in 1916 (see 174).

11 T. A. Bernshtam, *Molodezh' v obriadnoi zhizni russkoi obshchiny XIX–nachala XX v.* (Leningrad, 1988), 78.

12 Ibid., 77.

13 Quoted in Engel, *Between the Fields and the City*, 155.

14 Ibid., 155. For a general study of the subject, see C. Ruane, 'Clothes Shopping in Imperial Russia: The Development of a Consumer Culture', *Journal of Social History*, 28 (1995), 765–82.

[15] A. Frolov, *Probuzhdenie* (Kiev, 1923), 17.

[16] R. E. Zelnik (tr. and ed.), *A Radical Worker in Tsarist Russia: The Autobiography of Semën Ivanovich Kanatchikov* (Stanford, 1986), 71.

[17] *Komsomol'skii byt: Sbornik*, intr. E. Iaroslavskii (Moscow, 1927), 169.

[18] V. Andrle, *A Social History of Twentieth-Century Russia* (London, 1994), 61–2.

[19] Bradley, *Muzhik*, 27.

[20] Quoted in J. Brooks, *When Russia Learned to Read: Literacy and Popular Literature, 1861–1917* (Princeton, 1985), 56.

[21] Cited in V. I. Lenin, *Collected Works*, iii. *The Development of Capitalism in Russia* (London, 1972), 577.

[22] S. Frank, 'Confronting the Domestic Other', in Frank and M. D. Steinberg (eds.), *Cultures in Flux: Lower-Class Values, Practices and Resistance in Late Imperial Russia* (Princeton, 1994), 86.

[23] Quoted in B. Eklof, *Russian Peasant Schools: Officialdom, Village Culture, and Popular Pedagogy, 1861–1914* (Berkeley, 1986), 423.

[24] R. Rothstein, 'Death of the Folk Song?', in Frank and Steinberg (eds.), *Cultures in Flux*, 111–12; Frank, 'Confronting the Domestic Other', 97; Robert E. Johnson, *Peasant and Proletarian: The Working Class of Moscow in the Late Nineteenth Century* (Leicester, 1979), 74; and C. Kelly, 'Better Halves? Representations of Women in Russian Urban Popular Entertainments, 1870–1910', in L. Edmondson (ed.), *Women and Society in Russia and the Soviet Union* (Cambridge, 1992), 5–8.

[25] The figures on numbers of entertainments are taken from V. Leikina-Svirskaia, *Russkaia intelligentsiia v 1900–1917 godakh* (Moscow, 1981), 186; on pleasure gardens, books, and films, see the sources in the Suggested Further Reading.

[26] D. A. Zasosov and V. I. Pyzin, *Iz zhizni Peterburga 1890–1910-kh godov* (Leningrad, 1991), 118–19.

[27] *Polnyi russkii pesennik: 1000 pesen* (Moscow, 1893), 11.

[28] *Polnyi sbornik libretto dlia grammofona*, pt. 2 (n.p., [c.1910]), 220. On music-hall songs, see also Kelly, 'Better Halves?'

[29] C. Schuler, *Women in Russian Theatre: The Actress in the Silver Age* (London, 1996); I. Erenburg, *Liudi, gody, zhizn'*, i (Moscow, 1990), 68.

[30] L. Kleinbort, 'Ocherki rabochei demokratii', pt. 2, *Sovremennyi mir*, 5 (1915), 153.

[31] *Strashnyi razboinik Churkin. Prikliucheniia ego v ostroge, na katorge, v rudnikakh, ego begstvo iz Sibiri, zhizn' ego v gorodakh i strashnyi konets ego uzhasnoi zhizni* (Moscow, 1885), [3].

[32] N. A. Leikin, *Gde apel'siny zreiut: Iumoristicheskoe opisanie puteshestviia suprugov Nikolaia Ivanovicha i Glafiry Semenovny Ivanovykh po Riv'ere i Italii* (St Petersburg, 1892), 6–7.

[33] I. I. Miasnitskii, 'V Ermitazhe', in *Prokazniki: Iumoristicheskie ocherki, stsenki, kartinki i fotograficheskie snimki s natury dobrodushnogo iumorista*, 4th edn. (Moscow, 1904), 309. When the book was first published, the author of one snide review commented that merchant Moscow already had its bard, Boborykin, and did not need another (*Russkoe bogatstvo*, 10 (1896), 56–7).

[34] The information about the Korsh theatre here and below comes primarily from the archive on its activities maintained in the Bakhrushin Theatre Museum, Moscow, *fond* 123.

[35] Quoted in L. Engelstein, *The Keys to Happiness: Sex and the Search for Modernity in Fin de Siècle Russia* (Ithaca, 1992), 403.

[36] D. R. Brower, *The Russian City between Tradition and Modernity, 1850–1900* (Berkeley, 1990), 152.

[37] See D. Christian, *Living Water: Vodka and Russian Society on the Eve of Emancipation* (Oxford, 1990), ch. 3.

[38] P. Herlihy, 'Joy of the Rus': Rites and Rituals of Russian Drinking', *Russian Review*, 50 (1991), 131–47.

[39] Zelnik (tr. and ed.), *A Radical Worker*, 247.

[40] Ibid., 406 n. 2, and V. Dal', *Tolkovyi slovar' velikorusskogo iazyka* (4 vols.; St Petersburg, 1880–2), ii, 288, iii, 401.

[41] S. A. Smith, *Red Petrograd: Revolution in the Factories 1917–1918* (Cambridge, 1983), 93, and R. W. Thurston, *Liberal City, Conservative State: Moscow and Russia's Urban Crisis* (Oxford, 1987), 133.

[42] Christian, *Living Water*, 83; M. Davidovich, *Peterburgskii tekstil'nyi rabochii v ego biudzhetakh* (St Petersburg, 1912), 20; A. M. Buiko, *Put' rabochego: Zapiski starogo bol'shevika* (Moscow, 1934), 11; *Putilovtsy v 1905 g.: Vospominaniia* (Leningrad, 1930), 12; and A. Buzinov, *Za Nevskoi zastavoi* (Moscow, 1930), 73.

[43] Buzinov, *Za Nevskoi zastavoi*, 25.

[44] Smith, *Red Petrograd*, 93.

[45] S. G. Strumilin, *Voprosy truda* (Moscow, 1923), 200; on cards, see F. Wigzell, *Reading Russian Fortunes: Print Culture, Gender and Divination in Russia from 1765* (Cambridge, 1997).

[46] S. G. Lazutin, *Russkaia chastushka* (Voronezh, 1960), 61; see also Rothstein, 'Death of the Folk Song?'

[47] E. N. Eleonskaia, *Sbornik velikorusskikh chastushek* (Moscow, 1914), no. 2623.

[48] Quoted in Rothstein, 'Death of the Folk Song?', 117.

[49] E. Dune, *Notes of a Red Guard*, tr. and ed. D. Koenker and S. A. Smith (Urbana, 1993), 8–9.

[50] Recorded in the 1920s; for the Russian text, see Iu. Sokolov, *Russkii fol'klor*, pt. 4 (Moscow, 1932), 66.

[51] On fist-fighting see Buiko, *Put' rabochego*, 15; Zelnik, *A Radical Worker*, 60; and Frolov, *Probuzhdenie*, 64–5. On bird-catching, see ibid., 9. A rather pleasanter custom was that practised on a Sunday during Lent: purchasing a small caged bird in order to let it go free.

[52] Zelnik (tr. and ed.), *A Radical Worker*, 13.

[53] Kleinbort, 'Ocherki rabochei demokratii', 153.

[54] Letter 1 quoted from I. P. Bogdanovich, *Novyi i polnyi pis'movnik, ili podrobnoe i iasnoe nastavlenie, kak pisat' kupecheskie, kantseliarskie, prositel'nye, zhalobnye, odobritel'nye, druzheskie, uveshchatel'nye i voobshche vsiakogo roda delovye pis'ma; takzhe ob"iavleniia, raznye dogovory, zapisi, svidetel'stva, veruiushchie, obiazatel'stva, zaveshchaniia i proch. . . .* (St Petersburg, 1791), 101; letter 2 quoted from M. Sieff (comp.), *Manual of Russian Commercial Correspondence* (London, 1916), 149, 151; the third example is from *Noveishii pis'movnik, samouchitel'*

sostavliat' bez pomoshchi postoronnikh pis'ma, dogovory, akty, prosheniia i dr. delovye bumagi, soderzhashchii obraztsy i formy . . . (Moscow, 1882), 88–90.

55 See A. S. Mindel, *Russian Commercial Correspondence: Letters, Idioms, Grammar, Notes and Full Vocabulary* (Manchester, 1918), and K. Haller (comp.), *Phraseologisches Wörterbuch der deutsch-russischen Handelskorrespondenz* (Riga, 1912).

56 *Pravila svetskoi zhizni i etiketa. Khoroshii ton. Sbornik sovetov i nastavlenii na raznye sluchai domashnei i obshchestvennoi zhizni* . . . (St Petersburg, 1889; repr. 1991), 315–16. Another etiquette manual that has been reprinted is *Zhizn' v svete, doma, pri dvore* (St Petersburg, 1890; repr. 1990).

57 H. Pitcher, *The Smiths of Moscow* (Cromer, 1984), 63; on the elaboration of culinary traditions, see the observations by J. Toomre in her English translation of E. Molokhovets, *A Guide for Young Housewives: Classic Russian Cooking* (Bloomington, 1993), 63–5, 214.

58 On genteelism amongst lower-class Russians, see the first part of this chapter; Frank, 'Confronting the Domestic Other', esp. 92–107; and M. D. Steinberg, *Moral Communities: The Culture of Class Relations in the Russian Printing Industry, 1867–1907* (Berkeley, 1992), 84–102.

59 On Russian utopianism, see R. Stites, *Revolutionary Dreams: Utopian Vision and Experimental Life in the Russian Revolution* (Oxford, 1989), and I. Smirnov, *Bytie i tvorchestvo* (Munich, 1990).

60 I. Annenskii, 'O sovremennom lirizme', in *Knigi otrazhenii* (Moscow, 1979), 347.

61 The remarks here are taken from the preliminary matter in K. A. Haller, *Deutsche und russische Handelsbriefe für den Schulgebrauch und das Selbststudium*, 4th edn. (Riga, 1911): cf. 'Kommercheskaia perepiska', in *Russkii pis'movnik: Sbornik obraztsovykh pisem, delovykh bumag i kommercheskoi perepiski . . . v piati chastiakh* (St Petersburg, c.1910); N. Krakovskii and A. G. Komarovskii (comps.), *Teoreticheskoe i prakticheskoe rukovodstvo kommercheskoi korrespondentsii . . .* (St Petersburg, 1911); and T. von Kawraysky, *Russische Handelskorrespondenz* (Leipzig, 1907).

62 M. Kuzmin, 'O prekrasnoi iasnosti', *Apollon*, 4 (1910), 5–10. Amongst other landmark writings on poetics and poets of the period were A. Blok, 'O sovremennom sostoianii russkogo simvolizma' (1910); V. Ivanov, *Borozdy i mezhi* (1916); A. Belyi, *Simvolizm* (1910) and *Arabeski* (1911); and V. Briusov, *Dalekie i blizkie* (1912). See also R. E. Peterson (tr. and ed.), *The Russian Symbolists: An Anthology of Critical and Theoretical Writings* (Ann Arbor, 1986).

63 On the Russian educational system, see S. V. Rozhdestvenskii, *Istoricheskii obzor deiatel'nosti Ministerstva Narodnogo Prosveshcheniia (1802–1902)* (St Petersburg, 1902); N. Hans, *History of Russian Educational Policy (1701–1917)* (London, 1931); and the articles on *Gimnaziia, Real'naia gimnaziia*, and *Kommercheskoe uchilishche* in *Entsiklopedicheskii slovar' Brokgauza i Efrona* (St Petersburg, 1890–1907).

64 A very full study of the merchant stereotype in Russian literature is available in D. Buryshkin, *Moskva kupecheskaia* (New York, 1954; repr. Moscow, 1991); see also C. Kelly, 'Teacups and Coffins: the Culture of Russian Merchant Women, 1870–1917', in R. Marsh (ed.), *Women and Society in Russia and the Ukraine* (Cambridge, 1996), 55–77. Recent more balanced studies of the merchant ethic include A. J. Rieber, *Merchants and Entrepreneurs in Imperial Russia* (Chapel Hill, 1982), and Steinberg, *Moral Communities*.

65 V. Dmitrieva, 'Po derevniam', *Vestnik Evropy*, 10 and 11 (1896), 520–53 and 131–76; an extract in English is available in C. Kelly (ed.), *An Anthology of Russian Women's Writing* (Oxford, 1994), 153–65. C. A. Frierson (tr. and ed.), *Aleksandr Nikolaevich Engelgardt's Letters from the Country, 1872–1887* (New York, 1993).

66 Frierson (tr. and ed.), *Aleksandr Nikolaevich Engelgardt's Letters*, 165, 167. Among other writings on the Russian village which are typical both in their careful attention to oral history and local custom, and in their somewhat uncritical attitude to patriarchal tradition, are O. Semenova Tian-Shanskaia, *Zhizn' Ivana: Iz byta chernozemnykh krest'ian* (St Petersburg, 1914), and Dmitrieva, 'Po derevniam'.

67 See B. Nijinska, *Early Memories* (London, 1982), 44.

68 On the congruence of high culture and 'boulevard culture', see esp. Engelstein, *The Keys to Happiness*, and N. Zorkaia, *Na rubezhe stoletii: U istokov massovogo iskusstva v Rossii 1900–1910 godov* (Moscow, 1976).

69 On the particular features of Russian constructivism, see esp. C. Lodder, *Russian Constructivism* (New Haven, 1983). On the avant-garde more generally, see J. Bowlt (ed.), *Russian Art of the Avant-Garde: Theory and Criticism* (London, 1988); J. Bowlt, *The Silver Age: Russian Art of the Early Twentieth Century and the World of Art Group* (Newtonville, 1979; repr. 1982); J. Bowlt and B. Hernard, *Aus vollem Halse: russische Buchillustration und Typographie aus den Sammlungen der Bayerischen Staatsbibliothek* (Munich, 1993); and S. Compton, *The World Backwards: Russian Futurist Books 1912–1916* (London, 1979) and *Russian Avant-Garde Books, 1917–1934* (London, 1992).

70 Russian quoted from Z. Folejewski (ed.), *Futurism and its Place in the Development of Modern Poetry: A Comparative Study* (Ottawa, 1980), 214; English version our own.

71 A. Belyi, 'Sinematograf' (1907), in *Arabeski: Kniga statei* (Moscow, 1911), 350, 351, 353. In fact, as Iu. Tsiv'ian points out in his excellent study of the early Russian cinema, *Early Cinema in Russia and its Cultural Reception*, tr. A. Bodger (London and New York, 1994), social differentiation was imposed on the audiences of the 'cinematograph' by seating plans (the most expensive seats being at the back). However, the semi-darkness in which film showings were held made differentials less evident in the cinema than in the contemporary theatre.

72 See A. Blok, 'V kabakakh, v pereulkakh, v izvivakh', in *Sobranie sochinenii v 8 tomakh*, ii (Leningrad, 1960), 159–60; O. Mandel'shtam, 'Kinematograf', in *Stikhotvoreniia* (Leningrad, 1973), 80; and A. Chumachenko, 'V kinematografe', *Russkoe bogatstvo*, 1 (1911), 54. On literary reactions to the cinema, see also Tsiv'ian, *Early Cinema*, esp. chs. 1 and 2.

73 V. I. Gorianskii, 'Zhivopisets Pchelkin', in *Poety 'Satirikona'* (Moscow, 1966), 167–8.

74 On the Russian literary avant-garde generally, see V. Markov, *Russian Futurism* (London, 1969). On the Oberiuty, see N. Cornwell (ed.), *Daniil Kharms and the Poetics of the Absurd* (London, 1991), and B. Müller, *Absurde Literatur in Rußland: Entstehung und Entwicklung* (Munich, 1978).

75 See N. Gumilev, *Pis'ma o russkoi poezii* (Berlin, 1923), 173–5. On Teffi, see I. Odoevtseva's memoir in *Na beregakh Seny* (Paris, 1983), 79–123, which both summarizes and replicates the slightly patronizing attitudes of the literary *beau monde* to Teffi's work.

76 V. Nabokov, *Speak, Memory* (London, 1967); M. Dobuzhinskii, *Vospominaniia*, i (New York, 1976); Iu. Annenkov, *Dnevnik moikh vstrech: Tsikl tragedii*, i (New York, 1966); and A. Benua [Benois], *Moi vospominaniia*, i (Moscow, 1980). On the idealization of childhood in Russia, see esp. A. B. Wachtel, *The Battle for Childhood: Creation of a Russian Myth* (Stanford, 1990).

77 See M. Voloshin, 'Oslinyi khvost', in *Liki tvorchestva* (Leningrad, 1988), 287–9.

78 There is now a vast number of album-type publications with good reproductions of work by avant-garde artists: see Suggested Further Reading.

79 On the use of lettering in political slogans, see E. Waters, 'The Female Form in Soviet Political Iconography', in B. E. Clements, B. A. Engel, and C. D. Worobec (eds.), *Russia's Women: Accommodation, Resistance, Transformation* (Berkeley, 1991), 229.

80 Quoted from C. E. W. Petersson and W. Barnes Steveni, *How to Do Business with Russia: Hints and Advice to Businessmen Dealing with Russia* (London, 1917), 72. A fair number of Russian advertising agencies were listed in trade directories such as *Spravochnaia kniga o litsakh, poluchivshikh na 1915 god kupecheskie i promyslovye svidetel'stva po g. Moskve* (Moscow, 1915).

81 An excellent selection of posters, soap-packets, and other commercial art is reproduced in the catalogue of a Hayward Gallery exhibition, *The Twilight of the Tsars: Russian Art at the Turn of the Century* (London, 1991).

82 M. Tsvetaeva, 'Nataliia Goncharova' (section 'Pervaia Goncharova'), in *Izbrannaia proza v 2 tomakh*, i (New York, 1979), 311.

83 J. Berger, *Ways of Seeing* (London, 1972), 154.

84 On the art collectors of Russia, see B. W. Kean, *All the Empty Palaces: The Merchant Patrons of Modern Art in Pre-Revolutionary Russia* (London, 1983; repr. 1995); J. Bowlt, 'The Moscow Art Market', in E. Clowes, S. D. Kassow, and J. L. West (eds.), *Between Tsar and People: Educated Society and the Quest for Public Identity in Late Imperial Russia* (Princeton, 1991), 101–30; and C. Burrus, *Art Collectors of Russia: The Private Treasures* (New York, 1994).

85 L. Haimson, 'The Problem of Social Stability in Urban Russia', *Slavic Review*, 23 (1964), 619–42, and 24 (1965), 1–22.

86 R. Stites, *Russian Popular Culture: Entertainment and Society since 1900* (Cambridge, 1992), 12.

87 In *The Keys to Happiness*, Engelstein offers many interesting reflections on the relationship of the emergent public sphere to the liberal middle class, which have a bearing on consumption, but the relationship has not been studied in detail so far.

88 See Frank, 'Confronting the Domestic Other', 107, and I. Shcheglov, *Narodnyi teatr* (St Petersburg, 1898), 109.

89 See A. Moiseenko, *Vospominaniia starogo revoliutsionera* (Moscow, 1966), 70; Brooks, *When Russia Learned to Read*, 123–5; and Brower, *The Russian City*, 180.

3 Collapse and Creation: Issues of Identity and the Russian *Fin de Siècle*

Rosamund Bartlett and Linda Edmondson

Additional material by Catriona Kelly and Steve Smith

Introduction

THE late nineteenth and early twentieth centuries were a particularly unsettled and vexed era for Russia in terms of both national and individual expressions of identity. The country entered the three decades leading up to the First World War on a high note for military patriotism: the defeat of Turkey in the short-lasting Russo-Turkish War of 1877–8 had made Russia dominant in the Eastern Balkans, partly reversing the situation that had obtained since the Crimean War twenty years earlier. The Congress of Berlin in 1878 saw the Western powers, most particularly Britain, manœuvring to halt what was seen as an unstop-pable Russian advance, and forcing Russia to abandon its ambitions to set up a powerful Orthodox satellite state in Greater Bulgaria. The Russo-Japanese War twenty-six years later, in which the Russian Empire suffered a crushing defeat at the hands of an imperial power just emerging on to the international scene, raised some questions about Russia's military might, but it was still widely accepted that the country was a significant land power, if not a naval one. No one could have predicted even at this late stage of the Empire's history that the next decade would see Russia's forces failing to make headway against German and Austrian troops on the Eastern Front, and finally withdrawing ignominiously from the war after the Bolshevik Revolution, when Russia's new leaders, abandoning hopes of international revolution, bowed to popular pressure and pulled their troops from a conflict that had, for the past three years, brought the mass of the Russian population nothing but loss of life and physical hardship.

But military might (however flawed) was not the only element in Russia's international image. The country was also widely perceived as economically backward and intellectually oppressive. Western observers commented relent-lessly (and not without a degree of picturesque exaggeration) on the contradic-tions between the modernity and wealth of the cities and the primitive conditions in the countryside. The existence of Russian prison camps was reported, and political dissidents profiled. The February Revolution of 1917, understood as the downfall of tyranny, was celebrated by bonfires in many villages and small towns in Europe, including even rural Ireland. Given that the members of Russia's political and intellectual elites invariably had a command of at least one other European language, and that educated Russians had been painfully aware of how others saw them since at least the late eighteenth century, all this was bound to give Russian nationalism a more or less obvious defensiveness. This was evident, on the one hand, in the strong presence of Slavophile ideologies of various kinds, and on the other in increasingly strong pressure for the formation of alternative, outward-looking and internationalist, collective identities, which were particularly prominently expressed in the various colorations of socialism. Matters were further complicated by the fact that, like their 1840s predecessors, Slavophile thinkers were profoundly influenced by Western thinkers (in this generation, particularly by Nietzsche), while some socialists, for instance the anarchist Petr Kropotkin, looked in their collectivist theories towards traditional Russian institutions such as the peasant commune (*mir*). At the same time, the era saw numerous activists, thinkers, and artists turn from national to individual issues, struggling to force the Tsars to grant their subjects personal and civil rights. Finally, new pressures from the East, as Japanese imperialism pushed at Russia's Pacific borders, compounded the traditional sense of Russia as a 'Eurasian' nation, destined to act as saviour of the Occident from 'yellow hordes', but perhaps at the cost of her own autonomous existence.[1] The fissures in national identity were reflected in the proliferation of curious ideological fusions ('mystical anarchism', Nietzschean socialism, Weiningerian Judaism), in the violent shifting between political sympathies in some individuals (for example, the cubo-futurists, such as Maiakovskii, who enthusiastically produced propaganda in support of the imperialist First World War, and then of the anti-imperialist Bolshevik Revolution), and in the shrill, indeed at times vicious, arguments between small groupings which, from an objective viewpoint, often seemed to have much in common (typical were the disedifying disputes that erupted at the First Russian Women's Congress in 1908, at which Aleksandra Kollontai led a walk-out by socialist feminists).

Yet, as the two previous chapters of this section have made clear, the late nineteenth and early twentieth centuries also saw Russia go through an economic boom, attracting international investment and admiration, and saw Russian scholars, particularly scientists, making themselves reputations far outside their country's borders. What was more, this was an epoch in which the arts —literature, music, painting—flourished to an extraordinary degree. Though commonly known as the 'Silver Age' of Russian literature (as opposed to the age of Pushkin), it might more properly, if all the arts are taken together, be referred to as the 'Golden Age' of Russian culture. Unlike Pushkin's generation, moreover, this was one in which artists were able to make international, as well as national, reputations. Painters such as Serov, Kandinskii, Bakst, Benois, Goncharova, Larionov, and Malevich, composers such as Musorgskii, Tchaikovsky, Rimskii-Korsakov, Skriabin, and Stravinskii, writers, in particular Tolstoi, Dostoevskii, and Chekhov, became known all over Europe, as did other cultural figures of genius, such as Diaghilev and Meyerhold. Well-known foreigners (Matisse, Marinetti, Rilke) began to put Russia on the map of their

European tours; some Russians, particularly symbolists such as Valerii Briusov, Dmitrii Merezhkovskii, and Zinaida Gippius, contributed to foreign periodicals, for example *Mercure de France*, while adaptations of Russian spirituality were popularized by theosophist thinkers, such as 'Madame Blavatsky' (that is, Elena Blavatskaia, daughter of the 1830s writer Elena Gan, and cousin of the Finance Minister, and later Prime Minister, Sergei Witte). Russian painting, literature, music, ballet, opera, and thought, as well as that most dubious of national fictions, the 'Russian soul', became famous among readers, spectators, and enthusiasts for culture everywhere in Europe, America, and Asia (where the young Gandhi wrote fan letters to Tolstoi and saw in the latter's advocation of non-resistance to evil a powerful weapon against colonialism).

Official Nationalism: Russification and Rituals of Power

Official chauvinism by no means began with the accession to the throne of Alexander III. Throughout the nineteenth century, Russian law had discriminated against those subjects of the Empire who were not of Orthodox belief, and also against Orthodox sectarians, who were given a rest from persecution only with the reforms of 1905. Non-Christians were subject to especially harsh restrictions. Since the late eighteenth century, Jews had been allowed to live only in *mestechki* (shtetls, small towns) within the Pale of settlement, an area to the west of the Empire covering Poland, Belorussia, parts of the Ukraine, and the Baltic; exemption was granted only to merchants belonging to the First Guild (that is, those with a substantial capital), to army recruits, and to those with higher education.

Under Alexander III, however, the government began to pursue intensive policies of Russification, attempting to assimilate other parts of the population by directly coercive measures. In order to stop education becoming a route to Jewish emancipation, strict quotas on participation in secondary and higher education were introduced during 1886 and 1887. Jews might make up no more than 3 per cent of pupils at secondary schools in Moscow, no more than 5 per cent in St Petersburg, and no more than 10 per cent even in the Jewish Pale. The same quotas applied to students at universities and institutes, including the Higher Courses of Education for Women. Jews were banned altogether from some institutes, including the Moscow Theatre School. From 1891, restrictions on property ownership were also introduced in some *gubernii*, and in the same year non-Christians who proposed to practise as private attorneys (*chastnye poverennye*) began having to be cleared by the Ministry of the Interior before taking up employment. Jews who converted to Christianity, on the other hand, were immediately admitted to full civil rights. The intent, and in some cases the effect (the laws on settlement were not infrequently broken, and intellect and determination sometimes proved insuppressible), was to push Jews either into complete assimilation, or into isolation, as members of marginal, deprived communities denied the rights to education and involvement in the professions. Legal discrimination was ended only after the February Revolution, when a decree of 20 March 1917 finally terminated the Pale of settlement.[2]

Late imperial Russia was also to see official Russia embroiled in its unsavoury counterpart to the *affaire Dreyfus*, the 'Beilis case', when, in 1911, a Jew was indicted on a charge of ritually murdering a Christian child in Kiev. The grotesqueness of the accusation, with its overtones of medieval superstition, was evident to many observers; as in the case of Dreyfus, prominent writers intervened to defend Beilis and denounce his prosecutors. But the trial dragged on for two years before Beilis was finally acquitted in 1913.

Official nationalism was not only a question of legal regulation, but also of the way in which Tsarist power symbolically legitimated its authority. Here too Alexander III and Nicholas II reacted against the 'Tsar Reformer', and indeed against the practices that had obtained since the reign of Peter the Great. Whereas earlier rulers had emphasized Tsardom's remoteness from national tradition, its innovative, Westernizing character, Alexander III, whose tutors had included the nationalist historian Sergei Solov'ev, and the reactionary politician Konstantin Pobedonostsev, set out to emphasize the links between the ruling house and 'native Russian', pre-Petrine tradition. Dynastic intermarriages with other European royalty continued, and private tastes remained those of well-off aristocrats throughout Europe (French fashions, English furniture, hunting, shooting, and yachting). But court symbolism increasingly invoked the pre-Westernized past (albeit in elegantly transmuted form). This was particularly evident during the reign of Nicholas II, who had a strong personal reverence for Tsar Alexis Mikhailovich, after whom he named his own heir, and who, in 1903, organized a performance of *Boris Godunov*, followed by a costume ball, at both of which hosts and guests wore full seventeenth-century court dress.[3] Ten years later, celebrations for the three-hundredth anniversary of the Romanov Dynasty drew the analogy with pre-Petrine times still more forcefully, as the royal family toured Russian cities to be greeted by citizens with the traditional gifts of bread and salt, and ceremonial items, such as a pearl-and gold-embroidered *kokoshnik* (traditional Russian head-dress) presented to Grand Duchess Maria Nikolaevna in the city of Galich.[4]

Not only the pre-Petrine period, but also more recent legitimating ceremonial was invoked, sometimes with little regard for the needs of a rapidly changing society. One of the most poignant illustrations of the hiatus between the Tsarist image machine and the new reality was the 'Khodynka disaster' of 1896. It had been decided that the Tsar's coronation in Moscow should be followed by the traditional gift-giving ceremony at which food and mementos were presented to members of the public, and an entertainment programme took place in the presence of the Tsar. The organizers of the event had, however, failed to make proper preparations for the crowds that arrived to take part, from a now far larger city. Over half a million gathered at Khodynka field, the traditional site for the ceremony, which the authorities had decided to use although it was on the fringes of the now heavily populated Presnia area, and although it was still scarred with trenches after being used as an exhibition site. The spaces between the booths from which gifts were doled out were far too narrow to allow free passage of the crowds. Predictably, there was a stampede, as a result of which perhaps 2,000 were trampled to death (official figures of 1,350 are generally reckoned a significant underestimate).[5]

Of course, not all archaizing events were so fraught with disaster—the Translation of St Seraphim of Sarov, in 1903, when the removal of the saint's bones to a new site near Moscow was attended by crowds of 200,000 pilgrims as well as the Tsar, passed off without major incident. But rituals of solidarity presented Russian officialdom with almost insuperable problems: they stretched the resources of policing to, or sometimes beyond, the limit, and there was always the danger that they might turn into, or be understood as, demonstrations of disloyalty. This latter danger was spectacularly manifested when Father Gapon, head of the Assembly of Russian Workers, organized, in 1905, a mass deputation of workers to present a petition to the Tsar demanding constitutional change, including the formation of a democratic assembly. The hallowed right of petition was not, in this case, observed: in the incident that became internationally infamous as Bloody Sunday, unarmed petitioners were gunned down by troops as they approached the Winter Palace.[6]

As Russian cities became larger and more difficult to control, a much safer public manifestation of official nationalism was architecture, which in this period attempted to recapture a less problematic past in stone. The key architectural monument of Nicholas I's day, the Cathedral of Christ Redeemer in Moscow, not completed until 1883, but constructed in the pompous neoclassical style of the 1840s and 1850s, had commemorated national victory in a manner that stressed affinities with Western, rather than national, models. Surpassing St Peter's, Rome, in size if not in architectural merit, the church was a basilica-type construction that drew on Christian tradition before the tenth-century schism split the Church into Western and Eastern wings, suggesting Russia as the true inheritor of pre-schismatic might. The first important project of Alexander III's reign, by contrast (which, by a historical irony, was built in the supremely neoclassical city of St Petersburg), was the Church of the Resurrection (popularly known as 'The Saviour on the Blood'), built on the spot where Alexander II had been assassinated in 1881, and employing a series of quotations from pre-Petrine national architecture in order to underline a revival of the Tsar's role as keeper of ecclesiastical and temporal authority. Motifs in the building made allusion to the New Jerusalem Monastery near Moscow and to the Cathedral of the Protection (popularly known as 'St Basil's') on Red Square, and through these to the ideology of 'Moscow as New Jerusalem', while a display of the arms of every town and district in the country emphasized the ruler's authority over 'all Russia'. Beautiful but absurd in its backward-looking pastiche of styles, and intended as an image of dominance rather than of martyrdom (it was popular tradition, rather than official ideology, that drew analogies between the church and that of the murdered sixteenth-century heir, Dimitrii, at Uglich), the church was a harbinger of official patronage for Russian revivalist architecture, which was to be used, both in Alexander's reign and in Nicholas's, for a large number of important public projects, not only churches.[7]

The fact that some of the most famous sixteenth- and seventeenth-century architecture had been created in mercantile cities, such as Iaroslavl', may have prompted one of the more surprising features of Russian revivalist architecture —the use of pre-Petrine allusions in the construction of commercial buildings, such as banks, apartment blocks, and, above all, railway stations. The elegant neoclassical Nicholas Station on Kalanchovka Square in Moscow, housing the terminus of the earliest Russian main line, the link to St Petersburg, was joined in the early twentieth century by two famous *monstres sacrés*: the red-and-white Kazan' Station, looming over the square like the fortified walls of an oversized monastery, and Fedor Shekhtel's opulent Iaroslavl' Station (1902–4), resembling the gigantic chambers of a medieval *bogatyr'*. Less surprising was the adoption of a historicizing monumentalism for museum projects: the History Museum on Red Square, a nightmarish vision of fretted, liver-coloured brick completed in 1883 (though it had, in fact, been begun in 1875, during the reign of Alexander II), and the Tret'iakov Gallery in Lavrushinskii pereulok (1900–5), a design by Vasnetsov encrusted with motifs drawn from textiles, woodcarving, icon-painting, and other areas of traditional Russian visual culture.[8]

Encasing the Past: Museum Culture and 'Literary Classics'

The History Museum was significant, of course, not only for how it was built, but for what it contained: exhibits relating the history of Russia from prehistoric times up to the end of the pre-Petrine period. The enormous display of artefacts was intended not only to enlighten, but to impress: in late imperial Russia, as in most other countries, museum exhibits were a display of national authority and wealth, as well as the props of disinterested education. Though by no means the first museum dedicated to national history (earlier institutions included the Kremlin, whose cathedrals, palaces, and Armoury, with superb examples of applied art, made it the richest museum in Moscow, and the Rumiantsev Museum, founded in the 1820s), the History Museum represented a new and systematic approach to its material, making concrete the recovery of the past, and particularly the Muscovite past, that was being carried out in archaeological investigation and narrative reconstruction by historians such as Ivan Zabelin (the author of many influential studies, including *The Daily Life of the Russian Tsars* (1862) and *A History of the City of Moscow* (1906)) and Mikhail Pyliaev (whose entertaining, but widely researched, synthetizations, such as *Old St Petersburg* (1887), brought the history of Russia's younger capital to life).

So far as displaying the fine arts went, the government was relatively slow off the mark. It was only in the late 1890s that the Alexander III Museum (later known as the Russian Museum) was set up in St Petersburg as a showcase for Russian painting and applied arts in the capital, opening in 1898 with a display mostly made up of portraits and historical painting. In fact, the first important gallery for national painting had been founded two decades earlier not by a decree from the

Tsar or from a ministry, but by the private initiative of the textile manufacturer Pavel Tret'iakov, who in 1874 moved his collection of Russian painting from his own house into a purpose-built separate building, and opened it to the public. Tret'iakov was a conservative nationalist, one of whose ambitions was that his gallery should be a pantheon of national genius, including not only paintings by prominent Russians, but portraits of them. To this end he commissioned artists, such as Il'ia Repin, to capture the likenesses of suitable individuals, including Turgenev, Tolstoi, Musorgskii, and later Korolenko and Garshin. Tret'iakov had begun collecting works of Russian realism more than twenty years earlier; his financial support to the *Peredvizhniki* (Wanderers) group of painters had been instrumental in the evolution of realist representation in Russia. Some artists resented having to deal with a sponsor of his background because they worried lest their art be associated with middle-class values. Yet Tret'iakov's social network was wide: a brother served as Moscow's mayor, and Pavel's daughter studied with the playwright Ostrovskii's sister. Many of the top painters of the day, including Il'ia Repin, V. V. Vereshchagin, and V. G. Serov, socialized at the Tret'iakov home. In 1892, Tret'iakov was to donate his gallery and contents to the City of Moscow. As he told his daughter: 'My idea from my earliest years was to make money so that what had been accumulated by society should be returned to society, to the people, in some sort of beneficial institutions.'[9] His philanthropic gesture meant that each capital now had a 'national gallery' in public ownership. Western painting, on the other hand, had traditionally been better represented in St Petersburg, in the famous royal Hermitage collection; Ivan Tsvetaev, father of the poet Marina Tsvetaeva, and a distinguished classical philologist, long campaigned for a museum of Western art, as a result of which the Museum of Fine Arts (renamed the 'Pushkin Museum of Fine Arts' after the Revolution) finally opened in 1912, its nucleus then a collection of reproductions of famous classical sculptures, with some Egyptian antiquities and Italian primitive paintings.

Not only the visual arts and history, but also national literature, were the subject of monumentalization at this period. An early example of the type of 'museum apartment' that became ubiquitous after the Revolution was Tolstoi's house in Moscow, opened to the public as a museum not long after the writer's death. Statues were erected to Pushkin (in 1880, to mark the eightieth anniversary of his birth in 1799) and to Gogol' (in 1909); streets were named after these two writers, and also after the composer Glinka and other important cultural figures. The late nineteenth and early twentieth century also saw the publication of landmark editions of what were now called 'the Russian classics': the works of Pushkin, Gogol', Lermontov, Derzhavin, and other prominent writers of the late eighteenth and early nineteenth centuries.[10]

But the most significant event in national literary annals was the Pushkin Centenary Jubilee of 1899, which, unlike the rather decorous and high-minded celebrations of 1880, dominated by writers such as Dostoevskii and Turgenev, was, as Marcus C. Levitt has put it, 'broadly aimed at acculturating the Russian and non-Russian masses'. The bulk of the ceremonies commemorating the 'forefather of Russian literature' included not only the erection of statues and the issuing of presentation volumes, but also countless other occasions all over the Russian Empire:

> Jubilee events both in the capitals and the provinces included church services, public meetings with lectures, theatrical performances, school and university celebrations, public readings for the folk, the renaming of streets and the opening of libraries and schools in Pushkin's name, the state's purchase of Pushkin's family estate at Mikhailovskoe, the establishing of Pushkin scholarships and prizes, the issuing of commemorative medals, and so on. The state also mass-produced busts and pictures of the poet, as well as copies of his works which were distributed free to schoolchildren (in some cases, along with chocolate bars impressed with Pushkin's likeness) on the day of the anniversary.[11]

Even so circumspect and ironical a literary modernist as Innokentii Annenskii was drawn into the thick of events, contributing to the Tsarskoe Selo celebrations not only a speech, but also a 'Cantata', 'The Birth and Death of a Poet', in which the legendary Russian bard, Baian, invokes, in excruciating folksy-Old Russian pastiche, the birth of 'a brave young curly-haired lad', as 'little birds listen in their little gardens'.[12]

Alternative National Identities: Spiritualism and the Spiritual Renaissance

The Pushkin jubilee, an event which saw state and literary establishment more or less united in a celebration of national achievement (with the exception of some provocative outsiders, such as Tolstoi, who wondered rhetorically how the life of an aristocratic adulterer could be supposed to be instructive for the Russian people), was, however, a rare occurrence in late nineteenth-century history. By and large, the character of official nationalism under Alexander and Nicholas was profoundly alienating to intellectuals, most particularly writers, who were especially at risk from intensified censorship (the radical journal *Otechestvennye zapiski* (*Fatherland Notes*) was closed down altogether in 1884), as well as from moves against the universities, centres of liberal as well as radical thinking. Even the most Slavophile intellectuals were rarely overt monarchists, or supporters of the Church in its most reactionary manifestations: in any case, as Reginald Zelnik has pointed out, 'However much they purported to identify with Orthodoxy, new religious ideologies such as Slavophilism were heterodox and marginal when seen from the vantage point of church or state.'[13]

Yet, though Orthodoxy did not always play a direct role in oppositional representations of national identity (except as antagonist), there is no doubt that a major factor in the struggle for new forms of identity was the issue of faith, or rather the lack of it. In the largely secular world of late Tsarist Russia, where nothing was certain any more, some found it possible to revel in the emancipation from Victorian values by indulging in Nietzschean amorality, but there were many more people who found the idea of life being meaningless a truth too uncomfortable to face. Science, materialism, and atheism, it turned out, did not have all the answers, and the huge upsurge of interest among the intelligentsia at this time in mysticism, theosophy, the occult, and all kinds of religious sects is testament to the intense desire of many people to fill the spiritual emptiness of their lives with new beliefs.

Turning back to Christianity was not really an option. The Orthodox Church, weakened for ever when Peter the Great made it into a bureaucratic department of state, was hideously compromised as a moral authority by its failure to speak out against the government's repressive regime. Tolstoi's courage in exposing the apparent hypocrisy of the Church's stance in a series of devastating articles, and the honesty with which he confronted the complete irrelevance of its dogma and rituals to his daily life, despite a sincere desire to believe and follow its moral teachings, were rewarded with his excommunication in 1901.[14]

The chasm between the intelligentsia and the Church seemed unbridgeable, yet a group of intellectuals led by the symbolist writers Dmitrii Merezhkovskii and Zinaida Gippius, who had begun to debate religious questions on the pages of *Mir iskusstva* (*The World of Art*), set out to try to bridge it all the same, as they found their state of isolation intolerable. The result was the St Petersburg Religious-Philosophical Society, founded in 1901, which was soon one of the most influential forces in the capital's intellectual culture. If the society's efforts at mediation finally failed, the fact that they existed at all was of significance, for open discussions between the intelligentsia and ecclesiastical representatives in a country which allowed neither freedom of speech nor criticism of the Church, and where the majority of intellectuals had traditionally been anticlerically inclined, had previously been unthinkable. Not surprisingly, the twenty-one meetings, which were held between November 1901 and April 1903 (when they were shut down by Pobedonostsev), drew intellectuals of all persuasions, from Marxists to decadent aesthetes, all hoping that some real dialogue might be initiated, and that some kind of unification could take place which might lead to the revival of Russia and the establishment of social justice. Since neither side was prepared to back down in any substantive way, there were no tangible results, but both the Religious-Philosophical Society and its journal, *Novyi put'* (*The New Way*, 1903–5), succeeded in opening debate and honest communication on important and topical issues that lay at the heart of the identity crisis Russia found itself in at the beginning of the twentieth century.[15]

While the Orthodox Church lacked autonomy, there was no real chance of it reforming itself and winning back its lost flock: the hundreds of people who attended the meetings of the Religious-Philosophical Society seem rather insignificant when compared to the 20,000 converts to the bible-based Baptist faith by 1903. Though aristocrats had flirted with mystical pietism since the days of Alexander I, Protestant evangelism first took real root in Russia in the late 1860s, and, thanks to the fact that it could not in any way be identified with the state, did not preach standards it could not live up to, and offered the possibility of a new life, it had an appeal for all sectors of the population. As a result of the Baptists' energetic missionary activities and their dissemination of many thousands of Russian bibles (translated from the original Church Slavonic), their faith grew steadily in popularity, despite the harsh measures taken by the authorities in an effort to stamp it out. After the official declaration of religious freedom in 1905, the Baptist movement spread further, and had attracted about 100,000 people to its cause by 1914.[16]

The revival of interest in religion at the turn of the century was also intense in artistic circles, but here it was mysticism and the occult which held sway rather than Protestant fundamentalism. It is no surprise, for example, that the symbolist poet Aleksandr Blok's poems were first published in the pages of Merezhkovskii's religious-philosophical journal *Novy put'* in 1903, since under the potent influence of contemporary thinkers like Vladimir Solov'ev, artistic creation came to be regarded by many at this time as an innately religious activity, a way of communicating with the Divine. Indeed, for symbolist writers like Blok's contemporary Andrei Belyi, the belief in the existence of another superior reality which lay beyond the world of appearances led to art (in this case Russian symbolism) actually replacing religion as a world-view, and resulted in attempts to turn life itself into art.[17]

Along with the artists Kandinskii and Rerikh (Roerich), and the composer Skriabin, Belyi was one of the many seminal figures of Russian modernism whose preoccupation with metaphysical realities and the transfigurative powers of art drew him very naturally into the sphere of theosophy and the occult, the popularity of which began to soar at this time. In December 1903 the number of subscribers to *Novyi put'* had reached the two-and-a-half-thousand mark, but this is a figure which cannot but seem rather paltry when compared, for example, with the thousands who each week bought the Russian spiritualist journal *Rebus*, which by 1905 was attracting over five times as many readers. The appeal to the intelligentsia of both the Buddhist-inspired movement of theosophy, which was founded by Elena Blavatskaia, and the more Christian-orientated anthroposophy, led by the scientist and Goethe scholar Rudolf Steiner, was understandable, since their supposed synthesis of religion and science offered a way of combining the best of both worlds, rather than an invidious choice between the two. Both movements attracted a wide group of followers, particularly after 1905 when censorship was abolished and religious freedom granted to non-Orthodox associations.[18] Apart from such Westernized doctrines, other alternative forms of spirituality that attracted educated Russians included Orthodox sects. It was not the austere Old Believers who were the object of interest, but such weird and lurid cults as the *Khlysty*, 'Self-Flagellants', a group of people who, in their practice of ecstatic dancing (*raden'e*), were not unlike Islamic dervishes, but who believed that Christ and the Virgin Mary were constantly reincarnated in persons of exceptional spiritual gifts, and the *Skoptsy* (Castrators), a sect of extreme ascetic beliefs practising sexual self-mutilation (the 'small seal' of affiliation required removal of the testicles in men and the nipples in women, the 'great seal' removal of the penis in men and of the clitoris and labia in women).[19]

Until 1905, the small coterie of Russia's literary elite who called themselves symbolists were largely content to shut their eyes to the political situation and remain absorbed in their world of art, be it one tinged with decadence or one imbued with the new spirit of religious mysticism. This became more difficult after the 1905 Revolution, however, and some now made sincere attempts to assume the same degree of social responsibility that governed the behaviour of the artistically more conservative but politically more committed writers active at that time, such as Maksim Gor'kii (whose works were far more widely read than those of any symbolist writer). At the other end of the scale from Gor'kii was the outlandish doctrine of 'mystical anarchism' (1906–8) promoted by Georgii Chulkov and supported by Viacheslav Ivanov, which attempted to align symbolism with revolutionary ideology by advocating orgiastic, Dionysiac destruction on a world scale. Mystical anarchism was much ridiculed by most Russian symbolists, despite the fact that it represented a logical continuation of ideas they themselves had expressed.[20]

The ideas of Nietzsche, Schopenhauer, and Wagner were central to the development of Russian art in the modernist period, and responsible for its utopian dreams of cultural synthesis in the chaos and despondency which followed the 1905 Revolution.[21] But another German philosopher, Karl Marx, inspired utopian visions of a model society amongst the revolutionary intelligentsia. Of all the many new religions which flourished in pre-Revolutionary Russia, it was Marxism which ultimately proved to be the most influential in terms of social change, even if its congregation (the term is used advisedly: some, including Anatolii Lunacharskii, the Soviet Union's first Commissar of Enlightenment, actually viewed Marxism as the last great religion) remained relatively small. The establishment of social justice in Russia had been the dream of the intelligentsia ever since opposition to the autocracy and the barbaric institution of serfdom had united the educated classes into an identifiable group in the first decades of the nineteenth century. And since the 1860s, the establishment of socialism had been the goal of the radical wing of the intelligentsia, which had imbibed the utopian ideas of atheist thinkers such as Ludwig Feuerbach and Charles Fourier, Pierre Proudhon, and John Stuart Mill, and was determined to foist them on the Russian peasant.[22]

The populist movement of the 1870s (inspired by Herzen and Bakunin, and led by Lavrov and Mikhailovskii) was predicated on the assumption that the age-old peasant commune represented a primitive form of socialism, which, if refined, might enable Russia to bypass capitalism altogether. When the newly emancipated serfs proved resistant to the lure of a classless society, however, the populists' tactics hardened, with the ideas of Petr Tkachev (1844–85) playing a prominent role in the change. In the late 1870s, the umbrella group later known as Land and Liberty (*Zemlia i Volia*) began to practise a much more active manner of agitation; at the same time, a small splinter group known as The People's Will (*Narodnaia Volia*) (over a third of whose members were women) explicitly endorsed terrorist tactics, particularly the assassination of prominent officials, as a means of achieving their desired ends. At the beginning of the twentieth century, a new group, the Socialist Revolutionaries, some of them former populists from the 1870s, combined both types of political strategy: propaganda and terrorism. Playing a prominent part in the unrest of 1905, the Socialist Revolutionaries were the largest single political grouping at the time of the 1917 Revolution; their popularity was to make them a major target of repression by the Bolsheviks in the early years of their regime.[23]

The hostility among Russian Marxists, such as the Bolsheviks, to extreme forms of populism can be traced back decades. Indeed, the emergence of Marxism as a significant force in the Russian intellectual world-view dated from the moment when terrorist action was endorsed by some populists, while others, such as the earliest important Russian Marxist theorist, Tkachev, repudiated terrorism in order to dedicate themselves to a more economically and sociologically rigorous version of populism. The Russian Marxists devoted their energies to awakening a revolutionary consciousness amongst the industrial proletariat, under the initial leadership of Georgii Plekhanov. Furthermore, the activists were themselves, like the populists, riven by internal splits, which had concrete expression in 1903 when the major group of Marxists, the Social Democrats, split into two groups: the Bolsheviks, led by Lenin, and the Mensheviks. Therefore, unlike the Social Democrat parties in Germany or the Austrian Empire, which had become mass opposition parties by the time of the First World War, the Russian Social Democrats remained small cell organizations with little following among the mass of the people, or even the intelligentsia, right up to the Revolution.[24]

In its zeal to bring about the end of Russian absolutism through revolution, the radical intelligentsia sometimes seemed to care more about the moral righteousness of its cause than about the actual welfare of the country's long-suffering working-class and peasant populations, the supposed beneficiaries of its efforts. The callous dirigisme that could characterize Russian radicalism was a major theme of *Vekhi* (*Landmarks*), a highly important collection of articles published in 1909, which challenged the most fundamental ideas and assumptions of the revolutionary intelligentsia and predicted that the path of atheist socialism would lead to disaster.

Four of the seven contributors were former Marxists who eventually turned to Christianity, thus achieving the *rapprochement* of the intelligentsia and the Orthodox Church so longed for by Merezhkovskii. Their leader was the economist Petr Struve, initiator of the backlash against the radicals. Struve castigated the revolutionary intelligentsia for its failure to think beyond bringing about the destruction of the existing order, except in terms of utopian visions of a socialist paradise. Its anarchic abnegation of any sense of personal responsibility was, in his view, morally indefensible: 'It is no accident that the irreligious intelligentsia is fanciful, dreamy, unbusinesslike and irresponsible in politics. It is credulous without faith, combative without creativeness, fanatical without enthusiasm and intolerant without reverence; in short it has all the external forms of the religious mentality without its content.'[25]

The philosopher S. L. Frank criticized the radical intelligentsia for proclaiming the amelioration of the lot of the common man as its sole *raison d'être*, and for rejecting the legitimacy of other points of view. Its thinking, he argued, was simplistic in the extreme:

> The socialists are optimists from the conviction that all the misfortunes and imperfections of human life result from the mistakes and wickedness either of individuals or of exploiting classes. They believe that the natural conditions for human happiness

always exist. It is only necessary to suppress the injustice of the oppressors and to eradicate by education the stupidity of the exploited majority for the earthly paradise to be realized. Thus social optimism is based on a mechanical and rationalistic theory of happiness.[26]

Nikolai Berdiaev, also a philosopher, found fault with the radical intelligentsia's inability to confront its own limitations and to recognize that it had itself actually contributed to the country's problems. His recommendation was that the intelligentsia should begin to acknowledge its guilt, and cease blaming 'outside factors' for its own misfortunes. The economist-turned-theologian Father Sergii Bulgakov, meanwhile, focused on the radical intelligentsia's arrogance and dogmatism, and in particular on the contradiction between its theories of the brotherhood of man and its actual cult of the 'saviour-hero' which could only lead to rivalry and division:

> The intelligentsia in its desire to serve the peasant community is constantly vacillating between two extremes: between a sense of its spiritual aristocratic superiority and worship of the common people. Both these attitudes are false and harmful. The first is based on the idea that the common people are passive material to be reshaped in accordance with one or another of the most up-to-date western socialist theories; the second state of mind leads to abdication of that responsibility which belongs to a better educated and privileged minority.[27]

The rise of capitalism in Russia had brought about the final collapse of the identity of the intelligentsia as a coherent unit, as the variety of responses to the 1905 débâcle and its aftermath illustrated very clearly. If the intelligentsia's ranks had been swelled by new recruits to the professional classes who had been able to take advantage of the educational opportunities opened up in the great reforms of the 1860s, this enlargement had also led to a dilution of social character and of common intellectual purpose (the *raznochintsy*, non-gentry, recruits of the 1850s came from far more privileged backgrounds, intellectually and materially, than the *kukharkiny deti*, cooks' children, of the 1900s). The publication of *Vekhi* shattered for once and for all the illusion that the intelligentsia was a united group of individuals joined by a sense of community to the oppressed population.

It should be pointed out, however, that the contributors to *Vekhi* were not the only ones to voice such feelings at this time. The Russian symbolists may have remained outside the world of active politics, but their gifts of perception were often acute. Even before the publication of *Vekhi*, in November 1908, Blok had been shouted down for pointing to the impossibility of there ever being any real proximity between the post-Enlightenment world of conscience-stricken intellectuals and the essentially medieval world of the Russian peasant; his idea that the 'awakening' of the Russian people might not be wholly positive was considered nothing short of blasphemous.[28] And it was this same idea, the fallibility of Russian revolutionary ideology, which caused the huge uproar surrounding *Vekhi*. By 1910 it had run into five editions, and had provoked an avalanche of articles in response. The fact that there was such a show of indignation and outrage suggests that the ideas expressed in the collection had indeed touched a raw nerve.[29]

Predictably, the *Vekhi* articles were condemned as reactionary and erroneous, and their pessimism as unwarranted. The radical intelligentsia had no desire to revise its doctrines in any way, still less add any kind of spiritual dimension to them, preferring to cling instead to the materialist and positivist values of its teachers and ignore the signs that it was precipitating its own destruction. Few were those with the courage of the newspaper editor and politician I. V. Hessen, who was not afraid to look the future in the eye and admit that reading *Vekhi* had made him realize for the first time that his epoch was coming to an end.[30]

Non-Believers: Agnosticism and Pessimism in *Fin de Siècle* Literature

Divided by their views on what constituted the right 'signposts' for the new road to be taken by Russia, religious and revolutionary thinkers were united by their recognition that their ambitions were realizable only in the future. Constructing national identity in the present, rather than the future, was an agonizing task, as patriotism was increasingly identified with conservatism, and in particular with the preservation of the autocracy, and intellectuals painfully realized that 'the people' might not share the intelligentsia's 'Westernized' strivings for democratic change.

As early as the 1870s the alarm had been sounded by Tolstoi and Dostoevskii in their vigorously anti-rationalist and highly nationalistic, but also socially critical, late novels, which dissect the moral and social decay of society by depicting (in the case of *The Brothers Karamazov* (*Brat'ia Karamazovy*, 1880)) a disturbing world of crime, poverty, mental instability, and disintegration, and (in *Anna Karenina*, 1873–7) marital infidelity, the collapse of the family, the corrosive effects of capitalism, and the impotence of legalistic reform. Dostoevskii's doom-laden representation of contemporary society, here and in the anti-revolutionary *The Devils* (*Besy*, 1872, loathed by the radicals as a 'slur' (*paskvil'*) on their strivings), was at least as influential, before the Revolution, as his utopian doctrine of *sobornost'* (social renewal through a revival of 'native Russian', Orthodox and patriarchal, socio-religious collectives). In the 1890s and the 1900s, crime novels, sometimes involving revolutionary activists, became a favourite genre of fiction. More seriously, key literary texts of the day, such as Chekhov's 'Ward 6' ('Palata no. 6', 1892) and Garshin's 'The Red Flower' ('Krasnyi tsvetok', 1883), allegorized Russian society as an insane asylum, and one, moreover, run by incompetent, enfeebled doctors, abandoned to its fate by the world outside. Chekhov's last play, *The Cherry Orchard* (*Vishnevyi sad*, 1904), on the other hand, treats Russia's tragi-comic situation at the turn of the century with elegant irony, depicting a passive and thoughtless ruling class driven from its possessions by a young *nouveau riche* capitalist on the make (who is not unsympathetically portrayed), and, for all their attachment to the past, abandoning their old servant, Firs, a symbol of the country's peasant population, when they desert their former home. For its part, the cherry orchard is an eloquent symbol of traditional Russian culture—a thing of beauty, but utterly superannuated and unproductive.

Hostility among the Russian intelligentsia to censorship meant that it was rare for Russian writers to be out-and-out conservatives. It was only minor writers who responded to the Year of Revolution in 1905, as the Russian Empire erupted into open uprising, wringing promises of democratic change from the Tsar, and also significant relaxations in the censorship, with laments for the likely demise of civilized society.[31] But confidence in the future brought only a temporary respite. Under Petr Stolypin, Prime Minister from 1907, reactionary policies were again instituted, and stagnation set in once more. The mood among the Russian intelligentsia grew increasingly apocalyptic and inward-looking. The work of Aleksandr Blok, by far the most admired poet among Russian intellectuals in the 1900s and 1910s, and indeed right up to the 1960s, articulated disillusion for thousands:

> Рожденные в года глухие
> Пути не помнят своего.
> Мы — дети страшных лет России
> Забыть не в силах ничего.

> [Those born in the hollow years
> Do not remember their way.
> We—the children of Russia's frightful times
> Have the power to forget nothing.][32]

And Blok's 'Battle of Kulikovo' ('Na pole Kulikovom') cycle, composed in the aftermath of defeat in the Russo-Japanese War and of the 1905 upheavals, turned Dmitrii Donskoi's defeat of the Tatars at Kulikovo, an event traditionally seen as a peripeteia in the creation of national identity, into a lament for the disintegration of belief in national values, and the loss of hope in the future.

Not all visions of Russia's past, and future through her past, were so pessimistic. The First World War initiated a burst of literary triumphalism, in which even the formerly alienated cubo-futurists participated, with Maiakovskii producing patriotic agitprop representing the Germans as folklore bogies; other poets, such as Gumilev, saw in the war the opportunity to assert again masculine military values that had seemed devalued by the increasing prominence of feminism and of women's writing. Though disaffection with the war had set in by 1916, the Revolution of 1917 seemed to offer new possibilities of collectivism. Even the chaotic violence of the first months could seem an exhilarating expression of Russia's return to her essential, barbaric nature, as in two famous texts by Blok: in 'The Twelve' ('Dvenadtsat'', 1918), citations from urban folklore and from religious mythology are used to construct the narrative of a revolutionary force led by Christ, while 'Scythians' ('Skify', 1918) represents the onward march of Russia as the incursion by Eastern tribes into an inert Europe. These texts, like Khlebnikov's rather earlier excursions into Slavic paganism, such as his narrative of the Russian Pan, *Venus and the Shaman* (*Venera i shaman*, 1912), evoked an aggressive national pride that was far from the official Slavophile traditions of self-sacrifice and co-operation. The threatening undertone in this pride could, on some occasions, be expressed in an intellectual anti-Semitism that was the insidious counterpart to official policy of the day. A subtle and influential thinker,

Vasilii Rozanov, asserted in his work the moral superiority of the Russian nation to manipulative and feminized Judaism: thus did the theories of Nietzsche and Weininger give a new and unpleasant edge to Slavophile tradition. And the classicist F. F. Zelinskii (Tadeusz Zieliński), who dreamed of creating a 'Slavonic Renaissance' based on a return to classical Greek and Latin traditions, devoted much space in his popularizing essays on Greek culture to asserting the primacy of classical culture over every other in the ancient world, most particularly the Hebrew.[33] Partly for these reasons, and partly because its members shared the secular tastes of the nineteenth-century Russian intelligentsia, rather than the mystical ones of the *fin de siècle*, the Bolshevik government was to set its face against religious philosophy in all its forms, purging the libraries of idealistic and mystical texts (including even Plato!), and choosing to see the last years of the imperial regime through the eyes of Chekhov, Gor'kii, and Tolstoi, rather than of Ivanov, Berdiaev, Blavatskaia, or Merezhkovskii.

From National Pessimism to National Celebration: Russian Painting after 1881

In the visual arts, which were dominated throughout the late nineteenth century by followers of the *Peredvizhniki* (Wanderers) movement, expressions of national identity were rather different from those to be found in verbal texts. Rather than reflecting disillusion and cynicism, or hopes of a better world, the work of the most prominent painters, Il'ia Repin and Vasilii Surikov, moved, between the 1870s and the 1890s, away from social criticism and towards a celebration of the triumphs of national history. Over the same period, the Wanderers moved from being a marginal group set up in order to challenge the canons of academic art to becoming part of the Russian academic establishment, propagating their aesthetic and techniques in art schools and assaulting new artistic movements in critical articles. Significantly, work by the Wanderers was well represented not only in the collections of Pavel Tret'iakov, but also in the Alexander III Museum, whose original display was a showcase of patriotic painting (from portraits of rulers in Room 1 to Russian landscapes at the end of the display).

The transition had begun to become evident as early as the 1870s, when Repin's painting *The Archdeacon*, a study of a village priest, though perceived by conservative critics as an attack on the cloth, was in fact intended by the painter to represent a national type radiant with energy and earthy vitality ('a survivor of pagan gluttony').[34] A more famous painting by Repin, *Procession of the Cross in Kursk Province* (1883), was similarly ambiguous, reflecting at once the docile faith of plain, unwashed, sullen-faced peasants choreographed by repressive policemen, and a magnificent national pageant, uniting all classes and types in a traditional rite of social and religious solidarity. By the 1890s, Repin's historical set pieces evoked popular patriotism without any trace of alienation: *The Zaporozh'e Cossacks write a Letter to the Turkish Sultan*, begun in 1880, two years after the Russo-Turkish War, and completed in 1891, represents its subjects (supreme symbols of aggressive Orthodox patriotism since the publication of Gogol''s *Taras Bul'ba* in the 1830s) as colourful, barbarous expressions of Slavonic military strength, shown in the act of manifesting their derision for all external, and particularly non-Christian, authority. In the next decade, Repin, by now probably the best-regarded academic painter in Russia, was to embark on two canvases evoking autocratic power in the present day, one of which, *The State Council* of 1901–2, was later to become a model for ruler portraiture during the era of socialist realism.

A similar path can be traced in the work of Vasilii Surikov, who moved from portraying historical dissidence (in his famous paintings *Boiarynia Morozova* and *The 'Strel'tsy'* of the 1880s, where the seventeenth century is seen as a time of embittered social conflict, rather than of the harmonious consensus beloved of autocratic symbolism) to illustrating famous victories. His *Suvorov Crossing the Alps* (1899) was a work particularly in tune with official patriotism, showing as it did Russia's military might engaged for the 'salvation' of Western Europe. And *The Tsaritsa Visiting a Convent* (1912) returned to the pre-Petrine period in order to represent a tradition of official piety and philanthropy: the young central figure (who bears more than a passing resemblance to the reigning Tsaritsa, Alexandra) is shown as a pale and vulnerable figure, on display before the sympathetic or knowing looks of her subjects. It is autocracy, rather than hostility to it, which is now intended to evoke the viewer's sympathy.[35]

The 1890s was also to see the older Wanderers turn to ethnographical portraiture of an idyllic, rather than socially critical, kind. Repin's *Belorus* (1892), or Surikov's *Cossack Girl* (1898) are healthy, glowing specimens of improbable vitality, the human equivalents of cottages with roses round the door and allotments bursting with carrots. Only in portraits of private individuals, such as Repin's vision of a pale-faced, haughty, hollow-eyed, languidly powerful Baroness Ikskul, did he and Surikov escape the constraining pressure to treat individuals as embodiments of national virtue and as expressions of patriotic optimism. The earlier Wanderer tradition of representing national types and events critically, rather than idyllically, did continue, but its proponents were now minor realists, such as Bogdanov-Bel'skii, in whose work satirical force was often submerged beneath documentary detail (see chapter 1).

The fact that national triumphalism played a larger role in painting than in literature (it is hard to think of any writer of Repin's or Surikov's talent who would have endorsed their approach) may be partly attributable to the fact that the authorities were able to exercise greater control over the artistic establishment than over the literary one. The Tsarist government could censor literary works that were not to its tastes, but writers did not have to go through an officially sanctioned system of professional training, as artists did, and pass professional examinations before they were allowed to practise their craft. Repin, along with the landscape painters Kuindzhi and Polenov, was to be among the artistic representatives on a government commission which drafted new statutes for the Academy in 1893. After this, senior Wanderers dominated the teaching body of the institution too.[36] The Academy was increasingly despised by innovators after the mid-1890s, with the Wanderers now subject to the same kind of attacks with which they themselves began their secessionist movement in the 1860s.

The old oppositional tradition was to be revitalized after the 1905 crisis by a very different set of artists, as the relaxation of print censorship allowed the publication of graphic art that was ground-breaking not only in its violent denunciations of official brutality, but also in its sophisticated and economical use of line. Among many superb cartoons and caricatures, perhaps the best work was done by Mstislav Dobuzhinskii. *The Pacification*, published in the second edition of *Zhupel* (*The Bugbear*, 1905), is a brilliant image of the Kremlin as ark rising above a deluge of blood, with a blood-spattered, colourless rainbow in the background, black clouds promising to add to the deluge, and no dove. Dobuzhinskii's handling of biblical symbolism is strongly influenced by the work of Japanese printmakers, in particular Hokusai, who was widely admired among Russian artists in the late nineteenth and early twentieth century, being the subject, for instance, of a pioneering article by the poet and painter Maksimilian Voloshin.

As with the verbal arts, representations of national identity were not limited to simple 'pro' and 'contra' expressions of loyalty, or disloyalty, to official tradition. From the mid-1890s, painters such as Vasnetsov, Nesterov, Bilibin, and Rerikh began to produce work whose sources could be traced to folklore, to Old Russian history, and to religious art. The traditions of 'national art' were also to be revivified by modernist painters such as Goncharova and Larionov, in whose work neo-primitivism was at least as important a direction as was abstraction. It was the most 'Russian' of these painters' works, too, which earned them a reputation abroad, exciting considerable interest, for example, at Roger Fry's Second Post-Impressionist Exhibition in London in 1912.[37] Neo-primitivism was particularly well represented in Moscow; among St Petersburg artists, the key movement was the World of Art, whose founders included Diaghilev, Somov, Benois, Lanceray, Dobuzhinskii, and Bakst, and whose elegant canvases were imbued with nostalgia for the eighteenth-century Russian and European past (though neo-primitivist elements were prominent in the work of Bakst, while Dobuzhinskii's superb black-and-white images of St Petersburg, many produced as illustrations to Dostoevskii, still remain among the hardest and least nostalgia-ridden images of that dangerously appealing city ever to be produced). A quite different form of aestheticism was to be developed in the work of the great landscape painter Isaak Levitan, whose lyrical images of the Russian countryside included not only such obviously attractive subjects as autumnal birch groves (*Golden Autumn*, 1895), but also bleak fields crossed by muddy tracks, images at once of endless space and of monotony.

The applied arts were also strongly involved in the national revival. The pioneer here was the railway magnate Savva Mamontov, one of Russia's most successful new capitalists and the first of a new breed of art patron, who played a key role in the rediscovery and revival of medieval artistic traditions and peasant crafts at the end of the nineteenth century. Not only the falsity of official national ideology (whose lip-service to pre-Petrine tradition was accompanied by a commitment to industrialization), but a sense that urbanization posed a very real threat to the survival of national cultural traditions stimulated Mamontov, who with his wife Elizaveta set out to preserve peasant crafts by establishing a museum and workshops at the artists' colony they founded in 1874 at their estate

View of the private theatre at Talashkino, the estate of Princess Mariia Tenisheva, showing the auditorium and drop curtain, with decorations painted by Nikolai Rerikh (Nicholas Roerich).
The abundant use of woodcarving and the Old Russian references (the figure on the curtain represents Baian, the Russian Ossian, with his *gusli*) are typical of the *style russe* movement, but the handling of the leaf and flower designs is in the spirit of art nouveau more generally. This photograph is taken from a spread of photographs devoted to Talashkino in a 1901 issue of *World of Art*, the sumptuous art journal sponsored by Tenisheva, which acted as a showcase for Russian visual and applied art as well as a conduit by which Western 'new arts' passed into Russia.

at Abramtsevo, near Moscow. The artists who worked with Mamontov included Vasnetsov, Vrubel', Serov, and Nesterov; the estate buildings, including a magnificent private church, Russian bathhouse, kitchen, and workshops in idealized Old Russian style, were among the most significant achievements of Russian revivalist architecture. Later, in the early 1890s, another lover of the arts, Princess Mariia Tenisheva, turned her Smolensk estate Talashkino into a similar arts centre; the focus on native crafts and traditions at both colonies can be seen as part of a nostalgic wave that swept across all of Europe in the second half of the nineteenth century, as the effects of industrialization took their toll. The chief influence here was the English Arts and Crafts movement, led by William Morris, who hoped the revival of native traditions would serve to revitalize contemporary art.[38] At one end, the Mamontovs' project intersected with the modernist movement: artists who participated in the workshops included the extremely talented symbolist painter Vrubel', who designed some extraordinary ceramic sculptures, as well as Vasnetsov and Nesterov. At the other, the Arts and Crafts movement fed into industrial or semi-industrial production: folk and Old Russian motifs became ubiquitous not only in architecture, such as Shekhtel's Iaroslavl' Station, but also in artefacts produced by commercial workshops, most particularly in metalwork, furniture, and ceramics.

But the most significant kind of artwork rediscovered from the Russian past was the icon. Though sacred pictures had always been valued for their liturgical and religious associations in Russia, they had not traditionally been valued primarily for aesthetic reasons. The work of outstanding masters was valued as a model for later endeavours, but over-painting, even of the oldest and most precious icons, was frequent; images were frequently all but invisible under wrought metal and jewelled *oklady* (cases), leaving only the hands and face exposed, and even these might be covered by a thick layer of soot from the candles. What was more, to an educated Western sensibility of the late nineteenth century, the Eastern tradition of icon-painting seemed utterly barbarous: typical was the attitude of an Englishman, J. Beavington Atkinson, who visited the Kremlin in the 1870s, and described the frescoes in the Cathedral of the Assumption in most uncomplimentary terms: 'The columns of the chief church in the Kremlin are bedaubed with indifferent pictures.'[39] During the late nineteenth century, however, under the influence of the new upsurge of interest in national history, icons began to become the subject of closer and more respectful scrutiny. Exhibitions were organized, and academic studies began to be issued. Father Pavel Florenskii, an aesthetician as well as a religious philosopher, began, in the 1910s, to evolve extremely interesting theories of how the symbolism of the icon should be interpreted, arguing that the absence of perspective in traditional Byzantine and Russian religious painting derived not from a backward failure to understand this development, but from a conscious choice to eschew ordinary geometrical perspective, with its subordination of image to viewer, in favour of 'reverse perspective', in which the image draws the viewer in to its eschatological, metaphysical reality.[40] Interest in the icon, like that in craft industries, had varied effects: it led to the production of some superb copies of early icons, particularly those of the seventeenth century, which were sold for domestic use, but more importantly, it inspired a whole generation of Russian modernist painters, in whose work the icon's geometrical draperies, flat handling of colour, etiolated hands, limbs, and faces, and symbolic representations of the natural world were used in order to construct a new, uniquely Russian, but also determinedly modern, sensibility in figurative painting, as demonstrated by such artists as Filonov, Goncharova, Tatlin, and Petrov-Vodkin.

All in all, then, expressions of identity in turn-of-the-century painting were very diverse. Russia appeared as a military power, as embodiment of tyranny, as the site of true Christianity, as the homeland of barbarous, pre-Christian energies (and here there was a direct link—thematic if not formal—between Repin and Surikov on the one hand, and Goncharova and Larionov on the other), and as the repository of traditional craft industries, to be wrenched from the verge of the extinction with which industrialization threatened them. Abandoning the now hackneyed painting of social conflict to minor figures, the great painters of the late nineteenth and early twentieth centuries (whose numbers were unprecedented in Russian history) constructed images whose impulses were sometimes, in political terms, overtly reactionary, but which made a far more significant contribution to European culture than those of the Westernizers of the past, the chilly neoclassicists of the early nineteenth century.

Performing Identities: Music Theatre and Ballet

Though reaction against official nationalism played a considerable role in both literature and the visual arts, it was perhaps only in music that Alexander III's Russification policies had truly positive effects. This did not mean, of course, that nationalism was entirely unproblematic here: the crisis of national identity that was felt so strongly in literature and painting of the 1870s and 1880s was also the subject of Musorgskii's last opera *Khovanshchina*, which (like Surikov's *Boiarynia Morozova* painting) ostensibly explores unrest in Russia at the end of the seventeenth century, but is really about the edge of the abyss on which Russian society found itself teetering at the end of the nineteenth: yet again the seventeenth century, sanctified in official ideology, was seen as a period of painful conflict.[41] However, the decision to close the Italian Opera and end the monopoly of the imperial theatres in 1882 made possible the performance of a rapidly growing repertoire of operas by Russian composers, most of whom (Glinka apart) the establishment had hitherto regarded with contempt. Tchaikovsky, one of the first graduates of the St Petersburg Conservatoire, founded in 1862 (its Moscow counterpart had opened four years later), soon achieved immense popularity with his opera *Eugene Onegin* (*Evgenii Onegin*, first performed by students from the Moscow Conservatoire at the Malyi Theatre in Moscow in 1879, and at the Bol'shoi in 1881), which was followed in 1890 by *The Queen of Spades* (*Pikovaia Dama*); eventually operas such as Borodin's *Prince Igor* (*Kniaz' Igor'*), Rimskii-Korsakov's *Woman of Pskov* (*Pskovitianka*) and *Snow Maiden* (*Snegurochka*), and Musorgskii's *Boris Godunov* also found their place in the repertoire and became themselves new symbols of national identity (as mentioned earlier, a performance of *Boris Godunov* was one of the events organized for Nicholas II's Shrovetide celebrations in 1903). Musorgskii and Rimskii-Korsakov directed their energies to opera precisely for these reasons, though their vision of Russian national identity, inspired as it was by a Pushkin play whose theme of usurpation had made it unpopular with the Tsarist authorities since its original composition, by Old Russian history, and by folklore, was of course one that was remote from the vision promoted by Alexander III, Pobedonostsev, and other ideologues of official culture.[42] Borodin's *Prince Igor*, on the other hand, was a musical adaptation of *The Lay of Igor's Campaign* (*Slovo o polku Igoreve*), depicting the struggle between a medieval Russian princeling and the nomadic tribes at the borders of Rus'; written in a time of imperialist expansion in the East, the opera can be given a chauvinistic interpretation, making it in some senses the heir to Glinka's *A Life for the Tsar* (*Zhizn' za tsaria*) a generation earlier.

The ballerina Matilda Kshesinskaia in her boudoir.
The figure of Kshesinskaia exemplifies the erosion of cultural boundaries that took place in the early twentieth century. A star of the Imperial Ballet, and mistress of Nicholas II before his marriage, Kshesinskaia also worked with the Ballets Russes after leaving the Imperial troupe in 1904. One of her most famous roles was Esmeralda, in the ballet of that name, based on Hugo's *The Hunchback of Notre Dame*, in one production of which she had danced with the pet goat pictured here. The elegant art nouveau screen, up-holstery, and carpet, and the dancer's diaphanous neoclassical gown, could have come straight from a film by Evgenii Bauer, who presented similarly glamorous visions to a very different public from that subscribing to *Stolitsa i usad'ba* (*Town and Country Life*), the periodical in which this image first appeared.

It was precisely operas based on Russian folklore or Russian history which were championed by Savva Mamontov at his Private Opera in Moscow, which he opened soon after the imperial theatres' monopoly was ended, in 1885. It was also Mamontov who brought the music world the incomparable Fedor Shaliapin. Works by Russian composers made up over half the entire repertoire of the company. Thirteen of the fifty Russian operas performed at the Private Opera during its eleven seasons received their world premières there, including Rimskii-Korsakov's *Sadko* (1897), *The Tsar's Bride* (*Tsarskaia Nevesta*, 1899), *The Tale of Tsar Saltan* (*Skazka o tsare Saltane*, 1900), and *Kashchei the Immortal* (*Kashchei bessmertnyi*, 1902). In addition, ten received their Moscow premières here, including Musorgskii's *Khovanshchina* (1897), and Rimskii-Korsakov's *Snow Maiden* (1885) and *Woman of Pskov* (1896).[43]

As with literature and painting, so in music the beginning of the modernist movement was to introduce new versions of national identity, which contested those current in official ideology more directly. Stravinskii, for example, is often seen as the most 'cosmopolitan' of Russian composers, and for a while violently rejected the stereotyped image of Holy Russia, what he called 'vodka–izba–balalaika–pope–boyar'. Yet he drew extensively upon Russian folk texts, music, drama, and the traditions of folk entertainers, particularly in his early music. Perhaps the most remarkable instance of this was another music drama, the ballet *The Rite of Spring* (*Vesna sviashchennaia*), first performed in 1913. Composed with the help of Nikolai Rerikh, who had worked at Talashkino, and who was an expert on Russian pre-history, the combination of the pagan subject (based on material taken from the folk-tales collected by A. Afanas'ev, 'the Russian Grimm', in the 1850s, and the neo-pagan poetry of Sergei Gorodetskii) with Rerikh's fiercely coloured costumes, Nijinsky's revolutionary choreography, and music that drew on native folk melodies, had an explosive effect on its first listeners. One of the dancers, Anatole Bourman, complained afterwards: 'With every leap we landed heavily enough to jar every organ in us. Our heads throbbed with pain, leaving us continually with nerves that jangled and bodies that ached.'[44] Still more devastating to the audience's sensibilities, though, was the score.

In *The Rite of Spring*, as in Stravinskii's other early stage works, the themes were for the most part entirely original, though based on Russian archetypes. As much as anywhere else, his 'Russianness' lay in the deepest features of his musical language: 'a radical diatonic character, a powerful and varied rhythmic scansion, a firmly-drawn melodic line, clear, bitter harmonies, an assertive brilliance in tone: a "stripped" style in fact, transparent in texture and with a solid bone-structure—these are the fundamental constants in Russian music, to which should be added an inherited tendency to the hieratic.'[45] As with those Russian painters inspired by the icon, Stravinskii's affinities with traditional Russian culture lay in the abstract qualities of technique, rather than in concrete attempts to reproduce the subjects and motifs of folklore.

The Rite of Spring, first performed in Paris, was part of the 1913–14 season of the Ballets Russes, the brainchild of the great entrepreneur Sergei Diaghilev, an associate of the World of Art movement who had made it his cause to publicize to the world the hitherto unrecognized achievements of Russian art and music.

Rather than an original artist, Diaghilev was an administrator and impresario of genius, who was able to mediate successfully between the avant-garde aspirations of the artists he employed and the conservative tastes of a moneyed Russian and Western public. Though Diaghilev's associates, such as Larionov, sometimes waxed ironical about his tastes, implying that his greatest talent was a nose for what was fashionable, he was in fact a remarkable innovator. For example, it was Diaghilev who took the decision to exhibit Russian icons for the first time primarily as works of art, rather than as religious artefacts, at an exhibition that he organized in 1902, and it was Diaghilev who went on, from 1908 onwards, to export Russian operas and ballets to Europe, following Mamontov's example by employing professional artists to design the sets and costumes. It was a venture that was outstandingly successful. Diaghilev was interested not only in what was new, but in what was Russia, and he must take considerable credit for having the vision to bring about a strengthening of Russian cultural identity at a time when morale was generally very low.[46]

Diaghilev of all people knew that the death of the old world—of which he was very much part—was imminent. His own personal reaction to the gloom and despair of the political situation in pre-Revolutionary Russia was to escape into art. Aesthete that he was, he wanted the death of the old world to be beautiful if nothing else.[47] But Diaghilev was more broad-minded than some of his friends from the World of Art circle, such as Somov and Benois, who rather disapproved of the younger painters, including Goncharova and Larionov, and later such Western modernists as Picasso, whom Diaghilev sponsored. 'Beauty' for him was represented by *The Rite of Spring* as much as by the more easily picturesque *Petrouchka*, and by *Le Coq d'or* as much as by *Daphnis and Chloe*, or the quintessentially World of Art-style *Good-Humoured Ladies*, a balletic adaptation of Goldoni choreographed by Massine to arrangements of Scarlatti.

Popular Patriotism

Though some Ballets Russes productions, such as *Petrouchka*, or indeed *The Rite of Spring*, were loosely based on subjects taken from Russian folklore, the distance between these adaptations and their originals was nothing less than enormous. The beautifully camp decadence of the Ballets Russes had a wistfulness and refinement utterly missing from folklore; what is more, the ballets and operas staged by Diaghilev were beyond the economic reach of the primary consumers of folklore in its original state, the lower classes of Russian society. These new versions of 'Russianness', therefore, almost certainly had no effect on the lives of peasants or workers. They were far more likely to be directly affected by official nationalism in its various manifestations: official decrees and propaganda, public buildings and rituals, popularizations of history; and also by commercialized versions of national culture (commemorative pottery, *style russe* motifs as used in cafés and variety theatres, folkloric motifs in advertising).

This does not, of course, mean that the lower classes were solidly patriotic in the sense that they shared the Tsarist regime's own identification of 'Russia' with autocracy and Orthodoxy. There was, certainly, a strong reverence for the person of the Tsar among Russian peasants, and indeed among some town-dwellers. After the assassination of Alexander II, pilgrims pressed round the spot where the Tsar had fallen, trying to dip their handkerchiefs in the blood pooled on the snow, treating the Emperor's remains as they might have the relics of a saint. Pierre Gilliard, tutor of the last Russian heir to the throne, Tsarevich Alexis, recalled his pupil's embarrassment when a delegation of peasants insisted on falling to their knees in his presence. Among some members of the Russian lower classes — servants, some of the common soldiery — devotion to the Royal Family survived even the Revolution, the Tsar's abdication, and the imprisonment of the Romanovs.[48] Popular attitudes to authority retained a pre-modern flavour of supplication; rather than demanding rights, peasants (and even workers) often petitioned for patronage, favours, or mercy, as their ancestors had in medieval times, though formulas of patronage on occasion found themselves attached to radical demands, and the 1905–6 unrest saw some groups addressing directly confrontational demands to various authorities.[49]

One check to rebellion was the fact that the concepts of paternalism, 'fatherland' (*otechestvo, otchizna*), and Tsar were often linked in the popular mind, as in the following patriotic soldiers' song:

> Из отчизны мы идем, марш вперед!
> Прощайте, милые друзья, нас царь зовет!
> На них печаль, и дело правое возьмет:
> С горячею любовью за отечество идем,
> Бог знает, вернемся-ль мы в родной наш дом.

> [We're marching from the fatherland, forward march!
> Farewell, dear friends, the Tsar calls us!
> Confound them, and the righteous cause will be victorious:
> With burning love we march on for the fatherland,
> God knows whether we will return to the home where we were born.][50]

It is clear, too, that many members of the lower classes were far from averse to the policies of 'Russification', since chauvinism was common enough. The Russians who supported the overtly anti-Semitic policies of the 'Black Hundreds' movements that sprang up in reaction to the uprisings of 1905 might have been a small minority of the population, but their capacity for instigating violence was very real. Far more common, though, was low-level chauvinism, manifested in abuse directed at foreigners (*zhidovskaia morda*, Yiddish mug, for a Jew; *tsyganskaia rozha*, Gypsy chops, for a Gypsy). Popular audiences loved to watch serious spectacles reflecting Russia's glory (for example, pageants depicting famous victories); they also enjoyed humour directed at non-Russians, especially Germans and Jews. A German and a Gypsy, and less frequently a Jew, were among the traditional victims of the puppet-theatre hero Petrushka, while tortuous and unfunny jokes about Jews were a speciality of the Russian music-hall. In one example, a Jew goes into the office of the 'Russian Steam Packet and Trade Agency' and tries to book himself a steamer ticket. Once he has grasped that the steamer will not simply take him wherever he wants to go (which takes a fair while), and fended off a protest by the assistant about the salt fish he is carrying ('It's me that stinks, not the fish'), he begins negotiating for the cheapest fare, trying finally to book 'seventh class', and talking all the while in a thick Jewish accent.[51] Not all jokes were as nasty as this example, and some displayed a certain admiration for Jewish craftiness, but there is no doubt that the most positive image of a Jew for the average working-class Russian was a comical and harmless, if rather simple-minded and tight-fisted, joker.

But if the Russian subordinate classes shared some of the views of conservative Tsarist officials, they did not share by any means all of them. For one thing, uneducated Russians often had a foggy grasp of international affairs, so that they were unable to feel much resentment against Russia's foreign antagonists, except of the most generalized kind. Even when war erupted in the late 1870s against Russia's traditional antagonists the Turks, many of the peasants in Aleksandr Engelgardt's district were unable really to understand what was going on:

> They have no hatred for the Turk, all their hatred is directed at her, the British woman [i.e. Queen Victoria]. . . . They were already talking about the war a long time ago, three, four years ago. Various rumors circulated in which the 'Englishwoman' figured most prominently. . . . No matter how absurd these rumors and stories, their general idea was that the heart of the matter had to do with the Englishwoman. Something happened, and we had to ally with the Englishwoman, but in order to do so, we had to convert her to our faith. If we don't succeed in converting the Englishwoman to our faith, there will be war.[52]

Perhaps the confusion derived from folk memories about the Crimean War twenty years earlier, but any number of other explanations for it can also be adduced (for instance, antagonism against *bab'e tsarstvo*, 'women's rule'). Chauvinism, or national definition by negatives, formed an unstable and unreliable basis for nationalism of a positive kind, as Hubertus Jahn has demonstrated in a recent close study of nationalism during the First World War. Though bellicose propaganda reached heights not seen before in Russian history, and though lower-class resentment against Germans erupted in pogroms against German shop-owners, the Tsarist authorities were unable to drum up positive patriotism in the sense of support for what, once it became costly in terms of lives, soon turned into a deeply unpopular conflict.[53]

As Engelgardt's recollections suggest, religion, rather than ethnic origin or even language (though the popular Russian word for all foreigners, *nemtsy*, 'the dumb', suggests that the last played some role in perceptions), was probably the most important aspect of 'Russianness' for many peasant Russians. Here there was a strong possibility of intersection between official ideology and popular belief, since peasants were not only strongly loyal to the Church, but also likely, in the ordinary course of things, to have much contact with its teaching, to which they were exposed not only in sermons, but in basic literacy teaching, which still, in the late nineteenth century as in pre-Petrine times, adopted religious material—the breviary and the psalter—as the first practice texts. By law, one to two hours per week's teaching in all Russian primary schools had to concern religion (*Zakon Bozhii*, the Law of God), so that even the Sunday schools run by the Imperial Technical Society included extensive teaching of religious material (prayers, the Short Catechism, bible stories, lives of saints, and icon appreciation, among other things).[54] Even in cities, religion remained a not insignificant part of popular life. In the environs of St Petersburg during the late nineteenth century, for example, two religious figures attracted huge numbers of followers: Father John of Kronstadt, philanthropic activist, popular preacher, and author, and Kseniia the Blessed, a *iurodivaia* (holy fool) whose burial place in the Smolensk Cemetery became a spot for popular pilgrimages.

Of course, the Tsarist regime's insistence on indoctrination could not ensure that all Russian subjects remained devoted Christians, and there is considerable evidence that Russian peasants who left their villages, most particularly men, tended to be extremely lax in their religious observances when living in the city.[55] Uprooted from village life, where the parish church, with its services for saints' days and Sundays, and its annual *prestol'nyi prazdnik* (festival of the saint to whom the church was dedicated), was an important centre of activity, many workers also lost touch with their faith. Religious feeling was transferred to other objects: often, to radical political groups, which sometimes employed quasi-religious rhetoric in order to tap popular piety in a new cause, or sometimes directly propagandized against religion, or sometimes both together. Like Russian intellectuals, too, peasants and workers were attracted to evangelical forms of Christianity, particularly the Baptist movement. Thousands were also drawn to the teachings of Tolstoi, whose doctrines of salvation through self-restraint, sexual continence, pacifism, and manual labour fell on anything but stony ground among peasants and workers throughout Russia. The energy with which both churchmen (for example, John of Kronstadt) and Social Democrats (for example, Lenin) attacked Tolstoyanism is a clear indication of just how popular the movement was.

But it was not only new forms of collectivism that proved attractive. Some chose to use their new literacy in order to express their feelings in words. These included not only the worker poets discussed in our first chapter, but the so-called 'peasant poets', men from Russian villages whose verse gained them admiring readers and listeners among Russian educated circles in the 1910s, who, indeed, because of the intelligentsia's idolization of the peasantry, found themselves lionized in every literary drawing-room in both capitals. Two of the peasant poets, Sergei Esenin and Nikolai Kliuev, were men of exceptional literary talents. They were also expert poseurs who knew exactly how to manipulate the expectations of Russia's literary establishment. Asked, in 1915, to inscribe a comment and a signature in the album of the literary historian and collector F. Fidler, for example, Kliuev produced a well-turned, and suitably deferential, compliment to his host's interests: 'A Heine manuscript, Pushkin's pipe, the second part of the dead soul [*sic*] and . . . my ephemeral signature! It seems we have to believe in miracles, even in this century of iron and lies.'[56] Acquaintances, such as Georgii Ivanov and indeed Esenin, were later to remember Kliuev acting the peasant naif for all he was worth: changing out of a suit and into traditional clothing in order to go visiting, or insisting that he would not read his poems in 'the parlour', but only in the kitchen.

However, underneath his forelock-tugging act, Kliuev preserved a shrewd and contemptuous appreciation of just how much he was worth to those who for the moment chose to enthuse over his work, as the following scorchingly embittered letter to Esenin of 24 April 1915 indicates:

> I'm chilled by memories of the humiliations and patronizing caresses that I've had to endure from this pack of dogs, the public. I've collected about two hundred cuttings from papers and magazines about my work, which in time may serve as documentary evidence for researching their socially and intellectually snobbish [*barsko-intelligent-nyi*], pompous, and contemptuous attitudes to the pure word, and for demonstrating the fact that the spirit of Saltykova [a notorious serf-abuser at the time of Catherine II] and Arakcheev [court official of Alexander I] has still not disappeared even among the best members of so-called Russian society. I remember how [Sergei] Gorodetskii's wife sat there at one gathering where they were all praising me to the skies, waited for a pause in the conversation, and then was pleased to say, 'Yes, it must be wonderful to be a peasant.' Well, lad [*tovarishch*], doesn't that just sum up what you and I should most detest, what should cut us to the quick? You see, it's not your soul they're interested in, the immortal part of you, but the fact that you, a lackey and a boor [*kholui i kham*], a Smerdiakov [from the character in Dostoevskii's *Brothers Karamazov*], just managed to open your mouth and say something articulate.[57]

But for the time being Kliuev continued to produce well-turned 'peasant poetry' according to the accepted patterns, invoking seasonal changes, daily labour, izba *realia*, and the ritual practices of Orthodox sects (especially the *Khlysty*). It was only after the Revolution, when the new intellectual establishment soon indicated its preference for worker lyric over the poetry of the Russian village, that the anger he had expressed in his letter to Esenin made its way into his verse, and he began to produce some of the most magnificent laments for the destruction of rural life ever created in any European country.

It was not only *vis-à-vis* the intelligentsia that new identities were defined, but within the lower classes themselves: between skilled and unskilled workers, the employed and the unemployed in the cities, between those who had benefited from the Stolypin land reforms in the countryside, and those who had not; between migrant labourers and those who were permanent residents. Gender relations, too, came under increasing pressure: women in villages with high levels of male migrancy expected to participate more fully in public affairs than they had traditionally been expected to do, while those women in towns who had their own salaries, rather than being employed unpaid in the peasant households, could also exercise economic leverage in order to assert themselves. Social upheaval could contribute to altering the gender balance: as happened all over Europe, women workers began to be employed as substitutes for men in some traditionally male forms of employment during the First World War, while others exploited the need for workers in order to edge themselves unofficially into men's jobs. Even before the start of the war, in March 1914, the mass-market *Gazeta-kopeika* (*Copeck Paper*) reported on a case in Astrakhan':

> The Astrakhan' District Court has dropped the case of Mariia P., who had been charged with altering the name 'Mariia' to 'Mark' in her passport [i.e. identity papers] and living under the name 'Mark Pashin'. The discovery was made quite fortuitously. A young, beardless, and moustacheless sailor working as a cook on the Volga steamer *Nikolai* came to the attention of observers. [When challenged, she confessed

she had done this] to escape from the 'gallantry' of her employers and their customers, and so that she could earn more money. Having turned herself into a man, she
started earning 4–5 times as much as before. She had made the change in Nizhnii
Novgorod, where she had been employed in a cookshop, and had then moved on to
Astrakhan', where at first she had worked as a painter, and then got a job as a cook.[58]

Six months later, when the war had started, another woman made a still
more extraordinary transition: from nun to soldier. The same paper reported
that a 21-year-old novice from a convent in Kazan' had been caught in Vilno
'dressed in a private's full field dress, with her hair cropped'.[59] Alongside such
cross-dressers, the Russian Army also, unlike its counterparts in other European
countries, found room for women serving as women: the famous 'Women's
Battalion', founded in May 1917 during the death throes of Russia's involvement
in the First World War, attracted 2,000 recruits during the first two days of
enlistment, drawn from all classes, from the gentry and intelligentsia down to
workers, servants, and peasants. In its wake, battalions were formed in Moscow,
Perm', Odessa, and Ekaterinodar, with smaller units in Kiev, Saratov, and many
parts of the Black Sea coast. The Petrograd Battalion was to play a not inconsid-
erable part in fighting during the October Revolution, as the last detachment left
guarding the Winter Palace when the Bolsheviks stormed it.[60]

Though Aleksandra Kollontai mocked the Women's Battalion recruits as
women motivated by personal disappointment, especially in love, it is clear
that these women, like those who joined up in men's battalions, and, indeed, like
women soldiers at any period, had many more motives than forgetting personal
grief in fighting. Desire to have a share of men's sexual independence, earning
power, and social status was certainly the main impulse in some cases, such as that
of *Gazeta-kopeika*'s Mariia P. Another motive was the expression of patriotism:
Mariia Bochkareva, founder of the Petrograd Women's Battalion, stirred the
hearts of her listeners with a speech calling on women 'whose hearts are pure crystal, whose souls are pure' to set 'an example of self-sacrifice' and to help save the
motherland.[61] There were women who lived as men in some Russian villages
(dressing like men and doing men's work), the so-called *monatki*, but their position was less a question of choice than of necessity: they came from households
where there were no male relatives.[62] The conscious rebellion against gender
boundaries made by at least some women soldiers stemmed less from folk tradition, therefore, than from an unsettling of traditional gender boundaries in the
wake of urbanization: the promptings of these working-class women, none of them
educated feminists, were not dissimilar from those of the upper- and middle-
class activists who campaigned for women's liberation from legal, economic,
and cultural discrimination.

The Russian Women's Movement

Problems of terminology

To understand the history of the Russian women's movement we need both to
define it and to ask when it began and ended. The two questions are rather more

difficult to answer than they would seem; they are also inextricably linked, as will become clear in what follows.

Histories of women's movements in Europe and North America in the half century before the First World War come equipped with three apparently self-explanatory terms, all loaded with ambiguities and misconceptions: the 'woman question', the 'women's movement', and the always controversial term 'feminism'. First posed in the middle of the nineteenth century, the 'woman question' (in Russian, *zhenskii vopros*) was a catch-all phrase indicating a perceived crisis in relations between the sexes and the undermining of a long-established social hierarchy. It concerned issues that were both practical and philosophical—for example, whether society ought to educate girls as well as boys; whether girls were physically and psychologically capable of study, and, if so, whether their education should equip them for paid employment; how education would affect their future role as mothers, and what that role was; and how women's emancipation might affect the integrity and functioning of the nation and state. Discussion of the woman question ranged from education and work, to the role and structure of the family, to personal relations and sexual morality, to the balance between individual autonomy and responsibility to the community.

Although encapsulated as a question about women's place in society, the woman question in reality grouped together a host of interrelated issues that affected men as well as women—the very term betrays an anxiety about threats to male authority ('what shall we do with our women?') in a world undergoing massive social and economic upheaval and adaptation. In Russia, as elsewhere, the discourse on the woman question was largely a male one. It was mainly men who first defined it and initiated the public debates on female emancipation at the end of the 1850s, at a time when very few women felt sufficiently qualified (or were thought fit) to participate in public intellectual or political discussion. For these men the woman question had a certain abstract quality—a highly intellectualized subjectivity—whereas for women the subject also concerned the practical details of their day-to-day existence.

As a public and male-defined issue it was only one of several questions up for debate in the intoxicating air of the reform period, debate which was in some cases initiated by the government itself. The Jewish question ('what shall we do with our Jews?') was opened to the press for the first time after 1855, in an attempt to define the legal position of the Jewish communities incorporated into the Empire by Russia's conquest of its western territories in the eighteenth century: the ultimate goal was Jewish assimilation.[63] More immediately obvious as a question to be solved was the future of serfdom, which the new Tsar, Alexander II, addressed on his accession. In these few years of officially sanctioned *glasnost'*, the government's decision to emancipate the serfs generated an unstoppable debate about Russia's future, arousing dreams of transformation and regeneration that would inevitably be disappointed.

The male monopoly of the woman question in the world of published scholarship, journalism, and public affairs is all the more striking now that so much more is known about women's literary creativity in the half century before the women's movement developed. Prevailing cultural norms had made it possible for an exceptional woman ('the woman writer') to consider the woman question, so long as she confined her reflections and observations to a fictional or auto-biographical form.[64] While a number of female literary critics, most famously Mariia Tsebrikova, began to contribute to the public political discourse in the second half of the nineteenth century, their discussions of the woman question were still usually corralled into educational issues or discussions of literary works, rather than trespassing on the hallowed masculine ground of philosophy, political economy, or science.

A remarkable exception here was Mariia Vernadskaia, who ran a journal dedicated to free market economics with her husband. On her death in 1860, at the age of 28, Vernadskii penned a tribute to his 'modest' and 'self-sacrificing' wife, a highly gifted woman who had been 'the first and so far the only Russian woman to write on political economy'.[65] Vernadskaia's direct access to the printed medium evidently enabled her to take on such a role, although her modesty, according to her husband, extended to having many of her articles published under his name. In her own name she wrote a number of pieces on women and work; in a much-quoted passage, she exhorted women of her class to 'grow up' and 'stand on your own two feet' by earning a living.[66]

It was partly the virtual exclusion of women from public discourse—particularly striking when the issues being debated concerned them and their future—that first prompted a remarkable number of women to take action on their own behalf at the end of the 1850s and during the 1860s, thus creating what became known in Russia (as in the West) as the 'women's movement' (*zhenskoe dvizhenie*). Like the woman question, the term is difficult to pin down, but unlike it the phrase indicates female agency and initiative. The development of the movement in Russia was part of an international phenomenon which has been described by historians, but still not fully understood, largely because there are such clear explanations for its growth within each society, but much less identifiable causes across nations. In Russia it took shape after the disaster of the Crimean War (1854–6) and the accession of Alexander II, who immediately accepted the necessity of major social and economic change and substantial legal reform for Russia's survival as a major world power. The government's proposed educational reforms and the ending of serfdom were taken up by liberals hoping for an uninterrupted and controllable process of modernization, on Western models, and by a restless intelligentsia developing a radical critique of the existing hierarchical society.

This was the environment in which the women's movement grew. It began with the efforts of a rather small but committed group of women from the privileged classes to extend the restricted limits of their own lives, to end the legal and social subordination of women of all classes, to open up opportunities for education and work, and to provide practical help for women in poverty and distress. Over the next half century there was a significant widening in the scope of the movement (notably during 1905, when women's suffrage came on to the agenda), and its social base grew broader. Apart from its considerable practical achievements (above all in higher education, professional training, and work), it widened social perceptions of women's capacities and roles and punctured the pervasive misogyny of the dominant culture.

As it developed and became more confident, the movement also created its own literature, so that the earlier dominance of men in articulating the woman question receded, without disappearing altogether—few women, even by the early twentieth century, were contributing to theoretical writings on emancipation. It would be far too crude and sexually stereotyped, however, to suggest that the 'question' was entirely male territory and the 'movement' female; this would also diminish the complexities of the interrelationship between intellectual debate and practical activity. For example, Nikolai Chernyshevskii's didactic novel *What is to Be Done?* (*Chto delat'?*, 1863), with its central role for an emancipated woman, Vera Pavlovna, is often interpreted as a blueprint for the radicals of the 1860s; in reality, it was as much a commentary on, or documentation of, a phenomenon that it substantially influenced, but in no sense initiated.

Another point raised by *What is to Be Done?* is the question of deciding where to place the many 1860s women who, like the fictional Vera Pavlovna, called themselves 'nihilists', were closely involved in radical discussion of the woman question and committed to their own liberation as women, but who, at the same time as being actively (if intermittently) engaged in the women's movement, were intentionally detached from it. Because the Vera Pavlovnas of Russian society refused to consider themselves participants in the women's movement, labelling it 'aristocratic' and rejecting its leaders' moderation and willingness to compromise, it is difficult to include them; yet to leave them out wrongly conveys the impression that the movement was very narrowly focused and composed only of middle- and upper-class women leading lives in most respects genteel and in conformity with society's norms.

Though nihilism as such hardly outlived the 1860s, women continued to be involved in radical politics right up to 1917. The issue of where such women stood in relation to the women's movement became even more acute as first populists and later Marxists laid claim to solving the woman question via social revolution, and denounced the women's movement as an unwanted distraction from Russia's true needs.

Defining the boundaries of the woman question and the women's movement may not be straightforward, but at least the terms themselves are not heavily contested. The same cannot be said for feminism, whose use ever since the term was coined has produced a severe allergic reaction in large numbers of people, many themselves closely involved with a women's movement. The word was first used sometime in the mid-nineteenth century, but did not become at all common until the 1890s, and even then was often avoided.[67] In Russia it found favour almost nowhere, evoking all the negative connotations that Turgenev abhorred in the 'emancipated woman', mercilessly portrayed in *Fathers and Children* (*Ottsy i deti*, 1862) as the shrill, angry, over-intellectual, pretentious, and utterly unfeminine Kukshina. Like this anti-heroine, feminism appeared to be a denial of femininity, a rejection of the 'natural' polarities of sexual difference and therefore of the accepted sexual hierarchy. While there were many political quarrels over the validity of the women's movement, the term itself was not threatening; it emphasized co-operation and mutuality, not 'strident' individualism. Feminism was never associated with motherhood and emotional fulfilment, whereas the term 'women's movement' readily evoked a collectivity of nurturing and maternal figures.

Feminism also suggested women without a homeland, who failed to put the needs of society and nation before their own self-interest. In general this was a false perception—feminists aspired to internationalism, but also possessed a strong sense of their own nationality, and believed that women as equal citizens would have a central role to play in their nations' destiny. But in Russia (as in many other societies experiencing a political struggle for popular representation against an authoritarian state system, or for national autonomy against an imperial power), feminists' alleged lack of patriotism made them unacceptable both to the government and to the liberation movement struggling against it. Largely for this reason, separatist feminism never took hold in Russia; even when the women's movement became involved in the campaign for political rights in 1905, the majority continued to identify with the common struggle against autocracy and tyranny (*proizvol*). Significantly, the small number of separatists who then emerged were not afraid to call themselves feminists, but they remained among the very few in Russia who did use the term in a positive sense.

It cannot have been the foreignness of the word *feminizm* by itself that caused the problem, if we consider how easily many other 'isms' crept into the Russian language (*sotsializm* and *kommunizm*, to name but two). But it may have suffered from the dual handicap of being an alien word and of describing women who were already outsiders by virtue of their failure to conform to the expectations of Russian womanhood. It was not simply that they disrupted the conservative stereotype of submissiveness and self-abnegation. Women in the populist movement of the late 1870s—terrorists who engaged in violently unfeminine activities and were reviled by the right wing—were admired for their defiance of convention, in a way that feminists could never be, by liberals who otherwise abhorred terrorism. Terrorist women were worshipped for being willing to sacrifice themselves for a cause beyond their own narrow interests; feminists were never seen as self-sacrificing, even when they dedicated their entire lives to the cause of women's liberation.[68]

Historiographical problems

The problem of defining terms should not be dismissed as a scholarly obsession. It arises out of the need to look with new eyes at the history of women's emancipation in Russia before 1917, releasing it from a highly schematic interpretation that bound all Soviet historians and infused the entire subject for decades. This model divided the women's movement into two antagonistic forces: on the one hand, non-revolutionary women (termed 'bourgeois' by their revolutionary opponents before 1917 and by Soviet historians thereafter), pursuing female emancipation but rejecting any fundamental change in the social structure; and on the other, women closely involved in revolutionary organizations, for whom women's liberation went hand in hand with social transformation. According to this highly schematized interpretation, Marxists developed the nihilist and populist critique of Tsarist society into a scientific analysis of women's oppression, which they claimed was inextricably connected to the class relations of an emerging capitalist system, and could be resolved only by capitalism's overthrow.

As is clear from our own remarks above on the nihilists and their successors, there can be no doubt that the mutual antagonism of reformers and radicals was a constant factor in the Russian women's movement (as in other countries too), and that the lack of a stable middle ground profoundly affected the movement as it did every other aspect of Russian political life. At the same time, the crude categorization of 'reformers' and 'revolutionaries' ignored the reality of intermittent collaboration between many individuals in the two 'camps'; it also distorted the political history of Russian women by assuming the inevitable attainment of women's liberation after 1917, under Bolshevik rule. With the disappearance of the Soviet Union, this inevitability was exposed as historical myth: the much-vaunted sexual equality of Soviet society was admitted to be at best flawed, and the processes whereby women were understood to have achieved their own liberation during the last half century of Tsarist rule came to seem much less clear-cut and predictable.

As well as focusing almost exclusively on the split between left and centre, the Soviet model left out a host of other questions that arise in the study of women's movements around the world. In other national histories, as well as Russia's, it was not at all uncommon for women to be actively engaged in philanthropy, education, or child welfare, but consciously to stand aside from the women's movement, and even (as, say, in the case of the British writer Mrs Humphrey Ward) to express hostility to the pursuit of political equality. Whether historians should retrospectively include such women in a broader concept of the women's movement is a matter of current debate. Should the contribution made by all women in the public eye to changes in female self-perceptions and social assumptions about women's roles be acknowledged as an achievement of the women's movement? What of the role of women in national liberation movements, who did not see themselves as feminists and whose male leadership may have been unenthusiastic or obstructive on the issue of female equality? Should these women, too, be regarded as 'feminists despite themselves'?[69] Issues such as these were hardly acknowledged in the very limited Soviet historiography of women's liberation, nor in much of the Western writing on the subject.

Problems of periodization

This questioning of the stereotyped Soviet interpretation, along with the rediscovery of women's writing in the first half of the nineteenth century, leads necessarily to a reassessment of the established periodization of the women's movement, which has always been neatly fitted into the half century between the 1860s and 1917. Alexander II's reforms, with which the period opens, are followed by rapid industrialization and urbanization; the growth of radical political movements, including terrorism; the Tsar's assassination in 1881, followed by severe political reaction; the intensification of Russian nationalism and the upsurge of nationalist movements among the many non-Russian subject populations in a constantly expanding empire; the emergence of liberalism as a political force; a simmering social and political crisis that finally exploded in the 1905 Revolution; mounting international conflict which led to the catastrophe of the First World War; the fall of the monarchy in February 1917, the failures of the provisional government, and the Bolshevik coup in October.

There are a number of ways in which this framework might need adjustment. For example, women's writings of the late eighteenth and early nineteenth centuries raised topics in literary form that were to become central to the debates on the woman question in the 1860s. The very existence of these writings also represented a remarkable shift in the nature of women's presence in public life (before 1750, public written culture had been wholly dominated by men). Much of this early women's writing was overlooked by the men who defined the terms and provided the texts of debates on the woman question, whose denunciations of women's ignorance overlooked the fact that educated women had been writing in similar vein for more than half a century. But it is possible to see a direct connection between, say, Aleksandra Murzina's spirited poetic defence of women's intellectual capacities in the 1790s, Ekaterina Puchkova's articles on women's education and women's literature in the 1810s, the fiction of Mariia Zhukova and Elena Gan in the 1830s and 1840s, and the work of Nadezhda Khvoshchinskaia in the 1850s and 1860s.[70]

At the other end of the period, the watershed of 1917 merits new scrutiny. Most histories of Russia are still divided quite comfortably into 'pre-Revolutionary' (or 'late Tsarist', 'late imperial') and 'Soviet'. But if 1917 ceases to be an end-point, how will that affect the history of the women's movement?

On the one hand, there are grounds for arguing that 1917 was not a real divide: women had achieved little besides wider access to education and professional employment before that date. They had to wait for the downfall of the monarchy for any significant extension of their civil and political rights (universal suffrage for both sexes was one major legislative gain under the provisional government); until 1917 women were not recognized as equal before the law. The Bolsheviks, for their part, were formally committed to total sexual equality and initiated a range of legislation to that effect; they were also persuaded to establish a separate Women's Section (Zhenotdel) within the Communist Party, to mobilize the female masses for their own liberation and the success of the Revolution. Zhenotdel was a considerable triumph for Social Democrat women such as Aleksandra Kollontai and Inessa Armand who had waged a war on two fronts before 1917, against the 'bourgeois' feminist and against the predominately male leadership of their Party, which opposed separate work among the female proletariat.

Yet Zhenotdel possessed no real autonomy, surely essential for any definition of a 'movement'; it belonged to the ruling Party, and was closed down by Stalin at the end of the 1920s when, in a famous phrase, the woman question was declared 'solved'. Since the Bolsheviks also banned all opposition groups, including bourgeois feminist organizations, soon after their rise to power, it can equally well be argued that the women's movement, deprived by the October

Revolution of even the restricted scope for independent action that it had enjoyed under tsarism, really did cease to exist at the end of 1917.

Women's liberation after 1881

Whatever the conclusions of this necessary chronological reassessment, the fact remains that 1881 is in many ways a strange point at which to begin a history of the women's movement, representing as it did a disaster for both liberals and radicals. Those women radicals who were not rounded up by the police in the crackdown that followed Alexander II's assassination fled abroad, some abandoning politics altogether; the women's movement went into eclipse for more than a decade, and many of the hard-won gains of the preceding decade were snatched back only a few years after being granted. The Higher Courses of Education for Women (offering university-level or advanced secondary education in a wide range of subjects) were closed down everywhere but in St Petersburg; medical courses, sponsored by women since the early 1870s, were suspended until the late 1890s. Leading members of the women's movement lost their access to sympathetic ministers and bureaucrats; some suffered personally for their earlier outspoken behaviour. As early as the late 1870s, the well-connected Anna Filosofova had been put under surveillance for her alleged contacts with terrorists; in the wake of the assassination, her husband forfeited his post in the civil service. By that time the enthusiasm and confidence of the early women's movement had been dissipated; it never fully recovered, though it flared up during the 1905 Revolution and again just after the February Revolution of 1917.

But, though existing in a depressed cultural environment, in certain respects the women's movement can be said to have reached an equilibrium during the 1880s. For one thing, higher education for women was ceasing to be a matter of furious controversy, despite the closure of several higher courses and the narrowing of the curriculum in the one institution that survived (science was deemed to be incompatible with femininity). The very restrictions imposed on the running of the St Petersburg higher courses usefully transformed an unorthodox experiment into a secure bureaucratic edifice; its restrictions may have frustrated many of the students, but they made it more suited to hard political times. In any case, once the worst years of the reaction were past, schemes for new courses became acceptable. In 1897 medical courses were restored, this time in a purpose-built Women's Medical Institute in St Petersburg.

Furthermore, the rapid expansion of the Empire's major cities after 1881 was not halted by political reaction, and this had a profound impact on the women's movement. Peasant women migrated from the countryside to find work in factories, sweatshops, the retail trade, and domestic service; of more immediate concern to women from gentry and middle-class backgrounds, who were the mainstay of the movement, was the steady expansion of white-collar occupations, from clerical work to teaching. As the economy flourished, opportunities for educated women continued to increase. By the early twentieth century, primary education was not only expanding, but was becoming a female-dominated profession. Medicine, once the radical goal of a woman seeking her own liberation through service to 'the people', was becoming a respectable choice of career. Neither profession was likely to bring great status or financial reward for a woman, however. The prevailing sexual hierarchy determined pay levels and promotions, and permitted a range of demeaning restrictions on female autonomy, such as a marriage ban on women teachers in St Petersburg. Social isolation was the price paid by women teachers who went to work in rural schools, where they were often preferred to peasant men with equal qualifications, because women were expected to be politically docile. Not surprisingly, they were resented as middle-class intruders by many peasant communities.[71]

The newly sprawling cities not only brought work for migrants from the villages and for educated middle-class women, but also exacerbated a host of social, medical, and administrative problems, such as homelessness, disease, prostitution, illegitimacy, and alcoholism. From its earliest years the women's movement had involved itself in philanthropy, in an attempt to mitigate the worst effects of uncontrolled urban growth, though the government tended to be suspicious of all initiatives that were independently sponsored and not directed by a ministerial department (on women in philanthropy, see chapter 1). Such developments resulted in greater opportunities for women to train in new and existing professions. On graduation they were increasingly employed by rural and municipal councils, as teachers, doctors, and medical assistants, and in less obviously 'caring' professions such as statistics or agronomy.

Cultural priorities were also changing. The focus of the woman question moved away from ultra-rationalist approaches to education, work, and egalitarian relations between the sexes, to a concern with the undercurrents of sexual politics—the complexities of sexual desire and intimate relations between men and women, a new preoccupation with the nature of gender difference, and the revived cult of the 'eternal feminine'. This cultural shift should not be overemphasized, however. The institutionalization of science embraced many now middle-aged scientists who had been radicals in the 1860s and retained their ascetic and rationalistic ethics, and often their political sympathies too. The same values were also very evident in revolutionary circles. Marxists claimed to work on scientific principles and held the 'generation of the sixties' in great esteem for its clear-headed opposition to obscurantist religion and the cult of the irrational. Furthermore, male writers continued, as they had in the 1860s, to reveal assumptions (evidently derived from their own upbringing) about the 'natural' qualities of women that sat uncomfortably with their proclaimed sociological objectivity. When the embryologist Il'ia Mechnikov (a friend of women's education) declared that genius was a 'sex-related characteristic', like facial hair, he unwittingly indicated that attitudes had not much moved on since Chernyshevskii's portrait of the independent but 'womanly' Vera Pavlovna in the 1860s.

Besides, while discussions of the woman question had become more complex in society at large, the declared aims of the women's movement had not altered significantly. Changing intellectual and cultural fashions had not removed the need to establish women's autonomy and 'self-directed activity' (*samodeiatel'nost'*) and increase their still limited employment opportunities and status. Even education, which remained the greatest achievement of the women's movement before 1905, was not yet secure, or so widely available that the issue could be played down. Indeed, far from rejecting the recognized methods of achieving women's liberation, feminists if anything stepped up their struggle to break down the legal exclusions disabling women. The laws on inheritance, divorce, and custody and guardianship of children were still heavily weighted against women, while the statutory right to own property and retain earnings after marriage (unusual for European women before the end of the century) was in practice often negated by the obligation on married women to live with their husbands. (Freedom of movement was restricted for both sexes, but a married woman was inscribed on her husband's passport, so that his consent, as well as that of the authorities, was required for her to change her place of residence.) Pressure for reform of these laws—and many others—became stronger with the development of a self-confident legal profession dedicated to the modernization and liberalization of Russian law. Just as the women's movement benefited from the support of liberal university professors in the campaign for higher education, so they were aided by liberal jurists in their attempts to reform personal and property law.[72]

In the 1860s and 1870s, the women's movement in Russia had aroused the envious admiration of sympathizers abroad, impressed by its enterprise and achievement in a society legendary for being backward and conservative. In those years, contact between Western and Russian feminists was maintained, though proposals for collaboration always foundered on the government's hostility. After the Tsar's assassination, these contacts were frozen, and it was only in the early 1890s that Russians were able to resume them. By that time a network of women's organizations in Europe, America, and Australasia was in the process of forming the International Council of Women, and the Russians were invited to join.

This invitation served to emphasize their lack of independence. Repeated requests to the Russian government for permission to join the International Council were turned down. All attempts to organize a national association of women met with official refusal, and the feminists' only success was the St Petersburg-based Russian Women's Mutual Philanthropic Society (Russkoe zhenskoe vzaimno-blagotvoritel'noe obshchestvo), which was beset with restrictions from the moment of its foundation in 1895. Several attempts had been made to launch a feminist press, but none was successful until 1904. Hampered by these restrictions, Russian feminists had no chance of creating the sort of broad-based middle-class association already existing in the West. But in the circumstances, the survival of the Mutual Philanthropic Society and a few similar organizations in provincial towns is a testimony to the persistence of the women's movement leaders and a good illustration of the halting development of a civil society in Russia at the end of the century.

Women's political rights

For all these reasons it comes as no surprise that the right to political representation (women's suffrage)—a major issue for the women's movement internationally—could not yet be broached in Russia. It became possible only after 1900, when pressure for political change began to rise irresistibly. During the 1890s, radical political groups, shattered by a decade of government reaction, were slowly reforming. The mutual recriminations and theoretical disputes over populism and Marxism that characterized radical politics in the 1880s fitfully gave way to a revived interest in propaganda among the urban working class, though in most cases networks were rapidly broken up by the secret police. By the earliest years of the twentieth century, however, revolutionary polit- ical parties—the Russian Social Democratic Workers' Party and the Socialist Revolutionary Party—were putting down roots. Though dedicated to the ulti- mate overthrow of the existing system, both adopted 'minimum' programmes which in the interim would guarantee constitutional rights, including universal suffrage without distinction of sex, religion, or nationality. In these same years, liberal political organizations were also coalescing, with the eventual aim of introducing a constitutional order based on a representative national assembly and guarantees of civil rights. Those liberals willing to risk open confrontation with the government formed a broad alliance, the Union of Liberation, early in 1904, which eighteen months later became Russia's first political party, the Con- stitutional Democratic Party (Kadets). More moderate liberals subsequently formed smaller centrist fractions.

It would have been astonishing if the women's movement had not become politicized by this time. Russia had been plunged into an extended crisis by the outbreak of the Russo-Japanese war early in 1904. Like the Crimean War fifty years earlier, this was a military disaster for Russia; unlike the earlier conflict, it came near to overthrowing the government's authority. By the end of the year, after the assassination of the hated Minister of Internal Affairs, Plehve, public protest was intensifying. It took only the fiasco of the Bloody Sunday massacre of St Petersburg workers and their families in January 1905 for the protest to become virtually uncontrollable.

At the heart of the conflict between the government and the self-styled 'lib- eration movement' was the demand for a constitution. The discourse of civil and political rights and legal equality became ubiquitous, infusing protest in factories and peasant assemblies as much as in the universities, and underpin- ning claims for religious toleration and ethnic autonomy, for administrative independence in local government, professional autonomy, and so on. Within weeks, feminists were recruiting support for a Union of Equal Rights for Women—the first political organization of women in Russia's history—to campaign for uni- versal adult suffrage without distinction of sex, religion, or nationality. By the middle of 1905, it had been incorporated (against objections from some men unable to conceive of women in political life) into the main coalition of left- liberal political action in 1905, the Union of Unions. As well as joining in the general protest against the government, the women's union focused its cam- paigning on the suffrage issue, first to persuade the liberal opposition to support it (with overall success), and then to persuade the government to adopt it in law (with no success at all).

The Union of Equal Rights was the most energetic and uncompromising organization in the history of the Russian women's movement. But the politiciza- tion of the women's movement was not limited to the left-liberal opposition. At the end of the year, a group of feminists dissatisfied with the union for being too close to the liberation movement formed a separatist organization, the Women's Progressive Party, to push for women's rights in the forthcoming State Duma. It was led by Mariia Pokrovskaia, a doctor and committed campaigner against state-regulated prostitution, who had launched a feminist journal, *Zhenskii vestnik* (*The Women's Herald*) a year earlier. The new party did not thrive, however, though the journal continued publication until 1917. More conciliatory was the Russian Women's Mutual Philanthropic Society, which adopted women's suffrage as a cause in 1905, sending a mass of petitions and declarations to officials and leading political figures. It also took the initiative in planning a national congress of women, which (after many setbacks) was finally held in December 1908.

The mutual antagonism between Social Democrats and feminists had become particularly fierce over the issue of suffrage: the former accused the latter of betraying the needs of the working classes to the self-interest of upper- and middle-class women in their orientation towards the 'narrow goal' of women's emancipation. Feminists accused the Social Democrats of willingly sacrificing women's rights on the altar of class struggle. The congress of December 1908 represented something of a point of no return in these squabbles, as Aleksandra Kollontai led a walk-out by the Social Democrat delegation early in discussions, as an unmistakable signal of the left socialists' unpreparedness to engage in dialogue on the question of women's rights.

What is (still) to be done?

The strife between radicals and women's liberationists was, then, an insistent and continuing theme in the history of the Russian women's movement. It was to be vital in shaping Bolshevik policy on women (which addressed economic needs rather than personal rights). But however critical the radical/feminist split, preoccupation with this conflict in historical commentary has led to the overlooking of other important problems. The study of Russian women has generated some excellent social history, much of which has been acutely sensitive to issues of class; but the women's movement itself has so far evaded sociological analysis.[73] 'Bourgeois' and 'proletarian' are seen as pitted against each other, but a more subtle grasp of differentials is missing. Certainly, the bourgeois women's movement was predominantly made up of upper- and middle-class women, but what did those categories actually mean in practical terms? Within the movement were individuals from a wide variety of social backgrounds and with very different life experiences.

It is well known, for example, that some had established careers: in medicine (such as Anna Shabanova, a practising paediatrician and president of the Russian Women's Mutual Philanthropic Society), education (such as Mariia Chekhova, the mainstay of the Union of Equal Rights between 1905 and 1907), or journalism (Liubov' Gurevich, editor of *Severnyi vestnik* (*The Northern Herald*), a well-known 'thick journal'). But little has been written about their personal lives —whether they were married or lived singly, whether they had children, whether they were born in the city (like Gurevich, the daughter of a St Petersburg educationalist) or came there from a remote province (like Mariia Pokrovskaia, editor of *Zhenskii vestnik*). Even differences in generation have only been briefly mentioned, without any reflection on how they may have influenced attitudes and relationships.

So circumscribed was the Soviet view of Russia's history (and so unwittingly dependent were Western historians on that view) that a host of other vital questions was never addressed: for example, the influence of religion; issues of ethnic autonomy and nationalism and their effects on the women's movement; and the ambivalent relationship between women writers and artists and the women's movement. Religion is a crucial question. How significant, for example, were the tensions between the dogmatic agnosticism of the traditional Russian intelligentsia (to which many feminists belonged), and the sincere religious beliefs of some of them, and how was the women's movement affected by the increasing preoccupation with religion and spirituality in the *fin de siècle*? To take a couple of examples, what drew a woman such as Anna Filosofova to theosophy and spiritualism in the last years of her life, and did the rather moralistic Christianity of Pokrovskaia account for her lack of popularity among younger feminists, or was her separatism the stumbling block? There are much broader questions too, such as the role of the Orthodox Church in moulding and reflecting perceptions of gender difference and 'woman's place' in society, or the differing traditions and values of the many religious minorities—Old Believers, Protestants, Catholics, Jews, Muslims, and sects such as the *Skoptsy*.

One of the most pressing needs is to describe and analyse a movement that developed in a multi-national empire dominated in every respect by Russia. Russian feminists were acutely aware that they were speaking for women of all nationalities, but though they tried to maintain contact with women's movements in other parts of the Empire, in practice it was often easier to know what was happening in London or Berlin than to gather information about the Baltic provinces or the Caucasus. With few exceptions, Russian feminists were sympathetic to the persecuted minorities of the Empire (one individual at the All-Russian Congress of Women in 1908 was fiercely rebuked for her anti-Semitic remarks), and they identified with the nationalities' resistance to the government's heavy-handed Russification. They were particularly thrilled by the Finnish resistance, because women gained the vote in the successful struggle there twelve years before Finland won its independence from Russia.

Sympathy for the subject nationalities was a defining characteristic of the liberation movement in general, not least because contempt for these (above all for the Jews) was a guiding obsession of the right. Liberals supported the demands of Finns and Poles, for instance, to have their national identity recognized. However, there was a good deal less unanimity when national minorities held aspirations whose implementation might fracture the integrity of Russia. As the movements for national identity grew stronger, many liberals became fearful of the breakup of the Russian Empire and became increasingly antagonistic to calls for national self-determination. Socialists, on the other hand, while hostile to nationalism, were unanimous (before 1917) on the rights of subject minorities.

Russian feminists, being even further from political power than men in the liberation movement, perhaps felt less threatened by the nationalities' quest for autonomy from Russia. However, there were situations where interests were diametrically opposed, as when the liberal Kadets debated suffrage early in 1906, and the Muslim leader, whose support the Kadets needed, expressed unambiguous hostility to votes for women. On the whole, feminists did not have a distinct approach to national questions. Like members of the women's movement internationally, the Russian activists were dedicated to the renunciation of war and conflict between nations and peoples, but they also had a well-developed sense of their own Russianness. For all their denials of bellicosity, they submitted to the eruptions of patriotic fervour when war with Japan was declared, and similarly at the outbreak of the First World War, however they may have grieved in private. One prominent member of the Union of Equal Rights for Women, Zinaida Mirovich, precipitated a major crisis in the Union's more moderate successor, the League of Equal Rights, when she allegedly gave vent to an anti-Semitic comment about a fellow member with whom she had a feud. Anna Filosofova was incensed when the German feminist Käthe Schirmacher made offensive comments about the Poles, but it is not clear that all her fellows would have been so upset. In the case of the Muslim Duma leader, justifiable resentment at his misogyny may have been reinforced by a feeling of cultural superiority on the part of the Kadet feminists who argued against him.

Of all the questions that are still waiting to be asked about the Russian women's movement, though, the most elusive is the relationship between gender and power. Because of the severe restrictions on the Russian women's movement and on public political involvement in general, women's suffrage could never be debated before the turn of the century, though it was implicit in every discussion of female emancipation. Thus, a controversy addressed in Britain or America from the earliest years of the women's movement remained unopened in Russia until after 1900. The feminists' campaign for women's suffrage between 1905 and 1917 is well documented, but how they and their supporters conceived women's relationship to power is less clear. Looking beneath the liberal and socialist rhetoric of political rights, how was political equality actually envisaged? Did advocacy of women's suffrage mean simply 'the vote', or did it extend to women's equal participation in government? In Russia there was no parliamentary tradition, no elected assembly until the first State Duma in 1906. It was not a question of incorporating women into an already existing system. Tradition had to be established; some argued in favour of women's participation precisely because the new Russia needed every available resource, while others believed that women possessed unique spiritual and emotional qualities vital to a society overcoming centuries of oppression and violence.

This, however, was theory, persuasive rhetoric to be indulged when the chances of women actually exercising power were non-existent. Its real impact on Russian politics was slight, before and after 1917; power remained almost exclusively in men's hands (though the men belonged to different groups), with apparently little awareness on the part of those exercising it that sexual equality extended to an equal share in government. The particular traditions of Russian government might be invoked as an explanation for this, and the bloody circumstances of the Revolution. But Russia was hardly different from most other countries where women experienced a significant improvement in their legal status and a revolution of social expectations. Women's marginal position in relation to power is therefore not only 'political', in the specific sense, but imbricated with the whole cultural history of Russia. Though much still remains to be investigated, analysis of one key area of women's involvement in symbolic reality—their activities in art and literature—gives some sense of the forces in operation beyond the mechanisms of political government.

The Women's Movement and Women's Writing, 1881–1921: Social Change versus Self-expression

So far as the character of literary representations was concerned, the development of a Russian women's movement run by women for women seems at first glance to have left surprisingly few traces in women's writing of the same period. Feminist activists rarely, if ever, appeared in plays, stories, or poems; ironically, the officially sponsored Zhenotdel of the early Soviet regime was to spawn many more fictional descendants than the woman-centred feminism of the 1890s or 1900s. Feminist periodicals, such as *Drug zhenshchin* (*Women's Friend*) and *Zhenskii vestnik*, played an insignificant role in publishing women's writing when compared with mainstream journals and newspapers, such as *Russkaia mysl'* (*Russian Thought*), *Russkoe bogatstvo* (*Riches of Russia*), and especially *Severnyi vestnik*. Moreover, many prominent women writers were openly hostile to feminism. Zinaida Gippius, for example, one of the most important women writers of the twentieth century, described the woman question as 'really quite revolting'.[74] Though the realist fiction writers of the 1890s and the 1900s might not have gone so far, since many of them shared the radical left's sympathy to the general cause of women's liberation, few were active members of feminist groups, with such notable exceptions as Ol'ga Shapir, author of novels, stories, and plays, and an important activist in the moderate Russian Women's Mutual Philanthropic Society, Liubov' Gurevich, and Ariadna Tyrkova, member of the Union of Equal Rights for Women, journalist, literary biographer, and memoirist. In terms of participating numbers, populism was a far more significant rallying movement for women writers, attracting a spectrum from the realist Ekaterina Letkova to the modernist Lidiia Zinov'eva-Annibal.

At a deeper level, however, feminism in a broad sense, if not the feminist movement in a narrower one, was absolutely fundamental to the evolution of women's writing around 1900. It is notable, for instance, how many prominent women writers had been the direct beneficiaries of the new educational institutions for which feminists had campaigned. Among the *littératrices* who had attended the university-level Higher Courses of Education for Women were Letkova, Shapir, Gurevich, the realist writer Iuliia 'Bezrodnaia' (Vilenkina), the journalist and children's writer Tat'iana Bogdanovich, the critic Elena Koltonovskaia, as well as the poet Anna Akhmatova. So many others had come through the women's *gimnazii* that it is easier to name those who had not been educated there (for example, Gippius, Zinov'eva-Annibal, and the popular novelist Nadezhda Lappo-Danilevskaia).

What is more, feminist sympathies could be expressed in the actions of those who were not necessarily paid-up members of feminist groups. Letkova was an important supporter of educational charities for women; Gurevich, a skilled polemicist for women's rights since her student days, was publisher from 1891 of *Severnyi vestnik*, and was responsible for the favourable treatment given to women writers there; the best-selling author Anastasiia Verbitskaia used some of her earnings to found a women's publishing house. Such developments helped to make the late nineteenth century the era in which women's writing came into its own as a force in Russian literature. Few women now affected the male pseudonyms behind which their predecessors in the 1850s and 1860s had chosen to lurk: where pseudonyms were adopted (Akhmatova, Bezrodnaia), these were almost always explicitly feminine. More importantly, the years between 1881 and 1921 saw the production of an immensely diverse body of work, in which prose, poetry, and drama were produced in every conceivable genre and literary manner, and during which women proved every bit as artistically ambitious as their male contemporaries. In the late eighteenth century, and the first two-thirds of the nineteenth, women had generally avoided, or seemed uncomfortable with, the most prestigious literary genres, above all the epic (whether in its narrative-poetic or novelistic manifestation); now high-quality narrative poems and fiction of every length poured from the pens of women as well as men. Even male literary critics (increasingly challenged by women) were forced into less patronizing attitudes, with some, such as the poet Nikolai Gumilev, exercising a very positive influence on the reception and production of women's writing.

Rather than a cleavage between feminism and anti-feminism, or between feminism and literature, the years around 1900 were witness to an increasing divergence in ideology and artistic strategies between those women writers who favoured realism, in its different variants, and those who were attracted by the various 'new arts' tendencies that later came to be described as the modernist movement. While the former drew portraits of women battling against social repression and towards political and personal independence, the latter were far more concerned with women's self-expression, whether as sexual or as artistic subjects (or both). Undoubtedly, the realists were closer to the sympathies of the women's movement. Writers such as Mar'ia Krestovskaia, Anastasiia Krandievskaia, Shapir, Bezrodnaia, and Letkova all touched on issues drawn from the agenda of the movement: women's struggles for education and against discrimination at work, or within marriage and the family; participation in radical politics; reproductive rights (Ol'ga Runova's 'Nothing Sacred' ('Bez zaveta', 1913) even handled the explosive subject of abortion). Like their predecessors earlier in the nineteenth century, such writers showed women questing for personal satisfaction, as well as professional achievements; new in this generation was a concern with the lives of working-class women, who often (for instance, in the fiction of Shapir, Verbitskaia, or Krandievskaia) emerged as tougher and more determined than their more privileged sisters. Though a strong flavour of puritanism remained in much realist writing (female promiscuity was rarely presented as enjoyable, let alone commendable), there was also a strong emphasis on women's right to sexual fulfilment, and to end alliances in which they did not find it.

Most realist fiction was overtly didactic in character, whether exposing the status quo (as in Letkova's 'Lushka', a blistering depiction of poverty and oppression in the family of a village *soldatka*, wife of a conscript soldier, that is, effectively a single mother), or presenting incentive role models (as in Valentina Dmitrieva's 'Gomochka' (1894), the study of a feisty but self-sacrificing woman medical student). Though not necessarily more preachy than the fiction produced by many male writers of the day (Korolenko, Gor'kii, Garshin, and Boborykin all come to mind), women's realism carried particular weight because its writers, successful and prominent female professionals in the public eye, could be seen as models of enterprise (an interpretation suggested, for instance, by the admiring profiles of them carried in the feminist almanac *Pervyi zhenskii kalendar'* (*First Women's Calendar*)). It was, after all, during the early twentieth century that some Russian women writers managed to achieve a popular readership on a scale unforeseen by their predecessors. If Mar'ia Izvekova, author of early nineteenth-century soppy novels such as *Milena, or a Rare Example of Magnanimity* (*Milena, ili redkii primer velikodushiia*, 1811), had attained only a modest popularity, and been quite unable to rival foreign competitors such as Ann Radcliffe or Madame Genlis, Verbitskaia, Nagrodskaia, or Lappo-Danilevskaia were at least as well known in Russia as Ouida or Mrs Henry Wood. And Lappo-Danilevskaia's sensational tale of the Russian aristocracy, *A Russian Gentleman* (*Russkii barin*, 1914), was even translated into English (as *Michail, the Heart of a Russian*, in 1917), a tribute to the trashy appeal of this narrative of fatal love, infidelity, divorce, and suicide, spiced up with fashionable anti-Semitism (a minor character, the eponymous hero's lawyer, is gratuitously introduced in order to smear Jews as devious self-servers).

Quite different were the concerns of women modernists, who neither proposed role models in their writings nor suggested that their own lives should be imitated. Indeed, the work of self-styled 'decadents' such as Gippius, Zinov'eva-Annibal, or the poet Mirra Lokhvitskaia deliberately flew in the face of didactic tradition, presenting to the public alter egos who spoke openly of forbidden sexual desires, and turned a cold eye on all but their own passing fancies and impressions. Yet for all their distance from feminism and from the fiction of women's liberation, such writers, or the poets Tsvetaeva, Akhmatova, Poliksena Solov'eva, Sofiia Parnok, Adelaida Gertsyk, and Liubov' Stolitsa, to name only some of the more prominent associates of the 'new arts' groups, were also in an oblique sense artistic inheritors of the feminist movement. The successes of feminist activists in campaigning for women's rights led anti-liberal, Slavophile writers such as the poet Viacheslav Ivanov (in his essay 'On the Dignity of Woman') and Vasilii Rozanov (in 'Woman and Political Representation') to stress that 'true' liberation for women would be achieved not by granting them legal rights, but by encouraging them to look inwards to the spiritual forces of the 'eternal feminine'.[75] The 'eternal feminine' often appeared, in the representations of these and other writers (for example, Blok and Belyi), as the object of a contemplative male eye and interpretive male voice, but the new interest in the creative potential of 'femininity' facilitated the work of a new generation of women poets, as well as introducing 'androgynous' elements to men's writing. This was particularly important in a culture where women's creativity had been pushed firmly to the margins since romanticism by notions that 'genius' was a quintessentially masculine phenomenon. Furthermore, the eclectic cultural interests of the symbolists (from Orientalism to Western medievalism to the folklore of Russian villages) supplied women writers with a wide choice of languages and perspectives in and from which to articulate their particular 'eternally feminine' utterances.

Though the rise of post-symbolist movements such as acmeism and cubo-futurism led to something of a neo-romantic reaction against the 'eternal feminine', it could not suppress the work of women writers. Indeed, many were helped by the now more critical attitudes: in the years after 1910, some writers, such as Gertsyk, Nadezhda L'vova (before her suicide in 1913), and later Marina Tsvetaeva, began to scrutinize the question of what 'women's art' and 'women's language' might mean, while others, such as Akhmatova or Parnok, developed an unprecedentedly exacting attitude to their own use of the poetic word. However, the concept of 'androgyny' could be appropriated by women, as well as men; and so it was, notably in the work of Gippius and of Tsvetaeva (*The Tsar Maiden* (*Tsar'-Devitsa*), and *On a Red Horse* (*Na krasnom kone*)).

This is not to say that the early twentieth century should be seen as a paradise of free creation and artistic equality for women. 'Androgyny', depending as it did on a contrast between masculine/active/rational and feminine/passive/irrational elements, had considerable potential for reinforcing Russian *fin de siècle* culture's already strong tendency to essentialism. And the decadent cult of sexual freedom, with its emphasis on sexual behaviour as performance and as assault to conventional sensibilities, did encourage writing about alternative sexualities, but only where this could be seen as shocking and perverted. Lidiia Zinov'eva-Annibal's sensational tale of lesbian love, *Thirty-Three Freaks* (*Tridtsat' tri uroda*, 1907), was published and became so notorious it was even the subject of cartoons, but the erotic poetry that Tsvetaeva and Parnok wrote to each other (where lesbianism was seen from the inside, rather than put on show) was kept from the public gaze. Finally, women remained remote from the most avant-garde directions in the verbal arts (in contrast to the visual ones, where thoroughly radical work was produced by painters such as Popova and Stepanova). Part of the reason for this may have been women's under-representation in avant-garde groups (the cubo-futurists' only member was poet and painter Elena Guro), but it was also a question of the hostility that many women felt to what they saw as an extreme form of 'art for art's sake'. In her essay 'Natal'ia Goncharova', for example, Tsvetaeva pugnaciously attacked the whole notion of 'innovation' as a vulgarism and an irrelevance:

> Wanting to give 'something new' (tomorrow's 'something old') is much the same as wanting to be famous—if the latter means levelling down to your contemporaries, the former means levelling up to your predecessors; both are a preoccupation with self,

not with the thing—and therefore sinful. Wanting to give the truth is the only true justification for art—which does require (think of barracks, slums, trenches, factories, hospitals, prisons!) a justification.[76]

If even the most adventurous woman modernist could see things in these terms, it is not surprising that less confident women writers shunned devices such as *zaum'* (the use of 'transrational', that is, nonsensical, language). The appropriation of devices from folklore, of personae and masks from a variety of different cultural traditions, and what might be termed 'nursery neo-primitivism' (the preoccupations and vocabulary of childhood) were alternative ways of conveying 'the shock of the new' with which women felt fully satisfied.

However, such strategies were to prove dangerous, in a political sense, as men of the avant-garde came to prominence in some areas of Soviet artistic policy after 1918. It was all too easy for them to label women's work as retrograde (as Maiakovskii did with Tsvetaeva, or Mandel'shtam—in one aberrant essay—with Akhmatova). Confronted with, *inter alia*, demands for novelty at all costs, some established writers stopped publishing: Akhmatova and Parnok, for example, had considerable difficulty in placing work after 1925. Others stopped writing altogether: the veteran radical Tat'iana Shchepkina-Kupernik, worried that journals would no longer accept her work while putting out much worse material by other writers, anxiously asked why, and discovered that 'one had to write about new people, and I didn't know them. One had to write in a new language, and I didn't know it. . . . And so, after thinking deeply and painfully, I consciously renounced original writing, and decided to busy myself with "auxiliary work" '—that is to say, first library work, and then translation.[77] Yet the forcing-out of 'dead wood' was accompanied by no upsurge of young female avant-garde saplings to take its place (the poets produced by the proletarian arts movement, such as Anna Barkova, inclined to a full-blooded romanticism of theme, and modelled metrics and lexis on the popular ballad). At the same time, the Bolshevik hostility to bourgeois feminism and ideological commitment to a Party-led programme of women's rights tied the hands of women realists. With predictable schematism, Party activists and dynamic working-class heroines (remodelling those of pre-Revolutionary days) were opposed to 'class enemies' such as stick-in-the-mud peasant women, snobbish 'exes', and foolish, fashion-obsessed petites bourgeoises. Furthermore, the character of Bolshevik egalitarianism meant that there was a strong tendency for positively valued women to be seen as honorary men—crop-haired comrades in leather jackets who were prepared to devote themselves body and soul to the Party, and who had no use for child-bearing, home-making, or other such 'backward' feminine activities.

Jewish Writers and the (Re)construction of Identity

A rather similar progression can be seen in the case of Jewish writers: here, too, Bolshevik attitudes drew on, and reinforced, elements already present in pre-1917 Russian culture. The 1870s, 1880s, and 1890s had seen the rise to prominence

'The Cowboy Dance', a music-hall number whose gun-toting cowgirl heroine is one of the early twentieth century's many novel visions of femininity.
The act also illustrates the persisting Russian fascination with American culture, exemplified in high culture from Maiakovskii to Aksenov, and in popular tradition from 'American devils', trick toys that Nabokov recalled from his childhood, through Stalinist skyscrapers to the jeans and hamburger manias of the 1980s and 1990s.

of the first generations of Russian Jews really to make an impact on Russian culture, including the writers Nadson and Minskii, the painter Levitan, the sculptor Antokol'skii, the critic Volynskii, and the musician Anton Rubinstein. But Jewish themes did not necessarily play a greater role in the work of these individuals than in work by other liberal intellectuals of the same period (where the Jewish question had begun to challenge the woman question as a preoccupation in the late 1870s). Indeed, actual Jews were in some senses more restrained than non-Jews in invoking such material, because it might invite discrimination on the part of officials and patrons. Antokol'skii, for instance, had been sharply criticized for employing obviously Jewish allusions at an early stage in his career, in 1864, and thereafter stuck to subjects from Russian history, or to such safely universal ones as Spinoza.[78]

Yet the prominence of writers and artists of Jewish origin in the artistic establishment, like that of Jews in other professions, did have some effects on young people in the Pale. If Jews could be admitted to the Academy of Arts, as both Levitan and Antokol'skii were, the most conservative forum of artistic endeavour, they could surely make their way in more radical circles. Such aspirations were aided by efforts on the part of successful Jewish migrants to share their achievements with the communities from which they had come. In 1897, the painter Yehuda Pen opened an art school in Vitebsk, whose pupils included Chagall, Iudovin, and El Lissitzky. After Antokol'skii's death, a museum, industrial society, and school were opened in his birthplace, Vilna. Later, Jewish patrons such as Nadezhda Dobychina (also active as an art dealer between 1911 and 1919) and Iakov Kagan-Shubshai offered support to Jewish artists (though not only to them), while the Jewish Society for the Encouragement of the Arts, founded in 1916, did important work until closing down shortly after the October Revolution. In the verbal arts, the writer Semen An-skii (real name Shloime Zeinvil Rapoport) devoted much of his time, in the early 1900s, to the documentation of Jewish custom and to adaptations of folklore texts (for example, his play *The Dybbuk*, first performed in 1920).

Not only institutional, but intellectual change played its part. Early discussions of the Jewish question, like those of the woman question, had concentrated on the external, environmental forces shaping identity: legal and political discrimination. Furthermore, the most prevalent attitude among Jewish artists, as among Jewish intellectuals more generally, was summed up in the phrase 'a Jew at home and a man on the street': that is, Judaism and emancipation in the public sphere were incompatible. The Enlightenment attitudes expressed in the Haskalah movement, that emancipation would come about not only through legal change, but through Jews' own abandonment of their 'medieval' customs, were widespread, and were particularly well represented among socialists, where they were eventually to feed into the anti-Zionist 'internationalism' of Bolshevik official policy.[79]

The polarization of 'human' (general) and 'Jewish' (specific) markers of identity closely recalls the terms of debate espoused in Russian radical discussions of the woman question. As with the woman question, *fin de siècle* debates on the Jewish question led to a questioning of this polarization, a new sense

**Still from *The Keys to Happiness* (Protazanov and Gardin, 1913), a hugely pop-
ular film based on the bestseller of the same name by Anastasiia Verbitskaia.**
Here, the heroine Mania, posed with the Aryan 'superman' Nelidov, is threatened by the
mad uncle of her other lover, the Jewish Steinbach (turned by the film-makers into a
Shylockian caricature of gaberdine, yarmulka, and long beard). This vulgarization of national
identities was one reason why intellectual commentators found Verbitskaia's text, in its
various manifestations, so very irritating. However, as a being torn between authoritarian,
'German', and 'masculine' elements, and the 'feminine', 'oriental' elements of Judaism,
Mania was a potently mythic figure for a nation whose own identity was widely perceived
as divided along similarly 'Eurasian' lines.

of Jewishness (which was often, following Nietzsche, associated with femininity) as an intrinsic, metaphysical force. The writings of Rozanov, like those of his
Austrian precursor, the post-Nietzschean Otto Weininger, were preoccupied
with the autonomous essence of Judaism, and in the former case posited its
closeness to the interior, 'domestic' character of Russian culture. At the same
time, in representing Judaic culture as abject, 'feminine', primitive, Rozanov
and Weininger sharpened the painfulness in the situation of the young Jews
trying to break from the culture of their birth to try to establish themselves as
Russian writers. The conflicts caused by their subject position—the recognition
of being defined by a culture seen by others as inferior, a superciliousness they
had themselves internalized—are very evident in Isaak Babel''s superb quasi-
autobiographical cycle from the 1920s, *Red Cavalry* (*Konarmiia*). Babel''s alter
ego Liutov ('Savage', a wildly unsuitable *nom de guerre*) is torn between revul-
sion from and attraction to the Jewish culture that he encounters during the
Civil War, his perceptions transmuted by the internationalist political culture

and brutally masculinist Cossack militarism that he has espoused. The dilemma remains unresolved by the uneasy ending to the cycle (a later afterthought), in which Liutov learns at last to ride his fierce stallion and is accepted by the Cossacks as one of them.

Like Russia's women, then, Jews of the early twentieth century found themselves living a 'double life', caught between two cultures. Like Russia's women, too, Russia's Jews found visual culture more permeable than verbal culture. The superb early paintings of Chagall, such as *The Red Jew* (1915), are able to harmonize 'Hebraic' and 'Slavonic' elements as literature of the period could not. Here, a golden aureole (like that used in icons, which the palette used by Chagall also invokes) holds citations from Hebrew sacred texts, representing the internal, spiritual life of the believer, while the ramshackle *izba* and the tattered clothes of the central figure, placed in the lower part of the painting, stand for his external reality, indistinguishable from that of other village-dwellers. A tree, international symbol of enduring life, acts as mediator between spiritual and earthly domain—the tones of its foliage pick up shades used in each sphere of the subject's existence. Unlike Babel' or Tsvetaeva, but like Natal'ia Goncharova, Chagall neither feared, nor felt threatened by, the fragmentation of the world that he so poignantly represented.[80]

Conclusion: Triumph of the Arts

The creativity of the Russian modernists was largely inspired by prescience of the demise of their world and way of life; much of their art can be read as a death-wish in terms of its thematics. Yet what came out of this death-wish—music, literature, and art of genius—was ultimately creative, rather than destructive. The fact that the tensions of the era could be energizing, as well as frustrating, is clear in Belyi's great novel *Petersburg* (*Peterburg*, 1916), which captures the *fin de siècle*'s racism, erotic compulsiveness, snobbery, and intellectual vacuity, but which is also a peculiarly intense vision of a world about to vanish. But perhaps the richest and most deeply felt account of the era is a much shorter text written after the Revolution had (in the views of contemporaries) destroyed the old world. This is Mandel'shtam's memoir 'The Noise of Time', a dizzyingly virtu-osic evocation of the *fin de siècle* ('a term repeated more and more often with frivolous pride and coquettish melancholy'), with its 'talk of Dreyfus . . . and foggy quarrels about some book called *The Kreutzer Sonata*'.[81] Mandel'shtam brilliantly characterizes the tensions of his childish consciousness, internalizing the 'whirlwind of bellicosity, the ethic of the police state' as he watches a battleship crawl down its launching slip like a sea-caterpillar, and setting these against 'the kitchen fug of an absolutely average petit-bourgeois flat, with my father's study smelling of leather, glacé kid and calfskin, and Jewish business talk' (52). The ironies of this astonishing era are present everywhere, particularly in the flat of relatives whose military service has allowed them to live in 'Jew-free' Finland, and whose pride and joy is a sideboard carved with scenes from the life of Ivan the Terrible (63). A Jew who had internalized, like many of his contemporaries, the ideas of Nietzsche and Weininger, Mandel'shtam found the 'Judaic chaos' of his child-hood painful, even shameful, to recall. But, though insisting that 'my memory is hostile to everything personal', Mandel'shtam created a quintessentially *fin de siècle*, displaced portrait of a self in which boundaries melt, and incompatibilities shatter into a mosaic. The androgynous child of a father who represented what would now be understood as the 'feminine', 'semiotic' qualities of language (*kosnoiazychie, bez″iazychie*), 'the Talmudist's weird syntax', and of a mother who spoke with the 'impoverished, compressed vocabulary, the monotonous turns of phrase', of literary Russian (a supremely rational, masculine idiolect, in other words), the Mandel'shtam that is invented here can be understood as uniquely well qualified to invent the new language, fertilely miscegenating rather than sterilely hybrid, that will represent a world from which the snobbery, clutter, suffocating emotions, and sentimental art of the old world have vanished, leaving the thinking subject free to suffer 'nostalgia for world culture', but not for the circumstances of his own origin.

Suggested further reading

Philosophy, Religion, and Politics

BERDIAEV, N. A., BULGAKOV, S. N., GERSHENZON, M. O., IZGOEV, A. S., KISTIAKOVSKII, B. A., STRUVE, P. B., and FRANK, S. L., *Vekhi: Sbornik statei o russkoi intelligentsii* (Moscow, 1909); in English *Landmarks: A Collection of Articles About the Russian Intelligentsia*, ed. B. Shragin and A. Todd, tr. M. Schwarz (New York, 1977).

BOHACHEVSKY-CHOMIAK, M., and ROSENTHAL, B. G., *Revolution of the Spirit: The Crisis of Values in Russia, 1890–1918* (New York, 1982).

BURBANK, J., *Intelligentsia and Revolution: Russian Views of Bolshevism* (New York, 1986).

CLOWES, E., KASSOW, S., and WEST, J. L. (eds.), *Between Tsar and People: Educated Society and the Quest for Public Identity in Late Imperial Russia* (Princeton, 1991).

ENGELSTEIN, L., *The Keys to Happiness: Sex and the Search for Modernity in Fin de Siècle Russia* (Ithaca, 1992).

HAIMSON, L., *The Russian Marxists and the Origins of Bolshevism* (Cambridge, Mass., 1955).

JAHN, H. F., *Patriotic Culture in Russia during World War I* (Ithaca, 1995).

READ, C., *Religion, Revolution and the Russian Intelligentsia 1900–12: The Vekhi Debate and Its Intellectual Background* (London, 1980).

—— *Culture and Power in Revolutionary Russia: The Intelligentsia and the Transition from Tsarism to Communism* (London, 1990).

ROSENTHAL, B. G. (ed.), *Nietzsche in Russia* (Cambridge, 1986).

SABLINSKY, W., *The Road to Bloody Sunday: Father Gapon and the St Petersburg Massacre of 1905* (Princeton, 1976).

ZERNOV, N., *The Russian Religious Renaissance of the Twentieth Century* (London, 1963).

The 'Woman Question'

CLEMENTS, B. E., *Bolshevik Feminist: The Life of Aleksandra Kollontai* (Bloomington, 1979).

—— ENGEL, B. A., and WOROBEC, C. D. (eds.), *Russia's Women: Accommodation, Resistance, Transformation* (Berkeley, 1991).

EDMONDSON, L., *Feminism in Russia 1900–1917* (London, 1984).

—— (ed.), *Women and Society in Russia and the Soviet Union* (Cambridge, 1992).

FARNSWORTH, B., *Aleksandra Kollontai: Socialism, Feminism, and the Bolshevik Revolution* (Stanford, 1980).

MARSH, R. (ed.), *Women in Russia and the Ukraine* (Cambridge, 1995).

STITES, R., *The Women's Liberation Movement in Russia: Feminism, Nihilism and Bolshevism, 1860–1930* (Princeton, 1978), chs. 6–9.

WAGNER, W. G., *Marriage, Property and Law in Late Imperial Russia* (Oxford, 1994).

The 'Jewish Question'

BARON, S. W., *The Russian Jew under Tsars and Soviets* (London, 1964).

DREIZIN, F., *The Russian Soul and the Jew: Essays in Literary Ethnocentrism* (Lanham, 1990).

ELIASEVICH, D. A. (ed.), *Istoriia evreev v Rossii: Problemy istochnikovedeniia i istoriografii. Sbornik nauchnykh trudov* (St Petersburg, 1993).

GESSEN, IU., KEL'NER, V. E., and GESSEN, V., *Istoriia evreiskogo naroda v Rossii* (Moscow, 1993).

GRUZENBERG, O. O., *Yesterday: Memoirs of a Russian-Jewish Lawyer*, tr. D. C. Rawson and T. Tipton (Berkeley, 1981).

The Jews in Soviet Russia since 1917, 3rd edn. (Oxford, 1978).

KLIER, J. D., *Imperial Russia's Jewish Question, 1855–1881* (Cambridge, 1995).

ORBACH, A., *New Voices of Russian Jewry: A Study of the Russian-Jewish Press in the Era of the Great Reforms, 1860–1871* (Leiden, 1980).

SLIOZBERG, G. G., *Dela minuvshikh dnei: Zapiski russkogo evreia* (3 vols.; Paris, 1933–4).

ZIPPERSTEIN, S., *The Jews of Odessa: A Cultural History, 1794–1881* (Stanford, 1985).

Visual and Applied Arts

BORISOVA, E., and STERNIN, G., *Russian Art Nouveau* (New York, 1988).

BOWLT, J., *The Silver Age: Russian Art of the Early 20th Century and the World of Art Group* (Newtonville, 1979).

—— *Russian Art of the Avant-Garde: Theory and Criticism* (London, 1988).

BRUMFIELD, W., *History of Russian Architecture* (Cambridge, 1993).

GOODMAN, S. T. (ed.), *Russian Jewish Artists in a Century of Change* (Munich, 1995).

KAMENSKII, A., PETROV, V. N., and SHKAROVSKII-RAFFE, A., *The World of Art Movement in Early Twentieth-Century Russia* (Leningrad, 1991).

KEAN, B. W., *All the Empty Palaces: The Merchant Patrons of Modern Art in Pre-Revolutionary Russia* (London, 1983; repr. 1994).

SARABIANOV, D., *Russian Art: From Realism to Neo-Classicism* (London, 1990).

VALKENIER, E., *Russian Realist Art* (New York, 1977; repr. 1989).

Music, Music Drama, Ballet

BROWN, M., 'Skryabin and Russian "Mystic" Symbolism,' *19th-Century Music*, 3 (1979), 42–51.

BUCKLE, R., *Diaghilev* (London, 1979).

RIDENOUR, R., *Nationalism, Modernism and Personal Rivalry in Nineteenth-Century Russian Music* (Ann Arbor, 1981).

TARUSKIN, R., *Stravinsky and the Russian Traditions* (Berkeley, 1995).

Literature

CLYMAN, T., and GREENE, D. (eds.), *Women Writers in Russian Literature* (Westport, 1994).

KELLY, C., *A History of Russian Women's Writing, 1820–1992* (Oxford, 1994), chs. 6–8.

—— (ed.), *An Anthology of Russian Women's Writing, 1777–1992* (Oxford, 1994).

LEDKOVSKY, M., ROSENTHAL, C., and ZIRIN, M. (eds.), *A Dictionary of Russian Women Writers* (Westport, 1994).

MCVAY, G., *Esenin* (London, 1978).

NAKHIMOVSKY, A. S., *Russian-Jewish Literature and Identity* (Baltimore, 1992).

PROFFER, C., and PROFFER, E. (eds.), *The Silver Age of Russian Culture: An Anthology* (Ann Arbor, 1971).

PYMAN, A., *A History of Russian Symbolism* (Cambridge, 1994).

RICHARDSON, W., *'Zolotoe Runo' and Russian Modernism* (Ann Arbor, 1986).

SICHER, E., *Jews in Russian Literature after the October Revolution: Writers and Artists between Hope and Apostasy* (Cambridge, 1995).

Notes

[1] Western publications at this period range from jingoistic tosh such as *A Peep at Russia* (London, [1878?]), to the more serious J. W. Buel, *A Nemesis of Misgovernment* (Philadelphia, 1899). For information on Russian anxieties before and after the Russo-Japanese War, see J. T. Rimer (ed.), *A Hidden Fire: Russian and Japanese Cultural Encounters, 1868–1926* (Stanford, 1995).

[2] These details on legal constraints are taken from *Entsiklopedicheskii slovar' Brokgauza i Efrona*, xi (St Petersburg, 1898), 454–66, headword *Evrei*. A remarkable account of the period from a Jewish perspective is G. Sliozberg, *Dela minuvshikh dnei: Zapiski russkogo evreia* (3 vols.; Paris, 1933–4). See also Suggested Further Reading.

[3] See D. Lieven, *Nicholas II: Emperor of All the Russias* (London, 1993), 61; on Nicholas I and earlier, see R. Wortman, *Scenarios of Power: Myth and Ceremony in Russian Monarchy*, i (Princeton, 1995).

[4] For a photograph, see *Sotheby's Icons, Russian Pictures and Works of Art Sale Catalogue* (15 June 1995), lot 302.

[5] A first-hand account is V. Giliarovskii, 'Tragediia na Khodynke', *Russkie vedomosti* (20 May 1896).

[6] See W. Sablinsky, *The Road to Bloody Sunday: Father Gapon and the St Petersburg Massacre of 1905* (Princeton, 1976).

[7] See M. S. Flier's excellent study, 'The Church of the Savior on the Blood: Projection, Rejection, Resurrection', in R. Hughes and I. Paperno (eds.), *Christianity and the Eastern Slavs*, ii (California Slavic Studies, 17; Stanford, 1994), 25–48.

[8] See W. Brumfield, *A History of Russian Architecture* (Cambridge, 1993), 437, 412–20.

[9] Quoted in J.-A. Ruckman, *The Moscow Business Elite: A Social and Cultural Portrait of Two Generations, 1840–1905* (De Kalb, 1984), 96.

[10] See S. Moeller-Sally, 'Parallel Lives: Gogol's Biography and Mass Readership in Late Imperial Russia', *Slavic Review*, 54 (1995), 62–79.

[11] M. C. Levitt, *Russian Literary Politics and the Pushkin Celebration of 1880* (New York, 1989), 158.

[12] I. Annenskii, 'Kantata: Rozhdenie i smert' poeta', in *Stikhotvoreniia i tragedii* (Leningrad, 1959), 88–90.

[13] R. E. Zelnik, ' "To the Unaccustomed Eye": Religion and Irreligion in the Experience of St Petersburg Workers in the 1870s', in Hughes and Paperno (eds.), *Christianity and the Eastern Slavs*, 53.

[14] See the chapters about the church in Tolstoi's last novel *Resurrection* (*Voskresenie*, 1900), and his *Confession* (*Ispoved'*, 1879), as well as articles such as 'What I Believe' ('V chem moia vera', 1883).

[15] See A. Pyman, 'The Church and the Intelligentsia with Special Reference to the Religious-Philosophical Meetings in St Petersburg, 1901–1903', in R. Bartlett (ed.), *Russian Thought and Society 1800–1917: Essays in Honour of Eugene Lampert* (Keele, 1984), 181–219.

[16] See P. Steeves, 'Baptists of Russia', in *Modern Encyclopedia of Russian and Soviet History*, iii (Gulf Breeze, 1977), 76–81. On earlier evangelism, see A. N. Pypin, *Religioznye dvizheniia pri Aleksandre I* (St Petersburg, 1916), and M. V. Jones, 'Dostoevsky, Zasetskaya, and Radstockism', *Oxford Slavonic Papers*, xxvii (1994), 106–20.

[17] See A. Pyman, *A History of Russian Symbolism* (Cambridge, 1994), 183–225.

[18] See M. Carlson, *'No Religion Higher than Truth': A History of the Theosophical Movement in Russia, 1875–1922* (Princeton, 1993).

[19] See G. Ivask, 'Russian Modernist Poets and the Mystic Sectarians', in G. Gibian and H. W. Tjalsma (eds.), *Russian Modernism: Culture and the Avant-Garde 1900–1930* (Ithaca, 1976), 85–106, and 'Iz zapisok Iur'evskogo arkhimandrita Fotiia o skoptsakh, khlystakh i drugikh tainykh sektakh v Peterburge v 1819 godu', *Russkii arkhiv*, 2 (1873), 1434–53.

[20] See Pyman, *A History*, 279–84.

[21] For more information on Nietzsche's influence, see B. G. Rosenthal (ed.), *Nietzsche in Russia* (Cambridge, 1986), and E. Clowes, *The Revolution of Moral Consciousness: Nietzsche in Russian Literature, 1890–1914* (De Kalb, 1988). On Schopenhauer, see S. Maurer, *Schopenhauer in Russia: His Influence on Turgenev, Fet and Tolstoy* (Berkeley, 1966). On Wagner and Russian modernism, see R. Bartlett, *Wagner and Russia* (Cambridge, 1995), chs. 3–6.

[22] See N. Zernov, *The Russian Religious Renaissance of the Twentieth Century* (London, 1963), 1–34.

[23] See M. Perrie, *The Agrarian Policy of the Russian Socialist-Revolutionary Party from its Origins through the Revolution of 1905–7* (Cambridge, 1976).

[24] See L. Haimson, *The Russian Marxists and the Origins of Bolshevism* (Cambridge, Mass., 1955), 1–92.

[25] Quoted in Zernov, *The Russian Religious Renaissance*, 114.

[26] Ibid., 116.

[27] Ibid., 118.

[28] See A. Blok, 'The People and the Intelligentsia' ('Narod i intelligentsiia', 1908); see also A. Belyi, *The Silver Dove (Serebrianyi golub'*, 1909), V. Ivanov's article 'The Russian Idea' ('O russkoi idee', 1909), and Pyman, *A History*, 312, 426 n. 20.

[29] A good overview of the *Vekhi* debate is given in the introduction to J. Burbank, *Intelligentsia and Revolution: Russian Views of Bolshevism* (New York, 1986).

[30] See Zernov, *The Russian Religious Renaissance*, 129.

[31] See H. Baran, 'Religious Holiday Literature and Russian Modernism: A Preliminary Approach', in Hughes and Paperno (eds.), *Christianity and the Eastern Slavs*, 212–14.

[32] A. Blok, 'Rozhdennye v goda glukhie' [1914], in *Stikhotvoreniia. Poemy. 'Roza i krest'* (Moscow, 1974), 217.

[33] On Rozanov, see L. Engelstein, *The Keys to Happiness: Sex and the Search for Modernity in Fin de Siècle Russia* (Ithaca, 1992); on Zelinskii, see his own *Iz zhizni idei: Stat'i* (St Petersburg, 1905), and 'Drevnii mir i my', in *Zhurnal Ministerstva Narodnogo Prosveshcheniia*, sect. 3 (August–October 1903), 1–45, 18–47, 65–114.

[34] See E. Kridl Valkenier, *Il'ia Repin* (New York, 1990), 77–8.

35 On Surikov, see V. Kemenev, *Vasily Surikov* (Leningrad, 1979).

36 See E. Kridl Valkenier, *Russian Realist Art* (New York, 1977), 6–10, 132.

37 See B. Anrep, 'Po povodu vystavki s uchastiem russkikh khudozhnikov', *Apollon*, 2 (1913), 39–48.

38 See B. W. Kean, *All the Empty Palaces: The Merchant Patrons of Modern Art in Pre-Revolutionary Russia* (London, 1983; repr. 1995), and D. Elliott, *'Ruined Palaces': Twilight of the Tsars* (London, 1991). On the English movement, see G. Naylor, *The Arts and Crafts Movement: A Study of its Sources, Ideals and Influence on Design Theory* (London, 1971), and F. Murphy, *William Morris* (London, 1994).

39 J. Beavington Atkinson, *An Art Tour to Russia* (London, 1986), 236.

40 P. Florenskii, 'Obratnaia perspektiva', in *Sobranie sochinenii*, i (Paris, 1985), 117–92. On Florenskii's theological views, see B. Rosenthal, ' "The New Religious Consciousness": Pavel Florenskii's Path to a Revitalized Orthodoxy', in Hughes and Paperno (eds.), *Christianity and the Eastern Slavs*, 150–1.

41 See R. Bartlett, '*Khovanshchina* in Context', in N. John (ed.), *Modest Musorgskii: 'Khovanshchina'. English National Opera Guide* (London, 1994), 31–7.

42 For more information see R. Ridenour, *Nationalism, Modernism and Personal Rivalry in Nineteenth-Century Russian Music* (Ann Arbor, 1981).

43 For further details, see V. P. Rossikhina, *Opernyi teatr S. Mamontova* (Moscow, 1985).

44 Quoted in R. Shead, *Ballets Russes* (London, 1989), 70.

45 A. Boucourechliev, *Stravinsky*, tr. M. Cooper (London, 1987), 15.

46 See R. Buckle, *Diaghilev* (London, 1979).

47 See Elliott, *'Ruined Palaces'*, 13.

48 See P. Gilliard, *Trinadtsat' let pri russkom dvore* (Paris, 1978), 68, 223.

49 See M. Mommsen, *Hilf mir, mein Recht zu finden: Russische Bittschriften von Iwan dem Schrecklichen bis Gorbatschow* (Frankfurt, 1987); reference supplied by Sheila Fitzpatrick. On changes in attitude, see e.g. Sablinsky, *The Road to Bloody Sunday*.

50 *Polnyi sbornik libretto dlia grammofona*, pt. 3 (n.p., [c.1910?]), 127.

51 Ibid., 79–81.

52 C. A. Frierson (tr. and ed.), *Aleksandr Nikolaevich Engelgardt's Letters from the Country, 1872–1887* (New York, 1993), 144, 146, 147.

53 See H. F. Jahn, 'For Tsar and Fatherland? Russian Popular Culture and the First World War', in S. Frank and M. D. Steinberg (eds.), *Cultures in Flux: Lower-Class Values, Practices, and Resistance in Late Imperial Russia* (Princeton, 1994), 131–46.

54 See Zelnik, ' "To the Unaccustomed Eye" ', 60.

55 Ibid., 53.

56 N. Kliuev, *Sochineniia*, i (Munich, 1969), 195.

57 Ibid., 193–4.

58 *Gazeta-kopeika*, 25 March 1914, 6; reference supplied by Steve Smith.

59 Ibid., 21 September 1914, 3.

60 See R. Stites, *The Women's Liberation Movement in Russia: Feminism, Nihilism and Bolshevism, 1860–1930* (Princeton, 1978), 295–300; see also R. Abraham, 'Mariia L. Bochkareva and the Russian Amazons of 1917', in L. Edmondson (ed.), *Women and Society in Russia and the Soviet Union* (Cambridge, 1992), 124–44.

61 Quoted in Stites, *The Women's Liberation Movement*, 296. On female soldiers, see J. Wheelwright, *Amazons and Military Maids: Women Who Dressed as Men in Pursuit of Life, Liberty and Happiness* (London, 1989).

62 We have B. A. Uspenskii to thank for the information about *monatki*.

63 See J. D. Klier, *Imperial Russia's Jewish Question, 1855–1881* (Cambridge, 1995).

64 See C. Kelly, *A History of Russian Women's Writing, 1820–1992* (Oxford, 1994), ch. 1.

65 I. V. V-skii, [Obituary of Mariia Vernadskaia], *Ekonomicheskii ukazatel'*, 44 (1860), 753–5.

66 Quoted in Stites, *The Women's Liberation Movement*, 36.

67 See K. Offen, 'Defining Feminism: A Comparative Historical Approach', in *Signs: Journal of Women in Culture and Society*, 14 (1988), 119–57.

68 On women radicals, see B. A. Engel, *Mothers and Daughters: Women of the Intelligentsia in Nineteenth-Century Russia* (Cambridge, 1983).

69 See M. Bohachevsky-Chomiak, *Feminists Despite Themselves: Women in Ukrainian Community Life, 1884–1939* (Edmondton, 1988).

70 On these early women writers, see T. Clyman and D. Greene (eds.), *Women Writers in Russian Literature* (Westport, 1994), and C. Kelly, 'Sybil, Corinna, Niobe: Genres and Personae in Russian Women's Writing, 1760–1820', in A. Barker and J. Gheith (eds.), *A History of Women's Writing in Russia* (Cambridge, forthcoming).

71 See C. Ruane, *Gender, Class and the Professionalization of Russian City Teachers, 1869–1914* (Pittsburgh, 1994).

72 See W. G. Wagner, *Marriage, Property and Law in Late Imperial Russia* (Oxford, 1994).

73 For a good sample of recent social history on women, see B. E. Clements, B. A. Engel, and C. D. Worobec (eds.), *Russia's Women: Accommodation, Resistance, Transformation* (Berkeley, 1991).

74 Z. Gippius, *Peterburgskie dnevniki* (New York, 1982), 195.

75 V. I. Ivanov, 'O dostoinstve zhenshchiny', in *Sobranie sochinenii*, iii (Brussels, 1979), 136–45, and V. Rozanov, 'Zhenshchina i predstavitel'stvo', in *Kogda nachal'stvo ushlo* (St Petersburg, 1910), 87–95.

76 M. Tsvetaeva, 'Natal'ia Goncharova', in *Sobranie sochinenii v 7 tomakh*, iv (Moscow, 1994), 122.

77 T. L. Shchepkina-Kupernik, *Razroznennye stranitsy* (Moscow, 1966), 31–2.

78 Here and below see S. Tumarkin Goodman (ed.), *Russian Jewish Artists in a Century of Change* (Munich, 1995), esp. the articles by Z. Amishai-Maisels and J. E. Bowlt.

79 See E. Sicher, *Jews in Russian Literature after the October Revolution: Writers and Artists between Hope and Apostasy* (Cambridge, 1995), esp. chs. 1 and 2.

[80] Among Chagall's contemporaries, Iudovin, Rybak, Tchaikov, Altman, and David Shterenberg also did very interesting work on Jewish subjects: reproductions are available in Goodman, *Russian Jewish Artists,* and in Sicher, *Jews in Russian Literature.*

[81] O. Mandel'shtam, 'Shum vremeni', in *Sobranie sochinenii,* ii (New York, 1971), 47, 45 (references henceforth by page no. in main text).

PART III

Epilogue
Constructing a New Russia: Change and Continuity in the Aftermath of Revolution

Introduction: Iconoclasm and Commemorating the Past

Catriona Kelly

LIKE any violent social upheaval, the Russian Revolution was distinguished by iconoclasm in the most literal sense of the word, as crowds of peasants and workers subjected the symbols of the *ancien régime* to physical destruction. Country houses and city mansions were vandalized and burned, crowns were struck off the double-headed eagles on the wrought-iron fences of Petrograd, and church treasures were plundered ruthlessly. Eager to channel the 'spontaneity' of such gestures into a 'conscious' legitimating ideology, the Bolshevik regime made the effacement of Tsarist monuments one of its first priorities. The Plan for Monumental Propaganda of April 1918 decreed that such monuments be demolished and replaced with 'monuments to understanding persons in the field of revolutionary and social activity, philosophy, literature, science, and art'. A list of sixty-six appropriate figures was then drawn up, comprising thirty-one revolutionaries and activists, from Spartacus to Robert Owen, twenty writers, three scholars and philosophers, seven artists, three composers, and two performing artists. The internationalist character of the selection was matched by the choice of many artists working in the international modernist style to carry out the monumental sculptures required. The outstanding example was a project by Tatlin, later known as 'The Monument to the Third International', or 'Tatlin Tower', but even the works in figurative, rather than abstract, style, such as Viktor Sinaiskii's 'Monument to Ferdinand Lassalle', were far from being exercises in nineteenth-century academicism (Sinaiskii set a bust without pretensions to portraiture on an asymmetrical pedestal, the top of which was pushed back like the top building brick on a child's stack).[1] And, as is well known, the first twenty-five years of Soviet rule saw a rash of building projects in the most advanced architectural styles of the day: work by Russian architects, such as the Vesnin brothers, was published in Western Europe to international acclaim, while prominent Westerners, such as Le Corbusier, had buildings constructed to their designs in Moscow. The functionalist appearance of such architecture not only accorded with the new state's limited physical resources, but was symbolically representative of its commitment to progress and the machine age, and its determination to sweep away the unhygienic, disorderly, and socially divisive nature of the old city and replace it with a new collectivity based on the egalitarian and rational use of social resources. Accordingly, new housing blocks, many organized as dormitories with communal canteen and leisure facilities, and educational leisure facilities such as libraries, reading rooms, cinemas, theatres, and

A 250-rouble note produced by the White Cossack regime in Rostov-on-Don, 1918, with portrait of Matvei Ivanovich Platov (1751–1818, Ataman of the Don Cossack Host from 1801, and hero of the Napoleonic Wars).
The Russian Civil War, beginning in early 1918, led to a total breakdown of central control; non-Bolshevik local regimes held power in many places, among them Rostov-on-Don, a traditional Cossack stronghold, and seat of the Provincial Don Government from 21 April 1918, with Ataman P. N. Krasnov as military dictator from 11 May. In keeping with the broadly anti-Bolshevik, but not necessarily pro-monarchist, sympathies of the Volunteer Army, this banknote creates its own symbolism, allied to, but not simply replicating, pre-Revolutionary traditions. Neoclassical imagery (Minerva to the right, Victory with fasces to the left) and the use of the old orthography establish a link with the past, as does Platov's splendid uniform with bearskin and George Cross. However, the double-headed eagle is uncrowned, and the note pragmatically states that it is intended to be accepted 'alongside', not 'instead of', those issued by the Central State Bank.

multi-purpose 'palaces of culture' were among the key projects sponsored. The streamlined, functionalist appearance of the new buildings was an open reproach to the pre-Revolutionary tradition of urban architecture, with its love of extraneous detail, its emphasis on craft detailing, and its construction of interior spaces that underlined class privilege (as in the classic St Petersburg or Moscow apartment block, where only the best rooms faced outwards on to the street, leaving quarters for servants and the poor looking into grim internal courtyards). Now, every building, not only the new 'houses of rest' (*doma otdykha*) for workers on vacation, was meant to resemble a sanatorium, with huge windows to admit maximum sun and light, pale wood furnishings, white walls, and balconies and solariums where inhabitants might sun themselves when the weather permitted.

At the level of architectural aesthetics, then, one can see a dramatic break between the values of the 1910s and those of the 1920s. In other ways, too, the regime

1924 design by Aleksandr, Leonid, and Viktor Vesnin for a building intended to house 'Arcos' (a co-operative involved in Anglo-Soviet trade), published in *LEF*.

The Vesnins, with Panteleimon and Il'ia Golosov and Konstantin Mel'nikov, were among the leading exponents of constructivism, and this building exemplifies the movement's tenets, with the innovative exposed frame given lightness by the extensive use of plate glass in the lower storeys. All detailing is strictly functional, from the elegant lettering at the base to the chronometer at the top. Like many striking projects of the 1920s and 1930s, this building was designed for an architectural competition, and was never in fact erected. However, such designs were and remain vital symbolic expressions of Soviet architects' commitment to building a new rational environment for the urban population.

attempted to emphasize the Revolution as a 'clean break' with what had pre-ceded it. One straightforward and low-cost method of procedure was to alter city and street names with religious and royalist connotations. Thus 'Tsarskoe Selo' (actually derived from a Finnish toponym rather than the Russian word for 'Tsarist') was renamed 'Detskoe Selo', the 'Dvorianskaia ulitsa' (Gentry Street) to be found in every provincial town became 'Prospekt Revoliutsii', and a clus-ter of streets around the Winter Palace was renamed after nineteenth-century terrorists who had attempted to assassinate its inhabitants. Another method was the introduction, right from the beginning of Soviet power, of new festivals that commemorated revolutionary events: the uprisings of 1825 and 1905, and most particularly the Bolshevik Revolution of October 1917, which was com-memorated (according to the new, Gregorian, calendar) for the first time on 7 November 1918, when a monument to 'The Warriors of Revolution' was unveiled on the Champs de Mars in Petrograd, formerly the site of Tsarist mil-itary parades. From the first, too, Soviet propaganda emphasized the difference between life in the past and life in the present: as an exemplary text from an adult literacy reader produced in 1925 put it:

Знаем — долго итти нам.
Что же — не то видали.
Помним: по нашим спинам
Плети гуляли...

[We know that we have far to go,
But we have seen much worse things:
We remember how the scourges
Lashed down on our backs . . .][2]

Throughout the Soviet period, terms such as *peredovoi* (forward-looking), *radikal'nyi* (radical), *sovremennyi* (contemporary) would be used ubiquitously as terms of commendation, while words or phrases such as *otstalost'* (backwardness), *perezhitki proshlogo* (survivals of the past), and *reaktsioner* were used just as gen-erally in order to vilify.

The idea that the October Revolution was a 'clean break with the past' had enormous importance for Soviet ideology right up to the 1990s. It has also appealed to a very different group of commentators: anti-Soviet analysts and historians, from Vladimir Nabokov to Aleksandr Solzhenitsyn, who wished to underline the disconnection of Soviet power from Russian historical tradition, and hence to emphasize the possibility that its consequences might be excised from history. Its importance for large numbers of ordinary Soviet citizens was also enormous: the sense of participation in a radically new project helped to tide many over physical hardship and psychological suffering. But in whichever of its manifestations, the 'clean break' hypothesis does not facilitate the construction of sophisticated historiologies of the post-Revolutionary decades, first and fore-most because the notion that October 1917 was a once-and-for-all turning point masks the important discontinuities and contradictions observable in Soviet his-tory, as the regime moved between periods of accommodating pressures 'from below', and periods of challenging these.

The first four years of Bolshevik rule were a period in which pressures 'from below' were firmly repressed, first because the regime needed to establish its authority, and second because it soon found itself plunged into a debilitating Civil War, in which a huge variety of hostile forces, from peasant militias to Socialist Revolutionaries to former Tsarist officers, some backed by foreign interventionists of various hues, gained large areas of territory, fragmenting the former Russian Empire into dozens of short-lived republics and autonomous regions. Amid the disarray, it was important that the Soviet-controlled areas should stand for centralized authority and a clear political programme, which was assiduously disseminated to the public by the 'agitational and propaganda' sections subordinated to the new People's Commissariat for Enlightenment, whose founding in December 1917 had been one of the first acts of the Bolshevik government. The militaristic tone of 'War Communism' was entirely appropriate to the situation, given that there was a war to be won, and that the existence of Soviet Russia genuinely was threatened by opponents who sought to abolish the new order and impose an alternative regime.

In 1921, however, came a turning point in the fortunes of the new Soviet state. With the last of their opponents in the Civil War defeated, the Bolsheviks could now turn their attention to implementing the programme of cultural construction whose foundations had been laid immediately after the October Revolution. Yet there were still divisions and dangers evident everywhere. Much of the countryside still remained at best hostile to Bolshevik rule, and even the regime's key class of supporters, the urban proletariat, sometimes rebelled (most significantly, in the 'Kronstadt Mutiny' of 1921, in which the naval garrison stationed outside Petrograd, one of the most important forces in bringing the Bolsheviks to power, rebelled and demanded an end to one-party rule).[3] What was more, the Bolsheviks had attained power over a country devastated by seven years of war, in which industry was practically at a standstill. With the sense of a 'threat from outside' gone, political domination could be sustained only by a partial retreat from the economic policies that were the foundation of communist ideology. In 1921, Lenin pushed through his New Economic Policy (NEP) against considerable opposition from other dominant Bolsheviks. It modified the sweeping nationalization programmes of 1917–18, allowing some leeway to private enterprise in industry and commerce, and also softening the control over cultural forms that had been envisaged in the legislation of those years (private publishing, private theatres, and foreign-made films made significant contributions to the Russian cultural scene).

The NEP came under threat from 1925, when Stalin began to establish his authority as the dominant force in the ruling elite, and the successor to Lenin. It was definitively ended in 1928, as the First Five-Year Plan initiated a new industrialization drive, and initiated forcible collectivization of Soviet agriculture. The imposition of the Plan was preceded and accompanied by the so-called cultural revolution, which saw a return to the militaristic, class-war rhetoric of the early years. However, the institution of economic centralization was also marked by a rise in bureaucratization. Officials were needed to set planning targets, to see that these completed, and to oversee the workings of industry and agriculture. These new 'Soviet managers' would in time create a new class of state servants, with tastes and attitudes not too dissimilar to those of their Tsarist predecessors.

The combination of repression and bureaucratization set the tone for the next era of Soviet history, which ran from the early 1930s up to the death of Stalin in 1953. Reforms of the 1930s saw the reintroduction of the pre-Revolutionary internal passport, or identity card, system, suspended in 1917, and also of 'work books', personal records for factory workers that could be used to check prowess and to control movement from job to job. A variety of measures, ranging from the prohibition of male homosexual activity in 1934, to a ban on abortion in 1936, to the tightening of divorce regulations, also in 1936, substantially altered the libertarian sexual policy that had characterized the first decade and a half of Soviet rule.[4] These years also saw the onset of what was later to be called 'the cult of personality', in which 'dictatorship of the proletariat' was gradually replaced by personal dictatorship on the part of Stalin, who was increasingly celebrated in the Soviet press under such absurd titles as 'the coryphaeus of all knowledge', 'the friend of children', and 'the genius of geniuses'. The overtly internationalist character of early Soviet rule was replaced by an increasingly Russocentric atmosphere in political imagery and ideology, culminating, after the Second World War, in a period of overt chauvinism outdoing anything that had been seen even in the heyday of Nicholas II.

There is no doubt that the Stalinist era was an exceptionally repressive period of history, characterized not only by increasing control over the behaviour of citizens, but also by waves of political purges, most importantly in 1937–8. The victims came from every level of society, and fear of arrest was widespread; so, too, was righteous indignation about the activities of the 'enemies of the people' whom many supposed actually to exist. For a long time the dominant paradigm in Western studies of the period was that of the totalitarian state, held to extend its tentacles to every area of the culture, from politics to private life to the fine arts, and establishing its dominance above all by political terror.[5] The problem with this representation of Soviet history is that it remodulates the 'clean break' theory in a different key, ignoring the ways in which even an efficient dictator such as Stalin had to negotiate his way to authority by the tacit recognition of resistance from below that the most assiduous campaigns of repression could not entirely obliterate. As Vera Dunham put it in her classic study of 1940s Soviet fiction, *In Stalin's Time* (1976), 'in Stalin's time—and even in Stalin's worst times—the regime was supported by more than simple terror'.[6]

A more productive way of understanding the processes at work is through the hypothesis of a 'Great Retreat', evolved in the sociologist N. Timasheff's pioneering study of the pre-war USSR, first published in 1946. Timasheff suggested that there was a major historical discontinuity and a contradiction in the development of the Soviet system under Stalin. He documented a Great Retreat in all major spheres of life, which he saw as beginning in 1934, and which represented an all-out, albeit surreptitious, reversal of the communist revolutionary experiment. Once early Bolshevik values had been abandoned, the main pattern of the Great Retreat became 'the amalgamation of traits of the historical and national culture of Russia with traits belonging to the Communist cycle of ideas and behaviour patterns'. Yet the Great Retreat was also a 'return to normalcy' in politics and society: it meant a series of concessions in the spheres of distribution of wealth, education, consumption, family, religion, and leisure.[7] There were during this era extensive changes in everyday behaviour, manners, and tastes, which Timasheff read as an attempt to emulate some features of educated urban society under the old regime. Dunham herself, extending the Great Retreat hypothesis into the 1940s, argued that the Soviet system owed its regenerative power and stability (Stalin's regime had just survived a bitter and draining war with its authority enhanced) to what she termed 'The Big Deal'. This was an officially undeclared, but firmly observed contract between the Stalinist regime and its 'own indigenous middle class', whose values were accommodated by the regime in exchange for loyalty and efficiency. The Big Deal also included a conversion of public values: a transition from militant revolutionary asceticism and selfless devotion to public deeds to individual consumption, prosperous private life, and civilized conduct: 'Private values were converted into public values.'[8]

Perhaps the most imaginative development of Timasheff's hypothesis, though, came in Vladimir Papernyi's rich and fascinating study of early Soviet culture, *Kul'tura 'dva'*. Papernyi saw the move from Bolshevik to Stalinist culture in terms of a wide-ranging and detailed binary opposition between 'Culture One', which was machine-oriented, anti-ritualist, rationalistic, and scientific, and 'Culture Two', which was ritualistic, mythic, and characterized by 'scientific mysticism'. A vast amount of attractive detail was offered in support of the hypothesis, with reference to symbolic distinctions such as those between the earth-bound, anthropomorphic architectural structures of Stalinism, and the airy, geometrical buildings favoured in the 1920s.[9]

The Great Retreat hypothesis is persuasive because no one would deny that there was an increasing conservatism in Soviet life from the early 1930s. It was evident not only in political measures, but also in cultural politics, where the declaration of socialist realism, in itself something of an ambiguous concept, was accompanied by denunciations of 'modernism' and 'formalism' whose meanings were unmistakable. In architecture, too, no one could miss the contrast between the elephantine public projects of the 1930s and 1940s and their 'machine-age' 1920s predecessors. But the Great Retreat argument has come in its turn to seem simplistic, as more detailed research is done on the 1920s and 1930s. Sheila Fitzpatrick's studies in social history, for example, have traced the beginnings of the regime's accommodation with its middle classes to much earlier—the mid-1920s at the very latest—and she and other commentators on the 1930s (such as Roberta Manning and Lynne Viola) have emphasized the tensions that continued to run through the Party's accommodation of the Soviet bourgeoisie and the new values even as late as the 1940s.[10] The long-standing Russian tradition of public service did not suddenly disappear in the 1940s. Nor was private life annihilated in the 1920s; the pressures on private life after the Revolution, such as overcrowding and social atomization, derived as much from

1934 cartoon of Old Moscow by the 'Kukryniksy' group, the most famous cartoonists of the Stalin era (Mikhail Kupriianov, Porfirii Krylov, and Nikolai Sokolov).
The celebration of technological progress in the Stalin period required the mythologization of the past (as backward and obsolete) as well as of the present. The image of Old Moscow here, though amusing, is less than wholly accurate. Though pre-Revolutionary Moscow had been by no means so 'modern' as St Petersburg (Tverskaia Street, the central shopping street, was relatively narrow, and many side-streets in the middle of the city were tortuously winding), rebuilding after the Napoleonic invasion meant that most of its secular buildings were modern by European standards. A number of prestige contemporary projects (hotels, banks, department stores, and other commercial buildings) had also transformed areas of the medieval centre (for example, Red Square and Lubianka Square) by 1917. However, the rebuilding programme instituted in the 1930s was on a scale hitherto unseen, both in terms of its modernization of facilities (public transport, sanitation, public housing), and in terms of the destruction of architectural monuments.

the regime's practical difficulties as from its desire to engineer new kinds of human being.

Even the apparently straightforward area of political symbolism that we began by discussing has its historical complexities. The return to retrospectivity that can be seen in some areas of Soviet culture in the 1930s was accompanied by an upsurge in iconoclasm, which reached still greater heights than in the 1920s. In 1931, the Cathedral of Christ Redeemer was blown up in order to clear a site in central Moscow for a proposed new Palace of Soviets (never in fact built); newsreel film of the collapsing church was to become one of the most potent symbols of the transition to a new order not only in Moscow, but internationally. Other losses during the decade include the Church of the Assumption on Pokrovka, a pearl of the Moscow Baroque demolished to make room for Novokuznetskaia Metro Station; the Kazan′ Cathedral on Red Square, torn down on the three-hundredth anniversary of its building in 1935; and the seventeenth-century Sukharev Tower, cleared to make room for the expansion of the Sadovoe Ring Road in 1935. If seventeenth-century churches suffered particular onslaughts in Moscow, in Leningrad it was late nineteenth-century *style russe* that came under particular attack. Important ecclesiastical buildings that were destroyed included the Church of the Saviour on the Water, a beautiful exercise in twelfth-century Vladimir school revivalism built to commemorate the sailors killed during the Russo-Japanese War, and the Church of St Nicholas of Myra, a handsome and original Russian Art-and-Craft structure built to designs by S. S. Krichinskii in 1911–15. And the trope of 'clearing away the past' continued to be ubiquitous in 1930s propaganda too. As new buildings rose, they were featured in triumphalist magazine articles in seductively glossy photographs, and in idealized 'artists' impressions', while the 'backwardness' of the Russian past was relentlessly and hyperbolically evoked in cartoons and popular history.[11]

In any case, 'clearing away the past' was always an ideology fraught with contradictions. There was an uneasy paradox in the new regime's use of anniversaries as a manifestation of its attachment to the future, which was only partly resolved by the emphasis on novelty and youthful vitality in the 'demonstrations' of the Lenin and Stalin years. This became ever more apparent after Lenin's death in 1924, which was followed not only by the initiation of a cult of the dead ruler himself, with his mausoleum made the cynosure of Red Square, but also by the institution of a pantheon of Soviet leaders in the Kremlin Wall behind, and by the creation of various other prestige places of interment for Soviet society's most honoured dead.[12] These were often places, such as the Novodevichii Convent Cemetery in Moscow, and the Volkovskoe and Aleksandr Nevskii Cemeteries in Leningrad, which had been the most fashionable and aristocratic cemeteries in the cities before the Revolution. Though there was some attempt to 'Sovietize' these sites by clearing them of the insufficiently distinguished dead to make room for the famous political and cultural figures whose exhumed corpses were transferred from other, less honourable, places of burial, and by constructing suitably heroic monuments on their new graves, the process was less than wholly systematic. The result was that self-consciously secular monuments to Stakhanovite workers and pioneering Bolsheviks ('member of the Russian Social Democratic Party since 1902') often stood (and stand) within less than a stone's throw of marble angels, wrought-iron crosses, and neo-Byzantine funerary chapels emanating from quite a different *post mortem* sensibility.

Nor was conservationism by any means limited to commemoration of the dead. As well as the decree dictating the destruction of Tsarist monuments, 1918 also saw a decree placing historical monuments of a more neutral kind under state protection. The division between 'Tsarist' and 'historical' artefacts was, of course, wholly arbitrary; it meant that, for instance, a statue of Alexander III by P. P. Trubetskoi was transferred to the Russian Museum in Leningrad when taken down in 1937, while N. V. Sultanov's lavish Gothic monument to Alexander II was dismantled where it stood, even though the artistic value of the objects concerned was similar, and the standing of Alexander II considerably higher in Soviet historiography than that of his successor. However, the very fact that some pre-Revolutionary artefacts could be elevated to the canon of artistic achievement was significant. Continuity made itself felt also in the organization of Soviet museums: most of the major art galleries and historical museums continued their existence after the Revolution, albeit sometimes under different names (the Alexander III Museum became the Russian Museum, the Imperial Hermitage the State Hermitage, the Rumiantsev Museum the Pushkin Museum, and so on). And Russian bureaucrats took on some of the attributes of their successors at a very early stage. The fact that the Rossiia Insurance building, on the Lubianka in Moscow, could be considered appropriate to the dignity of the forces responsible for suppressing counter-revolution as early as 1918 (when it became the headquarters of the Cheka) indicates that civil servants, even if they attended work in revolutionary uniforms, did not wish to work, or to live, in 'crystal palaces' of steel and glass.

One should also bear in mind the strong weight of inertia that could lead to the surprising tolerance of 'survivals of the past'. For example, the Church of the Feodorovskaia Icon at Tsarskoe Selo should have been a prime candidate for dynamiting on a variety of grounds. It commemorated the three-hundredth anniversary of the Romanov dynasty; it had been the personal church of the Russian Imperial family; and it was in the turn-of-the-century *style russe* most abominable to Soviet taste. Yet the church survived, albeit in the suitably humiliating function of a milk factory.[13] In the same way, old wooden houses that should have vanished in slum clearance programmes sometimes continued to decline gently in the courtyards of stone-faced Stalinist blocks, even in the most prestigious central districts of the capital city.[14] And new housing projects often rose next to unlandscaped tracts of forest, or wildernesses of scrub and rough grass, an effect that hardly evoked the modern, 'forward-looking' nation that ideology and symbolism sought to achieve.

If the course of history ran far from smoothly even in the areas that were most subject to control by the state, it follows that reconstructing more complex aspects of culture proved tricky indeed. Further analysis of the themes that we examined in our discussion of pre-Revolutionary history gives some sense of the diverse historical processes at work in the decades after the Revolution, and of the many contradictions and U-turns that, contrary to an official rhetoric emphasizing consistency in Party dogma, were characteristic of every phase of Soviet history. Time and again the ruling elite was forced to temper its max-imalist aspirations in order to contain the bottom-up pressures that its policies purported to anticipate, and which official ideology—propaganda, imagery in media, literature, and film—and collective rituals—revolutionary festivals, show trials, mass meetings—were not always successful in manipulating. The result was less a Great Retreat at any one particular point than a gradual and haphazard retreat from the intentions and declarations of the early Soviet years, and from the hopes and ideals of Russian radicals before the Revolution.

New Boundaries for the Common Good: Science, Philanthropy, and Objectivity in Soviet Russia

Catriona Kelly

Introduction: the *'Mission Civilisatrice'* under Assault

THE collapse of the Tsarist regime in February 1917 was welcomed by many, if not most, members of the Russian intelligentsia. Since 1907 at the latest, it had been clear that Nicholas II's administration was incapable of serious reform, not least because of the Tsar's own misty-eyed idealization of autocratic rule. A change of government at last offered hope that the legal, social, and political reforms long desired by Russia's educated population might take place. By instituting change on such issues as women's rights (women were given the vote in March 1917) and the rights of ethnic minorities (the Jewish Pale was abolished immediately after the February Revolution), and by setting up plans for an elected parliamentary body (the Constituent Assembly), the Menshevik administration made clear its commitment to a reform programme that was widely supported by intellectuals, whether Social Democrats or not.

The rise to power of the Bolsheviks in October 1917 was traceable at least in part to the power vacuum opened by the Mensheviks' ineptitude on another level—their failure to placate grassroots opinion, as represented by the soviets and factory committees of the major cities.[15] The coup left the intelligentsia fragmented; many disapproved of the use of undemocratic means in order to seize power, and were hardly reassured when the dirigiste authoritarianism of the new regime made itself felt in a series of decrees establishing one-party control and suppressing political opposition (the Constituent Assembly was suspended in January 1918, non-Bolshevik political organizations outlawed, and a press censorship stricter than anything existing in Russia after 1905 imposed). The new regime's proclamation of the dictatorship of the proletariat also seemed to threaten the old notion of a common good guided above all by the values of the educated classes. It promised that the intelligentsia's *mission civilisatrice* might now be as obsolete as private ownership, or the State Council (advisory body to the Tsar).

Some aspects of the social contract were indeed altered irrevocably. The reorganization of local government, subordinating city and district organs to Party authority, ended the hegemony of merchant industrialists and gentry activists which had formerly held sway in Russian cities. The nationalization of cultural institutions made those who espoused the 'free professions'—doctors, lawyers, writers, teachers, academics—servants of the state, which was now in a position to exact obedience through institutional disciplinary structures, and through the regulation of pay and benefit. Intellectuals could now be reminded of their duties of loyalty through coercion, reprimand, or indeed in more sinister ways. When Alexander III observed to his Minister of the Interior in 1887, 'We must put an end to the disgrace of Lev Tolstoi', the writer emerged more or less unscathed, barring the censorship of some of his works in the Russian Empire (and these he published abroad without hindrance or punishment). Had Lenin or Stalin made such an observation, it would probably have been followed by Tolstoi's arrest and imprisonment, or even execution.

Purges against Russian intellectuals began soon after the Bolshevik ascendancy. In the appalling conditions of the Civil War, characterized by atrocities on all sides, the Cheka (emergency committee dealing with counter-revolutionary activity) had no monopoly of barbarity, but the execution in August 1921 of the Petrograd poet Nikolai Gumilev for purported involvement in a monarchist plot marked a watershed in the state's relations with dissent. A year later, a group of scholars and intellectuals (including the religious philosopher Nikolai Berdiaev) were summarily deported from Soviet Russia, and the early 1920s saw large numbers of intellectuals leave Russia voluntarily, because of wholly understandable anxieties for their safety. The cultural revolution, beginning in 1928, was accompanied by fresh rounds of purges, in which, for example, hundreds of researchers at the Academy of Sciences, and several full academicians, were arrested; some later perished in the prison camps of the far North. In 1930, about a quarter of the country's engineers were arrested, in another blow against perceived subversion. But the largest assault came in the Great Purges of 1937–8, as thousands of writers, doctors, academics, teachers, artists, actors, and scientists were rounded up, brutally interrogated, and either shot, or imprisoned in conditions that in many cases equated to slow execution.[16] Even those who survived state violence were often left significantly worse off by revolution. In the grim years after the Revolution, many intellectuals led a hand-to-mouth existence on handouts in cash and kind from the new authorities, and were subject to arbitrary incursions by local administrators who could brand them as 'exes' (*byvshie*) and have them expelled from their homes, or forcibly billet upon them strangers from favoured class groups who needed a home in the city.

These assaults left the Russian intelligentsia vastly reduced in strength as a force for political opposition or even criticism. In the late 1920s, some had still bravely spoken out against the regime's attempts to impose control on intellectual life. The veteran physiologist I. P. Pavlov, for example, had vehemently opposed the enforced candidature, in 1928, of 'politically correct' scientists for membership of the Academy of Sciences. Interpreting the government's actions only too accurately, he protested: 'If we admit such scientists to our Academy, it will not be a scientific institution, but God knows what it will be.'[17] By 1948, on the other hand, the only voice publicly raised against the triumph of the charlatan biologist Trofim Lysenko was that of Iurii Zhdanov, who happened to be the son of the Leningrad Party chief.[18] Among intellectuals who had dealings with state institutions (that is, anyone who needed to work in a laboratory, publish a book, make a film, teach a class, or exhibit a picture), careerism and self-interest had taken root as never before since the intelligentsia's emergence around 1840. Denunciation of colleagues (not unknown, but relatively rare, in the past) had become a standard technique among those wishing to climb to the top (though it was a technique that could rebound, since arrest for failing to denounce an 'enemy of the people' early enough was always a possibility).[19] Top-down rule meant the investiture of enormous authority in departmental and institutional heads, so nepotism and other forms of patronage became rife. Especially disabled were lawyers, who had played a crucial role in the evolution of concepts of a civic society, but now found themselves hobbled by a system that allowed defendants no right to proper legal representation, and according to which the law was understood as a mechanism for the imposition of Party policy, rather than as an expression of consensual social control.

What was more, the different waves of physical repression were preceded and accompanied by vitriolic campaigns of vilification directed at individuals, at institutions, and at character types ('*burzhui*', 'exes', 'Trotskyites'). Since the Revolution, in fact, some left-wing radicals had been voicing the view that 'bourgeois specialists' had no place in the new order. In 1918, the Communist Academy, a higher institute devoted to the social sciences, was set up as a revolutionary alternative to the old Academy of Sciences, with its bias towards natural sciences and the humanities. Attacks on the old scientific and scholarly establishment were frequent: indicative was an article by V. Pletnev, chairman of the Central Committee of Proletkul't, published in *Pravda* in 1922, which denounced 'bourgeois science' as characterized by self-serving individualism.[20]

Attacks on individualism had their effects on education too, as collaborative and anti-elitist forms of learning practice were urged on Soviet institutions; schools, for example, were directed by the Commissariat of Enlightenment (Narkompros) to incorporate 'labour training' and thematic learning in their curricula in order to suppress academicism and break down the opposition between manual and intellectual work that was held to bedevil Soviet life. They were also supposed to set up 'school councils', allowing children a chance to debate educational and disciplinary policy. Some of the same techniques made their way into adult education too, as the poet Vladislav Khodasevich, teacher of a course on Pushkin for the literary studio of Moscow Proletkul't, biliously recorded:

> Sensing that the studio participants were increasingly susceptible to influence from the 'specialists', the heads of Proletkul't decided to take things in hand. If they'd got rid of us completely, that would have meant admitting their powerlessness, showing their hand and provoking the lecture audiences against the Proletkul't soviet. Therefore, they decided to obstruct us. The first thing they thought up was this: I was told that formal lecturing made the studio participants too passive; I had to get them involved in active work on Pushkin, that is, to switch to the seminar system. . . . What happened was exactly what one would have expected. Even by the second seminar, some of the participants from the first had dropped out, while some new people had turned up, and I had to explain everything to them all over again. The students felt intimidated by me and each other; any 'active participation' had pretty well

to be extracted from them with forceps, and even then in microscopic doses. I ended up by 'acting out' not only the seminar leader, but the participants as well.[21]

For his part, Daniil Kharms was later (in a dialogue from *Happenings* (*Sluchai*), written in the mid-1930s) to caricature the 'levelling-down' process in which intellectuals lost their former authority:

WRITER: I'm a writer.
READER: I think you're sh—t.
[*The writer stands for a few minutes shattered by this new idea, then falls down dead on the ground. He is carted out.*]
ARTIST: I'm an artist.
WORKER: I think you're sh—t.
[*The artist goes white as a sheet, shakes like a leaf, and falls down stock dead. He is suddenly carted out.*]
COMPOSER: I'm a composer.
VANIA RUBLEV: I think you're a ....!
[*Composer, breathing heavily, collapses in a heap—he is suddenly carted out.*][22]

For some of his contemporaries, such material would have seemed less 'absurdism' than an accurate reflection of a world of inverted hierarchies and anti-intellectual barbarity.

Empowerment by the Back Door: the Soviet Regime's Absorption of Intellectual Values

What Kharms's sketch also illustrates is the theatricality of much 1920s and 1930s egalitarianism, apparent also in the work experience experiments of the late 1920s, when schoolchildren, dispatched to Soviet factories in order to observe work practices, made themselves thorough nuisances by ringing the fire-alarm to summon workers to agitprop presentations on the dangers of heavy drinking, or placing black pennants on the lathes of persistent absentees.[23] Such disruptions of the status quo had a quite different character from the actions of the adolescent Red Guards during the cultural revolution in the People's Republic of China, who subjected their victims to beatings and executions. In Russia, class war in action signified temporary misrule on the part of a proletariat and peasantry themselves kept well in control by Party regulation, rather than political purges achieved through manipulation of grassroots violence. Conversely, the social contract between the intelligentsia and the regime was a good deal more complicated than the ritual abuse of helpless Chekhovian intellectuals would have suggested.

The first reason for this was a high degree of overlap between the class interests of intellectuals as a group, and those of the regime. A representative number of the Old Bolsheviks—Lenin, Bukharin, Krupskaia, Zinov'ev, Lunacharskii —were themselves members of the intelligentsia by birth and education. Those who were not (for example Kalinin, Trotskii) had often come through a system of education and political training in which intellectual values were enormously influential. Party schools of the 1920s to some extent perpetuated the traditions of the pre-Revolutionary Sunday schools, so even when the Old Bolsheviks were decimated by the Great Purges, belief in the importance of progress, the value of education, the necessity of hygiene and efficiency, and the significance of service to society, persisted, if only as symbolic entities, components in a 'bright future' of efficiency and egalitarianism. Conversely, while educated and sophisticated observers might find it difficult to accept the paranoiac fantasies about 'Trotskyite-Masonic conspiracies' that filled the Soviet press in the 1930s and 1940s, many shared the state's secularist distaste for religious ritual and clericalism, its conviction that hooliganism should be stamped out, its detestation of disruptive work practices, and its commitment—at the ideological level—to social equality.

The fact that egalitarianism as such, if not aggressive social inversion, was an ideal common to most of the intelligentsia was reflected, for instance, in the fact that few regretted the demise of the old selective secondary school system, with its division into *gimnazii*, elite schools teaching classical languages and humanities to a microscopic fraction of the country's population, *real'nye gimnazii*, with a curriculum of science and practical subjects, and commercial schools (*kommercheskie uchilishcha*). Inflammatory though the precise content of the integrated curriculum might be (some observers, notably the Communist Youth League (Komsomol), favoured a practical and work-based education, while Narkompros itself preferred a more academic approach), the fact of an integrated curriculum was generally accepted (and remained so until the early 1960s).[24] And central control was not generally opposed as anti-democratic in itself. The majority of medical professionals welcomed the creation of a People's Commissariat of Health Care (Narkomzdrav), since some of them had been campaigning for a central health ministry since well before the Revolution, in order that emergency relief could be organized in major catastrophes (such as famines or epidemics), and health policy properly co-ordinated.[25]

For its part, the Academy of Sciences, which had always enjoyed cordial relations with the Tsarist state, was not opposed to the principle of state control. Moreover, while the academicians' concept of 'scientific neutrality' might lead them to reject what they saw as undue intrusion on the part of the authorities, the 'neutral' standpoint also hindered direct confrontation with these authorities. A further contributory factor to quiescence was the fact that many scientists remained convinced (however naïvely) that even vociferous critics could be contained within the margins of civilized debate; hence the biologist Vavilov's disastrous attempt to outflank Lysenko by supporting his candidature for the Academy of Sciences in 1935.[26]

Conversely, from the government side, pragmatic considerations could often be as important as ideology. Though Soviet officials were perfectly well aware that 'bourgeois specialists' were not necessarily natural political allies, they were forced to rely on them *faute de mieux*. Faced with a choice between competent scientists with stiff collars and bourgeois views, and boiler-suited radicals who lacked scientific expertise, whatever their grasp of Marxism, the government favoured the former. Though not one member of the Academy of Sciences was a member of the Communist Party at the time of the Revolution, the Bolshevik regime quickly negotiated a *rapprochement*: in 1918, its President, A. Karpinskii, agreed, in response to an approach from Lunacharskii, that the Academy was willing to aid in 'developing productive forces for material needs'.[27] In response, on 12 April 1918, the Soviet of People's Deputies passed a decree agreeing that the Academy should be guaranteed financial support.[28] By the early 1930s, the government was supporting the Academy of Sciences to the tune of many millions of roubles per year. Several million were devoted to one key project alone, the construction of a 'scientific village' at Koltushi, near Leningrad, as a site for the experimental work of I. P. Pavlov, complete with a substantial 'cottage' for the grand old man himself.[29] And in 1936, the Communist Academy was itself closed down, and some of its personnel absorbed into the old Academy of Sciences, which became the central organizing body for academic research, expanding all over the Soviet Union.[30]

In education, too, a *rapprochement* with the intelligentsia was dictated by practicalities, here above all the age structure of the teaching profession. As late as 1930, 33 per cent of primary and 45 per cent of secondary teachers had received their training before the Revolution. The older teachers also represented a relatively stable core in a profession plagued by a high drop-out rate.[31] Narkompros did not produce a coherent new syllabus until 1925, and even then many teachers failed to grasp what was meant by *komplektirovanie* (thematically integrated teaching), or the 'Dalton system' of project work. So, apparently, did their pupils, as suggested by N. Ognev's lively and plausible memoir of a fictional Soviet schoolboy, *The Diary of Kostia Riabtsev*:

> They're introducing the Dalton Plan in our school. It's a system that means the beaks do nothing and the students have to find it out all for themselves. . . .
>
> The Dalton Plan is turning out a real mess. No-one understands what's going on—not us, nor the beaks. The beaks discuss it all every evening. So far as we can see, the only new thing is that they've given us benches instead of fixed desks, so you've got nowhere to hide the books you want to read in boring classes.[32]

In such circumstances it is not surprising that, as one expert has commented, 'in primary and secondary schools throughout the Republic, teachers continued to teach, and students continued to learn, by means of the familiar cycle of dictation, memorization, and drill'.[33] Things did not go much better with pupil self-government—introduced in only two out of twenty-one reporting regions by 1923—or with marks and homework, supposedly abolished but in fact retained by many Russian schools.[34] The reintroduction of more 'old-fashioned' educational criteria in 1931, at which point the Central Committee began dictating policy to Narkompros, can therefore be seen as a recognition of the inevitable, rather than as a Great Retreat. In any case, though pointless experiments were now frowned on, a certain flexibility in educational method was still allowed to the more go-ahead schools. 'Pedology', the innovative and exciting school of Soviet educational psychology that had developed during the 1920s (its most famous exponent was Vygotskii), retained some influence until the late 1930s.[35] And informality persisted in at least some classrooms, as recorded by a British schoolteacher, Deana Levin, who spent time teaching in Moscow in the mid-1930s:

> I found the children very intelligent, rather noisy and uncontrolled, but very easily interested. The first lesson I had with them was arithmetic, and as I kept them very busy, they worked fairly quietly. But when it came to geography, I found it more difficult to control them. They were seemingly very much interested in this subject, but all began to ask questions at once, without any idea of order. I stopped the lesson to explain that unless we had some sort of discipline we should not be able to get on fast enough. One girl raised her hand. 'The trouble with our class is that although everyone knows the rules, we forget to keep them.'
>
> 'What are the rules?' I asked curiously. 'Well,' she answered, 'we know that we should raise our hands if we wish to ask questions, because if we all speak at once, it is impossible to hear. I think we should have socialist competition with the fourth class, as we did last term.'
>
> 'Yes, yes,' everyone agreed.
>
> These remarks seemed to serve as a reminder, for the class studied quietly until the end of the morning.[36]

In 1943, a new educational code tightened rules on conduct once again, imposing on every Soviet pupil the duty to stand up whenever a teacher or the director entered the classroom and when asked to speak in class, and to raise his or her hand before speaking. But even in this era of regimented discipline, there were some surprising aberrations, such as the survival of the Gnesin Institute, a formerly private music school, right through the Stalin era under its pre-Revolutionary director, E. F. Gnesina.[37] And individual teachers could, if they wished, moderate the unregulated aspects of class discipline, choosing, for example, a more or less authoritarian form of address, and moderating, or exaggerating, the harshness of their intonation. The fact was that though state regulation had been tightened up, teachers now enjoyed a great deal more social status than they had in the 1920s, particularly during the cultural revolution, when many unfortunate individuals had found themselves attacked, on the one side, as 'class outsiders' and 'kulaks', while, on the other, suffering verbal and indeed physical abuse when they actively involved themselves in official campaigns, for example the collectivization of agriculture.[38]

In medicine, *rapprochement* with the intelligentsia proved possible quite quickly, since state policy realized some long-standing objectives of the profession at an early stage. The influential Pirogov Society at first resisted the government's replacement of the *zemstvo* physicians' leading role in medical propaganda by the co-ordination and professionalization of prophylactic medicine. However, objections were in part outflanked by the incorporation of leading medics into the planning and policy-making of Narkomzdrav from the start (its formation was discussed at the First All-Russian Congress of Sanitary Sections, held in June 1918). And in fact the Sanitary Sections, later renamed Health Sections, allowed health professionals to play a significant role in health education, if they so wished.[39] Even as late as the 1940s, voluntary associations could still play some part in health policy: for instance, a campaign to clean up

Leningrad housing in 1945 drew on the resources of the Red Cross as well as of local sanitary committees.[40]

All of this seems to bear out the hypothesis put forward by Sheila Fitzpatrick in *The Cultural Front* that the 1920s and 1930s saw the formation of an uneasy understanding between intelligentsia and state, accompanied by a loss of independence on the intelligentsia's part, but also by a blunting of class-war rhetoric in recompense. If control over the intelligentsia increased from the mid-1920s, so, too, did the benefits available. In the early 1920s, a university professor's salary was no higher than that paid to teachers in elementary schools. But in 1924–5, academic salaries began to rise again, and academic personnel became more militant in demanding privileges to which they thought they were entitled.[41] Moreover, the civil-servant status of doctors, academics, scientists, and (after the creation of the Writers', Composers', Film-Makers', and Artists' Unions in the 1930s) creative artists entitled them to the benefits paid to Soviet civil servants, including special rations allocated through the place of work, annual visits to rest homes and sanatoria, relatively high pensions, and a more generous allocation of living space than that available to most members of the Soviet public, with some in the highest grades even allocated a *kazennaia kvartira*, the grace-and-favour residence also granted to high-ranking Party officials.

Reinscription of the intelligentsia's *mission civilisatrice* was to take on particular importance from the late 1920s, in connection with the Soviet government's attempts to effect a transition from the so-called dictatorship of the proletariat to socialist democracy. While on the one hand perpetrating purges against intellectuals, the authorities tried, on the other, to revive the old ideal of *obshchestvennost'*, the engagement in social change of politically aware citizens who were not professional politicians. Sofiia Smidovich argued in 1930 that the mobilization of *obshchestvennost'* was of the utmost importance for the reformation of everyday life; Nadezhda Krupskaia even went so far as to suggest that it might in time displace the state. *Obshchestvennost'* came to be associated with two main roles: the formation of a broadly based consensus supporting the mechanisms of local government, and the instrument of social regulation, a tool for monitoring public order and combating deviant behaviour.[42] Though the practical consequences of these discussions remained muted, they were an indication of a new readiness to recognize the traditional role of the intelligentsia as a force for cultural change (albeit an intelligentsia with a much broader social base than before). And one manifestation of *obshchestvennost'* which did get off the ground (the *obshchestvennitsa* movement, on which see below) represented a piquant reworking of the activities of women philanthropists on which Social Democrat activists had traditionally poured scorn.

The Price of Knowledge: State Centralization and the Reinstatement of Objectivity

The interaction between intellectuals and the state was to be dramatized in some Soviet writings (such as Bulgakov's *The Master and Margarita*) as a 'Faustian pact', but in truth there was no one moment at which the intelligentsia 'sold its soul', rather a slow process of integration in different areas. What was more, the contradictoriness of official policy meant that regulation had its gaps and loopholes. The Soviet state's ostensible objective was to professionalize all intellectual activities: that is, to ensure that every person practising an intellectual activity was properly trained, appropriately remunerated, and occupied a rational niche in the planning of the centralized state. This was straightforward enough with science and other areas of academia, and to some extent also with music, the visual arts, and the performing arts, where there was an established history of institutionalized training, and (in the case of painting) of state regulation via the 'gold medal' system. It was never more than partially achieved in literature. The Writers' Union was always an elite organization, as were the writers' training colleges, from which only a few hundred graduates emerged each year; and, since there was never any attempt to ban the circulation of paper and writing materials, non-unionized writers could and did continue to produce, filling the in-trays of Soviet journals with unsolicited manuscripts (the so-called *samotek*). Moreover, this process was actually encouraged by the admission to the Writers' Union only of writers who had already proved themselves, which meant that the journals were under pressure to publish suitable work by débutant, non-unionized writers. The result was that journal editors became still more powerful figures than in the pre-Revolutionary period, operating not only in the repressive role of censors (rejecting or cutting work that did not 'reflect Soviet reality', to cite the cliché that commonly appeared on rejection slips), but also in the productive role of patrons and literary advisers.[43]

The literary establishment was not the only area in which the conflicting objectives of state policy empowered intellectuals. Professionalization of academic subjects, particularly the natural sciences, had from the first a highly elitist and impractical character. Though the state constantly called on scientists to aid in improving industrial and agricultural production, the number of scientists actively involved in industry remained low. So far from encouraging specialists to work directly with industry, the Soviet government opted, in the 1920s, for the so-called German model, according to which prestige scientific projects were concentrated in specialized institutes. The admission of engineers to the Academy of Sciences in 1929 (they had not formerly been eligible to apply for membership) exacerbated the problem, by removing the most prominent applied scientists into the ivory tower.[44] One consequence was that scientific charlatans, such as Lysenko, who propounded cure-all practical solutions from within privileged institutions, could be dangerously successful. Lysenko's 'discovery' of 'wonder-working' strains of Soviet wheat (actually pre-existing inferior varietals) made his more cautious academic colleagues seem out of touch, and the practical agronomists who might have given the lie to his arguments lacked the status to contradict him. However, at bottom, professionalization and bureaucratic regulation were intrinsically contradictory: as activities became more complex, it became harder for outsiders to monitor them. Lip-service might be paid to Stalin's scientific genius as 'the coryphaeus of all knowledge', but the leader's semi-literate excursions into complex fields such as linguistic history could only dent his prestige among the experts that the Soviet system had created. Increasingly, too, specialists themselves saw their professional knowledge as a weapon, as the Czech poet and biologist Miroslav Holub has recalled. Holub, working as a pathologist in Sovietized Czechoslovakia during the late 1940s, was present at a meeting when a lecturer introduced colleagues to the theories of Ol′ga Lepeshinskaia, a quack trumpeted by the Soviet scientific authorities for her success in 'healing' tubercular sores by exposure to soda baths. With deadly irony, a pathologist asked from the floor for more details of Lepeshinskaia's experiment: 'Could you give us the concrete quantitative conditions of the soda bath, concentration, duration, etc.?' Lamely, the lecturer had to confess, 'I am sorry, but the volume of the bath-tub of Ol′ga Borisovna has not been published.'[45]

As Holub also points out, 'experimental and theoretical sciences were not only under the strictest surveillance, but also most vulnerable to the Russian orthodoxy'. The rise of highly specialized, complex disciplines, already furthered by the rarefied character of the Academy of Sciences institutes, was further enhanced by a growing tendency among scientists and scholars to perceive as 'objective' those areas which were most difficult to regulate in terms of Marxist-Leninist dogma. For orthodox Marxist-Leninists, on the other hand, objectivity meant precisely the opposite. According to Lenin's tract *Marxism and Empirio-Criticism* (1908), all intellectual activities had by definition to be politically engaged (*partiinye*), but it was only those informed by Marxist-Leninist theory that were *partiinye* in a positive sense, cataloguing phenomena through the processes of dialectical materialism, and so avoiding the 'dogmatism' and 'one-sidedness' that were held to be characteristic of 'bourgeois science'.[46]

In the Stalin years, Lenin's tenets were increasingly interpreted narrowly and crudely, forcing any accessible areas of intellectual activity to construct themselves according to the current interpretation of Marxist-Leninist (or Marxist-Leninist-Stalinist) ideology. So far from suffering 'epistemological crises', intellectuals hostile to Stalinist ideology began to perceive specialized knowledge and mandarinic density of expression as means of establishing their independence from state control. Crises of confidence were much more prevalent, and objectivity far more closely contested in the 1920s. At this point, state regulation of science and intellectual debate was less effective, but the status of knowledge was far less secure, and objectivity, in particular its links with visual observation and with materialism, was the subject of vehement debate. Attacks in the 1920s on 'individualism in science' had appeared to accept the nineteenth-century positivistic view according to which the acquisition of knowledge depended above all on the suspension of individual viewpoint, on the adoption of a panoramic representation of facts that transcended the limitations of subjectivity. But the fierce disputes about particular areas of scientific or scholarly investigation—eugenics, quantum mechanics, linguistics, to name but three—stressed the essential political engagement of all scientific discourse, the fact that every theory, however neutral, had to be the expression of some ideological viewpoint—in other words, that there was no such thing as a universal perspective. The result was the evolution of competing discourses that constructed objectivity in vastly differing ways. In the area of literary history, for example,

formalist theory, which aimed to adduce ideologically neutral rules governing cultural evolution, stood in radical opposition to the sociological approach,
according to which all cultural forms were produced by different phases of the
class struggle. The latter approach was later to be vilified, in the late 1930s, as
'vulgar sociologism', and replaced by a restoration of the literary canon as an
unassailable bastion of merit. Yet in the hands of talented and intelligent inter-
preters, literary sociology produced some work of exceptional merit, particularly
in areas such as the history of the Russian theatre and the study of literary institutions (publishing, journals, salons). Here, the emphasis on objectivity in the sense
of panoramic treatments of the historical context, rather than emphasis on the
personal characteristics of famous writers, was enabled rather than hampered
by literary sociologists' ideologized standpoint.

There was similar diversity in the world of artistic theory, which was divided
by disagreement about what constituted factual representation. At one level,
there was a split between documentary and mythologizing interpretations of
realism, expressed, for instance, in the distinction between monumentalizing
sculpture (in which figures towered over the observer, stressing their part in a
larger and more heroic struggle) and academic portrait painting (a key example
of which, Isaak Brodskii's *Lenin at Smol'nyi*, represented the leader seen from
above, as a small and physically frail middle-aged man on a self-consciously
drab and homely brown armchair). There was also a division between traditional views, which saw the artistic representation as objective when it represented reality in a manner satisfactory to common-sense perceptions, and the
more radical criteria of the avant-garde, which emphasized the need for objective representations to discard the conventional understanding of how reality
should appear to the naked eye. One of the most interesting statements of this
came from the film director Dziga Vertov, who argued from the necessary fallibility and subjectivity of the human observer to the notion of the camera as a
more qualified and objective recorder of reality:

> The most thorough investigation does not reveal a single film, a single piece of
> research that is correctly designed to *emancipate the camera* which has been pitifully
> enslaved and subjugated to the imperfect and none too clever human eye. . . .
>
> Our starting point is: *the use of the camera as a Cine-Eye, more perfect than the
> human eye for examining the chaos of visual phenomena that resemble space.* . . .
>
> Until now we have *coerced the film camera and forced it to copy the work done by our
> eyes.* And the better the copy, the more highly we thought of the photography.[47]

In a statement by another, more moderate member of the avant-garde—the
painter David Sterenberg, the first head of Narkompros's Representational Arts
section (Izo)—the notion of objectivity as a panoramic view was quixotically
combined with an assertion that objectivity depended on specific knowledge
beyond the image:

> The cultivated and keen eye can open up a world of phenomena in nature that is still
> infinitely vast yet remains closed for the majority of people. Thanks to this organ and
> their capacities for invention, artists have given these phenomena concrete reflection
> in works of art. But even the works of art themselves can be understood completely
> only by a cultivated eye.[48]

The 1920s saw an explosion of interest in adventurous work with the camera, not only in film, but also in still photography. A crucial direction was photo-montage, in which the notion of 'seeing round' a subject was expressed (rather as in cubist painting) by collages of multiple images seen from different angles. The tradition of off-centre shots continued well into the 1930s—the flagship thick journal *Nashi dostizheniia* (*Our Achievements*) has some remarkably adventurous images as well as quasi-documentary footage. Only in the 1940s did a sort of greetings-card soft-focus style take over.

Equally, in narrative (literature and film), objectivity was interpreted in very different ways by different groups of intellectuals. Among some, such as Serafimovich in his Civil War novella *The Iron Flood* (*Zheleznyi potok*, 1924), or Eisenstein, in *Strike* (*Stachka*, 1924), it signified a supra-individualist perspective according to which 'the Russian masses' were seen as the collective and undifferentiated heroes of revolutionary upheaval. Granted, Leninist emphasis on the need for 'conscious' direction of 'spontaneous' popular aspirations meant that the people always had their tribunes, but there was no attempt to characterize these—the military leader in *The Iron Flood*, for example, is known, metonymically, as 'Leather Jacket' (Kozhukh), while the strike organizers in *Strike* are nameless figures whose public and private existences are indistinguishable from those of their workmates. In texts of this kind, characterization was kept for the villains—the barrel-dwelling lumpenproletarian strikebreakers in *Strike*, or the lolling members of the Women's Battalion in their cropped hair and lacy camisoles in Eisenstein's *October* (*Oktiabr'*). For other writers and film-makers, however, the techniques adopted were to be those of a more conventional realism, with recognizable characters and omniscient narrator, a direction known, with considerable over-simplification of the alleged precedent, as 'the search for a Red Lev Tolstoi'.[49] For others again, objectivity was a question of representing a perspective that was limited by individual experience: in fiction, of speaking with a voice self-consciously differentiated from that of the biographical author. This was the case, for example, in the 1920s stories of Mikhail Zoshchenko, in which a working-class male city-dweller speaks with bewilderment of the trials that he undergoes at the hands of petty officials, or in Evgenii Zamiatin's 'Comrade Churygin Takes the Floor' ('Slovo predostavliaetsia tovarishchu Churyginu', 1928), where a narrator from a remote village describes how he and his neighbours attempted to plunge the locality into revolution without understanding what it was that the Revolution required of them.

Knowledge as Peril versus Knowledge as Power: Bulgakov's *Notes of a Young Doctor* and 'Heart of a Dog'

The voice of Zoshchenko's confused 'little man' was in a sense a distorted echo of the voice of many subjects far better educated than he. Under Soviet power, intellectuals themselves were much more pushed around than had ever been the case before. Now that philanthropy was derided as voluntarism, and public service was a duty imposed from the outside, as well as an activity prompted by the inner voice of conscience, some of the self-respect that had been inherent in the intelligentsia's subject position had evaporated. Now that objectivity was bedevilled by the intelligentsia's integration into state service, and by uncertainty about what the activity constituted in a new society, it was extremely difficult to construct a position from which to offer detached social commentary. Yet at the same time, the competence of 'bourgeois specialists', however derided by radical commentators, came increasingly to afford them social leverage. Racked by self-doubt about the morality of their social position though they might be, Soviet intellectuals could still feel a sense of pride, even arrogance, in the prestige that was afforded them by living in what one 1930s popular song called 'the land of heroes, dreamers, scientists, and scholars'. Nowhere is this paradox more closely reflected than in two 1920s texts by Mikhail Bulgakov: the short-story cycle *Notes of a Young Doctor* and the novella 'Heart of a Dog'.

Bulgakov was himself by all accounts rather a reluctant medic, and in *Notes of a Young Doctor* (*Zapiski iunogo vracha*) his *alter ego*, Dr Bomhardt, goes through a significant *crise de foi* when presented with his first patients in a remote village some forty miles distant even from the 'district centre', with its blandishments of cinema, street-lights, and educated company.[50] Bomhardt's overwhelming sense of his own uselessness is conveyed by the insistent polarization, in his mind, between the 'knowledge' to which he has been exposed as a medical student, and the practical situations with which he is confronted. Again and again, medical emergencies (the need to amputate the leg of a girl crushed in a beetling machine, a breech birth, a tracheotomy that must be performed to save a child from diphtheria) cause him to revert in his mind to the well-lit lecture hall where white-bearded professors demonstrated the appropriate techniques, or to the requisite page of the textbook he studied as a student. His experience of medical practice prompts him to a vivid sense of dislocation between the rational formulations of his education and the instinctive, indeed at times shamanistic process by which a physician actually achieves results. In the most striking story in the cycle, 'The Sideways Christening', the tensions are especially obvious. When confronted with a breech birth, Bomhardt first rushes terrified to Doderlein's textbook on obstetrics as a source of information about what to do, but the knowledge accumulated in the book cannot bring enlightenment, only confusion ('everything in my brain got totally muddled, and I realized immediately that I knew nothing' (136)). Help comes from elsewhere: from the advice offered spontaneously by Bomhardt's nurse, and from Bomhardt's own sense of what he should do:

> From [Anna Nikolaevna's] fragmentary words, her unfinished sentences and hints dropped in passing I grasped the essence, what you don't find in any books . . . All those learned words are no use in a moment like this. The only thing that matters is that I have to put one hand inside and use the other from outside to help the turn and, relying not on books, but on my own sense of proportion, without which a doctor is no use to anyone, carefully but firmly draw down one of the legs and behind it the infant. (137)

The nurse's inarticulacy emphasizes the fact that medicine is a magical practice, one beyond concrete communication, while Bomhardt's preference of the tactile to the visual underlines his retreat from the brightly lit world of academic discourse on medicine to an older and more mysterious reality. Significantly, too, the story elides the actual moment when the child is turned (in his mind, Bomhardt refers to it as a 'child', rather than the clinical 'foetus', *plod*, preferred in the textbooks). Instead, two rows of suspension points are inserted, so that the movement from Bomhardt's resolution of his crisis to his successful performance of the task he has feared is left undepicted, as though it too were beyond description.

The transition from an overwhelming sense of self-doubt in Bomhardt to serendipitous success is repeated again and again in the cycle. Medicine, it is clear, cannot finally be 'known', or encompassed by the eye; it must be learnt by feeling (the Russian word *chut'e* suggests both sensation and instinct, 'sixth sense'). Yet Bomhardt's rejection of contemporary medical epistemology is only partial. The fact that the doctor's knowledge is professional rather than fortuitous is suggested by another repeated motif in the cycle—the nurse's congratulation to the doctor in having dealt with an amputation or breech birth in a manner that would do credit to an experienced professional. And there are stories in the cycle where Bomhardt's reconciliation with the medical orthodoxy of his day seems more whole-hearted. In 'Starry Rash', for example, he has two chance encounters with patients who have been exposed to syphilitic infection: a man with the rash characteristic of secondary syphilis, and a woman whose husband may have infected her with the disease. The two encounters set up very conventional images of the 'good' and the 'bad' patient. The 'bad' patient is insouciant, rebellious, confident in his ignorance, reluctant to surrender his bad social practices, and male. The 'good' patient is terrified by her condition, aware that she is ignorant and helpless, and totally deferential before the doctor's knowledge. She is also innocent of any bad practice (her husband has contaminated her); finally, she is female (it is no accident that it is women's bodies on which the doctor performs his most successful acts of witchcraft). Bomhardt guides the 'good' patient through her crisis, but is at first defeated by the 'bad' one (who lambastes him about bothering over the rash, rather than doling out a cure for the sore throat which gives the patient himself more cause for concern). However, the defeat spurs Bomhardt to a crusade: he gets the authorization for a treatment centre, and interns patients in an isolation ward, bullying them into completing their treatment, and treating them to hair-raising homilies when they try to leave. The story is a tribute to contemporary ideals of hygiene and appropriate therapy, and to the doctor's absolute authority over his patients.

What weight one gives to 'Starry Rash' as a resolution of Bomhardt's 'epistemological crisis' depends on where one chooses to place it in the cycle. When first published, *Notes of a Young Doctor* ended with two stories in which the medical ideal is again ruptured: 'Morphine', portraying the addiction to the substance on the part of Bomhardt's friend Dr Poliakov, and 'I Killed', a story in which Dr Iashvin relates how he had to kill a 'patient' in Kiev, a brutal colonel in Petliura's forces. Some editors, however, have reordered the stories, and in one possible layout 'Starry Rash' is our last view of Dr Bomhardt. Whichever way, the key motif of the cycle, repeated again and again, is the impossibility of resolving medical problems through knowledge alone, a revelation that sits oddly with the emphasis on 'progress' and 'enlightenment' that some commentators have chosen to see in the cycle.

Notes of a Young Doctor is a powerful set of stories that is very much in pre-Revolutionary tradition. Not only is the Revolution itself hardly mentioned (a point that most critics have noticed), but the 'epistemological crisis' proceeds along the lines of those sketched in pre-Revolutionary texts, such as Valentina Dmitrieva's 'Round the Villages' ('Po derevniam', 1896), which also portrays a young *zemstvo* doctor's anxieties about her position. Bulgakov's eerie science-fictional fable 'Heart of a Dog' ('Sobach'e serdtse', 1924), by contrast, represents a thoroughly Soviet professional intellectual, morally compromised, but epistemologically empowered.

At first sight, to be sure, the story is a savage indictment of the liberal, professional intelligentsia, in the person of Professor Preobrazhenskii, member of the All-Russian Association of Surgeons, internationally renowned specialist on endocrinology, with a profitable sideline in rejuvenation techniques. Preobrazhenskii's attempt to upgrade his rejuvenation techniques by implanting the hypophysis and testicles of a human being into a stray dog, Sharik, goes horribly wrong when the creature, far from being rejuvenated, is transmogrified into a low-browed, small, and stocky subhuman, 'Sharikov', who, or perhaps better which, proceeds to wreak havoc in the professor's comfortable seven-room flat.

Preobrazhenskii's respectability as a professional is open to doubt throughout the cycle. Though he himself protests that he has pursued the experiment out of an abstract desire for knowledge, rather than a thirst for profit, he is portrayed in the story's opening scenes as a classic sleek bourgeois, smelling of cigars as well as hospitals, and his attempt to defend his right to seven rooms when this is under assault from the *domoupravlenie* (the building's management committee) hardly speaks of his disinterested love for science, or indeed his concern for other human beings. His experiment in vivisection can be seen as a form of pointless cruelty to animals: so much is suggested not only by the anthropomorphic treatment of Sharik before his transformation (we are shown his thoughts), but also by the use of the verb *rezat'*, to 'cut up', to describe Preobrazhenskii's activities (the verb has also been used in the opening paragraph of the story, in which Sharik bewails the fact that a cook has 'cut into' his side by throwing boiling water at him). The experiment is also a sublime example of scientific discourse stymied by the phenomena it purports to represent. Dr Bormenthal, Preobrazhenskii's assistant, keeps a record of events whose 'neutral' scientific language gradually fractures as the phenomena observed move outside the ordinary domain of experimentation. The result is a pointed parody of the scientist's pretence to objectivity:

> 2 January. The subject was flash-photographed while in the action of smiling. It got up from its bed and stood on its hind paws for about thirty minutes. It is nearly my height.
> (On a sheet of paper stuck into the notebook)
> Russian science has narrowly escaped a terrible loss.
> History of the illness of Professor Preobrazhenskii.

At 1.23 a.m. Professor Preobrazhenskii fell into a deep faint. In falling, he hit his head on the leg of a chair. Tincture of valerian was administered.

In my and Zina's presence the dog (if 'dog' is what it can be termed) told Professor Preobrazhenskii to f— off.[51]

Yet this Soviet version of *Frankenstein* is not just an anti-intellectual diatribe. Preobrazhenskii is himself an advocate of objective, neutral observation: 'I am a man of facts, a man of observations, the enemy of unfounded hypotheses' (165; ch. 3). Alone among the characters in the story, he has the self-knowledge to realize that the experiment he has performed was fundamentally misconceived:

'You see, doctor, that's what happens when a researcher, instead of going in parallel with nature and feeling his way, tries to force the issue and lift the curtain on the mysteries: there's your Sharikov, enjoy him!'

'But Filipp Filippovich, suppose you'd tried it with the brain of a Spinoza?'

. . . 'What the devil for, though? Answer me that. Tell me what on earth would be the point of confecting a Spinoza when any peasant woman can give birth to him in any case?' (217; ch. 8)

And if *Frankenstein* demands that we feel sympathy for the monster, the creation of a scientist's fantasy, Sharikov is never allowed to inspire readers' pity for a moment. Though his assertion that Preobrazhenskii is responsible for what he has created is undoubtedly just, he is himself a revolting embodiment of what Bakhtin called 'the lower bodily stratum' run riot. Drunken, foul-mouthed, and possessed of a low cunning, he represents 'hooliganism' (the word *khuligan* is used to describe him) and, still more abominably, a hooliganism that has come to pollute private, as well as public space. The transgression of boundaries is underlined by the fact that Sharikov is soon in league with the *domoupravlenie*, four young people whose appearance caricatures another shocking fact of Soviet reality—its abolition of gender boundaries:

'We've come to see you, Professor,' said the one with a quiff of the thickest curliest hair possible jutting above his forehead, 'on the the following business . . .'

'Gentlemen, it's an extremely bad idea not to wear galoshes in weather like this,' Filipp Filippovich interrupted him. 'For one thing, you'll catch cold, and for another, I have Persian carpets here.'

The one with the quiff was silenced, and all four visitors stared at Filipp Filippovich in astonishment. The silence lasted for several seconds, interrupted only by the sound of Filipp Filippovich's fingers drumming on the painted wooden dish on the table.

'For one thing, we're not gentlemen,' the youngest of the four, who had a vaguely Persian look, said eventually.

'For one thing,' Filipp Filippovich interrupted him in his turn, 'are you a man or a woman?'

The four were silent again, their mouths falling open. This time it was the first one, with the quiff, that answered.

'What's the difference, comrade?' he asked proudly.

'I'm a woman,' confessed the Persian youth in the leather jacket and blushed darkly. For some reason one of the other visitors blushed fiercely too—the blond one in the tall sheepskin hat.

'In that case, you may leave your cap on, but I would ask you, my dear sir, to remove whatever it is that you are wearing on your head.'

'I'm not your dear sir,' the blond asserted in a rude tone, removing his hat. (157–8; ch. 2)

Here, Filipp Filippovich restores order by giving the four juvenile upstarts a lesson in manners and sexual differentiation, which they seem surprisingly prepared to heed. At the end of the story, he unmakes the monster that he has created by turning 'Sharikov' back into the docile, endearing Sharik, who knows his place and rewards the care given to him with suitably canine devotion.

The viciously satirical portrayal of Sharikov—Bulgakov's story has a Swiftian force of hatred for the yahoos of Soviet society—illustrates that 'class conflict' in the 1920s was not only a question of anti-intelligentsia feeling. However, the story is not simply an expression of the desire that order, and the social order, should be restored. It is also an illustration of the part played by knowledge in restoring order. It is only Professor Preobrazhenskii who has the skill to rehabilitate the monstrosity that he has created; rather than feeling that his skill and knowledge are negated, he has his power to arbitrate over life and death confirmed by the action of the story. The story is a deeply ambivalent portrait of the Soviet scientist as self-interested, but also self-aware, and a representation of science both as an unlicensed meddling in the structures of nature, and as a fundamentally reliable way of understanding the universe.

Bulgakov's story, though wonderfully surreal, did have a curious real-life analogue: the biography of Pavlov, who shared not only Professor Preobrazhenskii's experimental relationship with dogs, but also his interest in the ageing process and its link with hormonal secretions. Like Preobrazhenskii, too, Pavlov had a privileged, yet wary, relationship with Soviet reality. He never made money out of private practice, and, as an émigré colleague put it, 'his integrity was beyond dispute'.[52] But his international reputation, as the first Russian scientist to win the Nobel Prize (in 1904), and his credentials as a 'materialist' ensured him a dominant position in the Soviet science establishment from the start. A complaint from Pavlov in 1921 that he was not getting appropriate funding for his work led to a decree by Lenin that his research should receive state support, and from then until Pavlov's death it was underwritten by the state. By the end of his life, in 1936, he was in charge of three huge laboratories, including the Institute of Experimental Physiology in Leningrad, which he headed from 1925, and the purpose-built facilities at Koltushi.

If Pavlov's position as an important critic, but also an important beneficiary, of the regime was ambiguous, so too was his pedagogical methodology. On the one hand, he imposed rigorous experimentation on his students, and named 'modesty' as one of the most important qualities in a scientist; on the other, he conducted his lectures in a self-consciously theatrical manner, in which seduction of the eye was as important as illustration: 'He demanded that the experimental table mounted on wheels with the ready-prepared experiment should appear before the eyes of his hearers at the exact moment required.'[53] There was also a contradiction in Pavlov between a view of nature as the indifferent material of experiment and a deeply involved, even sentimental attachment to the animals on which he experimented. At the end of his life, he addressed a letter of thanks to the Sechenov Physiological Society, which had organized his jubilee, and spoke of 'having acquired for the huge power of physiological investigation . . . the entire animal organism' as his major life's work: 'this is indisputably and wholly our Russian service to world science'.[54] But he also welcomed the construction, outside the Institute of Experimental Physiology, of a monument to the laboratory dogs who had been his unnamed collaborators in this 'investigation'. The resulting fountain, with a bronze of a dog on a cylindrical pedestal ornamented with quotations from Pavlov's works about the need not to cause unnecessary suffering, was a tribute to 'man's best friend' in his rightful place, as uncomplaining acolyte of human endeavour. It was a fittingly ambiguous monument to the divided career of one of Russia's greatest twentieth-century scientists and exemplary Soviet intellectual.

Conclusion: the Triumph of Knowledge

A full-scale 'epistemological crisis' can take place only in societies where freedom of information (in however limited a sense) is a given. Chekhov's agonizing over his Sakhalin project depended on the fact that there were no external obstacles to his gathering and publishing the totality of data relating to the study that he intended to make. In Soviet society, where the state maintained much tighter control over the production of knowledge, the subject position of a researcher was quite different. Objectivity became a key strategy in defending the neutrality formerly taken for granted; discussions about whether, in principle, it was possible to be objective were, therefore, out of the question. Chekhov's standpoint is in intriguing contrast to the position adopted by Pavlov, whose apparently modest instruction to his students that any hypothesis must be discarded on the basis of a single contradictory fact depends on an unspoken assertion that there might be such a thing as a hypothesis uncontradicted by even one fact. In this sense, the determination of Soviet leaders to keep the circulation of information under Party control undermined, rather than upheld their own authority, creating the potential for intellectual critics to emerge as a formidable opposition force once political terror was suspended, in the post-Stalin era.

Programmes for Identity: The 'New Man' and the 'New Woman'

Lynne Attwood and Catriona Kelly

ONE of the most characteristic features of Soviet society in the 1920s and 1930s was its obsession with two totemic figures, the 'new man' and the 'new woman'. Rational, independent, and resolute, eschewing the self-scrutiny and vacillation of purpose that the classics of Russian literature had so often seen as essential aspects of Russian identity, such figures were celebrated as playing a crucial part in the construction of a new reality, and the suppression of unwanted elements of the old—from the larger social evils of insubordination and corruption, to the small ones of superstition and unpunctuality. Tracing their lineage back to the 'new people' celebrated by 1860s Russian radicals, such as Chernyshevskii in his famous novel *What is to Be Done?* (*Chto delat'?*, 1863), the 'new man' and 'new woman' differed from their ancestors, however, in that their model characters were seen to have resulted not only from private moral choices, the espousal of utopian philosophies such as rational egotism, but from coherent programmes of socialization and behaviour transformation, what Lunacharskii referred to as 'the process of production' of new types of human being.[55]

An eminently representative movement of the 1920s was Fordism, an adaptation of the time-and-motion theories of the American industrialist Henry Ford to Soviet reality. In his polemic of 1926, 'Culture and Socialism', Leon Trotskii had adopted Ford's key image of rational factory labour, the conveyor belt, as a metaphor for the transformation of nature and human nature under socialism:

> In practice the 'norm' for Ford's 200,000 workers is not Ford's conduct but the gliding-past of his automatic conveyer: *it determines the rhythm of their lives, the movement of their hands, feet and thoughts.* For 'the well-being of your fellow citizens' it is necessary to separate Fordism from Ford and to socialize and purge it. This is what socialism does.[56]

Fordism was an indicative development both in its modernist emphasis on the harmony of man and machine, and in its manifestation of an insouciant conviction that ideologies might effortlessly be stripped of their harmful elements and transferred to Soviet society. In practice, decontextualization was of course more problematic than was suggested in early Soviet polemic.[57]

If Fordism can be seen as a direct link between Bolshevik theory and Stalinist practice, other blueprints for identity in the 1920s were more eccentric and unexpected, if also more short-lived. One of these was psychoanalysis. As Aleksandr Etkind has pointed out in *The Eros of the Impossible*, psychoanalysts enjoyed a warm relationship with the country's leadership during the first half of the 1920s. The

People's Commissariat of Enlightenment, Narkompros, had a psychoanalysis department, which sponsored, *inter alia*, a 'children's home-laboratory' in Moscow, attended by the children of many highly placed Party officials (including Vasilii Stalin). Many of Freud's works were translated, and came out in print runs that were large enough to be the envy of psychoanalysts in other European countries. Though psychoanalysis began to fall into disfavour in the late 1920s, and was finally to be castigated as a 'bourgeois science', not resurfacing until the 1960s, and then half-clandestinely, its ideals of self-transcendence through explication of the unconscious, and the role of sexuality in human development, were familiar to (if not necessarily warmly received by) many Soviet intellectuals of the 1920s and 1930s, inspiring, among other things, Voloshinov's Marxist critique of Freudian theory, *Freudianism* (*Freidizm*, 1927), and Mikhail Zoshchenko's remarkable pseudo-autobiographical story cycle *Before Sunrise* (*Pered voskhodom solntsa*, 1943). Other movements with some currency in the 1920s included Tolstoyan theory (Aleksandra Tolstaia remained in charge of her father's school in Iasnaia Poliana until the late 1920s, and there were a few Tolstoyan communes in existence till the mid-1930s); and Rudolf Steiner's creed of anthroposophy, with its emphasis on the importance of childhood as a foundation for creativity.

All these 'programmes for identity', however (with the possible exception of Tolstoyanism), were relatively localized and marginal in their effects, affecting, in the main, the metropolitan elite. All, too, were to disappear underground around 1930, as the atmosphere became increasingly hostile to forms of mysticism and idealism: the books of Freud and Steiner were purged from Soviet libraries, removed to 'special stores' where they could be consulted only by scholars accredited by the authorities, while Tolstoi's religious teachings were republished only in the huge Jubilee Edition of the writer's complete works, which had a print run of 1,000 copies, most of which went into libraries in Russia and abroad. Of much more significance in reshaping the identities of ordinary men and women, therefore, were rather more down-to-earth methods aimed at the indoctrination of the Soviet population.

One particular target group, from the beginning of the Bolshevik regime, was children. Soviet policy-makers would have heartily endorsed the famous observation of Ignatius Loyola, 'Give me a child, and let who will have the man'. Since the rise of vocational education in the early nineteenth century, Russian usage had distinguished between *obuchenie* (training) and *vospitanie* (moral education). Like their Tsarist predecessors, the Soviet authorities had a pressing need to create an education system that would deliver in the first sense, providing literate, skilled workers and managers to staff Soviet industry and technology. However, they were just as concerned as the Tsarist authorities with education's potential for co-ordinating social control. From a child's first arrival in school at the age of 7, therefore, teaching materials were designed to create a vision of Soviet power as the optimum form of government. Where reading primers of the past had taken material from the Gospels for early reading practice, Soviet reading primers disseminated revolutionary history at the earliest possible opportunity. As a 1925 first-form reader put it: 'The workers and the poor

peasants lived very badly under the Tsarist government. Only landowners, capitalists, kulaks, and the bourgeois generally lived well.' There was emphasis, too,
on the socialization rituals of the new culture: 'It is our holiday. We decorated the
school with flags. Then we went walking round the town with flags.'[58] Extended
exposure to such myth-making had its effects. A 1928 survey of 120,000 provincial schoolchildren established that most had only a shaky knowledge of
revolutionary history. Working-class children generally thought that the main
achievement of Soviet power was to have 'given land to the peasants', while the
majority of peasant children named 'the eight-hour day and worker ownership
of the factories' as the greatest boons brought by the new order.[59] However,
revolutionary patriotism was not in question, even if factual knowledge was:
the great majority of the group (whether peasants or workers) thought that the
Soviet government was the best in the world.

The political effectiveness of Soviet education was ensured also by the creation of school organizations that were supposed to act as preparatory groups for
the Komsomol. Young children were enrolled *en masse* in the Octobrist society,
whence older children could proceed, on the basis of merit (in which class origin, conduct, and academic prowess all played a role, roughly in that order), to
the Pioneers, which in the first decades of Soviet rule was not a mass movement,
but an elite organization on the lines of the Komsomol (though non-members
were allowed to attend meetings). The Pioneer organization, with its flags,
oaths, quasi-militaristic rituals, and motto of 'Always Prepared' (*Vsegda gotov*,
an adaptation of 'Be Prepared'), was deliberately modelled on the Scout and
Guide organizations (banned under Soviet rule), but members naturally swore
fidelity to the Soviet regime rather than to King and Empire. Furthermore, as
befitted the doctrine of sexual equality to which the Bolshevik regime had committed itself, the Pioneer groups were co-ed.

Pioneer, and later Komsomol, organizations skilfully exploited the peer pressure which is found in institutionalized education all over the world. As one
Pioneer leader put it in 1933, 'I have not yet met a child who, at the age of ten, did
not want to be a Pioneer.' Since membership was an honour, it could also be
withdrawn, an extremely effective form of discipline. Moreover, the Pioneer
and Komsomol organizations were powerful disseminators of the new class
ideology—conspicuously preferential treatment could be given to working-
class children. Interestingly, this does not seem to have been resented by children themselves. The memoirist Raisa Orlova, for example, recalls that she felt
no bitterness at all on being ejected from the Komsomol as the daughter of a
white-collar worker (*sluzhashchii*), and that she had earlier felt a thrill on reading aloud the oath to be sworn by all Young Pioneers, that 'I, a Young Pioneer of
the Soviet Union, do solemnly swear that I will firmly support the working class
in its battle for the liberation of the workers and peasants for all the world.'[60]

But the success of Soviet education as a disseminator of 'programmes for
identity' did not depend only on the exploitation of overtly politicized methods
of socialization. The regime needed to win over parents who were lukewarm
or hostile towards the new ideologies. This came about partly because of Soviet
schools' success in imparting basic literacy skills, which became an increasing

necessity in the search for work as the proportion of literate citizens increased. The late 1920s were a turning point, with a significant improvement in school attendance among the target groups—peasant and working-class children—who previously had made up the overwhelming majority of pupils in lower grades, but only a tiny minority of those in the higher grades.[61] Increasingly, too, the importance of *vospitanie* (moral education) in the broadest sense was emphasized: the 1943 educational code imposed on pupils not only duties related to class discipline, but also the duty to be punctual, to keep desks and personal possessions tidy, to greet teachers or the director 'with a polite bow', to behave politely in the streets, and to observe 'order and cleanliness' in the home.[62]

Another important factor in ensuring the effectiveness of Soviet education as a socializing force was that schools were at the centre of a network of welfare services. School doctors examined and identified problem cases, who could then be sent for treatment; low-cost holiday camps were made available for urban schoolchildren. An expanding, though still by no means universal, provision of nursery education offered similar facilities to pre-schools, while improvements in ante-natal and post-natal care reduced the appallingly high infant mortality rate that had been evident in Russia before the Revolution. Even those who had strong reservations about Soviet rule pointed to the care of children as one of its real achievements. The elderly writer Fedor Sologub, for example, observed of the Pioneers in 1925: 'Everything about them that's bad is old and thoroughly Russian; everything new is good.'[63] And later, many children felt no irony at all in thanking Stalin for a happy childhood, as they were taught to do in the late 1930s and 1940s. Black spots remained—for instance, the treatment of inmates in children's homes, penal colonies, and, especially, labour camps—but these were well out of sight of most Soviet citizens.[64]

Children's Literature

The Soviet authorities were aware that formal education and day care were only half the battle. Particularly from the early 1930s, there were increasing attempts to regulate the time that children spent out of school. Apart from its political activities, the Pioneer network also organized 'circles' (*kruzhki*) offering a whole range of extra-curricular pastimes, from folk-dancing to drawing, from ballet to football to drama. Another way of reaching children during leisure time was providing them with suitable reading material; therefore, the creation of a suitable Soviet juvenile literature was of the greatest concern to Soviet officials and writers almost from the moment that the Revolution happened.

Almost immediately after the February Revolution, the Petrograd Soviet published Kornei Chukovskii's verse tale *The Crocodile* (*Krokodil*), interpreted by leftists as an anti-tyrannical allegory, in a large print run, despite the acute paper shortage; and in January 1918, again despite practical difficulties, the first Soviet book for children, an almanac under the title *The Fir Tree* (*Elka*), appeared, also in Petrograd. Though this was intended as the first in a series that never in fact materialized, and though the development of children's publishing houses and magazines was delayed by the Civil War (Gor'kii's *Northern Lights* (*Severnoe siianie*), founded in 1919, was not destined to last), the years after the war had ended saw the publication of two books that were to become classics: Chukovskii's *The Cockroach* (*Tarakanishche*, 1923) and *Wash 'em White* (*Moidodyr*, 1923), brought out by the pioneering Raduga (Rainbow) publishing house, and Samuil Marshak's *Children in the Cage* (*Detki v kletke*, 1923), this time sponsored by Detizdat, the Children's Department of Gosizdat (the State Publishing House).[65]

In 1924, children's literature was given a further boost, when a decree passed at the Thirteenth Party Congress stated that it was 'essential to proceed to the creation of a literature for children under the careful control and supervisor of the Party'.[66] The decree was followed by the founding in 1924 of several children's magazines that long outlasted their predecessors: *Murzilka*, *Pioner* (*Young Pioneer*), and *Vorobei* (*Sparrow*), later *Novyi Robinzon* (*New Robinson*) magazines. Another intriguing offshoot of the new official interest in children's writing was the composition of a number of agitprop verse texts for children by Maiakovskii, including *The Tale of Petia the Fat Child and Sima, who was Thin* (*Skazka o Pete, tolstom rebenke, i o Sime, kotoryi tonkii*, 1925), and *Let's Take our New Rifles* (*Voz'mem novye vintovki*, 1927). In the late 1920s, two important new magazines (among the most interesting ever produced for children anywhere) were founded: *Ezh* (*Hedgehog*, issued from 1928) and *Chizh* (*Finch*, from 1930) were edited by Marshak, in collaboration with Daniil Kharms, Evgenii Shvarts, Aleksandr Vvedenskii, and Nikolai Oleinikov.[67] The high status now accorded to children's literature was reflected also in the publication of a specialist critical journal, *Detskaia literatura* (*Children's Literature*), which began coming out in 1931.

If Leningrad had been the centre of much early activity, the balance was redressed in 1933 with the founding in Moscow of Detskaia literatura publishers. This was to expand to the most important outlet in the Soviet Union, releasing 168 titles in its first year of operation, rising to 309 in 1940, and 692 in 1963; the large number of imprints included 'The Children's Library', as well as 'The School Library' of Russian and Soviet classics intended for textbook use.

Events in the children's theatre followed a rather similar pattern, with a policy declaration by Lunacharskii in 1918 that the founding of a children's theatre would be desirable, followed by the establishment of the Moscow First State Children's Theatre in 1920, and by the Petrograd Theatre of Young Viewers (TIuZ) in 1921, whose first director was Nataliia Sats.[68] Children's literature and theatre were the subject of a good deal of attention at the First Congress of Soviet Writers in 1934, at which a major address was given by Marshak, and shorter speeches by both Chukovskii and Sats.

As with cultural centralization in so many other areas, though, state reorganization had costs as well as benefits. The 'careful control and supervision' foreseen by the 1924 decree began to have a sinister resonance in the 1930s. As early as 1931, in the course of an assault on the Children's Section of Gosizdat, Kharms and Vvedenskii had been arrested. Though they were released the following year, further crackdowns were to follow. Oleinikov and Sats were arrested during the Great Purges of 1937–8. Finally, in 1941, Detizdat in Leningrad was mopped up completely, its editors dispersed (Marshak continued his career in

Moscow) or, in the case of Kharms and Vvedenskii, arrested and imprisoned (both writers died in captivity not long afterwards). Soviet children's writing had lost many of its most imaginative writers and organizers, and others had been given an unmistakable injunction to be cautious.[69]

Another effect of Stalinism was the construction of a historical myth that overstated the uniqueness of Soviet children's literature in a historical and a national sense: its difference from Western and pre-Revolutionary Russian tradition. As late as 1960, Lidiia Chukovskaia, daughter of Kornei Chukovskii and for long an editor with Detizdat (and a steadfast opponent of Soviet oppression), could write of the situation pre-1917:

> In contradistinction to literature for adults, pre-Revolutionary children's literature had a strong whiff of monarchism and of liberal sensuality. Indeed, it was hard to recognize as literature; it was closer to a commodity [*predmet torgovli*], something much on the same level as cheap prints and greetings cards; and it was just as far removed from life as from genuine art.[70]

Chukovskaia's statement is in accordance with views assiduously propagandized, at the First Congress of Soviet Writers and elsewhere, by pioneers of Soviet literature such as Chukovskii and Marshak. It is conventional not only in its refusal to recognize that genuine works of art might ever, in whatever circumstances, function as commodities, but also in its misrepresentation of the nature of pre-Revolutionary tradition. While Russian writing for children before 1917 had not produced many classics comparable to the work of Robert Louis Stevenson, Frances Hodgson Burnett, or Lewis Carroll, or indeed Marshak and Chukovskii, it was both varied and well developed; as with adult literature, the number and variety of titles had expanded in the late nineteenth century (as the commodification of the book market developed), and native products had been supplemented with translations, from the girls' stories of Madame Genlis and Madame Cottin in the early nineteenth century to the work of Beatrix Potter and Carroll in the 1900s. Genres ranged from adventure stories (with the home-grown Lidiia Charskaia rivalling Jules Verne in popularity, especially among girls), to verse (to which Sasha Chernyi, Poliksena Solov'eva, and Aleksandr Blok all turned their hands in the 1900s), adaptations or imitations of folk-tales (*skazki*), and illustrated books (the painter Bilibin's sumptuous editions of Pushkin were particularly notable achievements; the publisher A. F. Devrien also produced well-designed, though more modest, decorated books). Furthermore, so far from being cynically profit-making in character, children's literature was generally of an overweening worthiness, from Aleksandra Ishimova, whose retellings of Russian history were praised by Pushkin in the 1830s, through Tolstoi's stories and fables, Sof'ia Soboleva's stories advocating tolerance for Jews and national minorities, and the patriotic historical novels of Evgeniia Tur.

So far from being invented from scratch, Soviet children's literature can in many respects be seen as continuing pre-Revolutionary tradition, substituting a new political conservatism for the old. Censorship was put in place well before the decree of 1924: the works of Charskaia, for instance, were not republished between 1917 and 1989, and were purged from libraries in 1920 (though they went on being read by many girls until at least the 1940s). And if anti-Soviet values (even of the obliquest kind) were guarded against, Soviet ones were inculcated from the beginning: where reading primers had formerly harped on Christian precept, now they disseminated Party dogma and official morality. One consequence of the rise of the Lenin cult after 1924 was that the life of Lenin became as permanent a fixture of children's schools as pinafores and milk pudding. Not only textbooks, but leisure reading, most famously Zoshchenko's *Tales of Lenin* (*Rasskazy o Lenine*) delineated the great leader's virtues, which included stoicism, fairness, hard work, and healthy habits (cold bathing and early rising). Elsewhere, 'bourgeois' virtues such as cleanliness, tidiness, punctuality, and politeness were vaunted no less assiduously than in the past, with (among less didactic examples) Daniil Kharms's Ivan Ivanych Samovar refusing to serve tea to a child late for breakfast, and Marshak's version of the folk hero Petrushka turned into a naughty, but reformable schoolboy very like A. A. Milne's Bad Bear.

The official history of Soviet children's literature, with its emphasis on 'professionalization'—the creation of a properly paid, but somehow also financially disinterested, body of workers all producing work to a uniformly high standard—has some foundation, but it is also misleading. Certainly, the number of book titles produced rose, and cheap pot-boilers were forced out; in some areas, such as children's poetry and children's drama, a genuine revolution did take place. But Soviet adventure stories were similar in character to their 'monarchist' predecessors, advocating patriotism and philanthropy: in *Timur and his Team* (*Timur i ego komanda*, 1940), the most popular book of the extraordinarily popular writer Arkadii Gaidar, the hero founds a secret organization offering aid to the sick and to others in need, a theme that would have been perfectly in tune with the ethics of a Charskaia or a Soboleva. And even the best Soviet illustrated books seldom matched the standards of the most expensive pre-Revolutionary efforts. As before the Revolution, too, most creative energy was expended on the under-10s, with adolescents often turning to works originally aimed at an adult reader (Pushkin's *Captain's Daughter* (*Kapitanskaia dochka*), Tolstoi's *Hadji-Murat* (*Khadzhi-Murat*), or indeed production novels).

Centralization had its effects too on the gendering of authorship. The fact that pre-Revolutionary children's writing had been dominated by women, with such as Ishimova, Soboleva, and Solov'eva all running journals as well as publishing books, was a matter to which Soviet pioneers alluded with distaste. 'It has not been so easy to kill off [*sic*!] Charskaia, despite her feminine sex and her supposed airy-fairyness [*vozdushnost'*]', Marshak proclaimed at the First Congress of Soviet Writers.[71] Women still continued to be heavily involved in the production of children's literature after the Revolution (with Elizaveta Vasil'eva, Elizaveta Polonskaia, Tat'iana Gabbe, Elena Dan'ko, Tat'iana Bogdanovich, Frida Vigdorova, and later Elena Blaginina and Vera Panova among the better-known names), but institutional power was generally wielded by men—Marshak from the mid-1920s up to the 1950s, and the dramatist and poet Sergei Mikhalkov from the mid-1950s up to the collapse of the Soviet Writers' Union in 1991. It was also men—Chukovskii and again Marshak—who played the most prominent role in establishing criteria of literary taste, as critics, editors, and patrons. And, though Chukovskii's poetry came under severe assault from 'left pedologists' such as Nadezhda Krupskaia in the 1920s, such commentators disliking its fantastical anthropomorphism and supposed propagandization of bourgeois values, the formal if not thematic innovations of Chukovskii and Marshak were to dominate children's writing throughout the Soviet period.[72]

The attacks on Chukovskii, but also his eventual survival, exemplified the paradoxical status of children's writing. On the one hand it was an important pedagogical tool, the vehicle of indoctrination with socialist values. Official history and morality were relentlessly propagandized not only in primers, but in readers, and later in texts set for literary discussion (which generally involved lengthy dissection of ideology). Much attention was devoted to the production of popular books for children on science and technology, and also to magazines, such as *Iunyi naturalist* (*Young Naturalist*), founded in 1928. However, children's literature, even after 1934, was considered not only the repository of official values, but also a refuge for fantasy. Significantly, it was Chukovskii's ally Marshak, rather than a 'left pedologist' or a representative of 'proletarian' tendencies, who was asked to give the keynote address on children's literature at the 1934 Congress, an address which included not only a call for more children's books on science, but also a defence of fantasy and of humour: production novels for children must not be merely 'inventories of nuts and bolts' (*reestry gaek*), Marshak declared.[73] And children's books published after the Congress included material that satisfied Marshak's demands in the second sense, as well as in the first, for example A. Tolstoi's novel about Pinocchio, *The Little Golden Key* (*Zolotoi kliuchik*, 1936), or its sequel by Elena Dan'ko, *Karabas Defeated* (*Pobezhdennyi Karabas*, 1941). And for three years after the Congress, until the crackdown of 1937, Marshak's Detizdat in Leningrad was a refuge for modernist devices, such as *zaum'* (transrational language, nonsense), ritualistic repetition, and word-play, that could not have been used in adult literature. Indeed, Kharms's fantasy poem 'The Merry Finches' ('Veselye chizhi', 1930) remained in print long after the writer's own suppression, conveniently reattributed to Marshak. The real author's name may have been explosive, but the regulators of children's literature could still accept passages of pure sound-play that would not have been tolerable in adult writing, such as:

> Лёжа в постели
> Дружно свистели
> Сорок четыре
> Весёлых чижа:
> Чиж — трити-тити,
> Чиж — тирли-тирли,
> Чиж — дили-дили,
> Чиж — ти-ти-ти,
> Чиж — тики-тики,
> Чиж — тики-рики,
> Чиж — трюти-люти,
> Чиж — тю-тю-тю!

[In the bed flittered
Rustled and twittered
Twenty times twenty
Finches at once:
Some — tritty-tritty,
Some — tirly-tirly,
Some — dilly-dilly,
Some — tee-tee-tee,
Some — ticky-ticky,
Some — ticky-ricky,
Some — tooty-looty,
Some — too-loo-loo!][74]

Rather than indoctrinating children in the principles of socialist realism, texts like these inducted them in the techniques that were employed in the poetry and prose of such (then) unpublishable adult writers as Tsvetaeva, Khlebnikov, Belyi, or indeed Kharms, Oleinikov, and their OBERIU colleagues. Fairly tight lines were drawn round thematics (even the most 'advanced' children's writers eschewed the black humour and sense of real danger to be found in the work of, say, Hilaire Belloc, or, later, Maurice Sendak and Roald Dahl), but sound-play and other ludic elements often forced didactic purport to one side (or indeed, undermined it altogether). In the children's theatre, too, imaginative or ambitious effects were tolerated more readily than in the adult theatre, most particularly in genres, such as the puppet theatre, where the medium of representation already ran contrary to standard doctrines of realism.[75]

If anything, then, the besetting difficulty of Soviet children's writing was less formal timidity as such, or an unbearable constriction of theme, than the tendency to imitate the successful formulae invented by Marshak and Chukovskii rather than to break away from whimsy long made safe by familiarity. Like the child psychology and study of children's folklore that developed alongside it and fed into it, children's writing in Russia was at its most radical and innovative in the 1920s and 1930s, and its vitality was curbed if not completely stifled by Stalinism. Yet at the same time it should not be forgotten that the classics of Stalinist children's literature—Dan'ko, Tolstoi, Polezhaev, and especially Gaidar—have been read with genuine pleasure by generations of children, who in many cases seem to have screened out the more reactionary messages of the fables they consumed, just as Western children have often done when reading school stories or boys' adventure books, and as their pre-Revolutionary counterparts did while lapping up Charskaia and her contemporaries.

Moulding Adults: Education, Agitprop, Cinema

Great as the Soviet authorities' hopes for the indoctrination of children might have been, they were also conscious that this could only be a slow-acting method of changing society. The first generation of children entirely educated under Soviet rule began to emerge from schools only in the late 1920s. In any case, adults alienated from Soviet rule could undo much of the good work of social-ization once children returned home. Hence the Soviet government had an urgent need to win over adults as well as children. These included not only intel-lectuals, but also the peasants and workers in whose name the regime purported to speak.

It has sometimes been argued (for example, by Boris Mironov in a recent essay on patriarchy in the Soviet village) that Stalinist authoritarianism suc-ceeded because it was able to graft itself directly on to the traditional power structures of peasant society.[76] While it is certainly true that Soviet practices often directly invoked peasant precedent (up until late Soviet times, the leader of any delegation would be referred to as a *starosta*, the old word for a 'village elder'), such invocations could only have a limited effect in themselves, given that traditional power structures, already under assault during the wave of industrial-ization and urbanization that followed the emancipation of the serfs in 1861, had suffered still more erosion during the Russian Civil War, as fighting disrupted large areas of the Russian countryside, and during the vicious famine of 1921–2, which reduced swathes of land along the Volga to destitution. In the aftermath of these events, uprooted peasants and abandoned children poured into Russian cities, where unemployment and the housing shortage, euphemistically known as the 'accommodation question' (*zhilishchnyi vopros*), reduced many of them to begging in the streets and sleeping rough. The private sector's share of the construction industry was running as high as 65.2 per cent in 1926, and the same year also witnessed something of a denationalization of housing administra-tion, with the running of large numbers of state apartment blocks handed over to housing co-operatives. Many workers still lived in pre-Revolutionary barracks or factory hostels; others were forcibly resettled in flats owned by bourgeois 'exes' to form collectives often riven by class strife and cultural incompatibility. This method of procedure was more unpopular with those who had formerly enjoyed adequate living space than with workers and peasants transferred from still more overcrowded conditions in villages or factory barracks: it is unlikely that a Russian worker would have felt that the appropriation of living space was 'bestial', as Aleksandr Blok had called it in a diary entry of May 1921. But the fact was that overcrowding remained endemic, though it was now endured by a wider class range than before. In 1923, more than 90 per cent of the population of Moscow still lived in one room or less, an almost identical figure to that for 1912, though the numbers of those living two or more to a room had decreased significantly.[77] And the primitive division of pre-Revolutionary blocks—some of them decaying and ill-maintained—into units by means of crude plywood partitions or even curtains in no sense produced hygienic living conditions.

Nor did things improve under the First Five-Year Plan, given that the indus-trialization drive which it initiated was first and foremost concerned with the mobilization of population for work purposes, rather than with the provision of facilities for the new urban population. Between 1926 and 1939 the popula-tion of the cities grew by some 30 million; during the First Five-Year Plan alone the cities grew by 44 per cent, absorbing up to three million people, mainly former peasants, each year. This 'ruralization' (*okrest'ianivanie*) of the cities, as

Moshe Lewin has termed it, meant that conditions for the urban population were appalling.[78] Magnitogorsk, the city constructed round the largest metalworks in the Soviet Union, the Stalin Foundry, was founded in 1930, and by 1932 it already had 215,000 inhabitants, but until the mid-1930s most of these were living in temporary accommodation; proper housing and urban infrastructure were not set in place until the late 1930s.[79] And in the major cities, the communal flat (*kommunalka*) remained the standard form of accommodation until the 1960s. Throughout the 1920s and 1930s, worried press reports catalogued the social filth and anomie that characterized these dystopian collectives: gossip, domestic violence, foul language, and absence of even the most elementary grasp of hygienic principles.[80] A striking inverse image of the prevailing conditions is given by a pamphlet of 1945, *Towards Healthy Living Conditions*, which contains a long list of rules attempting to regulate domestic chaos. Inhabitants of communal flats were instructed that they must wash floors in private rooms and the common parts regularly, empty spitoons daily, keep fire exits free of firewood, report outbreaks of parasites (that is, cockroaches, bedbugs, fleas) to the local authorities, and that they must not store dirty linen in the corridors of the flat, or do their washing (apart, oddly enough, from nappies) in the communal kitchen.[81]

Naturally, bad living conditions impacted directly on work performance too. Industrial production suffered from the breakdown of labour discipline and from high labour turnover. The new urban masses, peasants by origin and workers by occupation, were theoretically the bastion of the new regime. But, uprooted by the regime's policies, they were marginal by culture and behaviour, and therefore endangered its very existence.

The brutality with which the Soviet regime acted to suppress intellectual dissent, or even the potential for such, has already been discussed. Still less could it afford to tolerate rebellion on the part of the working classes or peasantry, which would have threatened its legitimacy not only at home, but also abroad (where the prestige of the world's first 'worker state' would have been dangerously impaired by any all-out confrontation with the workers). A pattern was set very early: in March 1921, the Soviet government was faced with mutiny in Kronstadt, the naval garrison just outside Petrograd. No attempt was made to negotiate with the mutineers, whose demands included 'government by soviet' rather than the Bolshevik oligarchy; instead, a force was sent to suppress them, which it successfully did, at the cost of up to 15,000 lives. On later occasions, too, direct repression was used where necessary, perhaps the most striking instance being the forcible collectivization of agriculture, which involved mass arrests, and the deportation or execution of particularly recalcitrant objectors.[82]

Such methods were used in extreme cases, however. Ordinarily the regime preferred to rely on coercion by force of law. In 1932, the 'internal passport', or identity card system, suspended in 1917, was reintroduced, and in 1938 'work books' were again made mandatory in Soviet factories, allowing the authorities to keep tabs on disruptive workers. To clean up public space, a network of administrative regulations was set up, forbidding street-trading, busking, public drunkenness, the dispersal of litter, and other forms of 'hooliganism' (the pre-Revolutionary term was still current). The 1920s and 1930s also saw the accretion of a formidable list of measures aimed at 'counter-revolution', which embraced the dissemination of propaganda, sedition, sabotage, and participation in illegal organizations as well as terrorist activity *per se*. According to recent archival research into Soviet penal institutions under Stalin, the majority of 'socially harmful and dangerous elements' and 'counter-revolutionaries' detained and executed throughout the 1930s were in fact arrested for violent crimes, robbery, crimes against property, theft, swindling, hooliganism, and similar violations of public order.[83]

In their attempt to counteract serious violations, then, the authorities failed to differentiate clearly between political and public order, which in turn has led some historians to see the changes of the 1930s primarily in terms of direct political repression. However, for obvious ideological and pragmatic reasons they were unable to apply full-scale punitive and violent measures against the mass of Soviet workers; the logical alternative was to turn to more subtle and 'positive' (that is, non-violent) policies to restore and maintain public order, and weld together new urban identities.

Adult education was one effective vehicle by which new programmes could be transmitted, and one which the Soviet government did not neglect. Narkompros presided over a vast network of organizations and institutions, ranging from the mass movement Doloi negramotnost'! (Away with Illiteracy!), which had groups all over the Soviet Union between its foundation in 1923 and its dissolution in 1936, the *izby-chital'ni* (reading cottages) placed in villages, up to the *rabfaki* and *partshkoly* (worker faculties and Party schools) that gave training in political literacy at a higher level. The manuals used in classes to combat illiteracy were anthologies of the new reality. One example of 1925, *Our Strength is the Soviets*, neatly linked a message about socialist reconstruction with a message about the need for hygiene and urban transformation:

> It was hard to put the chaos back in order, to create everything afresh. But all the same we have put it back in order, we've got things going ourselves, without the capitalist bosses.
>
> Now we are going further. This summer we're going to build a sewer to take waste straight into the river Biiu. . . . We're going to build a new bathhouse.[84]

At best, though, adult education could occupy only part of the day. Hence, as in the world of children's education, there was a sense of the need to occupy time outside the classroom, and to inculcate 'rational leisure'. One important way of doing this was by encouraging 'physical culture' (*fizkul'tura*), a 'sport for health' movement which drew on the contemporary obsession with prophylactic medicine. The roots of the movement went back to the Civil War, during which an organization known as Vseobuch (the Central Board of Universal Military Training), founded on 7 May 1918, had been given the task of enrolling all men eligible, or shortly to become eligible, for military conscription, and bringing them to the requisite standards of physical fitness. Resources had been obtained by confiscating equipment and facilities from pre-Revolutionary sports associations, such as Sokol and the Boy Scout movement. These militaristic and masculine origins (only 4 per cent of Vseobuch's 143,563 members in

Parade of *fizkul'turniki* (physical culture enthusiasts) in Moscow, 1935.
The culture of the Stalin period required not only the reconstruction of cities (evident in the high-rise building going up in the background here), but also of the human body. The Fordism and biomechanics of the avant-garde now mushroomed into a mass cult of physical exercise and of *zakalennost'* (toughness, literally 'tempering of the body like steel'). Newspapers, books, and radio programmes exhorted the population to recognize the benefits of brisk exercise, cold baths, and fresh air; physical activity was propagandized in schools, pioneer camps, and through the Komsomol movement. Socialist realist art played a key part in glamorizing physical exercise, with sculptures, paintings, and especially photographs representing firm, muscular, youthful bodies in states of partial (rarely complete) undress. This image comes from the illustrated magazine *Nashi dostizheniia* (*Our Achievements*): the often excellent photographs published here belonged to a more imaginative strand of socialist realism than those appearing, for instance, in the immensely popular *Ogonek*.

1921 were women) were diluted during the later development of the *fizkul'tura* movement, after criticism from hygienists that Vseobuch was too 'sportist' in its emphasis. Thereafter, *fizkul'tura* had two branches: competitive sport, and what one of the most influential supporters of competitive sport, Nikolai Semashko, Director of the Supreme Council of Physical Culture, contemptuously described as 'the semolina pudding of hygienic gymnastics', that is, the mass performance of collective exercises.[85]

The *fizkul'tura* movement had both utilitarian and symbolic overtones. On the one hand, it was intended to bring the Soviet population up to the level of fitness required in the modern industrial state, and, more sinisterly, to ensure their preparedness for civil defence (*boevaia gotovnost'*). But the public parades by trim young *fizkul'turniki* with their human pyramids and mass exercises were also intended as powerful representations of a fit new society, of the healthy state of the Soviet body politic. As one Soviet popular song, 'The Sporting March' ('Sportivnyi marsh'), put it:

Чтобы тело и душа были молоды,
Были молоды, были молоды, —
Закаляйся, как сталь!
Физкульт-ура!
Физкульт-ура!
Физкульт-ура! Ура! Ура!
Будь готов,
Когда настанет час бить врагов,
От всех границ ты их отбивай!
Левый край! Правый край! Не зевай!

[So your body and soul can be young,
Can be young, can be young—
Don't shrink away from the cold or the heat,
Temper yourself, like steel!
Fizkul'tura! Hurrah!
Fizkul'tura! Hurrah!
Fizkul'tura! Hurrah! Hurrah!
When the hour comes to bash all our enemies,
To drive them from our borders, be prepared!
Left! Right! Don't hang back! Don't be slack!][86]

Besides the elite who took part in revolutionary festivals, *fizkul'tura* aimed its propaganda at ordinary Soviet citizens, who were subjected to compulsory physical education in schools from 1933, and exhorted to follow the exercise programmes printed in Soviet newspapers and magazines, and, later, to tune into exercise broadcasts on the radio.

Yet as a conduit of 'programmes for identity', *fizkul'tura* had its limitations. Though effective as rituals of solidarity, and as contributions to the movement for hygiene awareness, gymnastic displays could not transmit new roles that were useful outside the boundaries of physical culture itself. The same was true of the mass songs that often accompanied displays, and which disseminated messages of generalized patriotism, rather than individualized conduct. 'March

Still from Pudovkin's film *Mat'* (*The Mother*, 1926), an adaptation of Gor'kii's famous novel of the same title.

The Mother was not only an important contribution to the genre of films mythologizing revolutionary history, but also a cinematic masterpiece, described by the formalist critic Viktor Shklovskii as 'a unique centaur, an altogether strange beast'. It was also one of the biggest popular successes in the early Soviet cinema, a success helped by the moving performance of Pelageia Vlasova as the title character, a simple woman at first suspicious of her son's involvement in revolutionary politics, but eventually converted to the cause. (Taken from an article on Pudovkin in *Pechat' i revoliutsiia*, 1929, no. 9.)

of the Enthusiasts' ('Marsh entuziastov'), a typical example set to music by the most famous 1930s composer of popular songs, Isaak Dunaevskii, apostrophized 'the country of heroes, the country of dreamers, the country of scientists and scholars', which stretched 'from the poles to the tropics' across 'steppes and forests'.[87] Also urgently required, then, were genres that offered models for individual behaviour within the collective. Here, Soviet literature rushed into the breach: novels such as Dmitrii Furmanov's *Chapaev* (1923), the representation of a semi-legendary Civil War commander, or Aleksandr Fadeev's *The Rout* (*Razgrom*, 1925–6), built on the success of Gor'kii's *The Mother* (*Mat'*, 1906) by portraying the revolutionary masses not as 'undifferentiated forces', but as individuals contributing, in their own very various ways, to the heroic struggle. Yet, for all the prestige of literature among Party leaders, intellectuals, and self-improving workers, it had two disadvantages as a vehicle of propaganda. The first was that its effectiveness depended on the spread of fairly high-level literacy, and the second was that books could be consumed alone, so that their reception could not always be closely monitored. Because of this, genres which combined rituals of solidarity and models for identity had the greatest appeal.

Among the most important of these, in the early days, were the street festivals held to celebrate occasions in the revolutionary calendar (1 May, 7 November). The following description, from *Krasnaia gazeta*, 2 May 1925, describes the pattern that was followed in the early years:

> An entire tragic scene calls us to the aid of MOPR [International Organization for Aid to Workers]. A prisoner is waving a red handkerchief from behind bars. Nearby a fascist is crucifying a blood-stained worker. Further on a huge worker's fist is ceaselessly cudgelling a spineless bourgeois. A living Wilhelm [II] is hiding shyly behind a vast guy of Hindenberg.[88]

In the late 1920s, the dramatic scenarios of the early years vanished in favour of more general displays of marching and tributes to socialist construction. As Katerina Clark has pointed out, emphasis was now given to the area that was covered by the demonstrations, rather than narrative, or the numbers of those involved.[89] New parade spaces were created to cater for the lengthy columns of marchers. During the reconstruction of Moscow, the Sadovoe kol'tso (Garden Ring) was rebuilt as a vast inner-city highway, and Mokhovaia Street, renamed Prospekt Marksa, became an enormous avenue intended to lead up to the Palace of Soviets. Red Square was cleared of kiosks and market stalls, and also of extraneous buildings (the Kazan' Cathedral and the sixteenth-century Iberian Gates were demolished, and Martos's 1818 monument to Minin and Pozharskii, defenders of Novogorod from the Poles, moved from the middle of the square to a site next to St Basil's Cathedral; there were even plans to blow up St Basil's itself, though these came to nothing); strict regulations governed comportment within the precincts of Red Square. Gor'kii Street, the former Tverskaia, unrecognizably broadened by a programme beginning in 1937, became the equivalent in ambition, if not in architectural merit, of Paris's Boulevard Haussmann, with the unpretentious nineteenth-century buildings along its edges replaced by tall and uniform blocks as monotonous as they were dignified. Okhotnyi Riad, the former food market, was transformed into a square bounded at one side by the enormous Hotel Moscow. These innovations opened out the medieval plan of the city, giving it parade spaces that more than rivalled those of Tsarist St Petersburg; the pattern of straight avenue and square was imitated in provincial Soviet towns too, so that demonstrations could progress up through the centre of town on festival days before arriving in the central square to salute the tribunal of Party dignitaries on their dais.

The reshaped streets and squares also had other uses: they provided public spaces in which Soviet citizens might, on non-festival days, escape their often hellish domestic spaces, and participate in decorous mass promenades. During the 1930s, other facilities for rational leisure were developed as well. An important innovation was the Park of Culture and Rest (*Park kul'tury i otdykha*), a site for recreation where Soviet citizens were offered not only attractions of a kind that had been available in the pre-Revolutionary pleasure gardens (for example, variety performances on outdoor stages, shooting galleries, roller-coasters, and roundabouts), but also sports facilities, such as skating-rinks, tennis-courts, and boating lakes. Some of the most famous of these were laid out on the Krymskii val in central Moscow (Gor'kii Park), at Sokol'niki in the northern suburbs, and on Stone Island, renamed Pioneer Island, in Leningrad. But the best-known spot for 'efficacious recreation' of all was the All-Soviet Agricultural Exhibition opened near Ostankino in 1939, to whose enormous site flocked tourists from all over the Soviet Union, and where visitors wearied from consulting educational pavilions lauding the Stakhanovite deeds of industry and agriculture might refresh themselves in kiosks and cafés.[90]

In the Stalinist era, the slogan 'life has become jollier' (*zhit' stalo veselee*) underlay the treatment of other public spaces too. The first stretch of the Moscow Metro, opened in 1935, linked two of the culture parks, Gor'kii Park and Sokol'niki; many of the early stations, graced by marble benches, bronze statues, and sweeping staircases, resembled pleasure pavilions rather than the severely functional subway interchanges of Western transport systems. Statues and slogans stressed the dignity of the Soviet working classes, with whole stations, such as Komsomol'skaia, serving the three most important mainline rail stations bringing peasant visitors into the capital, turned into galleries of heroic bronzes and bas-reliefs.

The revolutionary festivals, and the restructuring of the two capitals, were illustrations of the Soviet government's decision to opt for a top–down, centre–periphery programme of reform, carried by media reporting from Moscow and Leningrad to other parts of the country. But there was also a need to carry new forms of solidarity and identity to other parts of the country. The theatre was one means of doing this: agitational drama groups, the most famous of which was Siniaia bluza (Blue Overall), carried on the work of the pre-Revolutionary people's theatre, taking sketches and agitational plays (for example, Sergei Tret'iakov's *Are You Listening, Moscow?!* (*Slyshish', Moskva?!*)) to parts of Soviet Russia far beyond the centre.[91] However, live theatre groups were relatively costly in terms of numbers involved and organization; as the strictness of censorship increased, the difficulty of monitoring individual performances also began to be seen as a drawback. Hence the appeal of the cinema, which Party leaders saw from early days as a counterweight to the backward forces stigmatized in a famous article by Trotskii, 'Vodka, the Church, and the Cinema'. Particularly after the advent of sound film, the cinema was to become the central genre of Russian popular culture, the means by which other genres were made familiar to a wide public. *Chapaev* became universally known through the film version by Georgii and Sergei Vasil'ev (unrelated, but generally known as the 'Vasil'ev brothers'); the most famous songs of the 1930s, 'Song of The Motherland' and 'March of the Cheery Lads', were made known all over the Soviet Union by Aleksandrov's massively popular musicals *The Circus* (*Tsirk*) and *The Cheery Lads* (*Veselyie rebiata*).[92] Of the other Soviet vehicles for propaganda, perhaps only the radio could compete with the cinema, and then only from the second half of the 1930s.[93] It is therefore important to consider in some detail what kinds of 'programmes for identity' the cinema offered its audience.

Women and the Cinema

Audience response and women's liberation

In line with their dirigiste orientation in other matters, Bolshevik theorists of mass culture conceptualized audience response in a highly generalized and unnuanced manner, seeing the views of the masses as polarized between the 'conscious' appreciations of the proletarian avant-garde, and 'elemental' or 'spontaneous' reactions of other sections of the lower classes (the peasantry, the lumpenproletariat). Such broad and overarching constructs did not facilitate the development of any sophisticated sense of the attitudes pertaining to different sectors of the masses. In his *Theatre and Revolution* of 1918, for example, the Proletkul't theorist Platon Kerzhentsev set out a plan for a propaganda cinema that was to work on very straightforward class-war lines:

> Suppose a newsreel were to show an orphanage in a former landowner's mansion. That would be very interesting, but how much more significant it would be to show it to the spectators in a more developed manner. First show a picture of that same nobleman's house and estate two years before the dictatorship of the proletariat. Show what kind of people used to live there, what frightful scenes of despoliation were played out, or maybe simply how irrationally and despotically the rooms in the house were used, how egotistically the garden exploited. Show what a contrast there was between the upbringing of the aristocratic brats and that of their peasant neighbours. Just a couple of scenes—well-scrubbed children playing croquet and little boys yelling by a scummy pond. And then this image:
>
> IN THE MANOR HOUSE AFTER THE REVOLUTION
>
> On the screen will be shown frames of an orphanage or a work commune in the former aristocrats' residence. The contrast with what has just been shown will be so clear and incontrovertible that no one will have room to doubt the advantages of the new order set up by Soviet power.[94]

Kerzhentsev's scenario leaves no room for a spectator too unfamiliar with a privileged existence to be able to comprehend what he or she is seeing; conversely, it cannot accommodate any viewer for whom, say, the institutionalization of private life under Soviet rule was a negative, rather than a positive feature. Class envy was assumed to be enough to pull the masses in. However, for all such oversights, there was an awareness among most Bolshevik activists that some sectors of the population had particular needs: for example, that young Russian men were more likely to be the Bolsheviks' natural allies than members of non-Russian ethnic groups, older people, or women.

The belief that women as a gender were inclined to 'backwardness', that is, to support for 'reactionary' forces such as the Church, traditional peasant customs, etc., underlay the Bolsheviks' organization of their campaign to give women equality with men. Campaigning was organized through women's sections of the Party (Zhenotdely), subordinate to the central leadership, and detailed to do consciousness-raising propagandistic work among lower-class women, including instruction in basic health care, legal rights, and political literacy. Besides face-to-face agitation, a good deal of centrally organized propaganda also took place, through the dissemination of posters, tracts, manuals, etc., and also through film, which was an especially convenient medium for propagandistic work among women, given the high rates of illiteracy in the female population. Only 13 per cent of women were recorded as literate in the 1897 census; though this figure had risen to 25 per cent by 1920, and the abysmally low average concealed considerable variations according to age, occupation, and place of residence (for instance, 67 per cent of younger women factory workers were literate by 1918), the task of combating illiteracy was a formidable one, and even by 1926, only 42.7 per cent of Russian women were able to read.[95]

Another factor that caused film to be seen as an excellent medium for proselytizing among women was their well-attested attraction to the genre; the cinema had already drawn in large female audiences before the Revolution, with some directors, notably Evgenii Bauer, known as 'women's directors'. As discussed in earlier chapters, the cinema had responded to and fed this enthusiasm with striking portraits of women, sometimes exercising power and autonomy, but just as often sorrowing and surrendering to the erotic power of scoundrels played by pre-Revolutionary matinée idols such as Vitol'd Polonskii. In reconstructing the Russian film industry, therefore, the Soviet authorities urgently needed to provide their audience with compelling alternatives to these seductive models; to represent 'new women', economically and sexually independent professionals, in ways that made them seem as attractive, and as inspiring of emulation, as the melodrama heroines played by Vera Kholodnaia, the star of the pre-Revolutionary cinema.

In doing this, they had also to accommodate Soviet policy on women's rights, and the official understanding of what constituted women's equality, with the further complication that this was not fixed and immutable, but underwent a number of significant alterations throughout Soviet history. These changes did not generally occur because of pressure from women themselves. Without an independent women's movement (suppressed by the Soviet regime in 1918), women's opportunities to express their views were circumscribed, and lobbying had to go on through Party channels, if at all. Nor, despite declarations to the contrary, were the changes necessarily in the interests of women. Rather, they were responses to changing economic and demographic requirements. When it was expedient to draw women into the workforce in large numbers, Soviet ideology backed this up with reference to women's equality. When increasing the birth rate became a greater priority, the understanding of women's equality was adjusted accordingly.

In the 1930s, for example, there were simply not enough men to carry out the drive to industrialize the country at the speed and on the scale envisaged; the banner of female equality disguised what was, in effect, the conscription of women into the labour force as a cheap army of workers.[96] In the Brezhnev era the so-called demographic crisis was to become a major cause for concern: the population was as a whole failing to reproduce itself, and the imbalance between the low birth rates of the European republics and the high birth rate in Central Asia was causing increasing alarm. A new version of equality was promoted —equal but different. As one pedagogical theorist explained, 'if a woman is granted the "right" (which in fact means she is forced) to do work unusual for her, this is also inequality'.[97] This new understanding of equality meant that women (at least those in the European republics) were supposed to put work in second place and devote more of their time to having children, yet still be considered notionally equal with men (whose family roles were not propagandized to anything like the same extent).

These changes in the understanding of equality were reflected in the representations of women and gender relations in film. The notion that women would take on new roles under socialism was not part of a genuine, sustained rethinking of gender roles; it was grafted on to a continuing essentialism, the insistence that nature had created men and women as different but complementary beings. Although woman's essential 'female' role—motherhood—could be allowed to slip into the background when it was more useful to emphasize her contribution to the workforce, it could be brought back into the limelight whenever required. This was facilitated by the eulogizing of motherhood which had long been part of Russian culture: the 'Mother of God' had been one of the most powerful images of the Orthodox Church. From the mid-1930s, an idealized image of maternity started to be an essential feature of the Soviet model of womanhood; but, as we shall see, many 1920s 'new women' in film are associated with maternal qualities as well. On the one hand, then, the Soviet woman was glorified for her capacity to work like a man: to drive tractors, to build roads, to operate complex machinery. On the other, she was celebrated for her traditional feminine, in particular maternal, qualities.

However, while the image of woman, and the ideology of women's equality, were certainly manipulated by the Soviet authorities to provide support for changes in economic and demographic policy, this does not explain the powerful emotional reaction which changes in gender roles and relations have elicited in Soviet and post-Soviet society. Nor are we suggesting that film-makers were government agents, consciously carrying out directives to promote certain

images of women at particular historical periods, though shifting ideological values certainly did get reflected in film texts, as they did in literary ones. It
would also be an over-simplification to see Soviet representations of women
as manifesting a male conspiracy to keep women in their place. Those who
evolved the Bolshevik programme of women's liberation included women, as
well as men (notably Aleksandra Kollontai and Inessa Armand), and women as
well as men worked to create film texts for the Russian cinema (most notably
Ol'ga Preobrazhenskaia, creator of a harrowing portrait of 'backward' women
in *The Women of Riazan'* (*Baby riazanskie*, 1927), and Esfir' Shub). Such women
genuinely believed that the new regime had given them, and would give all
women, unparalleled new opportunities (and their views were shared by the
many foreign visitors who rushed to inspect the new clinics, schools, nurseries,
and maternity hospitals set up under Soviet rule).

Rather than tracing institutional pressures, our concern here is to trace the
symbolic reality of early Soviet culture, and to show how, as E. Ann Kaplan has
put it in relation to the USA, representations reveal to us the 'mythic signifieds'
of a culture, existing on a different level to daily, conscious actions.[98] While
changes in representations of gender were influenced by their cultural and political contexts, they also indicated a discomfort about shifting gender boundaries
which was never resolved and which, in certain situations, was able to rise to
the surface and find expression.

Because of our restricted space, this 'gender angst', unease about shifting
borders between male and female roles, will be demonstrated on the basis of a
small number of key films, though reference will be made in passing to other
relevant texts. The focus is on the representation of women, although reference will also be made to images of men. This is because women's roles changed
rather more than those of men, and so they were more a subject of cinematic
concern; also because women were more often used as signifiers of abstract ideas
such as the motherland, the people, and morality. We have chosen these particular films because they are good examples either of women's roles (especially
the combination of motherhood and work), or because they offer clear examples
of the symbolic use of the woman.

The 1920s: public and private revolution

The early films of the Soviet period give little attention to women's role as such.
In Eisenstein's two famous films of 1924 and 1925, *Strike* and *Battleship Potemkin*
(*Bronenosets Potemkin*), for example, female characters play a muted and subordinate role as victims (the mother pushing her pram in the famous Odessa Steps
sequence), or as representative of 'backward' attitudes (the wives in *Strike* who
try to dissuade their husbands from continuing strike action when money runs
out, or the lightsome-living floosies of the counter-revolutionary camp). With
the possible exception of Protazanov's science-fiction film *Aelita* (1924), it was
not until the second half of the 1920s that the new Soviet woman started to make
herself felt in film as well as literature. A good example of this trend is E. Ioganson
and F. Ermler's 1926 study of a determined working-class heroine, *Kat'ka the
Reinette Apple Seller* (*Kat'ka, bumazhnyi ranet*, 1926), set in Leningrad during

NEP (when the city was apparently transformed into a huge open-air bazaar, remarkably like the St Petersburg of the *perestroika* era). There are two principal female and two principal male characters. Kat′ka and Verka are the two women, living in the same boarding house. Both are street-traders, selling very different products, a reflection of the different personalities, aspirations, and, indeed, class identifications of the two women. Kat′ka sells apples, a product produced from Soviet soil which meets basic human needs. She wears no make-up, dresses in an unostentatious way, and is always to be found in a headscarf, signifying that she is a good socialist woman. Verka, on the other hand, sells imported luxury items such as perfume; she wears plenty of make-up and likes fancy clothes. While Kat′ka's ambition is to get a job in a Soviet factory, Verka's is to open a private shop.

The two principal male characters are Semka and Vad′ka. Semka is a cad, who has made Kat′ka pregnant. We do not know how such a clearly sensible person succumbed to his charms, but presumably it was due to naïvety and inexperience: she is a country girl recently arrived in the city. (The type of the sensible young lower-class girl betrayed by love had in any case already been popular before the Revolution, appearing, for example, in Evgenii Bauer's 1914 weepie *Silent Witnesses* (*Nemye svideteli*).)

Vad′ka is a young homeless man who works as a lookout for the street-traders, warning them about the imminent arrival of the police. Kat′ka befriends him and lets him stay in her room, though their relationship is strictly platonic. Yet when her child is born he becomes its virtual father, baby-sitting while Kat′ka is out on the streets selling her apples. Vad′ka is good, kind, but shy and ineffectual; Kat′ka is by far the stronger of the two. Yet although Vad′ka comes across as a comic character, he is far from unsympathetic. Such role reversal was apparently acceptable in this era.

Meanwhile, Verka, with the help of her mother, sets out to ensnare Semka, convinced that he has money and will help set her up in a shop. He has other plans: to rob the two of them. He moves in, but ignores Verka's entreaties that they register their relationship and buy a shop. In fact, Semka seems more concerned with harassing Kat′ka and Vad′ka and threatening to take the baby. Kat′ka is able to stand up to him, but the feeble Vad′ka is not: when Semka insists he move out of Kat′ka 's room he meekly obliges, and then tries to kill himself. Yet, as the caption tells us, he finds it as hard to die as he does to live: when he finally plucks up courage to jump off a bridge, the water he lands in only reaches his knees.

Semka arranges for Verka's room to be burgled, getting his accomplices to tie him up to ensure that he looks innocent. The old lady gets killed in the bungled attempt. Meanwhile, despairing of Semka, Verka takes up with an older man from her home town in the hope that he will buy her the shop. Semka convinces her this is a fantasy, and persuades her they should rob him instead. Verka invites him home, and Semka knocks him out with a bottle. But the police turn up making enquiries about the old woman's murder, and the game is up. Semka manages to escape by going down to Kat′ka's room and disguising himself as her, taking the baby for added effect. At that moment Vad′ka comes back, followed, coincidentally, by Kat′ka. They struggle for the baby, and are saved when the police come out of Verka's flat. Semka and Verka are taken into custody, and Kat'ka announces to Vad'ka that she has achieved her ambition: she has got a job in a factory. He hugs her; and the relationship, we are led to believe, is about to move on to a new plane.

This, then, is the 'new Soviet woman': an independent woman whose life is a combination of work and motherhood. She does not need a man's protection, and certainly does not need the biological father of her child. It does not matter, then, that her male partner is so ineffectual. The state will look after her and her child. The latter's future becomes clear when Kat'ka sees a troupe of young Pioneers marching past, and smiles a maternal smile.

A more honest view of motherhood, which looks at its pitfalls as well as its joys, is conveyed in the openly didactic *Prostitute* (*Prostitutka*, O. Freilikh, 1927). There are three principal female characters, Liuba, Nadezhda, and Man'ka. At the start of the film, Liuba and Nadezhda are neighbours. Liuba lives in one room with her step-mother, Nadezhda in another with her husband and two children. Then Liuba is thrown out by her mother after she spends the night with another neighbour, which her mother actually arranged and was paid for. Liuba is taken in by a 'benefactress', who in fact runs a brothel. Now, when she runs into Nadezhda on the street, the latter will not allow the children to talk to her: Liuba is a 'bad woman', she tells them. She is forced to change her attitude when her husband dies, and the family is thrown into poverty. The children get ill. In due course, Nadezhda is forced on to the streets herself.

Man'ka is a long-term prostitute, who meets both Liuba and Nadezhda, at different times, as they are all plying their trade. She was once a servant, she tells Nadezhda, but was seduced by the son of her family, whose doting mother blamed her for what had happened and threw her out. She realizes that Liuba will never adjust to this kind of work and helps her get a job at a sewing workshop attached to the hospital where the prostitutes have their medical examinations. Liuba is ecstatic. At a lecture after work one day, a female doctor talks about the causes of prostitution: poverty, unemployment, homelessness, alcoholism. She explains that the government should fight not against prostitutes themselves, but against the social conditions which give rise to the phenomenon. The best 'cure' is to ensure that women can find good jobs. Liuba adds that men who treat women's bodies like merchandise should be punished.

While Liuba enjoys her new life and new friends, Nadezhda sinks to such depths of despair that she attempts suicide. Liuba and her friends manage to save her, and set her up in a job in a tram depot; her daughter is given a place in a state nursery, where she happily draws pictures of her mother at work on the trams. For Man'ka there is no chance of a new beginning, however, since she discovers she has syphilis.

In *Prostitute*, then, as in *Kat'ka the Reinette Apple Seller*, one of the principal messages is that women must be independent and earn their own money. They cannot rely on the support of men: the good ones are not immune from dying, and most are only interested in exploiting women (even the colleagues of Nadezhda's late husband refuse to help her unless she will sleep with them). Yet, curiously, the most negative representations in the film are of women: the solidarity of Liuba and her female friends is contrasted with the cruelty and abuse of Liuba's step-mother, of the brothel-owner, and of the matriarch of the family for which Man′ka once worked. This exemplifies a general trend. Female characters in films of the 1920s were often used as a touchstone of morality: both the goodness of the ordinary people and the brutality of the bourgeoisie were represented in female form.[99]

In many of the films of this era, women are also used to signify the progress of the new society, the people's potential for change. This is rather ironic since the Bolsheviks had, before the Revolution, expressed concern about the political backwardness of women, noting, for example, the inverse correlation between the number of women employed in a particular industry and its level of political radicalism. In *The Old and the New* (*Staroe i novoe*, Eisenstein and Aleksandrov, 1929), the female protagonist is also a progressive force, but in this film she functions as a symbol of the people and the country moving towards an understanding of the importance of the new society. This film is interesting for our purposes not because of what it says about gender roles, then, but because it is a classic example of the symbolic use of woman, something we will find in a less blatant form in the Stalin era, particularly in films made during or about the Second World War.

The Old and the New is concerned with the setting up of a milk co-operative, a forerunner of the collective farm. Begun in 1926, it was originally going to be called *The General Line* (*General′naia liniia*, a title by which it is still sometimes known), a reference to the Party's general line on agriculture. However, work on the film was interrupted when Eisenstein was commissioned to make *October* for the tenth anniversary of the Revolution; then *October* needed considerable reworking because Stalin insisted that the images of Trotskii be edited out; and when, in 1929, Eisenstein was finally able to return to *The General Line*, the Party's policy on agriculture had changed—forced collectivization was about to begin. So Eisenstein's very positive image of collectivization as a grassroots movement jars with the reality. This is one of the things that has had modern critics accusing him, somewhat unjustly, of being an apologist for Stalin.

While the masses were the hero in Eisenstein's earlier films (*Strike* and *Battleship Potemkin*), in *The Old and the New* he has an individual hero—or heroine—played by a real peasant woman, Marfa Lapkina, also called Marfa in the film. However, Marfa functions primarily on a symbolic level. First of all she symbolizes the peasantry, which comes to recognize its class interests and the importance of class unity. It is she who persuades the peasants to join together and form a co-operative, and when they have done so they are given credits by the government which allow them to buy a cream separator. The ecstasy Marfa experiences when the cream separator proves to work represents, as James Goodwin suggests, the birth of class-consciousness. Furthermore, when the co-operative applies for credits to buy a tractor, and the application is delayed by bureaucracy, her impatience and anger signify 'a consolidation in class consciousness and militancy'. Marfa also represents the land: in the words of Jacques Aumont, she is 'an earth-mother par excellence . . . What is also evoked here is the overwhelming female sensuality of The Earth.'[100]

As representative of land and peasantry, Marfa is crucial in depicting the growing harmony between the rural and the urban. By the end of the film she has turned from peasant women into someone who looks indistinguishable from a 'city slicker' into a chic young woman, wearing make-up and dressed in leather, as if she is about to drive off on a motorbike. Instead, she is aboard a tractor. The difference between city and country has been erased. As symbol of nature and fecundity, another of Marfa's functions is to facilitate the sexual metaphors with which the film abounds. During a terrible drought, the priests attempt to persuade God to send rain by means of a giant religious procession. It does not work; to demonstrate the impotence of religion, Eisenstein shows a burning candle suddenly bending over and going limp. In contrast the milk separator does have an orgasm, showing the superiority of technology over religious superstitions. It does this with Marfa's help; just before it sends an explosion of milk over the faces of the expectant peasants, she is seen stroking its spout. Marfa later dreams that milk is raining from the sky, making a direct link between the scenes of the milk separator's orgasm and the religious procession's impotence. The falling milk is, of course, redolent of semen.

While it is Marfa who persuades the peasants to join together, it should be noted that the initial impetus comes from the local Party agronomist, who looks remarkably like Lenin. The Party, then, has a male form, and is responsible for guiding the people, represented by Marfa, to class-consciousness and co-operation.

Tractor-drivers in lipstick: heroines in the Stalin era

If work was difficult to come by in the harsh conditions of the NEP, this ceased to be the case once Stalin was firmly in power. In the 1930s women were drawn *en masse* into the workforce. This was hailed as irrefutable evidence of their new-found equality under socialism, especially when they entered jobs which were not traditional for their sex. The magazine *Rabotnitsa* (*Woman Worker*) congratulated its readers in 1936 on the news that women 'are more than one quarter of all metal workers and machine construction workers, almost a quarter of all workers in the coal industry . . . In collective farms women are the main force.'[101] Their success was reflected on cinema screens, with the heroine emerging from a humble background and, in keeping with the tenets of socialist realism, going through a process of development to become a prize-winning worker, the chair of a collective farm, even a member of the government.

As well as being workers and builders of communism, women also had to be mothers, especially with the Civil War, and later the purges and the Second World War, claiming vast numbers of male lives. This was a social duty they were persuaded to embrace with the help of a dearth of contraceptives and, from 1936, a ban on abortion.

In women's lived experience, success in the workplace was inevitably hindered by motherhood, especially 'multi-motherhood'. As Lewis Siegelbaum has pointed out, the relatively small number of female Stakhanovites achieved their records at the expense of the family.[102] On the representational level, however, scant attention was paid to the contradictions between women's roles.

Stalinist mythology depicted the new Soviet woman as a happy amalgam of the old and the new. It was her right as well as her duty to divide herself between production and reproduction. In films of the 1930s, work took centre stage. The heroine was usually childless; she would have her children in the future. If she was already a mother, the children remained firmly in the background, not interfering with what was currently her primary function.

However traditionally masculine a job, it did not distort a woman's natural femininity. *Rabotnitsa* assured its readers that female workers on the Metrostroi (the metro-building organization) exchanged their overalls for fashionable dresses at the end of the working day: 'If you were to meet one of our female metro-builders at the theatre or a party, you would not be able to guess that she works underground.'[103] All the same, the emphasis on work, combined with the puritanism about sex that prevailed in the Stalin era, necessitated some rewriting of the old formulas of female beauty. The new Soviet woman portrayed on cinema screens was strong, healthy, and largely asexual. She was the socialist 'girl next door'; a 'mischievous, snub-nosed, energetic, cheerful member of the Komsomol'.[104] In Ivan Pyr'ev's collective-farm comedy *Tractor Drivers* (*Traktoristy*, 1939), the hero falls in love with a woman whose photograph he has come across in a newspaper: a crop-haired, dungareed, prize-winning tractor-driver, a tomboy whose femininity still comes across in the form of girlish vivacity.

That love must not get in the way of social duty was made very clear as early as 1931, in *Alone* (*Odna*), directed by Kozintsev and Trauberg. The protagonist, Kuzmina, has just graduated from a pedagogical institute and is looking forward to a great future; 'how good life will be', trills the song playing in the background, reflecting her mood. She is shortly to marry, and she and her fiancé are window-shopping for furniture and crockery. She dreams of teaching radiant children in a bright, airy classroom. So infectious is her mood that the tram she is riding on suddenly bursts into flower. But her joy turns to despair when she learns of her work placement. At first we do not know what she has been told: we only know it is bad news because when she leaves the employment office, the building casts a shadow over half the screen, enveloping her. It turns out she has been placed in a school in the Altai, in the far east of Siberia. When she has got over the shock she decides to try to change the placement, explaining to the administrators about her forthcoming marriage. Her plea is partially successful: she is given an official letter to take to a higher body requesting a different placement. But she now finds herself torn between the desire for personal happiness and a sense of socialist duty: 'Do I have the right to think about my own personal life at a time like this?' she asks herself. She runs into another young woman at the administration centre who wants to go to Siberia but has been rejected on health grounds and is as miserable as Kuzmina. An old man reads her valuable letter over her shoulder and says she is quite right to ask for a transfer; why would she want to go to such a stupid, backward place? He is, of course, a symbol of the past. Kuzmina realizes what she is doing: betraying the Revolution. Decisively, she tears up the letter and sets off, alone, to the Altai.

The village to which she has been posted is clearly locked in the past. It is based on a combination of superstition, apathy, and corruption. At the entrance is a pagan symbol, a skinned horse on a wooden frame intended to ward off evil spirits. Medical treatment consists of a dance conducted by a feather-clad shaman. All that exists of Soviet power is one apathetic representative who wants to do nothing to interfere, and instructs Kuzmina to do the same. Neither he nor the villagers have any interest in education: 'What can you teach them?', asks one of a group of women shearing sheep with their children. The school-house is virtually in ruins. But Kuzmina forces herself to get on with it, and does begin to make headway, until an old toothless man (another symbol of the past) insists on taking the children out of school so they can look after his sheep. Kuzmina goes to see the president of the village soviet. The camera focuses on the symbols of national backwardness which fill his house: samovars, bulgy teapots, not a Lenin in sight. This presumably suggests that he is clinging to tra-dition, to his ethnic past, rather than embracing the Soviet future. He tells her not to interfere. Kuzmina, however, symbol of the new society, cannot be held back. If the children cannot come to the school, the school will go to them: she goes out to the fields and teaches them while they are tending the sheep. While there, she learns that the old man is planning on selling the sheep for meat. She protests, demanding to know how the villagers will live when their livelihood is gone, and sends one of the children back to the village to warn everyone. The old man takes drastic steps to stop her interference: he instructs her sledge-driver to take her away from the village and make sure she freezes. She almost does. As she hangs between life and death, the children at her bedside, it is clear that she has won over the villagers. The woman who was once her greatest adversary is now her fiercest supporter. She tackles the president of the soviet for not defending the villagers' interests, and declares that since the existing soviet is doing nothing for them they will set up a new one, and sets about doing so. She also notifies officials in Leningrad about Kuzmina's condition, and a plane is sent to get her. As she is taken away, she declares that she will be back. She has apparently forgotten her fiancé: her own needs and desires have merged with her social duty. The final scene has the plane flying over the horse-skin totem, a symbol of European technology winning over Asiatic superstition.

Women, then, once again, are the embodiments of the new society. Men, on the other hand, are symbols of the past, of inertia and corruption. Mother Russia has embraced the new ways; duty has triumphed over selfish personal concerns.

A rather different image of womanhood was presented in *Chapaev*, one of the supporting characters in which is a female machine-gunner Ania, who became one of the most famous images of the new woman in Stalinist cinema. Accord-ing to Sergei Fomin, 'the woman warrior, or, forgive me, the woman killer', of whom Ania is the prototype, was 'the only original female type created in the Soviet cinema'; it was repeated in film after film.[105]

Ania is, indeed, a curious forerunner of the female war heroes who became so prominent in films about the Great Patriotic War. She retains her femininity even in this most masculine of domains, and duly develops a romantic attach-ment to a male machine-gunner, Pet'ka. It is under his tutelage that she learns to use her weapon, which at one point she is shown happily polishing as if it is a piece of household furniture. When the White Army launches a 'psychological attack' on the smaller forces of the Red Army, smartly uniformed officers marching inexorably towards them in strict formation like a machine (reminiscent of the Tsarist officers in the famous Odessa Steps sequence of *Battleship Potemkin*), Ania's nervousness is palpable, although she steels herself to fire only at the last possible moment in order to save the Red Army's bullets. When Chapaev comes to the rescue her relief pours out in a display of rapturous emotion impossible to imagine in a male character.

The relationship between Pet'ka and Ania is flirtatious but comradely. Nor is there any suggestion that children will ever result from the union. When Chapaev looks forward to the glorious future of socialism, he paints a picture of an idyllic life in which Ania and Pet'ka will live together, and both will work, but here his prophecy ends. Fomin has suggested (rather unfairly) that Ania's relationship with her machine gun is charged with rather more erotic feeling. He writes:

> I am not speaking just of the scene in which the psychological attack is repulsed, a scene permeated with ecstasy [*ekstaz*], in which the heroine and her mechanical partner form a single emotional unit. I am thinking of a different scene, that in which Pet'ka carries out his own initiation ritual by opening up to An'ka the construction of the machine gun. . . . Pet'ka's swagger, An'ka's coquettishness, all these normal parts of an erotic game are directed towards the details of a complex machine designed for destruction.[106]

In films about the Great Patriotic War, the woman soldier was again well represented, now appearing above all as a member of the partisan movement. Stories of female snipers taking their revenge on the Nazi oppressors dominated cinema screens (as well as short stories in the women's magazines). Again, killing people did not prove incompatible with femininity. Indeed, it was precisely their feminine traits which had induced these women to take up arms. As an article in *Krest'ianka* (*Peasant Woman*) explained, these were 'wives and mothers, they passionately love children, their families, their hearths. But they do not want to see their loved ones turned into slaves. . . . Love and motherhood . . . do not deaden their urge to fight to the end for the independence of the motherland, but fan it into a terrible flame.'[107]

In war films, allegorical transparency reached new heights, as women were insistently associated with Russia's heroic campaign of self-defence. Zoia, in the film of that name by Lev Arnshtam (1944), and based on the real-life (though much mythologized) figure of Zoia Kosmodem'ianskaia, is the classic representation of the female partisan. The film starts with her being captured by the Germans: she is dressed in a thick jacket and trousers and her hair is cut short, so it takes them some time to realize she is female. The Germans are astonished; the Russian woman in whose house they have taken up residence is horrified. Zoia refuses to tell them who she is, or to give any information about the partisan movement, and they torture her in an attempt to make her talk. First they beat her. Then, apparently for fun, one German soldier burns her face with a candle. As Zoia lies in a state of semi-consciousness, the camera focuses on a newspaper cutting on the wall behind her. It is a photograph of Lenin's funeral, and suddenly it comes to life, turning into newsreel footage of the event. Thus begins a lengthy flashback which forms the main substance of the film. We follow Zoia through her life, which interweaves with key events in socialist history. Even her first (chaste) love is tied into the events of the time: her boyfriend's father is killed fighting in the Spanish Civil War. There is continual emphasis on the beauty of Russia. In a stroll through an idealized Moscow, across a strangely deserted Red Square, Zoia and her boyfriend are pictured against a series of pre-Revolutionary monuments. Clearly these images of old Russia are meant to encourage patriotism and loyalty; this is a curious contrast to the pre-Revolutionary symbols of Russia portrayed in *Alone*, which were signifiers of a dangerous clinging to the past. Then the Germans invade. Zoia's school (another wonderfully idealized image: a building awash with light, and full of mighty columns and noble statues) is bombed. The innocence of childhood is over: the schoolchildren rush to enter the fray. We see Zoia commit herself to the partisan movement. Then we are back to the present day, where she is still being tortured. She is being marched along in the snow by a German soldier: while he is wrapped up in coat, hat, and scarf and yet still shivers from the cold, she wears only a thin nightdress. Finally she is taken to the gallows to be executed. (The female protagonist being marched to her execution is a ubiquitous scene in wartime films: see, for example, *Rainbow* (*Raduga*, Mark Donskoi, 1944) and *Marite* (Vera Stroeva, 1947). It is clearly intended as a Soviet version of Christ's procession to Calvary. The gallows have a marked similarity to the cross, and the woman always bears a beatific expression as she takes her last look at the wondrous Russian landscape. She is dying, like Christ, so that others may be saved.) When Zoia arrives at the gallows, surrounded by the local Russians who have been forced to come to witness her death, one of the soldiers decides to take a photograph as a souvenir. He asks the men holding her to stand back, and this moment of freedom gives Zoia the chance to turn to the Russians and declaim. They should not pity her, she tells them. It is a joy to die for your country. Stalin is with them, he will save them. After an inexplicably long pause the soldiers step forward to silence her. Then, as they are attaching her to the gallows, she manages to push them away (despite having been tortured for days) and addresses the crowd again. What this clearly signifies is Russian and Soviet superiority, physical as well as moral.

These cinematic representations of the new Soviet woman in the Stalin era, above all a worker and warrior, committed to social duty, still did not challenge the Soviet Union's continuing essentialism about gender. Womanly traits and desires could be temporarily suppressed in times of need, but they were not destroyed. There was no suggestion that women's entry into traditional 'male' domains, even taking up arms when required, damaged their inherent femininity. A faint discomfort about women's new roles, and the effect these might have on their personalities, did occasionally poke through the surface of Stalinist literature, however. In a short story by the popular socialist realist writer Fedor Panferov, published in *Krest'ianka* in 1937 and *Rabotnitsa* in 1938, a journalist is sent to interview the female director of a collective farm. He is expecting 'a simple country woman with a long wide skirt, a blouse with gathered sleeves, a blue headscarf on her head, and a shy and modest manner'. He is confronted instead by an alarming creature wearing a khaki shirt and jacket and heavy boots; she has a wide stride, 'like a man's', and when she speaks she has 'a deep, throaty voice . . . [and] it struck me that she talked not in her natural voice but in a deliberately masculine way, that she . . . strode in an intentionally masculine manner'. The journalist is alarmed by the woman's mannish style, and the story seems at first to be expressing concern that Stalinist policy on equality was having an unpleasant effect on women. By the end, however, it transpires that this woman had developed her hard shell after an emotional crisis; it was not her social role that had damaged her. Stalinism was redeemed.[108]

Moulding Collective Identities: Soviet Conceptions of *Narodnost'*[109]

The allegorical character of Soviet films meant that women were always more (or less) than real women: the fates of Kat'ka or Zoia were also those of a whole class and a whole nation. The Soviet cinema, therefore, mediated between programmes for transforming personal identity and official conceptions of national character, which were to become increasingly important as the internationalist ideals of the 1920s were eroded by the rise of a new Russian imperial spirit in the 1930s.

The term *narod*, because of its populist connotations, did not feature prominently in Soviet discourse in the first decade and a half after the Revolution. The urban proletariat was the favoured class of the new regime, and during NEP the peasantry was regarded as petit bourgeois and hence a potential obstacle to the implementation of socialism. It was only in the 1930s, after the forcible collectivization of agriculture and the liquidation of hundreds of thousands of kulaks and their henchmen, that the new Soviet peasantry began to be regarded as a politically reliable social category, and the term *narod* could again be used for the broad masses of society: the factory and collective farm workers.

One aspect of the new cultural policy that was adopted in the mid-1930s was a stress on folklore. In the relatively free intellectual atmosphere of the 1920s, the academic study of folklore had flourished, with various schools of thought coexisting. During the cultural revolution of the period of the First Five-Year Plan (1928–31), however, leftist cultural organizations such as RAPP (the Russian Association of Proletarian Writers) and RAPM (the Russian Association of Proletarian Musicians) attacked folklore and folk music as the products of the backward and reactionary rural classes. When the Union of Soviet Writers was founded in 1932, the leading role played by Maksim Gor'kii, who had returned from emigration in 1931, contributed to the official rehabilitation of folklore. At the First Congress of the Union of Writers, in 1934, Gor'kii claimed that many major works of world literature had been influenced by oral folklore, and he extolled the value of folk literature as an expression of the values of ordinary working people. A campaign was launched for the collection and publication of folklore, and the definition expanded to include not only traditional genres (such as the *bylina* or *starina*, folk-epic, and the *skazka*, or folk-tale), but also oral history, the biographical narratives of ordinary people about the events of their lives, including their experiences of war, Revolution, Civil War, and the construction of socialism. A new 'industrial folklore' was created, in the form of collective worker memoirs of the history of a factory or enterprise.[110]

At the same time, there appeared an officially sponsored genre of pseudo-folklore (or 'fakelore'), the new folk-epic about Bolshevik heroes such as Lenin and Stalin, composed in a style that was a pastiche of the old *stariny* about the warrior-heroes of ancient Kiev and Novgorod.[111] Professional folk-dance and folk-music ensembles, such as those of Igor' Moiseev and Nikolai Osipov, were awarded high status, while amateur folk choirs and dance ensembles were encouraged to form all over the Soviet Union (official sponsorship was granted not only to Russian folklore, but to that of all the nations of the USSR).

Folklore—or rather 'folklorism'—also influenced mainstream literary and artistic productions, not only because of Gor'kii's strictures at the First Congress of Soviet Writers, but also because the cultural conservatism of the mid-1930s onwards involved a return to the canon of nineteenth-century classical literature, whose leading figures (such as Pushkin and Tolstoi) had themselves incorporated 'folklorism' into their works. Folklorism was particularly common in Soviet historical novels and in films about collective farms. In music, the official attack on 'formalism' in 1936 was combined with a recommendation that composers incorporate folk melodies into their works.[112]

The concept of *narodnost'* does not appear to have been formally incorporated in Soviet expositions of socialist realism until the post-war period, when it became part of a 'holy trinity'—*narodnost'*, *partiinost'*, *ideinost'* (national populism, Party spirit, and political orthodoxy)—with studied echoes of Nicholas I's proclamation of *narodnost'*, *samoderzhavie*, *pravoslavie* (national populism, autocracy, Orthodoxy) a century earlier. But it was silently present from the outset. *Narodnost'* in culture meant not only folklorism of the type described above, but also accessibility and comprehensibility (in contrast to formalism). *Narodnost'* required that literature and the other arts should depict the lives of members of the 'socialist *narod*' rather than that of the 'vacillating, reflective intelligentsia', and simplicity was to be a major feature of the new aesthetic.[113] Thus, *narodnost'* might be equated with popularity, except that the 'popularity' of a Soviet work of literature or art was intended to be determined from above, by the tastes of the Party leadership, rather than from below, by the operation of market forces.[114]

Some commentators have suggested that *narodnost'* in the Soviet context could also mean 'nationalism'.[115] It is certainly true that the shift towards *narodnost'* in cultural policy occurred at the same time as a turn to Russian nationalism in, for example, the writing of history. But two qualifications have to be made. First of all, as we have seen, cultural *narodnost'* was a pan-Soviet phenomenon, rather than a narrowly Russian one; second, Russian nationalism in the 1930s and 1940s was almost always linked with a broader concept of Soviet patriotism and defence of the socialist motherland. It would perhaps be most accurate to say that Soviet patriotism was embellished with *narodnost'* in the sense of a folklorism that reflected the national traditions of all the peoples of the Union. This was particularly true during the Second World War, when folk choirs and music and dance ensembles made extensive tours of the front. The promotion of folklorism persisted in the post-war era, when folk melodies were again held up as a model for Soviet composers.[116] Yet, in a sense, Soviet propaganda always perceived the Russian people as 'first among equals', representing the 'back- ward' people of the East in much the same patronizing way that it represented women. A propaganda porcelain dish of the early 1920s, for example, shows a European-featured soldier in the Red Army, bearing a banner marked RSFSR (Russian Soviet Federative Socialist Republic), descending from the skies to bring the torch of enlightenment to a group of figures in Eastern costume.[117] Much the same pattern is evident in Kozintsev and Trauberg's film *Alone*, discussed above, and it was to be intensified in the late Stalinist era, as emphasis on the inventive powers of Russian scientists and the genius of Russian writers and artists was trumpeted in an international context.

Heroism and the Everyday: the Reception of Soviet Culture by Mass Audiences

Soviet films were coherent vehicles for the ideologies of gender, class, and national identity. They had the clarity that is a *sine qua non* for effective propa- ganda. Much the same could be said of other official campaigns to transmit *narodnost'*. Yet the reception of texts never depends simply on their content in a discrete sense; it is also a product of social forces beyond the texts themselves, of the diverse and sophisticated forces of cultural consumption. How did the Soviet state's 'programmes for identity' go down among those at whom they were aimed?

In accounts of the history of the Soviet period, the term *lichnost'* (personal- ity/selfhood) has figured in two main ways. Analysis has concentrated either on the *kul't lichnosti*, the 'cult of personality', or self-aggrandizing dictatorship of Joseph Stalin, or else on the self-expression of those outstanding writers and artists—Akhmatova, Mandel'shtam, Shostakovich, Eisenstein—who fell foul of the regime during the 1930s and 1940s. In 1936, André Gide, deploring the in- creasing standardization of Soviet high culture, wondered whether a Rimbaud, Baudelaire, or Keats might not 'vegetate unheard' in such a society.[118] Since 1956, and particularly since the opening of formerly closed archives in the late 1980s, the 'vegetative silence' of non-conformist writers censored after 1932 has been compensated by a flowering of interest in their works and lives. But we know a great deal less about the many other 'selves' who made up Soviet society—the peasants, factory workers, shop assistants, public service workers, and others who composed the *nizy* (lower strata) of Soviet society, or the minor Party officials, provincial schoolteachers, technicians, and low-level medical workers who lacked the privileges (ideological and practical) enjoyed by their Party bosses, and also by many members of the 'old' intelligentsia.

Attempts to record the oral histories of working-class Russians, such as Maksim Gor'kii's *History of Factories* (*Istoriia fabrik i zavodov*), inevitably concentrated on the 'revolutionary proletariat' at the expense of other sectors of the population. Published versions of autobiographies also censored details that did not accord with the Party's own legitimating myths. Yet they were a way of paying at least selective attention to bottom-up versions of pre-Revolutionary history. And, until the early 1930s, numerous *muzei byta*, or 'museums of daily life', gave space to pre-1917 material culture, including even that of Russian capitalists.[119] But the oral history of the Soviet period itself, with the exception of the Great Patriotic War, is poorly documented, and the views of workers and others must be reconstructed from second-hand accounts of events and opinions, the few scarce memoirs, and from archival texts (autobiographies, confessions, denunciations) that are often formulaic in character and which have yet to be properly assimilated by historians.[120]

Evidence from such sources suggests that ordinary people were often genuinely convinced that the Revolution would change their lot for the better. The painter Kuz'ma Petrov-Vodkin, himself from a provincial working-class background, was moved by such a conviction to write, in a letter to his mother of November 1917: 'The Russian, despite all the torments he must endure, will create a free and honourable life that is open to everyone. Layabouts will be the only people who will live in disgrace, no matter what titles they may be covered in or what *gimnazii* [elite high schools] they graduated from.'[121] A religious believer who had graduated from an elite art school himself, Petrov-Vodkin could nonetheless identify with the egalitarian utopianism of the Bolshevik Revolution. Those who benefited more directly from the educational and cultural programmes offered by the new regime were still more likely to take slogans of equality at their face value.

The genuine grassroots character of some Soviet 'programmes for identity' should also not be underestimated. The festivals, though carried out according to careful planning by cultural activists, and choreographed and designed by artists, involved thousands of workers and peasants who acted as participants as well as audience, helping to construct floats and to act in sketches and pageants. Some of those who helped organize them, such as the former fairground theatre manager A. Alekseev-Iakovlev, had wide experience in the commercial theatre, and the sketches performed included robust skits whose manner of performance resembled practices in the pre-Revolutionary popular theatres and circuses, even if the ideological loading was now rather more obvious. Nor did populism disappear when the festivals changed character in their later days. Indeed, revolutionary festivals in some ways became more populist in character during the 1930s, as artist-designed murals and giant puppets were replaced by floats constructed by factory workers themselves (albeit to an overall plan organized by the city authorities). Similarly, many 1920s plays drew directly on pre-Revolutionary popular art forms—the circus, the fairground, the music-hall. Exemplary were Maiakovskii's revolutionary *estrada* play *Mystery-Bouffe* (*Misteriia-buff*, 1918), or Meyerhold's production of Ostrovskii's *The Forest* (*Les*, 1924). That this was not simply a question of 'radical chic' is suggested by contemporary accounts. 'There are only two things that are working all-out at the moment,' Petrov-Vodkin wrote to his mother in December 1920, 'the churches and the theatres: the difference is that you can just squeeze into the churches, but the theatres are packed to the doors.'[122]

Ceremonies associated with the cult of Lenin's memory, while directed assiduously from above, were undoubtedly of huge importance for a lot of ordinary Russians, many of whom felt a quite sincere (if misplaced) appreciation of the leader as an unpretentious friend to ordinary people. Ekaterina Strogova's 1927 story 'Womenfolk' offers a very plausible description of how the official celebrations for Lenin's death become an intense ritual for many participants, who break into stretches of formal lament (*prichitanie*):

> The womenfolk have a special feeling and love for Ilich. When they went out on stage and started talking about him and the Party, they choked on their tears and couldn't finish, they would toss their applications to join the Russian Communist Party down on the black crape laid over the boards. Shtakelberg came out on stage, too. She began whirling around hysterically, flailing her arms, crying and laughing:
> 'Comrades . . . my dears . . . Our bright sun has set! Our Ilich has passed away . . . Women, why are you wailing? . . . Let us vow, women, my comrades, let us vow: let us stop our wailing and take up action. Let us join the Party in triumph!'[123]

A well-attested manifestation of popular identification with the Revolution was the naming of children after leaders. Vladimir remained one of the commonest names for boys right up to the 1970s, while the more esoteric Ninel' (Lenin spelt backwards) for girls, and Vladlen for boys, were also widely used in the 1920s, 1930s, and 1940s, as was Stalina. Other names celebrating historical or technological change were Maia (from 1 May), Mirra (from *Mirovaia revoliutsiia*, World Revolution), Diesel, Metallina, and Elektrina.[124]

What, though, of the reception of Soviet literature, mass song, and film, in the creation of which ordinary people did not have a hand? Intriguing evidence comes from the memoirs of Khava Volovich, a printworker from the Ukraine, who asserts that the propaganda images to which she was exposed in her youth made her long to sign up for a stint in the far North, or at the very least start work in a factory as soon as possible. Volovich also indicates that shared experience of Soviet songs and Soviet literature was very effective in creating social bonding. Promoted at work, she rapidly found herself disliked by workmates with whom she 'had read [Nikolai Ostrovskii's classic account of revolutionary consciousness gained] How the Steel was Tempered [*Kak zakalialas' stal'*, 1932–4] and sung "The Cool Morning Greets Us" [a hit number from Ermler and Iutkevich's 1932 film Counterplan (*Vstrechnyi*)]'. The reference intriguingly encompasses both the effectiveness of shared experience, and its limitations: Volovich's colleagues were later to denounce her for counter-revolutionary activity.[125]

By no means all Russian citizens, however, were inspired to dreams of heroism by heroic representations. Novels and films could also convey something quite different: a fantasy world of refinement, a place of escape very like that offered by pre-Revolutionary bestsellers or Evgenii Bauer weepies. In the next section, we will describe how such apparently unpromising material was shaped by the authorities in order to shore up social solidarity in quite a different way. However, it is fair to say that heroism made an immense contribution to the dissemination of Soviet patriotism. Many who did not have it in them to become Stakhanovites could still feel a disinterested sense of pride in living in a land of supermen and superwomen.

Directed Desires:
Kul'turnost' and Consumption

Catriona Kelly and Vadim Volkov

As was clear in our account of late imperial consumer culture, Russian intellectuals have a long and sturdy tradition of contempt for what is understood
as commercialism. The Bolsheviks, who as Marxists recognized capitalism as
a historically logical and unavoidable stage in the country's evolution, at the
same time fully shared the intelligentsia's contempt for trade as a degrading and
immoral activity. The writings of Lenin and other major Bolshevik thinkers
abound in splenetic denunciations of *meshchane* (petits bourgeois) and *lavochniki*
(small shopkeepers), terms used indiscriminately to brand those engaging in
commercial activities, and their supposedly self-serving and philistine mentality.[126]
Some utopian thinkers associated with Bolshevism dreamed that the future
would belong to communal forms of living that would leave no place for market
economics. The essentials of life—housing, lighting, heating, food, clothing—
would be provided without the need for monetary systems of exchange. Living
in state-run communes equipped with canteens, nurseries, and washing facilities,
dressed in rational workwear, citizens of the future would have no need of shops,
markets, or traders of any kind. The consumer would disappear along with the
capitalist; producers and users of goods would be engaged in perfectly rational
relations based on the supply of immediate and genuine needs.

It follows that the onset of NEP, whose effects were most far-reaching in the
consumption sector, rather than the production sector, was widely seen by Russian observers, and not only by Bolshevik supporters, as a disgraceful reversal
of revolutionary ideals. The poet Aleksandr Blok, for example, was reduced to
extreme distress by hearing once more the 'crawling noises of the foulest vulgarity,
repulsive foxtrots, pseudo-gypsy music', that he thought 'had disappeared from
our life long ago'.[127] Blok was one of many observers to see the NEP period, with
its proliferation of street-traders, beggars, balladeers, and NEP-men (entrepreneurs grown rich on the profits of trade) as treachery to the Revolution; the
sense of betrayal in him and others was enhanced by the fact that the corralled
capitalism of NEP was so conspicuously successful. The most glamorous and
elegant shops in major cities remained in private hands until economic centralization began again in the late 1920s, and privately made films and other entertainments were in wide circulation during NEP. The Soviet state attempted
to compete with private enterprise by encouraging co-operative ventures,
by launching a vociferous agitprop campaign to preach the virtues of state-
manufactured goods, and by sponsoring commercial or semi-commercial cultural

objects—films such as Perestiani's *The Little Red Devils* (*Krasnye d'iavoliata*, 1923), Ermler and Ioganson's *Kat'ka the Reinette Apple Seller* (1926), and Eggert's *The Bear's Wedding* (*Medvezh'ia svad'ba*, 1926) and popular fiction, such as the 'Red Pinkerton' detective novels. However, such ventures had only limited success. Many Soviet citizens continued to watch foreign films, just as they continued to buy foreign and privately made goods and to patronize private doctors, and Mary Pickford and Douglas Fairbanks were infinitely better known than their Soviet competitors, though films such as those mentioned above attracted decent audiences without such 'star actors' as draws.[128]

The high standing of the products of private enterprise, if not of entrepreneurs (NEP-men were universally detested) with Soviet consumers tempered the assault on commercialism that began with the First Five-Year Plan. It was one thing to clear the flea markets, such as the notorious Sukharevka in Moscow, a cornucopia of stolen, defective, and insanitary wares, in order to make room for more 'dignified' public spaces, and to nationalize private firms and shops. It was quite another to put an end to trade altogether. As the *Great Soviet Encyclopaedia* succinctly stated in 1975, 'the persistence of goods and money relations under socialism makes the preservation of the market inevitable'.[129] Even after NEP had ended, the *rapprochement* with capitalism continued to have its effects on the way that the state organized the commercial sector. As late as 1940, state-owned shops were responsible for only 66.8 per cent of retail transactions; co-operative ventures made up 24.5 per cent and collective farm markets 8.7 per cent.[130] Certainly, the activities of non-state ventures were rigidly controlled, making many co-operatives (such as village shops) indistinguishable in all but name from state enterprises. But the recognition of non-state participation in retailing was ideologically significant, especially when set against the dissolution of co-operatives in the production sector (such as building co-operatives) during the late 1930s.

What was more, the institutions of Soviet retailing directly aped capitalist institutions, rather than offering new-world alternatives. The Upper Trade Rows, nationalized in 1921 as the flagship GUM (State Department Store) continued to function like a bazaar, with rows of separate stalls selling state goods in the manner that private ones had been sold before the Revolution. And Muir and Merrilies, nationalized as TsUM (the Central Department Store), became the pattern for new Soviet department stores, a concerted programme for building which was launched in 1933. Like their capitalist equivalents, Soviet department stores were grandiose structures, with plate-glass display windows, solid masonry, and architectural flourishes, positioned at the cynosures of squares or main streets. The intention was that they should make shopping a pleasurable experience: studios for dress and suit fittings, cafeterias, and goods ordering points (*otdely zakazov*) were all provided. Admittedly, what was available in the stores often did not live up to the elegant surroundings: many Soviet-made goods remained of low quality, and shortages were persistent (rationing systems were in operation between 1930 and 1936, and again between 1941 and 1947). But the intention was that the appearance of Soviet shops, like the advertisements carried in Soviet periodicals, such as *Ogonek*, for watches, perfumes, and later cars and ice cream, should generate a feeling of security and plenty. In time,

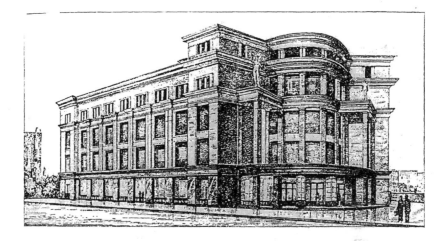

Design for a department store in the model city of Stalingrad, 1936.
The building is far closer to pre-Revolutionary commercial buildings such as that for Muir and Merrilies (see illustration 4) than to constructivist projects, though the opulence of the decoration (complete with pinnacles and caryatids) exceeds that of the Muir and Merrilies building by quite some way. Such *univermagi*, located at the cynosures of main streets, emphasized the growing importance of consumer goods in Soviet society, and promised a 'bright future' of commercial prosperity, even if the goods themselves remained poor-quality and subject to shortages in the meantime. (Reproduced from *BSE*, 1st edn., *Univermag*.)

Soviet citizens were supposed to think (and often did think, according to much of the memoir literature), there would be goods worthy of the shops that had been built to hold them. The new glamour was also propagandized by some Soviet films of the 1930s and 1940s, such as Aleksandrov's massively popular *Circus*, which aped the production values of Hollywood: in this case, a properly socially conscious subject (the emigration of an American circus star to Russia with her small mixed-race son to escape American racism) was turned into a glittering vehicle for Liubov' Orlova, the 'Soviet Greta Garbo'.

Consumption as a Way to Culture: *Kul'turnost'* and the Creation of a New Middle Class

The evolution of Soviet commercial culture, then, was as much to do with the manipulation of desires as with their satisfaction. In order to understand this process, it is important to look more closely at the other side of industrialization—not at the social problems caused by the construction of a new proletariat, but at the rapid growth of a new administrative and managerial hierarchy, made up of Party officials, technocrats, doctors, official writers, artists, and artistic administrators. The enormous programmes of educational opportunity set in motion

1949 advertisement for ice cream, published in the popular illustrated journal
Ogonek.

Though rationing in the major cities had officially ended when this image was published, and ice cream had been one of the first minor luxuries to reappear after the war, severe food shortages continued. Hence, the purpose of such images, as with Western slogans such as 'country fresh', was less to suggest real possibilities than to create a roseate idyll of plenty, suggested here by the glowing dream vision of tranquil cows and tidy *kolkhoz* on the left. At the same time, the creation of public spaces in which refreshments might be consumed in orderly fashion by happy families (ice-cream parlours, patisseries, cafés set in parks) was an important concern of the Soviet state from the early 1930s right up to its collapse in 1991, as part of the propagandization of *kul'turnost'* and the continuing battle with undesirable phenomena such as drunkenness and hooliganism.

during the 1920s had created a pool of literate and ambitious Party members who had been recruited from below, educated in colleges and high schools, promoted to command positions in the economy or cultural and social spheres, and granted vast material benefits and privileges. The 1930s were characterized by sudden reshufflings in the top leadership, purges of the old cadres, and consequent spectacular promotions of the new proletarian-peasant intelligentsia. Many members of the new elite were workers or peasants by origin, but upper-middle class in terms of their newly acquired place in the social hierarchy and the material benefits available to them. The contrast between these two formal attributes had to be resolved in practice—without questioning the basic ideological tenets of the 'worker-peasant's socialist state'.

When, in 1935, the right to a prosperous life (*zazhitochnaia zhizn'*) was officially sanctioned, Soviet existence was linked to new, higher standards of individual consumption. While, in reality, material well-being and civilized life were mainly accessible to the new administrative elite, the ideology of *kul'turnost'* stressed that the possibility of a prosperous and cultured life was available to everyone in exchange for efficient work. As Sheila Fitzpatrick puts it: 'One of the great advantages of the concept of *kul'turnost'*, in a post-revolutionary society burdened by the hangovers of revolutionary puritanism, was that it offered a way of legitimizing what had once been thought of as "bourgeois" concerns about possessions and status: one treated them as an aspect of *kul'tura*.'[131] The policies of *kul'turnost'* met at least two complementary objectives, pragmatic and ideological: to discipline the new masses by shaping everyday behaviour in accordance with uniform social, 'cultured' norms, and to integrate the values of the lower strata with those of the elite. In what follows it is the pragmatic dimension that will principally concern us.

Kul'turnost' was never a clearly defined concept, and no Party authority gave coherent instructions on how to become cultured. Concrete applications of the term, scattered across the pages of official and popular texts and periodicals between 1935 and 1938 as they sought to answer the question 'what should one do to become cultured?', do not conform to a single pattern. Rather, they point to a complex of practices aimed at transforming a number of external and internal features of the individual. If we put them together, we can arrive at a model of the cultured person (*kul'turnyi chelovek*). In itself this model is nothing new; many of the hints on behaviour could have been taken from any etiquette manual going back to Erasmus's famous *De civilitate morum puerilium* (1530). The campaign for *kul'turnost'* represented a Soviet variation of the process described in Norbert Elias's classic analysis, *The Civilizing Process*, which described the evolution of a concept of the individual needed in a modern society. Externally, this individual would conform to normative patterns of behaviour; internally, he would be committed to the values required by the state. What is unique is the way that this model functioned in the particular social conditions of Soviet culture.

The simplest and least demanding aspect of *kul'turnost'*, and the first to be associated with the concept, in 1933–4, was dress. The once popular military uniforms and their derivatives, such as leather jackets, manifestations of a style engendered by a combination of scarcity and early Bolshevik 'revolutionary' values, gave way to civilian clothes. The ascetic ideal was dropped as official propaganda endorsed smart clothes, clean shaving for men, the use of perfumes and make-up for women.[132] By 1937, a young male worker could dream of a 'Boston' suit, yellow shoes, and nice shirts, while a young *udarnitsa* (female shock-worker) from the Kirov plant in Leningrad might plan to spend her salary on a *crêpe de Chine* dress, beige shoes, an 'Oxford' suit, and a nice winter coat.[133] In January 1936, the new trend was supported by the opening of the first Soviet House of Fashions in Moscow and the publication for the Soviet market of a number of French fashion magazines, *Saison Parisienne* (*Parisian Season*), *Grande Revue des Modes* (*Grand Review of Fashions*), and *Votre Goût* (*Your Taste*), as well as their Soviet equivalents, *Zhurnal doma mod* (*The Journal of the House of Fashions*), *Mody oseni* (*The Fashions of Autumn*), and *Vesna 1936* (*Spring of 1936*).[134]

Care for one's appearance came to include other aspects of the public self. At the beginning of 1936, the press claimed that the Soviet Union had surpassed France in the gross production of perfumes, and had moved up to third place in the world after the USA and Britain. Towards the end of 1936, the Institute of Cosmetics and Hygiene was opened in Moscow, its ostensible purpose 'to satisfy the great interest of the population in the hygiene of facial and bodily skin'.[135] Regular use of perfumes and facial massage was perhaps not quite the working-class pattern. Nonetheless, there was no ideological problem with advertising these and other 'cultural skills', as long as they remained part of the ideologically positive notion of *kul'turnost'*.

Concern with appearance at a superficial level was followed by the need to keep the body clean and to wear fresh underwear. 'Cleanliness and tidiness are rightly considered attributes of *kul'turnost'*. A person cannot be referred to as cultured if he does not keep his body clean.'[136] As more attention was paid to bodily hygiene, practices underwent gradual modification. The traditional public bathhouse with large communal washing-rooms gradually evolved into a more complex washing space, partitioned and equipped with individual showers. In official language this tendency, which also involved installation of 'individual bath-shower complexes' in new apartment blocks, was referred to as 'the substitution of individual bath-shower washing for the communal bath'.[137]

Bodily hygiene was part of a wider practical framework of personal care. The latter also required 'equipment', such as bedlinen, underwear, and handkerchiefs. A study of young Leningrad workers conducted between 1934 and 1936 took the use of bedsheets and underwear as the main indicator of *kul'turnost'*. It found that all the workers surveyed had, in 1936, at least one set of bedlinen; 5 per cent of respondents had two, 38 per cent three or four, and 57 per cent five or more sets. This, the study claimed, indicated a steady growth of *kul'turnost'* in comparison with 1934, when 2 per cent of the workers used no bedlinen, 17 per cent had only one set, 34 per cent two sets, and 47 per cent three to four sets. A similar tendency was discovered in possession and use of underwear.[138]

It was no accident that the growing attention to personal hygiene coincided with the campaign for labour efficiency, the Stakhanovite movement, which reached its peak in 1936. Cleanliness testified to self-discipline and efficient organization of one's activities. *Kul'turnost'* in private life (*v bytu*) corresponded to efficiency and discipline at the workplace. 'Strict discipline, elimination of sloppiness [*raspushchennost'*]' characterized the true Stakhanovite, who 'must be the model of cleanliness, tidiness, and culturedness at work and in private life'.[139] The connection between personal hygiene and the culture of production (*kul'tura proizvodstva*) was central to press discussion of *kul'turnost'* in April 1936. As *kul'turnost'* was persistently associated with individual achievement, personal dignity, and pride, it was, at the same time, integrated into the system of industrial labour as one of the major conditions of its efficiency: 'The white collar and the clean shirt are the necessary working instruments providing for the fulfilment of production plans and the quality of products.'[140] Georgii Ordzhonikidze, the Minister for Heavy Industry, underscored the need to look tidy and to shave regularly. Thereafter, a number of enterprises issued orders compelling all engineers and managers to make sure that they were clean-shaven and their hair was appropriately styled. Some factories were specially provided with mirrors so that the personnel could monitor their appearance. In the last of a series of articles on the topic, *Pravda* stressed that the discussion of *kul'turnost'* was not a passing campaign, but the beginning of 'a long, systematic effort, in the sphere of cultural self-education, to inculcate cultural skills in the widest possible layers of the working population. The struggle for culture and cleanliness must embrace all spheres of our life.'[141]

Objects and Symbols of Private Life

The privatization of life was a long and complex process which conditioned the formation of the modern individual and society in Western Europe.[142] It implied a rearrangement of almost all the existing elements of everyday life and the introduction of new ones. Similar tendencies were present in the pre- and post-war Soviet Union.

The idea of mobilizing the wives of top managers and engineers in order to introduce workers to the basic skills of *kul'turnost'* was born, so the legend says, in the head of Ordzhonikidze in 1934 when he visited a Ural factory and saw, in the yard, a flower-bed, cultivated by a manager's wife (Surovtseva, later one of the leaders of the movement). There followed an All-Union Meeting of Wives of Industrialists and Engineering-Technical Personnel of Heavy Industry in May 1936 and a number of similar meetings in other branches of industry, the Red Army, and the communal services. This started a movement for the all-out civilization of everyday life. The journal *Obshchestvennitsa* became the printed organ of the movement, and the women involved were further referred to as *obshchestvennitsy*. No straightforward translation of the word is possible; it derives from the term *obshchestvennost'* (literally, 'socialness'), which came to signify the public as an active social force (see Prologue). In this particular case, the name *obshchestvennitsy* attached to the wives of members of the administrative-professional stratum (engineers, factory directors, etc.) who engaged in voluntary social work or agitation.

The *obshchestvennitsy* set out to reform the everyday life of workers along the lines of *kul'turnost'*. Initially, their work had nothing to do with propagandization of high ideas or ideals. Their fundamental principle was straightforward: 'a cultured environment raises the culturedness of those who live in it'; 'environment compels and edifies'.[143] 'Environment' here means the things proximate to one's daily existence: the arrangement of space, the structure of 'things at hand' (the term used, *obikhod*, can also mean 'equipment'), and elementary self-care techniques, such as hygiene routines and diet. It was these aspects of daily life that the *obshchestvennitsy* attempted to reform.

Workers' barracks, which accommodated up to several hundred workers with their families, all in one space, were one especial focus of criticism: they were seen as repositories of deviance, violence, filth, offensive smells, and coarse speech, problems to which the state had become more sensitive as a source of 'unculturedness'. Complaints that workers' domestic life and time outside sites of production were beyond the field of vision of *obshchestvennost'* had been heard before. But little was done to address this until the imperative of culturedness grew stronger.

On the pages of their journal the *obshchestvennitsy* shared their experience in erecting partitions and dividing the space of barracks into smaller living areas. (Where it was impossible to build new workers' hostels, changes in the living space were achieved through elementary partitioning of this kind.) There were numerous reports about how the bosses' wives planned and directed the rebuilding of barracks. New standards were implemented for 'these large, filthy halls':

> Each room must accommodate not more than four people. One bed must not touch another, even with its head; common bunks are unacceptable. . . . There must be a free passage between the beds not less than 0.35 m. wide, and a common passage at least 1.5 m. wide along the beds. . . . From which it follows that the norm for each bed must be not less than 4 square metres.[144]

Such norms were introduced with a twofold motivation: improving physical hygiene and ensuring public order. They also made living space more private. Social activities were now separated from physical ones. There were special and separate rooms for shared leisure and cultural activities; the occupants of the barracks were prohibited to sit or to eat on their beds. Special isolated 'hygiene rooms' were constructed. Their purpose was to improve hygiene, but at the same time they served to remove the natural functions of the body from public view.

The objects that surrounded people, their material environment, became instrumental in changing their habits and attitudes. The constant presence of certain objects was supposed to instil *kul'turnost'*. Among the items of everyday equipment associated with the norms of civilized life, three became fetishized, and are mentioned repeatedly in journal after journal: curtains, lampshades, and tablecloths. Sometimes the set included flowers and carpets. The following is a typical description of *kul'turnost'* achieved: 'There are snow-white curtains on the windows, tablecloths and flowers on the tables. There appear things never known before: bookshelves, wardrobes, and silk lampshades.'[145] Wives of Red Army officers reported how barracks and canteens were equipped with portières, curtains, and tablecloths made by the caring hands of women. The obsession with the objects of *kul'turnost'* took them as far as the North Pole. In 1938 the ship *Taimyr* went to rescue the members of the heroic Papanin Arctic expedition. Women decided to take care of the ship's interior: 'It was decided to make two beautiful lampshades and a tablecloth for a gramophone. . . . Many nice things were made by our women: portières, tablecloths, napkins, carpets, and lampshades.'[146]

What were the social significance and effects of these small symbols of culturedness? Curtains became a universal symbol of *kul'turnost'*, serving as a device that symbolically constituted one's home, one's cultured dwelling. The 'curtain effect', then, consisted in the creation, both real and symbolic, of a private space through limitation of its observability. Curtains accompanied the partitioning of large communal spaces; they functioned as a diaphragm that controlled the degree to which private space was secluded from the outside world (a person shutting or opening the curtains is a widespread symbolic image in the arts, a cliché in cinema). Curtains were often described as 'snow-white', which implied cleanliness and proper hygiene (the adjective has also a resonance of the *volshebnaia skazka*, magic tale).

A lampshade has the combined function of regulating the tonality of lighting and the aesthetics of the interior. Lighting, however, is also part of the social microstructure. To a certain extent, it defines the genre of an event or activity, it creates dispositions. We know, for example, that festive lighting excites joyous dispositions, when the lights are bright and everything is rendered completely visible; we are familiar with lighting techniques in the theatre and cinema; we talk of mournful lighting or intimate lighting. Techniques of lighting create and maintain certain social dispositions, but are themselves barely discernible in everyday life, because their function is to render other things discernible and to present them in 'this or that light'. The introduction of lampshades (the journal *Obshchestvennitsa* provided instruction in how to make them from different fabrics) was fundamental to producing such effects. Delimiting and condensing living space, soft lighting helped to make one's dwelling more comfortable, private, and self-contained.

The tablecloth was the third normative element of a cultured setting. An article giving instructions on 'rational diet' concluded: 'If the table is draped with a white tablecloth, the dinner tastes good and is digested perfectly. To live in a cultured way also means to eat in a cultured way.'[147] The white tablecloth figured as a symbol of *kul'turnost'*, and also tied together diet, hygiene, and manners. The introduction of tablecloths in workers' canteens implied further changes. Long wooden tables and benches were removed, to be replaced by tables for four or six with separate chairs. One could no longer eat in the same way at a small table covered with a white tablecloth as at a crude wooden table shared with a dozen other people. The 'snow-white' tablecloth would immediately testify to the person's table manners: 'I can't sit down at a table like that with my hands dirty', wrote one worker.[148]

Kul'turnost' implied systemic changes in material environment. The things associated with *kul'turnost'* were not just discrete objects which people encountered in the course of their daily lives. Rather, they tended to form a specific 'object-system' or an 'equipmental matrix', wherein all the elements presupposed one another and, being assembled together, constituted the material infrastructure of *kul'turnost'*. This material infrastructure contained an implicit concept of its user, including the user's practical skills, rhythms of activity, level of self-discipline, and basic habits; people used the elements of this infrastructure not only for practical purposes but, beyond that, to constitute themselves as cultured individuals. And in so doing they were bound to develop new habits which derived from the patterns of usage carried by the objects of *kul'turnost'*. Thus, once such an equipmental matrix had been introduced, the moulding of individuals would in the long term require neither permanent persuasion nor external coercion.

Brought to life by the policies of *kul'turnost'* in 1936, the *obshchestvennitsy* movement had changed its objectives by 1939. As Europe witnessed the outbreak of the Second World War, a different set of policies aimed at military build-up and mass mobilization was launched in the Soviet Union. Everyday life, including the cultural sphere, was reorganized to meet the needs of defence. The original civilizing pursuit of the *obshchestvennitsy* was also redirected. The inculcation of cultural skills was supplanted by military training. But even though the movement did not revive after the war, the processes that it had helped to set in motion continued, and norms of hygiene, manners, the culture of private life, which in the 1930s were still largely ideals awaiting realization, were beginning, by the 1950s, to become ingrained.

Word and Thought

Another sphere to be embraced by *kul'turnost'* was that of speech. In March 1936 the Komsomol press began a campaign against 'dirty talk', arguing that it was incompatible with the norms of *kul'turnost'*. Denouncing the impoverished, bureaucratic, low-life jargon of the Komsomol leaders, an article in a popular youth magazine proceeded to ask: 'Is it possible that culture only means that Stakhanovites wear cheviot suits and "attend theatre and cinema at least three times a month"?'[149] Proper appearance alone was no longer enough to meet the demands of *kul'turnost'*. This was stressed by the Secretary of the Komsomol Central Committee at the movement's Tenth Congress in April 1936: 'We have now a breed of people who mistake various petit-bourgeois [*meshchanskie*] attributes for a prosperous, cultured life. Their thoughts do not extend beyond a suit of foreign make, a gramophone, and books published by "Academia" [publisher of translations of light foreign novels].'[150]

That external attributes and formal criteria expressed in attending theatre and cinema were no longer evidence of culturedness signified a shift in the locus of the concept. From now on it would be increasingly sought in, and projected on to, the individual's inner world. The value of inner *kul'turnost'* grew, and this corresponded to a subtle change in the method of its acquisition. The mastery of correct, literary speech required greater self-monitoring and more sustained effort than buying smart clothes and gramophones. This linguistic aspect of *kul'turnost'* was further articulated during the celebration of the centenary of Pushkin's death in early 1937. Planned and prepared long in advance, this celebration marked a specific fusion of two grand cultural traditions, the old Russian and the new Soviet. Pushkin, it was declared, had given truthful expression to the Russian national spirit. On an individual level, however, the significance of Pushkin was more pragmatic, and was associated with correct patterns of speech: 'There can be no doubt about the positive effect of Pushkin's speech on the struggle for a cultured, correct, precise language.'[151]

In 1938 reading was proclaimed a central method of political self-education; before this, however, it had been associated mainly with the acquisition of *kul'turnost'*. At first, the word 'literate' was synonymous with 'cultured', but later, as more people read more books, 'educatedness' (*obrazovannost'*, a word from Pushkin's vocabulary) superseded 'literacy' (*gramotnost'*, which in Russian can apply to very low levels of literacy skills) as a designation for the primary characteristic of the cultured individual. Literacy was more of a technical skill; while educatedness implied knowledge and, significantly, the existence of a common cultural horizon acquired through reading. In a speech in 1936 the Secretary of the Moscow Komsomol organization presented a model of the cultured and educated person, a 20-year-old fitter from Leningrad, Nina Elkina: 'In the course of the year she read seventy-eight books by authors such as Balzac, Hamsun, Goncharov, Hoffmann, Hugo, Rostand, Flaubert, France, Chekhov, Shakespeare, Veresaev, Novikov-Priboi, [Galina] Serebriakova, Aleksei Tolstoi, Tynianov, Chapygin, and Iasenskii.'[152]

While retaining its earlier 'surface' manifestations, *kul'turnost'* gradually came to signify possession of this standard stock of cultural knowledge. The cultural world of the new Soviet man was formalized to the extent that it could be presented as a quiz with the title 'Are you a Cultured Person?', published in every issue of the popular weekly magazine *Ogonek* in 1936. Each quiz contained ten questions, accompanied by the following instruction: 'Remember, if you are not able to answer any one of the ten suggested questions, you evidently know very little about a whole sphere of science or the arts. Let this compel you to WORK ON YOURSELF [*PORABOTAT' NAD SOBOI*].'[153] The instruction also suggested testing one's friends and colleagues. Here is the first questionnaire:

> 1. Recite by heart at least one poem by Pushkin. 2. Name and describe five plays by Shakespeare. 3. Name at least four rivers in Africa. 4. Name your favourite composer and his three major works. 5. Name five Soviet automobiles. 6. Convert 3/8 into a decimal. 7. Name the three most important sports tournaments of the last year and their results. 8. Describe the three paintings which you liked most at last year's exhibitions. 9. Have you read Stendhal's *Scarlet and Black* and Turgenev's *Fathers and Children*? 10. Explain why the Stakhanovite movement became possible in our country.

Let the educated reader answer. There are grounds for supposing that by the end of 1936 many contemporary Soviet readers could. The *Ogonek* questionnaires were mentioned in other periodicals, and culture clubs were advised to copy and hang them up as posters; so it seems likely that in 1936–7 they were a popular topic of conversation and form of self-education. They are remarkable documents, representing an original matrix of the cultural and ideological knowledge required of the contemporary Soviet citizen, reflecting its breadth and its limits. The first question of the first questionnaire implied the necessity of reading Pushkin, the last the desirability of acquaintance with Stalin's speech of 1935 on the Stakhanovite movement. Other issues of the journal assumed knowledge of the gods of war, love, and trade in ancient Greece and Rome, three types of warplanes, and seven Stakhanovites (no. 2); or of two British newspapers and two representatives of utopian socialist thought (no. 3). Within a single questionnaire the reader might be asked to name two poems by Heine and two Soviet icebreakers (no. 23).

The *Ogonek* questionnaire is evidence of further evolution of the concept of *kul'turnost'*. To become a cultured person one must read classic literature, contemporary Soviet fiction, newspapers, works by Marx, Engels, Lenin, and Stalin, and poetry, and visit the cinema and exhibitions for purposes of self-education. A cultured person must have a cultured inner world and a broad (if historically very specific) cultural horizon. It was in this sense that the notion of individual *kul'turnost'* came closest to the impersonal concept of culture as specific values accumulated by past generations which are to be appropriated and augmented by their successors.

Although *kul'turnost'* continued to figure in the language, and preserved its main features and effects until well after the Great Patriotic War, as a semi-official concept it began to wane around 1937–8, when the 'acquisition of culturedness' was absorbed into a broader concept of political self-education articulated via the doctrine of 'mastering Bolshevism' (*ovladenie bol'shevizmom*). This called for extensive theoretical education in dialectical materialism, and implied the cultivation of Bolshevik consciousness. The tendency that preceded and, to some extent, legitimated this new demand to master Bolshevism was what might be called the problematization of the external aspects of *kul'turnost'*. Smart clothes, elegant behaviour, and even refined speech became associated with the image of the enemy. In the summer of 1937 the sphere of leisure and private life was subjected to sustained criticism which reached its peak in late August at the Fourth Plenary Meeting of the Komsomol Central Committee. The Komsomol press launched vigorous attacks on the sphere of leisure. The enemies, it was declared, operated in youth hostels and on dance floors; dressed in smart clothes in the 'Harbin' style (*Kharbinskii stil'*), they introduced young Komsomolers to their 'beautiful and joyous lifestyle', and eventually recruited them into the ranks of spies.[154] At the Komsomol Congress of 1936 young men were still urged to acquire *kul'turnost'* and to treat one another, and especially women, gallantly. Later, the external aspects of *kul'turnost'*, including refined speech, were condemned, and internal convictions and healthy consciousness demanded in their place. In 1938 the Komsomol periodical summed up the new vision of the enemy: 'The image of the hooligan has changed! The enemy is dressed according to the latest fashion. He is gallant. He dances nicely, speaks beautifully. He knows how to charm women. But if you delve into such a person, you will uncover his bestial, alien interior [*zverinoe, vrazhdebnoe nutro*].'[155]

This evolution of the image of the enemy is indicative of the dynamic of *kul'turnost'*. In 1934–6 (the first phase of *kul'turnost'*), the 'hostile elements' were dirty, badly dressed, ill-mannered, and illiterate people, while the model heroes of the popular press were neatly dressed, clean, well bred, and lived a joyous cultured life. In 1936–7, as culturedness became increasingly associated with inner culture, with broad knowledge and education, those obsessed with superficial attributes could be labelled 'petit bourgeois'. Finally, in 1937–8 the earliest aspects of culturedness became suspect, and, although there was no official rejection of personal hygiene and educatedness, the true virtues of the Soviet man now resided in the sphere of Bolshevik consciousness and private ideological commitment. If the semi-official beginning of the age of *kul'turnost'* was marked by Stalin's motto of November 1935, 'Life has become better, life has become jollier' (*Zhit' stalo luchshe, zhit' stalo veselee*), its official decline coincided with the new motto 'Master Bolshevism!' (*Ovladet' bol'shevizmom!*), unveiled in September 1938 upon publication of the *Short Course of the Communist Party*.

A Central Committee decree of 14 November 1938 prescribed the correct method of mastering Marxism-Leninism: individual reading (*samostoiatel'noe chtenie*). Dialectical materialism, the decree assured, was now accessible to all rank-and-file communists and intelligentsia, provided they undertook a continuous individual (this word was repeatedly invoked) programme of self-education through reading the *Short Course*, in classes and at home. A month earlier the Party's chief spokesman on cultural matters, Andrei Zhdanov, addressing Komsomol activists in the Bolshoi Theatre, emphasized that the Komsomol 'must make a very serious turn in the sphere of propaganda, concentrating on the quality, on the individual bookwork of Komsomol members'.[156]

The process of becoming cultured now had three stages. First, personal *kul'turnost'* was acquired through a combination of public effort (*zabota obshchestvennosti*) and self-transformation (*rabota nad soboi*, work on oneself). This entailed a dynamic relationship between the public and the private, wherein social engagement would normally result in individual ability to live in accordance with the norms of *kul'turnost'* without explicit external compulsion. Second, the process of becoming cultured moved from the external to the internal: beginning with a requirement of external propriety and manners, it went on to articulate and colonize the internal world, demanding intellectual and spiritual commitment. Third, all aspects of *kul'turnost'* were integrated, becoming a system of organic units which formed the elementary structure of public order.

In 1935–6 Stakhanovites were presented as models of *kul'turnost'*. They were initially associated with a kind of 'conspicuous consumption', purchasing expensive suits, overcoats, gramophones, furniture, and other accessories of cultured life.[157] Later, in the life-story of the Stakhanovite A. Busygin, published in 1939, we find that another vital ingredient has been added. After describing his comfortable, self-contained apartment, and his involvement in cultural life, he tells the reader about his new pursuits:

> At present I am working on the history of the Party [that is, the *Short Course*]. Slowly, in the dead of night, I read it line by line, paragraph by paragraph. Dozens of questions and new ideas emerge; I write them down. It is only recently that I started this way of working with the book. When you work with the book by yourself, when you think over every line, you feel that you are learning the Bolshevik way of thinking.[158]

This sketch creates an image of extreme privacy, of a quiet dark room with curtains drawn and a table lamp casting light on the book, an ideal setting for careful reading and reflection. Busygin's new experience, which the press sought to popularize, hints at the two vital components associated with the origins of private life: private living space, and silent reading, intensifying individual reflection.

Mixing Cultural and Material Goods: *Kul'turnost'* as Social Glue

The brilliance of the *kul'turnost'* ideology lay partly in the fact that it was a fusion of two value systems previously thought incompatible, those of the bourgeoisie and the intelligentsia. The reading lists, self-improvement programmes, and directions on hygiene that it set out would have been approved by any pre-Revolutionary intellectual (apart, perhaps, from one on the Bohemian fringe, such as Maiakovskii, whose revolutionary farce *Mystery-Bouffe* had seen the class struggle as a war of the 'clean' bourgeoisie and 'dirty' proletariat). The advice on good manners and home management provided, though, could have been taken from any manual of etiquette published in the late nineteenth or early twentieth century, oracles which had been relentlessly pilloried by intellectuals of the day.

In the nineteenth century, and indeed in the 1920s, *kul'turnost'* had been used to signify 'cultivation' in the sense of education, and particularly the use of educated, rather than popular speech. The only pattern of contextual usage regularly cited in dictionaries comes from Plekhanov's *The Russian Worker in the Revolutionary Movement*, first published in the 1890s: 'The more I get to know Petersburg workers, the more I am impressed by their *kul'turnost'*.'[159] Similarly, in Ognev's novel *The Diary of Kostia Riabtsev*, a schoolgirl who asks what good her command of written Russian will do her in later life receives the following reply: 'Z. P. [Zinaida Pavlovna] says that I write good literary Russian. I asked her, what you need that for in the real world, and she said, that style is what distinguishes a cultivated [*kul'turnyi*] person. The cultivated person has broader horizons.'[160] In the 1930s, this earlier concept of *kul'turnost'* was absorbed into what would previously have been called *vospitannost'*, 'good behaviour, *politeness*', a quality that 1920s radicals would have found distressingly bourgeois.

Kul'turnost' also achieved the hitherto impossible feat of equating consumer goods and cultural artefacts, both now respectable appurtenances of the new Soviet citizen. Before 1917, the humorous magazine *Satirikon* (*Satyricon*), aimed at the St Petersburg intelligentsia, had poked fun at the new Russian middle classes by crediting them with a lust for material acquisition unmatched by any grasp of high culture. One cartoon of 1910, published in an entire number dedicated to *poshlost'* (vulgarity), showed an obese couple in their over-decorated bedroom, accompanied by a 'Hymn to the Double Bed', as a sarcastic evocation of conventional family life. While poets might dream of illicit love, the text asserted, the double bed represented a truer and nobler kind of human existence:

> Пружинная! Нужней ты вицмундира!
> Дубовая! Ты жизнь нам можешь дать!
> Да сгинет та семейная квартира
> Где не в почете ты, двуспальная кровать!

> [Springy double bed, more necessary than a dress uniform!
> Oaken double bed! You can give us life!
> May the family flat rot in hell
> Where you are not honoured, O double bed!][161]

Another cartoon in the same number illustrated a parvenue complaining of the difficulties that she had had in furnishing her room: 'First the pictures wouldn't fit in the alcoves, then we couldn't get hold of an undamaged Venus de Milo, and then the oil paintings stank so much of paint that it was murder sitting in here for the first week!'[162]

The point of all this rather puerile humour was, of course, that classical sculpture was *not* the same as a new portière, and that one might be a fan of the double bed or intellectual pursuits, but not of both. The ideology of *kul'turnost'* deconstructed the binary opposition, creating a world in which a nicely bound collection of Tolstoi's works could, with perfect dignity, stand next door to a lustreware teaset, looking down on a tea-table laid with lace doilies and a table lamp. It also created a world where highly commercial cultural products—for example, Soviet musicals—could be seen as offering a radically new, 'Soviet' culture totally free of commercial values.

One way in which this was achieved was by the judicious use of the antonyms to *kul'turnyi*, *meshchanskii* (petit bourgeois), *poshlyi* (vulgar), and *nekul'turnyi* (uncultured). Of the three, much the simplest was *nekul'turnyi*, which was used to signify breaches of the new rules of etiquette—for example, failing to wash your underwear, biting your nails in public, not having heard of Pushkin, and never changing your sheets. The remaining terms suggested more subtle differentiations. It was, for example, permissible to have house-plants, but rubber plants, branded by *Satirikon* as 'vulgar' in 1910, remained taboo (the impeccably socialist realist painter Aleksandr Laktionov was reprimanded for introducing one into his canvas *The New Apartment* in 1952).[163] Dogs and cats were permissible (for those who could afford them), but canaries were not (Leningrad housing rules published in 1945 precluded the keeping of any pets bar cats and dogs).[164] But above all, the abusive terms 'petit bourgeois' and 'vulgar' were used in order to lambaste the capitalist West and late imperial Russia.[165] This technique was perhaps the most significant contribution to the process by which the profoundly bourgeois doctrine of *kul'turnost'* could appear to be class-free.

For all that, it would be simplistic to see *kul'turnost'* as an expression *only* of Soviet petit bourgeois values; this would over-value its 'etiquette manual' content at the expense of its 'cultural goods' content. The campaign was potent because it tapped the desires of the intelligentsia as well as the new elite. Not only magazines, but literature, paintings, etc. disseminated the doctrine. The third part of Anna Karavaeva's Stalin-prize-winning trilogy, *The Motherland* (*Rodina*, 1950), for example, opens with a scene in which Ol'ga Chelishcheva and her family return to the house from which they have been evacuated during the German invasion to find it in a shocking state:

> Ol'ga could hardly recognize the big room where the Chelishchev family loved to gather in the evenings. Instead of cheery wallpaper with pink bouquets on a green background, the walls were covered with brownish patches, the results of a botched attempt at whitewash. The embroidered net curtains had gone from the windows . . . All the doors were missing from the old oak sideboard, made by Ol'ga's late grandfather, a keen amateur wood-carver. The walnut sofa, lacking its cushions and both front legs, the armchairs, crippled in the same way, and the oval table were pushed into the corners, useless and ugly, with shreds of upholstery hanging off them. The floor was badly scratched; all the carpets and druggets had gone, and kitchen stools were mixed up with the dining chairs by the long dining table, over which a bit of old oil-cloth had been flung.[166]

As Vera Dunham asserts, textual representations such as this were likely to have been read by Soviet citizens in much the same spirit in which turn-of-the-century workers had gazed through the windows of department stores: 'Petunias in imaginary gardens or printed on imaginary fabrics acquired promissory significance.'[167] But they also catalogued goods that *were* available to some members of Soviet society, and for such readers, as well as painters and writers, they functioned as badges of genteelism. When the veteran painter Bogdanov-Bel'skii portrayed his much younger second wife, Antonina Maksimilianovna Höflinger, in 1932, he produced a canvas that is a positive sampler of desirable, *kul'turnyi* domesticity. Antonina Maksimilianovna sits in a plain but elegant Biedermeier mahogany chair, upholstered in a bright, and distinctively Russian, flower print. The room is flooded with light and is spotlessly clean; garlanded wallpaper can be seen in the background, and in the middle distance, to left and right, stand flowering plants on special Karelian birch stands. The *pièce de résistance* is a striking antique half-moon table to the rear of the room. Through the window can be seen a sunny, blossom-filled, trafficless street. It is the suburban idyll craved by the inhabitants of overcrowded industrial cities everywhere in Europe and America. Antonina Maksimilianovna herself is dressed with discreet opulence, and a whisper of decorous eroticism, in a fashionable green mesh top with gold braiding, its top left open to show marmoreal shoulders (but no cleavage), a pair of striped wool slacks, and a fair amount of casual jewellery. Her hair is elegantly permed, and round her shoulders is draped a fur tippet. On one level, the painting distantly alludes to Rubens's famous painting of his second wife, Hélène Fourment, draped in fur, with the insider's joke that Hélène (unlike Antonina) is nude underneath her cape. On another, Bogdanov-Bel'skii's use of a highly conventional treatment of the half-length (seated in an armchair) recalls the solid virtues of such modestly talented mid-nineteenth-century portraitists as Vasilii Tropinin. The result is an identifiably Russian celebration of family happiness as conjugal bliss plus material comfort.[168]

Lest anyone suppose that idylls of this kind were the province only of the talentless, here is Mikhail Bulgakov's vision of earthly paradise, the secret abode of his heroes, the Master and Margarita:

> A divan here and a divan opposite, and a little table in between, with a wonderful reading-lamp on it, and closer to the window a row of books, and in the main room—a huge room, 14 metres square—books, and more books, and a stove . . . [Margarita] would arrive and put on an apron, and they would light the paraffin stove in the narrow hall . . . and prepare a meal and set it out in the main room on the oval table . . . Then the man who called himself 'the master' would work, and she, sticking her slender fingers with their nails filed to points into her hair, would read what he had written, and when she had read it, would go on embroidering his little cap.[169]

Modest, conservative comfort, tended by a woman's loving hands—that is, serviced by her unstinting and always uncomplaining labour—was wholly in the spirit of the official remodelling of reality. The fact that this idyll could be seen as an escape from Soviet life is a remarkable illustration of the pervasiveness of the new values. This was a society where many had come to feel that the maximum reward was that finally granted to Bulgakov's hero, not enlightenment or joy, but *pokoi* (tranquillity).

The Poetics of Manipulation: Consumption and Popular Resistance

The *kul'turnost'* campaign was not simply about changing values: it also related to actual patterns of acquisition. An intriguing portrait of consumption habits among the privileged is painted by Elena Bonner, daughter of two Comintern officials, in her memoir *Daughters and Mothers* (*Dochki-materi*, 1994). Until the 1930s, the family often depended on remakes of Elena's grandmother's cast-offs for their clothes, but from then on they began to shop at Torgsin, and later at the newly opened GORT outlet for Party officials, with admission by card only (at first at the less exclusive 'B' section, later at the 'A' section). Significant items acquired by Elena before her parents were arrested in the Great Purges included an elegant beige knitted suit and red blouse, and a leather coat. The family also replaced its battered aluminium knives and forks with new stainless steel ones, and for one birthday Elena was given a handsome new Parker fountain-pen, the first she had ever seen.

The Bonner-Alikhanov family continued to live quite modestly, by the standards of the contemporary Western bourgeoisie. Though they had a private flat (in the Hotel Luxe, no less), with a maid, accommodation was fairly cramped; idealists like many other Party members of their generation, Elena's parents were slightly embarrassed by their *ex officio* privileges (chauffeur-driven car and dacha), and made little use of the latter (though the children and their grandmother summered there regularly). But their case illustrates that purchasing non-essential items, albeit in small quantities, was a fact of life for even the most high-minded.

For those outside the Party, rationing, and later shortages, were less comfortably buffered, but even here the better-off had resources. They could shop in Torgsin, where payment was made in vouchers granted to customers in exchange for valuable items (for example, jewellery or antiques), so that the store acted as the Soviet equivalent of a pawn shop. (The singer Galina Vishnevskaia, who saw the 1930s from a rather different social angle from Bonner's, recalls in her memoirs, *Galina* (1986), melting down an icon's precious metal *oklad*, decorative covering, in order to shop at Torgsin.) They could, in the 1920s and 1930s, petition foreign relatives to send them scarce items (Bulgakov wrote to relatives in France to see whether they would get his wife some lisle stockings), or indeed visit one of the 'speculators' (black market dealers) whose existence is clear from Western travelogues, if not from official statistics. The writer E. M. Delafield, who visited Russia in 1936, recalls how she was approached at a private gathering by a woman asking for 'silk stockings, aspirin, lipsticks, cotton frocks and nail scissors'; she duly agreed to sell some things to the woman in question, who proved a remarkably persistent buyer, having eventually to 'get her out of the room at last by giving her a lip-stick as a sort of bonus, like a pound of tea for a cash sale'.[170]

Stratification of the market-place was acknowledged not only by the provision of different retail outlets, but also by the grading of goods in terms of price and packaging. Most items were sold loose in shops called, say, 'Bread Shop no. 45', or 'Household Goods Shop no. 6', but the most prestigious, and expensive, shops and goods were allowed titles and brand names. The grandest and most elegant dress shop on Nevskii Prospekt was entitled 'The House of Fashion', rather than 'Women's Clothes', as a less pretentious equivalent would have been, and luxuries such as cakes, sweets, and chocolates, perfumes, fur hats, etc. all had individual names, albeit often ones with uplifting revolutionary connotations, such as 'Dawn' or 'October'. Moreover, the capacity of the privileged to afford such luxury goods was enhanced by the fact that the rationing system had built-in differentials. While unskilled workers in the provinces lived at levels only just above starvation (and peasants in many parts of Russia were literally starving), skilled workers, most particularly shock workers, army officers, OGPU and Party officials, policemen, and, above all, government officials had far more substantial provision. In 1930, for example, Moscow and Leningrad workers in heavy industry were due a maximum of 800 grams of bread and 200 grams of meat per day, and three kilos of meal (*krupa*), 800 grams of salt fish, 1,500 grams of sugar, 50 grams of tea, 600 grams of butter, and 750 grams of oil per month. In 1932 the meat ration had been reduced to two kilos per month, and no butter or oil was supplied. In reality, supplies often fell below even the miserly official allocations, and Moscow workers' diet deteriorated substantially in real terms between 1932 and 1935; the situation in the provinces was still worse. At the same time, privileged groups such as Party officials and shock workers were able to obtain far superior supplies of food (four kilos of meat per month, three kilos of meal, and so on) on their ration cards, and could buy better meals for less in the canteen.[171] There was therefore more left of their already larger salaries for the purchase of non-essential items. Though the situation improved slightly with the end of rationing, it was still only the privileged who could be described as Soviet consumers; the rest spent what they had to in order to survive.

How did the 'have-nots' in Soviet society react to this situation? There is evidence that food shortages in particular caused deep resentment. In January 1933, three textile workers from Ivanovo wrote to *Izvestiia* complaining about the appalling conditions in the town:

> We senior workers didn't live like we do now under the capitalist system. Textile workers get 100 roubles a month and all we can buy at a fixed price is bread, the rest comes from the market. Our children are withering from hunger, they never see milk or sugar, they sell potatoes at the market by the piece, the canteens only have frost-bitten potatoes and water. You can't live like this, there's muttering and dissatisfaction among the masses. People are talking about demonstrations like the ones at the Vichugi and Teikov factories [in April 1932].[172]

As the letter suggests, overt protests, such as demonstrations or even strikes, were not unknown in such circumstances. However, workers who resorted to measures of this kind risked further exacerbating the hardship in which they lived. After strikes were banned in 1921, those who resorted to stoppages as a means of voicing disaffection risked military intervention, lockouts, or at the very least suspension of wages in retribution. As the Ivanovo letter suggests, walk-outs were resorted to only *in extremis*, and workers preferred different tactics—threats of disruption, lobbying the press. A letter sent to *Izvestiia*, *Pravda*, or another Soviet paper would not reach a Soviet mass readership, but it would be carefully processed by the journals concerned, sent on to the appropriate government agency, and might sometimes result in action.[173]

If pleading with the authorities did not appeal, other forms of manipulation might be resorted to. Not for nothing was Il'f and Petrov's NEP trickster hero, the Odessa rogue with the speaking name Ostap Bender, one of the most popular fictional characters of the Stalin and post-Stalin periods. Crime against state enterprises—embezzlement, theft, and vandalism—might be played up in official campaigns against 'Trotskyite' saboteurs, but there is no doubt that it was a real social problem, and that some of the inmates of Soviet prison camps would have been incarcerated in any country (if not in such inhumane conditions). One of the livelier plays of the 1930s, Nikolai Pogodin's *Aristocrats* (*Aristokraty*, 1934), was an account of criminal prisoners on the White Sea Canal forced-labour project which, despite its didactic 're-education' plot and wholly mythologized portrayal of a campaign in which thousands died of starvation and overwork, still gave, in a famous production by Sergei Okhlopkov, a reasonably convincing portrayal of the criminal world, with its peculiar songs, mores, and slang.[174]

Apart from roguery, there were many other possible ways of giving laws a run for their money. Though alternative types of manipulation are not well represented in Soviet literature, more humdrum sources attest them widely.

Workers might not strike, but they could slow down their work pace so as to threaten the norms of production set up under the planned economy, and, by extension, their managers' jobs.[175] They also could, and did, exploit the system of formal denunciation in order to get rid of unpopular foremen—a ruse whose force was recognized by the Party authorities, who tended to be chary, rather than appreciative, of the efforts exerted by specialists in the denunciation genre. The denunciation system required the authorities to negotiate the tensions between the likely benefits to Party standing when it was recognized as a mediator in disputes, and the detriments to this standing when officials came under assault from below. And in domestic contexts, denunciations could be used to acquire *Lebensraum* in communal flats, to settle private scores such as property disputes, and to exact revenge on enemies or even occasionally family members—in other words, to exploit the criminal law in order to settle disputes that would have been taken to the civil courts in Britain or America.[176] Given this background, Il'f and Petrov's 1930s sketch 'A Recipe for a Quiet Life', in which the narrator proffers advice on how to deal with people who annoy you when you are shopping—take their names down in your pocketbook, and then denounce them—seems sharp satire indeed:

> First find out who jostled you. Then demand he produces his documents. Of course the guilty party will say he didn't do it on purpose, and refuse to show them. Even better. You call the manager and say very quietly, but firmly, that you demand the instant expulsion of this hooligan from the territory of the trading area. The manager, of course, will tell you that he doesn't give a —— for your pocketbook. He doesn't give a ——! Wonderful! You mobilize the consumer collective, sort things out with it, and send it into action against this official who has lost his sense of reality.[177]

The fact that this satire on denunciation as personal revenge was first published in *Pravda* during 1934 is an indication of the authorities' suspicion of 'voluntarist' denunciation. On the whole, they preferred to use the relatively clinical evidence provided by those Soviet citizens whom they recruited to act as paid informers, and whose denunciations could be directed from above.[178]

There were also milder forms than denunciation by which one might parade dissatisfaction. One was by being more or less subtly rude to one's superiors, social or professional, a possibility which workers in the Soviet service industries, particularly, exploited for all that it was worth. In the late 1940s, competitions between stores were organized, and the raising of sales levels rewarded, in order to promote helpfulness and amiability, but by all accounts relations remained much as they had in the 1920s, when Mikhail Zoshchenko graphically recorded the frustrations of lower-class Russians with the petty tyranny, small-minded officiousness, and indifference of minor public servants.

All in all, manipulation of Soviet reality was much commoner not only than protest or confrontation, but even than open grumbling, which would have invited prosecution under Article 58 of the 1926 Criminal Code, which covered a wide range of subversive and counter-revolutionary activities as well as sabotage and armed resistance. Perhaps commonest of all, though, was total indifference to the procedures of authority, and alienation from the realities beyond friends and family. A fascinating glimpse of this is given by an anthology of letters found in the pockets of Soviet soldiers fighting in the Soviet–Finnish War, and published in 1944 by the émigré journalist, and former Socialist Revolutionary, V. Zenzinov. The vast majority of the letters were written by workers and peasants. Though a good many indicate familiarity with the Soviet media (references to listening out for news 'on the radio' are common), few display any concern about the political or ideological aspects of the war. The majority of correspondents are completely parochial in their interests. They report the conscription of friends and relatives, complain about the problems of raising money to pay taxes, report with relief that there are no food shortages, and ask their soldier husbands, sons, and brothers to keep an eye out for scarce goods (notebooks, shoes, clothes). This indifference to politics and ideology is found even in letters written by petty officials. Mikhail Naumov, a sniper with the NKVD, for example, appears to have been barely more literate at a political level than he was at the level of grammar. His astonishingly badly spelt and inaccurately punctuated letter ends with 'a warm red army greeting' to his brother, and contains a few ritual exhortations to 'bash the Finns', but is otherwise entirely taken up with family affairs:

Hallo, dear brother Mr P. I. Naumov.

In the first lines of my letter I hasten to inform you that I have received your letter for which Im very greatful and for the good news about your life there and all. Petia now let me tell you wot Ive seen here that is in Moscow, I spoke to her but not for long she came into the shop they bought wot they came in for then they left Petia she looks deadbeat real bad she really misses you so you come soon but their OK at the moment no real problems by the way I bought myself a wrist watch one of them Kirov factory ones Petia I heard on the radio on 26 November there been standoffs wot those fins there up to eh hope nothing happened to you now Petia let me tell you wot I been up to things been going real good for me at the moment that is 26 November they let me off on a gymnastics course at Dynamo [Moscow] and it goes on till 1st May 1940 Ill be doing it from 1 Janury and when I get through that I wont have to attend the tech any more the moneys better here, by the way the weathers not too good some snow falling

Petia write and tell me wots going on spec youll be having a go at them fins soon an all But thats all Ive got to say for now things are fine my healths good and I wish you all the best in your young red army life their if they lay a finger you make sure you hit them three times back

I send you and all the soldiers and commanders a warm red army greeting from the NKVD section from us snipers

Bye for now wishing you all the best, written by
Mikhail Ivanovich Naumov.[179]

However, the letter also indicates that the idea of acquiring suitably 'cultured' goods was perfectly in tune with grassroots reality: here, it is a wristwatch that forms the centrepiece of Naumov's news. More confirmation of kul'turnost' in action comes from a rather different source: Nadezhda Mandel'shtam's embittered, but not implausible, description of her own denunciation at a workplace meeting in 1953:

People began to speak from the floor, some with prepared texts and others spontaneously. A woman technician with a perm asserted that she had once seen me sitting on a windowsill—though everybody had seen in films that you were only supposed to sit in chairs or armchairs. (Their ideas of 'good manners' all came from the movies, just as their notions of love and honour did. But the way that they laughed came straight off the radio—they imitated the silvery cadenced tinkling sound affected by the female announcers.)[180]

The genius of the *kul'turnost'* campaign, then, was that it directed aspirations as effectively as a successful Western advertising campaign, promoting desirable goods, and investing these with an aura of luxury and mystique. But it achieved far more than that: it reached across classes to construct an ideal collective in which those spurning the new values could be seen as riff-raff ('hooligans', 'bohemians'), but those who were too overt in their material attachments might be lambasted as 'vulgar'. By providing not only a pattern of conduct, but also a model for day-to-day living, and by harnessing, rather than challenging, the self-betterment aspirations that had been obvious among working people well before the Revolution, as well as satisfying the desires of the new and old bourgeoisies, it was to prove far and away the most successful 'programme for identity' evolved in the Soviet period.

Eventually, the very success of the *kul'turnost'* campaign was to prove its undoing. The idea of material acquisition as a perfectly justifiable reward for honest toil cut across a key tenet of Soviet labour ideology: that work should be its own reward.[181] Progressively, the doctrine of *kul'turnost'*, supposedly both spiritual and material in character, undermined the disinterested, purely spiritual doctrine of labour as self-sacrifice that was propounded in other areas of Soviet propaganda. Though consumer demand began increasingly to impinge, however discreetly, on Party policy, the production-led ideology of successive Soviet leaders would never allow full consideration to be given to consumer demands, and hence the supply of consumer goods, *tovary shirokogo potrebleniia* ('goods of broad consumption'), was always poorly regulated.

The Soviet system's inability to control the desires that it unleashed was to become acutely problematic in the post-Stalin period, as differences between the elite and the masses widened, as the cumbersome bureaucracy controlling production became increasingly incapable of responding to consumer demand, and as Soviet goods began to be spurned by many people in favour of foreign products. But for the time being, the new institutions and facilities seemed, to many people, to bear out Stalin's announcement that 'life had become jollier'. Material conditions might be hard, but working-class inhabitants of Moscow and Leningrad (if not villages or provincial cities) were at least no worse off than they had been before 1917 (when a rented bunk in a barracks and a diet bordering on malnutrition had been the norm for many). The regime's failure to eradicate poverty quickly struck outsiders, such as André Gide, a good deal more forcefully than it did many Soviet citizens themselves.

The resentment inspired by another aspect of Soviet society that shocked outsiders—social stratification, which became increasingly entrenched in the 1930s—was also containable for the meantime. Though domestic service persisted right up to the 1970s in many better-off families (when new opportunities for rural women, rather than changed preferences among employers, caused its decline), and though the Soviet upper intelligentsia and Party elite enjoyed far better living conditions than workers, let alone *kolkhozniki*, differences were discreetly enjoyed, rather than openly paraded. Ordinary people (unless in domestic service) never entered special Party apartment blocks or penetrated dacha compounds, and in any case old-fashioned intelligentsia tastes retained a hold.[182] By and large, Party activists did not collect Fabergé; they certainly did not sit at the opera in gold and diamond jewellery. Envy was also damped down by the fact that aspirations were relatively homogeneous across classes. A hand-embroidered evening dress or a dinner-jacket, a limousine or a Sèvres vase were much less likely 'wants' in the 1930s and 1940s than adequate living space, a Sunday suit, a magazine subscription, a radio, a chess set, a portière, or any of the other items associated with the *kul'turnost'* ethic. Foreign luxury foods might be available only to the elite, but indigenous ones could grace most tables on public holidays, such as New Year and the anniversary of the October Revolution. Given that a private car was an almost unheard-of possession until at least the late 1940s, when the Pobeda ('Victory', a sort of Soviet Volkswagen) came on the market, and that efficient public transport was a vaunted Soviet achievement, official cars inspired no more ill-feeling than ceremonial carriages might do in a monarchy. Though envy was far from absent in Stalinist society—the use of denunciations as a means to self-advancement is indication enough of its presence—'neutral' sources, such as the private letters collected by Zenzinov, are remarkably free of resentment on material grounds. They give the impression, rather, that the battle to keep afloat was so taxing that little energy remained for anything else.

Furthermore, most Soviet citizens had some tiny personal privilege—special rations, a professional skill, an unusually favourable allocation of living space—which allowed them to participate in the unofficial network of exchange and private purchase (*blat*). Peasants without the right to reside in cities could trade their labour as nannies or cooks for living space; workmen could gain access to a professor's rations in return for mending a lavatory; a seamstress might be the final recipient of a doctor's gifts from his grateful patients. And, since the privileged were regularly pilloried in newspaper articles and satirical plays and fiction, and since high-ups were most likely to come under fire in the various rounds of Party purges, those at the bottom of the heap could feel self-righteous if they wanted to, as they watched those above them go through the ruthless process of *samokritika*, the process of public self-vilification combined with general abuse from the spectators, that was urged on all Soviet enterprises during the Stalin era.[183]

Conclusion: From 'Russian Empire' to 'Soviet Union'

Catriona Kelly

IT would be wrong to suggest that Soviet society in the 1930s and 1940s, let alone in the 1920s, was homogeneous. Much of Central Asia, and outlying parts of European Russia and the Caucasus, remained more or less untouched by Sovietization until after the Second World War.[184] The attendant republics could also be notable centres of direct resistance, with the Baltic States and the Western Ukraine, the last territories to be accreted by the Soviet State, particularly important in this regard. In Russia itself, open rebellion, though rare, was not unknown, despite the appalling penalties that it exacted. The drive to collectivize agriculture was violently resisted in many Russian villages (including *bab'i bunty*, or women's rebellions, in which peasant women attempted, often successfully, to stop officials confiscating goods, animals, food, and tackle). In the late 1940s, riots between groups of prisoners turned some camps into civil war zones. However, in all these cases, resistance was effectively crushed. Mass deportations, executions, and the artificial famines created by the confiscations finally brought the countryside to its knees.[185] Similar methods—forced starvation or shooting—were used to suppress rebellions in the prison camps. The importance of the regime's capacity to threaten citizens with violence as a way of suppressing discontent is indicated by the fact that millions of Soviet citizens chose to throw in their lot with the Germans after the invasion of the Soviet Union in 1941, naïvely assuming that the Nazis' promises of support were genuine, and that their shift of allegiance would lead to an overthrow of Stalin's domination of the country.[186]

The extent of inner resistance is imponderable, but is suggested, for example, by the liking among camp criminals for sarcastic parodies of Stalin's official titles such as 'the best friend of children and Mongolian horned cattle'—cracks on the surface that may point to larger fissures underground. Even in the 1930s and 1940s, when telling a political joke was punishable by at least five years in a labour camp, political anecdotes still circulated. Two surviving examples both relate to the Pushkin Jubilee of 1937. In the first, Stalin says, 'If Pushkin had lived in the twentieth century, not the nineteenth, he'd still have died in '37.' In the second, the prizes are awarded for a competition to design a Pushkin memorial —third prize: Pushkin reading the works of Stalin; second prize: Stalin reading the works of Pushkin; first prize: Stalin reading the works of Stalin.[187] In her memoir *My Path* (*Put'*, 1993), Ol'ga Ivanova-Sliozberg recalls how a fellow prisoner in 1936 had denounced her professor at university after he said in jocular fashion, when she lit a splint during a power cut: 'Yes, life has got better, life has got jollier: look, now we've even got as far as lighting splints [a traditional peasant method].'[188] But the melancholy tone of such jokes, more grim reflections of reality than flights of fantasy, indicates how hopeless opposition seemed to be, closer to 'resistance' in the psychoanalytical sense than in the political sense. For ordinary Russians, the realities of life were summed up in two lines from a camp song: 'In the prison camps you dream of freedom / But to talk about it would be daft' ('V lageriakh mechtaiut o svobode / No o nei ne smeiut govorit').[189]

The sporadicism and marginality of actual rebellion could only contribute to the force of representations in which dissent was seen as the preserve of sinister, shadowy outsiders—from the 'Trotskyites' and 'enemies of the people' of the 1930s to the 'rootless cosmopolitans' (that is, Jews) of the late 1940s. Such representations were, indeed, so effective that they retained their hold even over many arrested and imprisoned during the purges. The uneasy encounter with 'genuine' criminals and subversives during the memoirist's first night in the cells is a *topos* of prison camp chronicles. For some, enlightenment about the true nature of their experience took days to filter through; for others, it took longer than a lifetime.

In any case, the Stalinist regime did succeed in imposing a broad consensus regulating life and mentality in Russian cities and large towns, if not all over the Soviet Union. As well as the governing role of the Party, and the duties of obedience exacted by it, this consensus took for granted the importance of 'culture'. In the 1920s and 1930s, this signified above all technological and scientific progress, but in the late 1940s it came primarily to signify nineteenth-century Russian art, with Pushkin, Gogol', Tolstoi, Gor'kii, the painters Ivanov, Repin, Shishkin, and Levitan, the composers Glinka, Tchaikovsky, and Rimskii-Korsakov, elevated to the new national pantheon. The key significance of the intelligentsia, above all writers, in expressing cultural values through moral pronouncements was also accepted; by the 1940s the dictatorship of the proletariat had become a dead letter. Even if those outside educationally privileged circles had a knowledge of the classics that was superficial at best (Pushkin meant Tat'iana's Letter from *Eugene Onegin*, which generations of Soviet school-girls learned by heart; Tolstoi, above all *War and Peace*; Gogol' *The Overcoat*; Levitan *Golden Autumn*; and Tchaikovsky *Swan Lake*), the names and biographies of such famous cultural figures entered into popular consciousness as never before, with exposure via the school syllabus reinforced by coverage in popular illustrated magazines, newspapers, and on the radio. The propagandization of the Russian classics was effective far outside its native culture: from the late 1940s, acquaintance with Russian literature became an obligatory part of self-fashioning among ambitious members of subaltern ethnic groups in the Soviet Union, such as the Chukchi and Nenets peoples of the far North-East, occurring as a *topos* in autobiographical narrative. Conversely, Sovietized adaptations of artefacts from traditional non-Russian cultures, most particularly those that could be viewed through an Orientalizing prism, were used in order to evoke otherness for Russians, and also to create a focus of identification, both traditional and modern, in the cities of the various Republics. From the Uzbek or

The house in Bagdadi, near Kutaisi, Georgia, where the famous Russian futurist and 'poet of the Revolution', Vladimir Maiakovskii, was born in 1893. The house became a museum in the 1930s.
The survival of this humble family dwelling (though of aristocratic descent, Maiakovskii's father was impoverished, and was working as a forester when he was born) is exemplary of the Soviet regime's meticulous preservation of places connected with those writers and artists whom it wished to honour. The bilingual sign (in Russian and Georgian) is a symbolic artefact of Soviet imperial culture, which was multi-lingual and multi-cultural, but which also asserted the central significance of Russian culture (no non-Russian poet or writer was accorded as glorious a status as that given to Pushkin, Tolstoi, or indeed Maiakovskii).

Azerbaijani pavilions at the All-Soviet Agricultural Exhibition to the department stores, stations, and Party buildings of Baku, Erevan, or Tashkent, to the traditional pottery, rugs, and jewellery bought by well-off Russians as decorations for their flats or themselves, a panoply of buildings and objects in a sort of Soviet Raj style attractively demonstrated the unity in difference of Stalin's empire.[190] But the main traffic flowed only in one direction: famous non-Russian cultural figures, such as the Georgian poet Shota Rustaveli, remained exotic curiosities, but Tolstoi or Pushkin were pan-Soviet figures, their fleeting visits to other parts of the Empire subject to assiduous mythologization.

The Russification of the 1940s reconciled at least some of the Soviet regime's opponents, not only inside but outside the country. The years after the Second World War saw numerous Russian émigrés taking up Soviet citizenship for the first time, a gesture of solidarity with their country in which the Soviet Union's retreat from internationalism sometimes played as large a role as did the country's achievement in defeating Nazism. Some émigré figures did remain steadfastly opposed, such as Vladimir Nabokov, who produced a viciously funny portrait of a Soviet-sympathizing émigré, all bogus populism and phony Cossack clothing, in his 1957 novel *Pnin*. Others, however, welcomed at least some aspects of the new reality, as indeed did certain Western commentators, for whom the puritanism of Soviet culture could seem a refreshing alternative to the ubiquity of 'trivial' material in the West: 'The rigid censorship, that with so much else, suppressed pornography, trash, and low-grade thrillers such as fill railway bookstalls in the West, served to make the response of Soviet readers and theatre audiences purer, more direct and naive than ours.'[191] Pride in national achievements—not least the defeat of a particularly brutal invading army—was felt all over Soviet society, no less among workers and peasants than among more privileged sectors of society.

Indeed, with foreign art removed from all major museums bar the Hermitage, with foreign languages not taught in ordinary schools, with few translations and only the most vestigial international news, and a burgeoning stream of overtly chauvinistic popular novels and films, ordinary Soviet citizens had little choice but to accept the idea of Russia as the centre of the world, a bulwark against exploitative capitalism, and a nation headed by the world's greatest leader. In any case, many, if not the majority, genuinely believed in the myth of the Party's concern for those at the bottom: 'Glory to our beloved Party, eternal glory to wise Stalin! In every action carried out by the Party is evident concern for the humble Soviet man', wrote a visitor to a newly opened metro station in April 1953, a month after Stalin's death.[192] Therefore, the post-1956 assault on the authority of 'The Boss', and erosion, especially from the mid-1960s, of belief in the virtue of all things Soviet, would be both painful and shocking for the parts of the population that had not personally endured repression, and had no first- or even second-hand experience of a world beyond Soviet society's respectable façade. While not undervaluing the experience of those Russians, of every class, who were steadfastly opposed to the regime, there is no doubt that those who could see no alternative to the system under which they lived formed the overwhelming majority of the country's population.

Suggested further reading

Education, Science, Cultural Institutions, the Urban Environment

BRUMFIELD, W., *A History of Russian Architecture* (Cambridge, 1993).

—— and RUBLE, B. A. (eds.), *Russian Housing in the Modern Age: Design and Social History* (New York, 1993).

BOWN, M. C., and TAYLOR, B. (eds.), *Art of the Soviets: Painting, Sculpture and Architecture in a One-Party State, 1917–1992* (Manchester, 1993).

DUNSTAN, J., *Soviet Schooling in the Second World War* (Basingstoke, 1997).

FITZPATRICK, S., *The Commissariat of Enlightenment* (Cambridge, 1970).

—— *Education and Social Mobility in the USSR 1921–1934* (Cambridge, 1979).

—— *The Cultural Front: Power and Culture in Revolutionary Russia* (Ithaca, 1992).

GARRARD, J., and GARRARD, C., *Inside the Soviet Writers' Union* (London, 1990).

GRAHAM, L. S., *Science in the Soviet Union: A Short History* (Cambridge, 1993).

—— *The Soviet Academy of Sciences and the Communist Party, 1927–1932* (Princeton, 1967).

HOLMES, L. E., *The Kremlin and the Schoolhouse: Reforming Education in Soviet Russia, 1917–1931* (Bloomington, 1991).

KOTKIN, S., *Magnetic Mountain: Stalinism as a Civilization* (Berkeley, 1995).

MICKIEWICZ, E. P., *Soviet Political Schools: The Communist Party Adult Instruction System* (New Haven, 1967).

MUCKLE, J., *Education in Russia Past and Present: An Introductory Study Guide and Select Bibliography* (Nottingham, 1995).

VUCINICH, A., *Empire of Knowledge: the Academy of Sciences of the USSR* (Berkeley, 1984).

'Programmes for Identity' (Agitprop, Cinema, Children's Literature)

BOWLT, J. E., and MATICH, O. (eds.), *Laboratory of Dreams: The Russian Avant-Garde and Cultural Experiment* (Stanford, 1996).

CHUKOVSKAIA, L., *V laboratorii redaktora* (Moscow, 1960).

CHUKOVSKII, K., *From Two to Five*, tr. and ed. M. Morton (Berkeley, 1968).

ETKIND, A., *Eros nevozmozhnogo: Istoriia psikhoanaliza v Rossii* (St Petersburg, 1993).

GELDERN, J. VON, *Bolshevik Festivals* (Berkeley, 1993).

GLEASON, A., KENEZ, P., and STITES, R. (eds.), *Bolshevik Culture: Experiment and Order in the Russian Revolution* (Bloomington, 1985).

KENEZ, P., *The Birth of the Propaganda State: Soviet Methods of Mass Mobilization 1917–1929* (Cambridge, 1985).

LEIGHTON, L. G., 'Homage to Kornei Chukovsky', *Russian Review*, 31 (1971), 38–48.

MALLY, L., *Culture of the Future: The Proletkult Movement in Revolutionary Russia* (Berkeley, 1990).

MARSHAK, S., *My Life's Beginning: Some Pages of Reminiscence*, tr. K. H. Blair (London, 1964).

MILLAR, A., ' "Chudesnye Ezhi" i "Veselye Chizhi": Two Soviet Children's Magazines and their Poetry, 1928–1941', unpublished MA dissertation (London, 1995).

RIORDAN, J., *Sport and Soviet Society: The Development of Sport and Physical Education in Russia and the USSR* (Cambridge, 1977).

Russkie detskie pisateli: Bio-bibliograficheskii slovar' (1917–1957) (Moscow, 1961).

SOKOL, E., *Russian Poetry for Children* (Knoxville, 1984).

TAYLOR, R., and CHRISTIE, I. (eds.), *The Film Factory: Russian and Soviet Cinema in Documents 1896–1939* (London, 1994).

TROTSKY, L., *Problems of Everyday Life* (no translator credited) (New York, 1973).

Populism and Popular Resistance

ANDREYEV, C., *Vlasov and the Russian Liberation Movement: Soviet Reality and Emigre Theories* (Cambridge, 1987).

BOREV, IU. (comp.), *Staliniada* (Moscow, 1990).

CONQUEST, R., *The Harvest of Sorrow* (New York, 1986).

FILTZER, D., *Soviet Workers and Stalinist Industrialization: The Formation of Modern Soviet Production Relations, 1928–1941* (London, 1986).

FITZPATRICK, S., *Stalin's Peasants* (New York, 1994).

McAULEY, M., *Bread and Justice: State and Society in Petrograd, 1917–22* (Oxford, 1991).

MANNING, R. T., and GETTY, J. A., *Stalinist Terror: New Perspectives* (Cambridge, 1993).

TOLSTOY, V., BIBIKOVA, I., and COOKE, C. (eds.), *Street Art of the Revolution: Festivals and Celebrations in Russia, 1918–1932* (London, 1990).

TUMARKIN, N., *Lenin Lives! The Lenin Cult in the Soviet Union* (Cambridge, Mass., 1983).

VIOLA, L., *Peasant Rebels under Stalin: Collectivization and the Culture of Peasant Resistance* (New York, 1996).

Consumption, *Kul'turnost'*, Commercial Arts

BOYM, S., *Common Places: Mythologies of Everyday Life in Russia* (Cambridge, Mass., 1994).

DUNHAM, V., *In Stalin's Time: Middleclass Values in Soviet Fiction* (Cambridge, 1979).

OSOKINA, E. A., *Ierarkhiia potrebleniia: O zhizni liudei v usloviiakh stalinskogo snabzheniia 1928–1935 gg.* (Moscow, 1993).

PAPERNYI, V., *Kul'tura 'dva'* (Ann Arbor, 1985).

STARR, S. F., *Red and Hot: The Fate of Jazz in the Soviet Union* (New York, 1983).

STITES, R., *Russian Popular Culture: Entertainment and Society since 1900* (Cambridge, 1992).

YOUNGBLOOD, D., *Movies for the Masses: Soviet Popular Cinema in the Twenties* (Cambridge, 1992).

Notes

[1] See C. Lodder, 'Lenin's Plan for Monumental Propaganda', in M. C. Bown and B. Taylor (eds.), *Art of the Soviets: Painting, Sculpture and Architecture in a One-Party State, 1917–1992* (Manchester, 1993), 16–32.

[2] A. Anson and V. Pulyshev, *Nasha sila—sovety. Sibirskii bukvar' dlia vzroslykh* (Novonikolaevsk, 1925), 3.

[3] On working-class rebellion generally, see J. Aves, *Workers against Lenin: Labour Protest and the Bolshevik Dictatorship* (London, 1996); on attitudes among the peasantry, O. Figes, *Peasant Russia, Civil War: The Volga Countryside in Revolution* (Oxford, 1989).

[4] These attempts to regulate sexuality and private behaviour are discussed in more detail in C. Kelly and D. Shepherd (eds.), *Russian Cultural Studies: An Introduction* (Oxford, 1998), ch. 5.

[5] The term 'totalitarianism' was already in use by the late 1930s, and classic studies of the concept include H. Arendt, *The Origins of Totalitarianism* (London, 1951); F. A. Hajek, *The Road to Serfdom* (London, 1944); C. J. Friedrich, *Totalitarian Dictatorship and Autocracy* (Cambridge, Mass., 1956); and E. Fromm, *The Fear of Freedom* (London, 1960). The term is in no sense obsolete in the West; indeed, the collapse of the Soviet Union to some extent effaced old battle-lines and inspired a fresh look at the resemblances between fascist Germany and Italy and Stalin's Russia. However, 'totalitarian' theories dominate less in the West than among Russian cultural theorists, some of whom use the term in an unproblematized way: see e.g. I. Golomstock, *Totalitarian Art* (London, 1990) and L. Gozman, *The Psychology of Post-Totalitarianism in Russia* (London, 1992).

[6] V. Dunham, *In Stalin's Time: Middleclass Values in Soviet Fiction* (Cambridge, 1979 (reprint)), 13.

[7] N. Timasheff, *The Great Retreat: The Growth and Decline of Communism in Russia* (New York, 1946), 354.

[8] Dunham, *In Stalin's Time*, 18.

[9] V. Papernyi, *Kul'tura 'dva'* (Ann Arbor, 1985).

[10] See S. Fitzpatrick, *The Cultural Front: Power and Culture in Revolutionary Russia* (Ithaca, 1992), and R. T. Manning and J. A. Getty, *Stalinist Terror: New Perspectives* (Cambridge, 1993).

[11] On the destruction of churches in Moscow, see *Razrushennye i oskvernennye khramy: Moskva i Sredniaia Rossiia* (Frankfurt, 1980); in Leningrad, A. P. Pavlov, *Khramy Sankt-Peterburga: khudozhestvenno-istoricheskii ocherk* (St Petersburg, 1995). The periodical *Nashi dostizheniia* is a particularly good source for idealized visions of the future and caricatures of the past.

[12] See N. Tumarkin, *Lenin Lives! The Lenin Cult in Soviet Russia* (Cambridge, Mass., 1983). A very interesting recent study of religious imagery in the early Soviet period is M. D. Steinberg, 'Workers on the Cross: Religious Imagination in the Writings of Russian Workers, 1910–1924', *Russian Review*, 53 (1994), 213–39.

[13] See Pavlov, *Khramy Sankt-Peterburga*, 227–30.

[14] The memoirist Raisa Orlova recalls that the families in the old house where she lived, just off Gor'kii Street, campaigned successfully to have the house spared

when the street was reconstructed in the mid-1930s: see her *Vospominaniia o neproshedshem vremeni* (Ann Arbor, 1988), 31.

15 See S. A. Smith, *Red Petrograd: Revolution in the Factories, 1917–1918* (Cambridge, 1983).

16 The most detailed account of the 1930s purges is R. Conquest, *The Great Terror Revisited* (London, 1990). Among the many memoirs devoted to the subject, Evgeniia Ginzburg's *Krutoi marshrut* (translated into English as *Into the Whirlwind* and *Within the Whirlwind*) is perhaps the most compelling.

17 B. P. Babkin, *Pavlov: A Biography* (Chicago, 1949/1979), 156.

18 L. S. Graham, *Science in the Soviet Union: A Short History* (Cambridge, 1993), 131–2.

19 A harrowing account of this side of Soviet life is given in Iu. Trifonov's novel *The House on the Embankment* (*Dom na naberezhnoi*, 1976).

20 Graham, *Science in the Soviet Union*, 88.

21 V. Khodasevich, 'Proletkul't', in *Proza* (New York, 1982), 266. On Proletkul't generally, see L. Mally, *Culture of the Future: The Proletkult Movement in Revolutionary Russia* (Berkeley, 1990).

22 D. Kharms, 'Chetyre illiustratsii togo, kak novaia ideia porazhaet cheloveka, k nei ne podgotovlennogo', in *Polet v nebesakh: Stikhi, proza, drama, pis'ma* (Leningrad, 1988), 372.

23 L. E. Holmes, *The Kremlin and the Schoolhouse: Reforming Education in Soviet Russia, 1917–1931* (Bloomington, 1991), 128.

24 Ibid., 5–11.

25 See J. F. Hutchinson, ' "Who Killed Cock Robin?" An Inquiry into the Death of Zemstvo Medicine', in Hutchinson and S. G. Solomon (eds.), *Health and Society in Revolutionary Russia* (Bloomington, 1990), 3–26.

26 The Academy of Sciences is extensively discussed in Graham, *Science in the Soviet Union*; see also A. Vucinich, *Empire of Knowledge: The Academy of Sciences of the USSR* (Berkeley, 1984).

27 Graham, *Science in the Soviet Union*, 84.

28 *Dekrety Sovetskoi vlasti*, ii (Moscow, 1959), no. 50.

29 Y. P. Frolov, *Pavlov and his School: The Theory of Conditioned Reflexes*, tr. C. P. Dalt (London, 1938), 266–72.

30 L. S. Graham, *The Soviet Academy of Sciences and the Communist Party, 1927–1932* (Princeton, 1967); see also Vucinich, *Empire of Knowledge*.

31 See Holmes, *The Kremlin and the Schoolhouse*, 129–32.

32 N. Ognev, *Dnevnik Kosti Riabtseva* (Moscow, 1927), 9, 11 (diary entries of 27 September and 3 October); English translation by A. Werth, *Diary of a Communist Schoolboy* (London, 1929).

33 Holmes, *The Kremlin and the Schoolhouse*, 37.

34 Ibid., 40, 38.

35 See A. Etkind, *Eros nevozmozhnogo: Istoriia psikhoanaliza v Rossii* (St Petersburg, 1993), ch. 8.

36 D. Levin, *Children in Soviet Russia* (London, 1942), 18–19.

37 See D. Paperno, *Zapiski moskovskogo pianista* (Ann Arbor, 1983), 125.

38 Holmes, *The Kremlin and the Schoolhouse*, 132–3.

39 See Hutchinson, ' "Who Killed Cock Robin?" ', and N. B. Weissmann, 'The Origins of Soviet Health Administration: Narkomzdrav 1918–1928', in Hutchinson and Solomon (eds.), *Health and Society in Revolutionary Russia*, 97–120. Ironically, recruitment to prophylactic posts, especially in the countryside, was to prove something of a problem throughout the 1920s, an indication that intelligentsia commitment to the common good was not always wholly selfless.

40 See *Za zdorovoe zhilishche* (Leningrad, 1945), 5.

41 Fitzpatrick, 'Professors and Soviet Power', in *The Cultural Front*, 55–64.

42 See Iu. Steklov, *Sovetskaia demokratiia* (Moscow, 1929), 12–15; S. Smidovich, *O kul'ture i byte* (Moscow, 1930); N. Krupskaia, *O bytovykh voprosakh* (Moscow, 1930).

43 Among the sources on this are V. Panova, *O moei zhizni, knigakh i chitateliakh* (Leningrad, 1975), and Iu. Trifonov, 'Zapiski soseda', in *Kak slovo nashe otzovetsia* (Moscow, 1985), 138–74. See also J. Garrard and C. Garrard, *Inside the Soviet Writers' Union* (London, 1990).

44 Graham, *Science in the Soviet Union*, 182.

45 In M. Holub, 'What Was it Like: Lepeshynskaya's [*sic*] Tub', *The Guardian* (11 Jan. 1996), sect. 2, 13.

46 V. I. Lenin, *Polnoe sobranie sochinenii*, xviii. *Materializm i empiriokrititsizm* (Moscow, 1961), 7–384.

47 D. Vertov, 'The Cine-Eyes. A Revolution. *LEF*, 1923', quoted in R. Taylor and I. Christie (eds.), *The Film Factory: Russian and Soviet Cinema in Documents 1896–1939* (London, 1994), 93 (emphasis in original).

48 Quoted in K. Clark, *Petersburg: Crucible of Revolution* (Cambridge, Mass., 1996), 50.

49 For more detail on the 'Red Lev Tolstoi' campaign and early Soviet literary debates generally, see Kelly and Shepherd (eds.), *Russian Cultural Studies*, ch. 1.

50 The entire *Zapiski iunogo vracha* cycle is available in M. A. Bulgakov, *Polnoe sobranie sochinenii*, i (Ann Arbor, 1982); all subsequent references to this edition in text. On Bulgakov's biography, see L. Milne, *Mikhail Bulgakov: A Critical Biography* (Cambridge, 1990) and J. A. E. Curtis (comp.), *Manuscripts Don't Burn: Bulgakov, a Life in Letters and Diaries* (London, 1990).

51 Bulgakov, 'Sobach'e serdtse', in *Khanskii ogon': Povesti i rasskazy* (Moscow, 1988), 183; ch. 5. All subsequent references to this edition in text.

52 Babkin, *Pavlov*, 95.

53 Frolov, *Pavlov and his School*, 248.

54 Babkin, *Pavlov*, 352.

55 On the 'new woman', see e.g. B. E. Clements, 'The Birth of the New Soviet Woman', in A. Gleason, P. Kenez, and R. Stites (eds.), *Bolshevik Culture: Experiment and Order in the Russian Revolution* (Bloomington, 1985), 220–37. On the 'new man', see e.g. A. Etkind, 'Psychological Culture', in D. N. Shalin (ed.), *Russian Culture at the Crossroads: Paradoxes of Post-Communist Consciousness* (Boulder, 1996), 109–23.

56 L. Trotsky, 'Culture and Socialism', in *Problems of Everyday Life* (no translator credited) (New York, 1973), 243, emphasis added.

57 On 'biomechanics', Dalcroze Eurythmics, and other forms of identity-formation through movement, see the special issue of the journal *Eksperiment*, 2 (1996), and also J. E. Bowlt, 'Body Beautiful: The Search for the Perfect Physique', in Bowlt and O. Matich (eds.), *Laboratory of Dreams: The Russian Avant-Garde and Cultural Experiment* (Stanford, 1996), 37–58.

58 P. O. Afanas'ev, *Pishi, chitai, schitai. Bukvar'* (Moscow and Leningrad, 1925), 90, 36.

59 Levin, *Children in Soviet Russia*, 23.

60 Orlova, *Vospominaniia*, 20, 54.

61 Holmes, *The Kremlin and the Schoolhouse*, 98, 134.

62 N. Grant, *Soviet Education* (Harmondsworth, 1974), 56.

63 See K. Chukovskii, entry for 10 Apr. 1925, in *Dnevnik 1901–1929* (Moscow, 1991), 336.

64 On children's homes in the 1930s, see the interesting memoir by M. Nikolaev, *Detdom* (New York, 1979). The early Soviet period is dealt with in A. Ball, *And Now My Soul is Hardened: Abandoned Children in Soviet Russia, 1918–1930* (Berkeley, 1994).

65 On the institutional history of children's writing in the 1920s, see Elena Sokol, *Russian Poetry for Children* (Knoxville, 1984), chs. 1, 4, 5, and A. Ivich, 'Detskaia literatura', *Kratkaia literaturnaia entsiklopediia*, ii (Moscow, 1964), 611–12.

66 Ivich, 'Detskaia literatura', 611.

67 On *Ezh* and *Chizh* see A. Millar, ' "Chudesnye Ezhi" i "Veselye Chizhi": Two Soviet Children's Magazines and their Poetry, 1928–1941', unpublished MA dissertation (London, 1995). On the OBERIU writers' involvement with children's writing, see also G. Roberts, *The Last Soviet Avant-Garde: OBERIU—Fact, Fiction, Metafiction* (Cambridge, 1997).

68 On the children's theatre, see *Teatral'naia entsiklopediia*, v (Moscow, 1967), headword *Teatr dlia detei*.

69 A. B. Ustinov, 'Delo detskogo sektora Gosizdata 1932 g.: Predvaritel'naia spravka', in G. A. Morev (ed.), *Mikhail Kuzmin i russkaia kul'tura XX veka: Tezisy i materialy konferentsii 15–17 maia 1990 g.* (Leningrad, 1990), 125–36, and I. Mal'skii, 'Razgrom OBERIU: Materialy sledstvennogo dela', *Oktiabr'*, 11 (1992), 166–91. On Sats, see N. Sats, *From a Woman's Viewpoint: An Interview with Il'ia Kucherenko* (Moscow, 1989).

70 L. Chukovskaia, *V laboratorii redaktora* (Moscow, 1960), 220–1. This point is not intended to undermine the importance of Chukovskaia's book, which contains vital information on Detizdat as well as on many other areas of Soviet publishing practice.

71 *Pervyi vsesoiuznyi s"ezd sovetskikh pisatelei: Stenograficheskii otchet* (Moscow, 1934), 22.

72 On the pedologists, see e.g. N. Krupskaia, 'O *Krokodile* K. Chukovskogo', *Pravda* (1 Feb. 1928); English translation in Sokol, *Russian Poetry*, 207–9.

73 *Pervyi vsesoiuznyi s"ezd*, 25–6, 32.

[74] Kharms, *Polet*, 238.

[75] On the puppet theatre in the 1920s, see N. Simonovich-Efimova, *Zapiski petrushechnika* (Leningrad, 1925), and N. I. Smirnova, *Sovetskii teatr kukol, 1918–1932* (Moscow, 1963); on the 1930s and later, see S. Obraztsov, *Moia professiia* (Moscow, 1981).

[76] B. N. Mironov, 'Peasant Popular Culture and the Origins of Soviet Authoritarianism', in S. P. Frank and M. D. Steinberg (eds.), *Cultures in Flux: Lower-Class Values, Practices, and Resistance in Late Imperial Russia* (Princeton, 1994), 54–73.

[77] Statistics in *Bol'shaia sovetskaia entsiklopediia* (hereafter *BSE*), 1st edn., xxv (1930), cols. 447 ff., headword *zhilishche*. The 1912 person-per-room figure had been adjusted to exclude those who owned their own homes, otherwise the achievement of the Soviet authorities would have looked still more modest.

[78] M. Lewin, 'Society, State, and Ideology during the First Five-Year Plan', in S. Fitzpatrick (ed.), *Cultural Revolution in Russia, 1928–1931* (Bloomington, 1984), 55.

[79] *BSE*, 1st edn., xxxvii (1938), cols. 651–2, headword *Magnitogorsk*; on Magnitogorsk generally, see S. Kotkin, *Magnetic Mountain: Stalinism as a Civilization* (Berkeley, 1995).

[80] See N. Lebina, 'Tenevye storony zhizni sovetskogo goroda 20–30-kh godov', *Voprosy istorii*, 2 (1994), 30–2.

[81] *Za zdorovoe zhilishche, passim*.

[82] On collectivization, see S. Fitzpatrick, *Stalin's Peasants* (New York, 1994), and L. Viola, *Peasant Rebels under Stalin: Collectivization and the Culture of Peasant Resistance* (New York, 1996).

[83] A. Getty, G. Rittersporn, and V. Zemskov, 'Victims of the Soviet Penal System in the Pre-War Years: A First Approach', *American Historical Review*, 99 (1993), 1032–3.

[84] Anson and Pulyshev, *Nasha sila—sovety*, 13.

[85] This account is based on J. Riordan, *Sport in Soviet Society: Development of Sport and Physical Education in Russia and the USSR* (Cambridge, 1977), chs. 3–4; for the Semashko quotation, see p. 96.

[86] See A. Ivanov (ed.), *Pesni sovetskogo naroda* (Leningrad, 1948), 137.

[87] See ibid., 147. On 'mass song', see also G. S. Smith, *Songs to Seven Strings* (Bloomington, 1984), ch. 1; R. Stites, *Russian Popular Culture: Entertainment and Society since 1900* (Cambridge, 1992), 66–7; S. Boym, *Common Places: Mythologies of Everyday Life in Russia* (Cambridge, Mass., 1994), 110–20.

[88] V. Tolstoy, I. Bibikova, and C. Cooke (eds.), *Street Art of the Revolution: Festivals and Celebrations in Russia, 1918–1932* (London, 1990), 151; translation slightly adapted. On the festivals, see also J. von Geldern, *Bolshevik Festivals* (Berkeley, 1993).

[89] See Clark, *Petersburg*, ch. 5.

[90] See B. A. Keller, 'K vsesoiuznoi sel'skokhoziaistvennoi vystavke', *Oktiabr'*, 7 (1939), 3–10. The writer enthuses about everything, from grain yield statistics to super-sized tomato plants. This exhibition was a successor to various temporary agricultural displays, on the first of which, in 1923, see M. Shaginian,

'Sel′skokhoziaistvennaia vystavka', in *Sobranie sochinenii v 9 tomakh*, ii (Moscow, 1971), 626–47.

[91] F. Deák, 'Blue Blouse', *Drama Review*, 17 (1975), 35–6; on the revolutionary theatre generally, see R. Russell, *Russian Drama of the Revolutionary Period* (Basingstoke, 1988), and K. Rudnitsky, *Russian and Soviet Theatre* (London, 1988).

[92] On mass song in film, see K. Clark, 'Aural Hieroglyphics?', in N. Condee (ed.), *Soviet Hieroglyphics* (Bloomington, 1995), 1–21. The songbook *Pesni sovetskogo naroda* has a list of songs from films and operas, so that users could work out where to find the text of hit songs (272).

[93] On Soviet radio, see Kelly and Shepherd (eds.), *Russian Cultural Studies*, ch. 3.

[94] P. Kerzhentsev, *Teatr i revoliutsiia* (Petrograd, 1918), 42–3.

[95] See Smith, *Red Petrograd*, 34–5, and R. Stites, *The Women's Liberation Movement in Russia: Feminism, Nihilism and Bolshevism, 1860–1930* (Princeton, 1978), 397. By 1939, the figure had risen to 83.4 per cent (ibid.).

[96] See N. Funk and M. Mueller, *Feminism and Post-Communism* (London and New York, 1993); G. W. Lapidus, 'Sexual Inequality in Soviet Policy', in D. Atkinson, A. Dallin, and Lapidus (eds.), *Women in Russia* (Hassocks, 1978), 127; and Z. Khotkina, 'Women in the Labour Market: Yesterday, Today and Tomorrow', in A. Posadskaya (ed.), *Women in Russia* (London, 1994), 85–108.

[97] D. V. Kolesov, *Besedy o polovom vospitanii* (Moscow, 1980), 178.

[98] E. A. Kaplan, *Motherhood and Representation: The Mother in Popular Culture and Melodrama* (London, 1992), 16.

[99] For a fuller discussion of this theme, see L. Attwood, ' "Rodina-Mat′" and the Soviet Cinema', in M. Liljestroom, E. Mantysaari, and A. Rosenholm (eds.), *Gender Restructuring in Russian Studies* (Tampere, 1993), 15–28.

[100] J. Goodwin, *Eisenstein: Cinema and History* (Urbana and Chicago, 1993) 117, and J. Aumont, *Montage Eisenstein* (Bloomington, 1987), 94.

[101] *Rabotnitsa*, 36 (1936), 4.

[102] L. H. Siegelbaum, *Stakhanovism and the Politics of Productivity in the USSR, 1935–1941* (Cambridge, 1988), 237–8.

[103] 'E.F.', in *Rabotnitsa*, 2 (1937), 15.

[104] O. Bulgakova, 'The Hydra of the Soviet Cinema', in L. Attwood (ed.), *Red Women on the Silver Screen* (London, 1993), 158.

[105] S. Fomin, 'Zelenyi seks', *Iskusstvo kino*, 7 (1991), 102.

[106] Ibid.

[107] V. Ketlinskaia, 'Zheny i materi . . .', *Krest′ianka*, 4 (1944), 19.

[108] F. Panferov, 'Tat′iana Khrebtova', ibid., 20 (1937), 11–13, and *Rabotnitsa*, 12 (1938), 17–18.

[109] This section was mostly written by Maureen Perrie.

[110] See F. J. Oinas, 'Folklore and Politics in the Soviet Union', *Slavic Review*, 32 (1973), 46–8.

[111] See ibid., 49–53, and F. J. Miller, *Folklore for Stalin: Russian Folklore and Pseudofolklore of the Stalin Era* (Armonk, 1990).

112 See S. Fitzpatrick, 'The *Lady Macbeth* Affair: Shostakovich and the Soviet Puritans', in *The Cultural Front*, 183–215.

113 V. Kirpotin, 'Narodnost' i prostota', *Pravda* (3 Apr. 1936), 4.

114 See A. Kemp-Welch, *Stalin and the Literary Intelligentsia, 1928–39* (Basingstoke and London, 1991), 260.

115 See e.g. ibid., 260–1.

116 See Stites, *Russian Popular Culture*, 108–9, and Fitzpatrick, 'The *Lady Macbeth* Affair', 210–13.

117 Nina Lobanov-Rostovsky, *Revolutionary Ceramics: Soviet Porcelain 1917–1927* (London, 1990), plate 44.

118 A. Gide, *Retour de l'URSS* (Paris, 1936), 90.

119 Walter Benjamin recalls visiting one such *muzei byta* in his *Moskauer Tagesbuch* (Frankfurt am Main, 1980), 156–7. Other museum history sources include *Obshchestvo 'Staryi Peterburg' 1921–1923* (St Petersburg, 1923), and the commentaries by A. M. Konechnyi, K. A. Kumpan, and D. S. Likhachev to N. P. Antsiferov, *Dusha Peterburga* (St Petersburg, 1991).

120 Among rare lower-class memoirs are W. Edgerton (ed.), *Memoirs of Peasant Tolstoyans in Soviet Russia* (Bloomington, 1993), and *Sud'by krest'ianskie* (Moscow, 1993).

121 K. S. Petrov-Vodkin, letter to A. P. Petrova-Vodkina, in *Pis'ma. Stat'i. Vystupleniia. Dokumenty*, ed. E. N. Selizarova (Moscow, 1991), 200.

122 Petrov-Vodkin, letter to A. P. Petrova-Vodkina, 22 November–5 December 1920, ibid., 210.

123 E. Strogova, 'Womenfolk' ['Baby'], tr. M. Schwartz, in C. Kelly (ed.), *An Anthology of Russian Women's Writing* (Oxford, 1994), 278; see also Tumarkin, *Lenin Lives!*

124 B. I. Kolonitskii, ' "Revolutionary Names": Russian Personal Names and Political Consciousness in the 1920s and 1930s', *Revolutionary Russia*, 6 (1993), 210–28.

125 See Kh. Volovich, 'My Past', in J. Crowfoot (ed.), *Russian Women's Camp Memoirs* (forthcoming).

126 Clark, *Petersburg*, 19.

127 See A. Pyman, *The Life of Aleksandr Blok*, ii (Oxford, 1980), 372.

128 On the Soviet popular cinema see D. Youngblood, *Movies for the Masses: Soviet Popular Cinema in the Twenties* (Cambridge, 1992), and Stites, *Russian Popular Culture*, chs. 2 and 3.

129 *BSE*, 3rd edn., xxii (Moscow, 1975), 453.

130 Ibid., v (Moscow, 1971), 166.

131 See Fitzpatrick, *The Cultural Front*, 218.

132 *Gigiena i zdorov'e*, 21 (1936), 7.

133 See *Obshchestvennitsa*, 1 (1937), 63.

134 *Ogonek*, 5 (1936), 19.

135 *Gigiena i zdorov'e*, 8 (1937), 9.

136 *Stakhanovets*, 2 (1937), 53.

137 *Sotsialisticheskii gorod*, 1 (1936), 35. These changes did not put paid to the traditional *bania*, but turned it into a facility that was less important for hygiene than for relaxation (on which see N. Condee, 'The Second Fantasy Mother, or All Baths are Women's Baths', in H. Goscilo and B. Holmgren (eds.), *Russia: Women: Culture* (Bloomington, 1996), 31–62).

138 *Gigiena i zdorov'e*, 20 (1936), 12–13.

139 *Pravda* (28 Oct. 1935).

140 Ibid. (24 Apr. 1936).

141 Ibid. (6 May 1936).

142 See R. Chartier (ed.), *A History of Private Life*, ii–iv (London, 1989).

143 *Obshchestvennitsa*, 4 (1938), 12.

144 Ibid., 2 (1936), 9, and 3 (1937), 30–1.

145 Ibid., 2 (1936), 9.

146 Ibid., 4 (1936), 13.

147 Ibid., 5 (1936), 12.

148 Ibid., 3 (1937), 12.

149 *Smena*, 3 (1936), 26.

150 *X s"ezd VLKSM: Sbornik materialov* (Moscow, 1938), 41.

151 *Klub*, 1 (1937), 4.

152 Ibid., 6 (1936), 1.

153 *Ogonek*, 1 (1936), 22.

154 *Smena*, 8 (1937), 25–6.

155 Ibid., 12 (1938), 20.

156 Ibid., 10 (1938), 5.

157 See Siegelbaum, *Stakhanovism*, 225–33.

158 A. Busygin, *Zhizn' moia i moikh druzei* (Moscow, 1939), 70.

159 Quoted in *Slovar' sovremennogo russkogo iazyka*, v (Moscow, 1956), headword *kul'turnost'*.

160 Ognev, *Dnevnik Kosti Riabtseva*, 216.

161 A. Radakov, 'Gimn dvuspal'noi krovati', *Satirikon*, 6 (1910), back cover.

162 Re-mi, 'Priiatnyi ugolok', ibid., 5.

163 See Boym, *Common Places*, 5–11.

164 *Za zdorovoe zhilishche*, 25. From a different point of view, the regulations on pets were no doubt meant to stop flat-dwellers from introducing pigs, hens, or goats to their living quarters.

165 For example, in E. Sidel'nikov, *Russkoe narodnoe tvorchestvo i estrada* (Moscow, 1950), in which the Soviet variety theatre is seen as a genuinely 'popular' form, unlike its 'vulgar' (*meshchanskii*) counterpart before 1917.

166 A. Karavaeva, *Rodnoi dom* (Moscow, 1950), 22–3.

167 Dunham, *In Stalin's Time*, 54.

[168] The Bogdanov-Bel'skii portrait is illustrated in colour as lot 134, Sotheby's catalogue, *The Russian Sale, London, Wednesday 17 July 1996* (London, 1996) (sale LN 6347).

[169] Bulgakov, *Master i Margarita*, in *Romany* (Moscow, 1973), 553–4, 558; ch. 13.

[170] E. M. Delafield, *I Visit the Soviets: The Provincial Lady in Russia* (London, 1937), 181.

[171] E. A. Osokina, *Ierarkhiia potrebleniia: O zhizni liudei v usloviiakh stalinskogo snabzheniia 1928–1935 gg.* (Moscow, 1993), 24, 33–5, 39.

[172] Ibid., 42.

[173] See S. Fitzpatrick, 'Supplicants and Citizens: Public Letter-Writing in Soviet Russia in the 1930s', *Slavic Review*, 55 (1996), 78–105.

[174] On Okhlopkov's production, see N. Worrall, *Modernism to Realism in the Soviet Theatre* (Cambridge, 1990), 161–6.

[175] For an excellent detailed treatment of Stalinist industrial relations, see D. Filtzer, *Soviet Workers and Stalinist Industrialisation: The Formation of Modern Soviet Production Relations, 1928–1941* (London, 1986).

[176] See R. T. Manning and J. A. Getty (eds.), *Stalinist Terror: New Perspectives* (Cambridge, 1993), and S. Fitzpatrick, 'Signals from Below', *Journal of Modern History*, 68 (1996), 831–66.

[177] I. Il'f and E. Petrov, 'Retsept spokoinoi zhizni', in *Sobranie sochinenii v 5 tomakh*, iii (Moscow, 1961), 294.

[178] A rare case of a paid informer who has recorded the fact is Margaret Wettlin, an American married to a Soviet citizen who had herself taken Soviet nationality: *Sixty Russian Winters* (London, 1994).

[179] V. Zenzinov (comp.), *Vstrecha s Rossiei: Kak i chem zhivut v Sovetskom Soiuze* (New York, 1944), 419. Our thanks to Martin Dewhirst for this reference.

[180] N. Mandel'shtam, *Vtoraia kniga* (Paris, 1970), 429. There is some evidence that the language of *kul'turnost'* became common currency: cf. a visitor to the recently opened Novokuznetskaia metro station in 1953: 'It is tender and blindingly white as the first snowdrop of spring!' (quoted in S. Garniuk, A. Kats, and A. Sonichev, 'Kusok kommunizma: Moskovskoe metro glazami sovremennikov', *Moskovskii arkhiv*, 1 (1996), 360).

[181] On this see V. S. Magun, 'Labor Culture', in Shalin (ed.), *Russian Culture at the Crossroads*, 279–98.

[182] Orlova, *Vospominaniia*, 182, reveals that the author only learned about the existence of Party dachas as late as 1955.

[183] See Manning and Getty, *Stalinist Terror*, *passim*, and R. W. Thurston, *Life and Terror in Stalin's Russia, 1934–1941* (New Haven, 1996).

[184] Cf. the account of Central Asia in the 1930s by F. Maclean in *Eastern Approaches* (London, 1949).

[185] On collectivization, see Viola, *Peasant Rebels under Stalin*; R. Conquest, *The Harvest of Sorrow* (New York, 1986); and Fitzpatrick, *Stalin's Peasants*. On revolts in the prison camps, see the Vozvrashchenie publications *Soprotivlenie v GULage* (Moscow, 1992, and continuing), and *Resistance in the GULag* (Moscow, 1992); and E. Bacon, *The GULag at War: Stalin's Forced Labour System in the Light of the Archives* (Basingstoke, 1994).

186 C. Andreyev, *Vlasov and the Russian Liberation Movement: Soviet Reality and Emigre Theories* (Cambridge, 1987); there were about one million Soviet citizens serving in the Wehrmacht alone by 1944.

187 On Stalin's sarcastic titles, see Z. Rossi, *Spravochnik po GULagu* (London, 1987), headword *Stalin*, 390; on Stalin jokes, see Iu. Borev, *Staliniada* (Moscow, 1990), 34, 36.

188 O. Sliozberg, *Put'* (Moscow, 1993), 21.

189 Ia. Vaiskopf (ed.), *Blatnaia lira* (Jerusalem, 1981), 28.

190 On the 'Long Journey' autobiographical narratives of writers from the 'Extreme North', see Y. Slezkine, 'Primitive Communism and the Other Way Around', in T. Lahusen and E. Dobrenko (eds.), *Socialist Realism Without Shores* (*South Atlantic Quarterly*, 94 (1995)), 947–76; on Orientalism in Soviet architecture, see G. Castillo, 'Peoples at an Exhibition: Soviet Architecture and the National Question', ibid., 715–46.

191 I. Berlin, *Personal Impressions* (London, 1980), 162.

192 Quoted in Garniuk, Kats, and Sonichev, 'Kusok kommunizma', 348.

Index

Analytical Index of Names and Places

Personal names are glossed only in the cases of those individuals whose contribution to the development of Russian culture is discussed in the text. The category of 'places' includes important named sites of cultural activity, such as museums, theatres, etc. Movements and associations are listed in the Index.